Library of
Davidson College

Echoes and Influences of German Romanticism

Echoes and Influences of German Romanticism

Essays in Honour of Hans Eichner

Edited by
Michael S. Batts
Anthony W. Riley
Heinz Wetzel

PETER LANG
New York · Berne · Frankfurt am Main · Paris

Library of Congress Cataloging-in-Publication Data

Echoes and influences of German romanticism.

"Hans Eichner – a bibliography": p.
  1. Romanticism – Germany. 2. German literature –
18th century – History and criticism. 3. German
literature – 19th century – History and criticism.
4. German literature – 20th century – History and
criticism. I. Eichner, Hans. II. Batts, Michael S.
III. Riley, Anthony W. IV. Wetzel, Heinz, 1935–
PT362.E25   1987   830'.9'145   87–3634
ISBN 0-8204-0511-6

CIP-Kurztitelaufnahme der Deutschen Bibliothek

Echoes and Influences of German Romanticism:
Essays in Honour of Hans Eichner / Ed. by Michael
S. Batts ... – New York; Berne; Frankfurt am
Main; Paris: Lang, 1987.
ISBN 0-8204-0511-6
NE: Batts, Michael S. [Hrsg.]; Eichner, Hans:
Festschrift

© Peter Lang Publishing, Inc., New York 1987

All rights reserved.
Reprint or reproduction, even partially, in all forms such as
microfilm, xerography, microfiche, microcard, offset strictly prohibited.

Printed by Lang Druck, Inc., Liebefeld/Berne (Switzerland)

Contents

Preface 7

Abbreviations 9

Ernst Behler (University of Washington, Seattle).
Nietzsche und die romantische Metapher von der Kunst als Spiel 11

Frank Jolles (University of Ulster).
August Wilhelm Schlegels Metamorphose des Sommernachtstraums . 29

Friedrich Gaede (Dalhousie University, Halifax).
«Hüte dich, das wilde Tier zu wecken» (Eichendorff). Beobachtungen zum Verhältnis Mensch-Tier in der Literatur des 19. Jahrhunderts 53

Raymond Immerwahr (University of Western Ontario, Emeritus).
Mörike's *Maler Nolten* as a Romantic Novel: The Problem of Unity .. 63

Lilian Furst (University of North Carolina).
Double-Dealing: Irony in Kleist's *Die Marquise von O*............. 85

Heinz Wetzel (University of Toronto).
«Guillotinenromantik»: Zu Verständnis und Wirkung der Romantik bei Georg Büchner 97

Charles N. Genno (University of Toronto).
Novalis and Musil 105

Theodore Ziolkowski (Princeton University).
Hermann Hesse and Novalis: A Portrait of the Artist as a Young Dilettante 115

Hans Reiss (University of Bristol).
Thomas Mann and Novalis: On Thomas Mann's Attitude to Romantic Political Thought during the Weimar Republic 133

Rodney Symington (University of Victoria, B.C.).
Music on the Magic Mountain: «Fülle des Wohllauts» and Hans Castorps «Selbstüberwindung.» 155

Martin Swales (University College, London).
Narrative Accommodations: The Legacy of the Romantic Künstlernovelle 183

Roman Struc (University of Calgary).
Nachdenken über Christa T. and the Bildungsroman 195

Linda Dietrick (University of Manitoba).
Appropriating Romantic Consciousness: Narrative Mode in Christa Wolf's *Kein Ort. Nirgends* 211

Hildegard Nabbe (University of Waterloo).
Von romantischer Kunstandacht zur nationalen Kunsterziehung. Die Politisierung eines ästhetischen Begriffs um die Jahrhundertwende ... 225

Hans Schulte (McMaster University, Hamilton).
«Wer hat Euch Wandervögeln die Wissenschaft geschenkt?» Zur Deutschromantik der Jugendbewegung 243

Wolfgang Frühwald (Universität München).
Kunststadt München: Von der Entstehung und der Dauerfähigkeit eines romantisch-literarischen Mythos 271

Hans Eichner – A Bibliography 287

Preface

The contributions by North American and European scholars that have been brought together in this volume are intended to provide new insights into the long-lasting influence of Romanticism on German culture in the nineteenth and twentieth centuries. It is generally agreed that Romanticism was one of the most seminal movements in German literature, and it is not surprising that a very large number of writers and poets have, as it were, used Romanticism as the lodestar to guide them through the troubled waters of the past two centuries.

The connections and relationships of these later writers with Romanticism are, however, as diverse and numerous as the authors themselves – as a glance at the table of contents of this volume will reveal. Reflections and echoes of Romanticism are to be found in writers as dissimilar as Nietzsche and Musil, Thomas Mann and Christa Wolf, or Georg Büchner and Hermann Hesse; and the range and scope of Romantic influence extend from the «unconscious» use of Romantic (or romantic!) themes, motifs, and forms, to a deliberate critique or even rejection of them. Nor is the influence of Romanticism confined to *belles-lettres:* the political and philosophical implications of Romantic thought and ideas, as well as their influence on the fine arts, are examined in some of the contributions that follow.

In view of the multiplicity of the after-effects of German Romanticism, the editors have not striven for completeness in the treatment of this extraordinarily rich and complex topic; such would of necessity be a multi-volume undertaking. Rather, we wished to present a series of individual essays, all written by experts in their various fields, but linked by the common theme. The diversity of critical approaches employed by the contributors is in our view advantageous, reflecting as it does the variety of research methods applied in both North America and Europe. All of the articles presented here are the fruits of original research and were written expressly for this volume.

At the same time this book is intended as a tribute to the truly outstanding achievements of the leading Canadian scholar in the field of German Romanticism, Hans Eichner, who has taught generations of Canadian students (at Queen's University from 1950 to 1967 and thereafter at the University of

Toronto), and who is recognized internationally as one of the most distinguished colleagues in our discipline as a whole. Thus, this collection of essays is not only a recognition of Hans Eichner's work, but is also intended to complement and continue it by adding new perspectives and fresh approaches to a field of scholarly enquiry which he himself pioneered in Canada.

The book has been published with the help of a grant from the Canadian Federation for the Humanities, using funds provided by the Social Sciences and Humanities Research Council of Canada.

MSB, AWR, HW

Abbreviations

ABnG	Amsterdamer Beiträge zur neueren Germanistik
CLS	Comparative Literature Studies
CRCL	Canadian Review of Comparative Literature
DDR	Deutsche Demokratische Republik
DR	Deutsche Rundschau
Droste Jb	Jahrbuch der Droste-Gesellschaft
DU	Der Deutschunterricht
DVjs	Deutsche Vierteljahrsschrift für Literaturwissenschaft und Geistesgeschichte
ES	English Studies
FRG	Federal Republic of Germany
GBJb	Georg Büchner Jahrbuch
GDR	German Democratic Republic
GLL	German Life and Letters
GQ	German Quarterly
GR	Germanic Review
GRM	Germanisch-Romanische Monatsschrift
HAR	Humanities Association Review
hrsg.	herausgegeben
Hrsg.	Herausgeber
Jb	Jahrbuch
JbDSG	Jahrbuch der Deutschen Schillergesellschaft
JbIG	Jahrbuch für Internationale Germanistik
JEGP	Journal of English and Germanic Philology
Kunst	Die Kunst
KW	Der Kunstwart
LJbGG	Literaturwissenschaftliches Jahrbuch der Görres-Gesellschaft
MLN	Modern Language Notes
MLR	Modern Language Review
NdL	Neue deutsche Literatur
NDR	Neue Deutsche Rundschau
NG	Neue Germanistik

NGC	New German Critique
NR	Neue Rundschau
OGS	Oxford German Studies
PEGS	Proceedings of the English Goethe Society
PMLA	Publications of the Modern Language Association of America
PolVj	Politische Vierteljahrsschrift
QQ	Queen's Quarterly
repr.	reprint
UTQ	University of Toronto Quarterly
WB	Weimarer Beiträge
WW	Wirkendes Wort
ZdPh	Zeitschrift für deutsche Philologie

Nietzsche und die romantische Metapher von der Kunst als Spiel

ERNST BEHLER, *University of Washington*

Wegen vieler gemeinsamer Merkmale hat es immer eine natürliche Tendenz gegeben, zwischen den Phänomenen des Spiels und der Kunst einen grundsätzlichen Zusammenhang anzunehmen. Solche Merkmale bestehen zum Beispiel im Heraustreten aus zweckrationalen Zusammenhängen, in der freien Selbstorientiertheit und der eigenen Regelhaftigkeit, welche den besonderen Charakter der spielerischen wie der künstlerischen Tätigkeiten kennzeichnen. In der Geschichte der Theorien über die Kunst, vor allem der Dichtkunst, tritt deshalb die Metapher von der Kunst als Spiel oder von dem Spiel der Kunst auch in zahlreichen Ausprägungen auf. Sie zeigt sich im Bild der Kunst als Repräsentation vom Spiel der Welt, vom großen Welttheater und Schauspiel des Universums, in dem die Metapher des Spiels in eigentümlicher Verflechtung in Erscheinung tritt. Denn sie gilt hier für die durch die Kunst repräsentierte Welt wie für die Kunst, welche das Spiel der Welt in Szene setzt.

In der durch Jahrhunderte vorherrschenden klassizistischen Tradition der *ars poetica* erscheint das freie Spiel der Kunst dadurch begrenzt, daß das Angenehme im Kunsterlebnis mit dem Nützlichen in einem angemessenen Zusammenhang stehen soll, ganz abgesehen davon, daß hier ein hierarchisches Gattungssystem und eine normative Poetik das Spielen beschränken. In dem Text aber, der am Anfang der klassischen Doktrin steht, der *Poetik* des Aristoteles, klingt die Metapher von der Kunst als Spiel bereits deutlich an. Aristoteles sagt dort, daß die Menschen von ihrer Kindheit an eine Neigung zum imitativen Tun haben und solche Nachahmungen Vergnügen gewähren.[1] Die Bezeichnungen, welche hier auf das Spiel zu weisen scheinen, bestehen in der Konfiguration von Kind, imitativem Tun und Vergnügen. In der Tat gewinnt das Kind eine wichtige Dimension im Bild der Kunst als Spiel. Und der griechische Begriff der *Mimesis* bildet für den Spielcharakter der Kunst «die eigentliche Basis,»[2] wenn man ihn nicht im Sinne klassizistischer oder naturalistischer Naturnachahmung auslegt.

---

1 *Poetik*, IV: 1448 b, 2-3.
2 Hans-Georg Gadamer, «Das Spiel der Kunst,» Hans-Georg Gadamer, *Kleine Schriften IV. Variationen* (Tübingen: J.C.B. Mohr (Paul Siebeck), 1977), S. 237.

Aber erst in der Zeit der Romantik ist die Metapher vom freien Spiel der Kunst zur vollen Ausprägung gekommen. Dies verbindet sich mit einer deutlichen Privilegierung der Dichtkunst, die ihrerseits gerade aus diesem Bild der Kunst als Spiel hervorgeht. Dieser Vorgang hängt genau mit der Autonomisierung der Ästhetik, dem Heraustreten der Kunst aus allen anderen Zusammenhängen als denen der Kunst selbst zusammen, die gegen Ende des achtzehnten Jahrhunderts bemerkbar werden. «In dem Augenblick aber,» sagt Gadamer, «in dem der Begriff „Kunst" die uns eigene Klangfarbe annahm und das Kunstwerk begann, ganz auf sich selbst zu stehen, herausgelöst aus allen Lebensbezügen, und Kunst zur Kunst, d.h. zum „musée imaginaire" im Sinne Malraux' wurde, als Kunst nichts als Kunst sein wollte, setzte die große Revolution in der Kunst ein, die sich in der Moderne bis zur Ablösung von allen Bildinhaltstraditionen und verständlichen Aussagen gesteigert hat...»[3] Der Ursprung dieses Prozesses führt zu Kant und zum Erscheinen der *Kritik der Urteilskraft* von 1790 und 1793.

Die Konzeption des Spiels als grundlegendes ästhetisches Phänomen ergibt sich bei Kant unmittelbar aus der Unabhängigkeit des ästhetischen Bereichs von der wissenschaftlichen Theorie und der Moral, den Bezirken der reinen und der praktischen Vernunft. Dies war bekanntlich der große Wendepunkt, den Kant in der Geschichte der Ästhetik herbeiführte und was seine Pionierleistung in der Bestimmung des Schönen ausmacht.[4] Die Vorstellung eines «freien Spiels» erfolgte direkt aus dieser Autonomie des ästhetischen Bereichs, und zwar in zwei grundsätzlichen und miteinander korrespondierenden Betrachtungsweisen: von Seiten des den ästhetischen Eindruck empfangenden und in ästhetischen Geschmacksurteilen formulierenden *Betrachters* und von Seiten des die kunstschönen Gegenstände hervorbringenden *Künstlers*.

Bereits Nietzsche hat klar gesehen, daß Kants Beschreibung des ästhetischen Zustandes als interesseloses Wohlgefallen aus der Perspektive des «Zuschauers» erfolgt war und daß Kant, wie Nietzsche es ausdrückt, «dabei unvermerkt den „Zuschauer" selber in den Begriff „schön" hinein bekommen hat.»[5] Interesselos bedeutet hier selbstverständlich, daß man sich auf den dargestellten Gegenstand weder in theoretischer noch in praktischer Absicht bezieht. Diese Interesselosigkeit und Zweckfreiheit, die unser Wohlgefallen am Schönen kennzeichnet, hatte Kant als einen «Gemütszustand» bestimmt, in

---

3 Hans-Georg Gadamer, *Die Aktualität des Schönen. Kunst als Spiel, Symbol und Fest* (Stuttgart: Reclam, 1977), S. 23.
4 Siehe hierzu René Wellek, «Immanuel Kant's Aesthetics and Criticism,» René Wellek, *Discriminations. Further Concepts of Criticism* (New Haven: Yale University Press, 1970), S. 122–42; Hans Georg Gadamer, *Die Aktualität des Schönen*, S. 23–28; Odo Marquardt, «Kant und die Wende zur Ästhetik,» *Zeitschrift für philosophische Forschung*, 16 (1962); aber bereits Friedrich Schlegel, *Kritische Ausgabe*, Bd. I (Paderborn: Ferdinand Schöningh, 1979), S. 357. (Stellennachweise aus dieser Ausgabe sind direkt in den Text eingetragen.)
5 Friedrich Nietzsche, *Kritische Studienausgabe* (Berlin: de Gruyter, 1980), v, 346. (Stellennachweise aus dieser Ausgabe sind direkt in den Text eingetragen.)

dem sich die beiden hier wirksamen Erkenntniskräfte (Einbildungskraft: Mannigfaltigkeit der Anschauung und Verstand: Einheit des Begriffs) in einem «freien Spiele» miteinander befinden, «weil kein bestimmter Begriff sie auf eine besondere Erkenntnisregel einschränkt,»[6] eben weil kein theoretisches Ziel oder kein praktischer Zweck sie leitet.

Aus der Perspektive des künstlerischen Hervorbringens ist Kunst für Kant «Kunst des Genies» (v, 307). Das bedeutet zunächst «Originalität im Unterschied zum Talent, insofern das Genie seine Produkte nicht durch Nachahmung, noch nach vorgegebenen Regeln hervorbringt und nicht einmal anzugeben weiß, «wie sich seine phantasiereichen und doch zugleich gedankenvollen Ideen in seinem Kopfe hervor und zusammen finden» (v, 309). Auf der höchsten Stufe ist Genie aber das «Vermögen der Darstellung ästhetischer Ideen.» Unter einer ästhetischen Idee versteht Kant, wie er in immer wieder variierenden Wendungen formuliert, «diejenige Vorstellung der Einbildungskraft, die viel zu denken veranlaßt, ohne daß ihr doch ein bestimmter Gedanke, d.i. Begriff, adäquat sein kann, die folglich keine Sprache völlig erreicht und verständlich machen kann» (v, 314), «die also zu einem Begriff viel Unnennbares hinzu denken läßt» (v, 316), «die kein Ausdruck, welcher einem bestimmten Begriff angemessen ist, völlig erreicht» (v, 316). Das «belebende Prinzip im Gemüte», das diese Darstellung erlaubt, ist wiederum das freie Spiel zwischen der Einbildungskraft und dem Verstande. Dieser «Gemütszustand» gestattet es dem Genie, «das schnell vorübergehende Spiel der Einbildungskraft aufzufassen und in einen Begriff ... zu vereinigen, der sich ohne Zwang der Regeln mitteilen läßt» (v, 317). Künstler und Zuschauer, Genie und Betrachter stehen hier in einem untrennbaren Zusammenhang, wobei noch hervorzuheben ist, daß sich Kant vornehmlich auf die Dichtkunst als besonders privilegierte Form der Kunst bezieht (v, 314).[7]

Schillers Konzeption des Spieltriebes als Vermittlung von Stofftrieb und Formtrieb ist nach dieser Kantischen Sehweise der Kunst als «Verbindungsmittel» und «Mittelglied» zwischen dem Reich der Natur und dem der Freiheit entworfen. Aber unter dem Einfluß Fichtes, der sich besonders in den Briefen *Über die ästhetische Erziehung des Menschen* von 1795 bekundet,[8] wurde diese Mittlerrolle der Kunst nicht nur in der Terminologie von «Trieben» vorgetragen, sondern ebenfalls nach den Fichteschen Begriffen der «Wechselwir-

---

6 *Kants Werke. Akademie Textausgabe* (Berlin: de Gruyter, 1968), v, 217. (Stellennachweise aus dieser Ausgabe sind direkt in den Text eingetragen.)
7 Zur hermeneutischen Deutung dieses Verhältnisses siehe Hans-Georg Gadamer, *Wahrheit und Methode* (Tübingen: Mohr, 1975), S. 39–51.
8 *Schillers Werke*, Bd. 20: *Philosophische Schriften,* hrsg. Helmut Koopmann und Benno von Wiese (Weimar: Böhlau, 1962), S. 316, 348. (Stellennachweise aus diesem Band der Ausgabe sind direkt in den Text eingetragen.)

kung» (aus der *Grundlage der gesamten Wissenschaftslehre* von 1794[9]) und des «Schwebens» zwischen theoretischen und praktischen, sinnlichen und vernünftigen Trieben als ästhetischer «Nullpunkt» (S. 377) gedacht. Fichtes Bestimmung des Menschen als völlige Selbstverwirklichung seiner selbst (III, 32) liegt Schillers Gedanke zugrunde, daß der Mensch nur da spielt, «wo er in voller Bedeutung des Wortes Mensch ist,» und er nur da «ganz Mensch» ist, «wo er spielt» (S. 359). Mit den Begriffen des Nullpunktes und der Unerreichbarkeit der Selbstverwirklichung war Schiller der romantischen Konzeption des freien Spiels und der Ironie beträchtlich nahe gekommen.

Bei genauerer Betrachtung zeigt sich jedoch, daß das Spiel bei Schiller zweckgebunden ist und der Erziehung des Menschen dient. Ebenso ist die «schöne Kunst» ein «Werkzeug» zur Überwindung der Wirklichkeit und der Natur. Das Spiel erweist sich bei Schiller letztlich als Arbeit, als Kampf, der auf einen Sieg hinaus will und den Stoff durch die Form vertilgen soll. Das Kunstwerk erwächst somit für Schiller aus einer «Verbindung von Ernst und Spiel,»[10] wobei aber das Spielerische lediglich die niedere Wirklichkeit abgrenzt, das Wesen des Kunstwerks selbst jedoch im Ernst der Wahrheit besteht. Diese Auffassung bekundet sich auch in Schillers Briefen an Goethe, wenn er diesem am 17. Oktober 1797 versichert, daß nach seinem Begriff «das Ästhetische Ernst und Spiel zugleich ist,» oder wenn er Goethe am 8. Mai 1798 mitteilt, daß es nach seinen Begriffen zum Wesen der Poesie gehöre, «daß in ihr Ernst und Spiel immer verbunden seien.»

Wie wir aus Goethes Skizze über die *Einwirkung der neueren Philosophie* wissen, sah er sich im Gegensatz zu der Auffassung der Kunst, die Schiller aus der *Kritik der Urteilskraft* gewann und verargte diesem besonders die Verkürzung der «Rechte der Natur,» wobei er Schiller freilich zugestand, daß dieser «in den ästhetischen Briefen die gute Mutter nicht mit jenen harten Ausdrücken» behandelt hatte, die Goethe den Aufsatz *Über Anmut und Würde* so «verhaßt» gemacht hatten.[11] Für Goethe leitete die *Kritik der Urteilskraft* «eine höchst frohe Lebensepoche» ein (XIII, 27), und er betonte es immer wieder als die Befreiungstat des Alten aus Königsberg, daß dieser «die Kunst von dem absurden Gedanken der Endzwecke gelöst habe.»[12] Einer der wesentlichsten Aspekte von Kants *Kritik der Urteilskraft* bestand für Goethe darin, daß «das innere Leben der Kunst so wie der Natur, ihr beiderseitiges Wirken von

---

9 Johann Gottlieb Fichte, *Werke,* hrsg. Reinhard Lauth und Hans Jacob, Bd. 2 (Stuttgart-Bad Cannstatt: Frommanns, 1966), 173-451. Dieser Begriff beherrscht auch die Schrift *Einige Vorlesungen über die Bestimmung des Gelehrten von 1794,* die ebenfalls für Schillers Briefe von entscheidender Bedeutung war: Fichte, *Werke,* III, 37-41; Schillers Werke, XX, 348.
10 Wolfgang Kayser, *Kunst und Spiel. Fünf Goethe-Studien* (Göttingen: Vandenhoeck & Ruprecht, 1961), S. 35.
11 Johann Wolfgang von Goethe, *Werke,* Hamburger Ausgabe in 14 Bänden (München: dtv, 1982), XIII, 28-29. (Stellennachweise aus dieser Ausgabe sind direkt in den Text eingetragen.)
12 Zitiert nach Wolfgang Kayser, «Goethe und das Spiel,» *Kunst und Spiel,* S. 41.

innen heraus» in diesem Buche deutlich ausgesprochen war. Und mit einer Betonung der zweckfreien Eigengesetzlichkeit dieser Welten fuhr Goethe fort: «Die Erzeugnisse dieser zwei unendlichen Welten sollten um ihrer selbst willen da sein und, was neben einander stand, wohl *für* einander, aber nicht absichtlich *wegen* einander» (XIII, 28).

Wie Wolfgang Kayser gezeigt hat, erhält das Wort von der Dichtung als Spiel bei Goethe «einen ganz neuen und ungleich tieferen Sinn als bei Schiller.»[13] Spielen äußerte sich bei Goethe in einer selbstbefreienden Hingabe an die Dinge, im Motiv der «Verwandlung» und in einem «mystifizierenden Versteckspielen» mit Masken.[14] In ästhetischer und poetologischer Hinsicht begegnet uns die Metapher vom Spiel zum Beispiel in den *Noten und Abhandlungen zu besserem Verständnis des West-östlichen Divan*. Hier wird die Dichtung als freies Spiel der Einbildungskraft charakterisiert, und Goethe sagt über ihre Produkte: «Ihr eigentlicher Charakter ist, daß sie keinen sittlichen Zweck haben und daher den Menschen nicht auf sich selbst zurück, sondern außer sich hinaus ins unbedingt Freie führen und tragen» (II, 146). In der Unterhaltung, welche *Das Märchen* einleitet, finden wir die Bemerkung über die Einbildungskraft: «Sie muß sich, deucht mich, an keinen Gegenstand hängen, sie muß uns keinen Gegenstand aufdringen wollen, sie soll, wenn sie Kunstwerke hervorbringt, nur wie eine Musik auf uns selbst spielen, uns in uns selbst bewegen, und zwar so, daß wir vergessen, daß etwas außer uns sei, das diese Bewegung hervorbringt» (VI, 209).

Mit solchen Formulierungen umschreibt Goethe Aspekte der Kunst, die auch für die romantische Sehweise charakteristisch sind. Ein wichtiger Unterschied zu der romantischen Konzeption vom freien Spiel der Kunst scheint aber darin zu bestehen, daß für Goethe in diesem freien Spielen der Phantasie eine «geregelte Einbildungskraft» wirksam ist, die eine «innere geregelte Organisation» hervorbringt, was sich in Goethes Worten, übrigens mit einer deutlichen Kantischen Wendung, auch so ausdrücken läßt, daß wie die «große allgemeine Natur die organischen Gesetze tätig bewahrt,» die Kunstgesetze «ebenso wahr in der Natur des bildenden Genius» liegen.[15] Freilich verlangt diese Unterscheidung eine genauere Spezifizierung, wie denn die Begriffe Kunst und Spiel in der Romantik gebraucht worden sind.

Henry Crabb Robinson hat wohl als erster klar gesehen, daß Friedrich Schlegels früher Essay *Über das Studium der Griechischen Poesie* (1795-97) direkt aus der *Kritik der Urteilskraft* erwachsen war und die Formulierung vom «interesselosen Wohlgefallen,» das der Eindruck des «Schönen» im Ge-

---

13 Siehe zum folgenden den in Anmerkung 12 genannten Aufsatz, S. 37ff.
14 Siehe hierzu Georg Simmel, *Goethe*, 4. Aufl. (Leipzig: Klinkhardt & Biermann, 1923).
15 Goethes Kommentar zu Diderots Aufsatz über die Malerei. Zitiert nach Wolfgang Kayser, S. 43.

müt hervorruft, in den Bereich der Geschichte der Literatur umbildete.[16] Die beiden großen Epochen der europäischen Poesie, die Schlegel in diesem Essay unterscheidet, die der «Alten» und die der «Neuern,» und denen die bedeutende Distinktion der klassischen und der romantischen Poesie zugrundeliegt, sind nämlich genau nach diesen Kantischen Begriffen kategorisiert. Die Poesie der «Alten,» d.h. der Griechen, wird dort als «schöne,» «ästhetische» oder «objektive» Poesie charakterisiert. Sie «weiß von keinem Interesse, und macht keine Ansprüche auf Realität. Sie strebt nur nach einem *Spiel,* das so würdig sei als der heiligste Ernst, nach einem *Schein,* der so allgemeingültig und gesetzgebend sei, als die unbedingteste Wahrheit» (I, 211). In konzentrierter Zuspitzung dieser Ansicht sagt Schlegel: «Der *spezifische Charakter* der schönen Kunst ist freies Spiel ohne bestimmten Zweck» (I, 241–242). Was aber jenseits dieses «ästhetischen Horizonts» (I, 328) liegt, d.h. nicht im zweckfreien Spielen der Einbildungskraft befangen ist, gehört letztlich nicht zur Welt der Schönheit. Es ist die «interessante,» durch einen bestimmten Zweck gebundene, z.B. «philosophisch» orientierte oder «subjektive» Poesie der «Neuern,» d.h. der Modernen, ungefähr seit dem Ausgang des Mittelalters. «Nichts kann die Künstlichkeit der modernen ästhetischen Bildung besser erläutern und bestätigen, als das große *Übergewicht des Individuellen, Charakteristischen und Philosophischen* in der ganzen Masse der modernen Poesie. Die vielen und trefflichen Kunstwerke, deren Zweck ein philosophisches Interesse ist, bilden nicht etwa bloß eine unbedeutende Nebenart der schönen Poesie, sondern eine ganz eigene große Hauptgattung...» (I, 241).

Während allen «Barbaren» die »*Schönheit an sich selbst nicht gut genug*« war, bilden die »*Heiligkeit schöner Spiele*« und die »*Freiheit der darstellenden Kunst*« die eigentlichen *Kennzeichen echter Griechheit*» (I, 175). Das Prinzip dieser im freien Spiel sich konstituierenden Schönheit ist die vollständige Ausbildung der «ganzen menschlichen Natur,» die sich «im glücklichsten Ebenmaß, im vollkommenen *Gleichgewicht*» von «einseitiger Beschränkung» oder «künstlicher Mißbildung» weit entfernt hält (I, 279). Ein solcher Schein von Schönheit zeigt sich uns zum Beispiel bei Homer. «Der *Umfang* seiner Dichtung,» sagt Schlegel, «ist so unbeschränkt, wie der Umfang der ganzen menschlichen Natur selbst. Die äußersten Enden der verschiedensten Richtungen, deren ursprüngliche Keime schon in der allgemeinen Menschennatur verborgen liegen, gesellen sich hier freundlich zueinander, wie im unbefangnen, kindlichen Spiel» (I, 279). In noch höherem Maße kommt dieser ausgewogene Charakter der Schönheit im ästhetischen Spiel des Sophokles zum Ausdruck (I, 296–301). Spiel als Wesenselement der Einbildungskraft und Poesie zeigt sich selbst in Grenzfällen der griechischen Literatur, d.h. in nicht rein poetischen Werken wie der Geschichte des Thukydides, den «Demostheni-

---

16 Henry Crabb Robinson, *Letters on German Literature,* No. [IV]. «Kant's Analysis of Beauty,» unveröffentlicht (Dr. Williams's Library, London, Bundle 1. III. 28).

schen Reden» oder den «Sokratischen Gesprächen,» wo die «dichtende Einbildungskraft zwar durch einen bestimmten Zweck des Verstandes beschränkt, aber doch nicht aller Freiheit beraubt, und also auch der Pflicht, schön zu spielen, nicht entbunden» ist (I, 205-06).

Schlegel gibt zu, daß die Grenzlinien der Poesie in einzelnen Fällen oft schwer zu bestimmen sind, der entscheidende Punkt aber in der »*Anordnung des Ganzen*» besteht. Er sagt: «Der bestimmte Gliederbau eines didaktischen Werks läßt sich am wenigsten verkennen. Ist es die gesetzlichfreie Ordnung eines schönen Spiels, so ist das Werk ästhetisch» (I, 244). Damit wird deutlich, daß aus diesen im Medium der Griechen sich vollziehenden Betrachtungen über das Schöne, die Einbildungskraft und das Spiel eine Theorie der poetischen Einheit erwächst, die der gerade von Goethe zitierten durchaus nicht unähnlich ist. Genau diesen Begriff einer sich in Mannigfaltigkeit und Fülle auffächernden Einheit hat Schlegel auch in seiner Rezension von Goethes *Wilhelm Meister* von 1798 weiter ausgeführt (II, 126-146), und Goethe lobte den jungen Kritiker dafür, daß dieser «immer auf den Bau des Ganzen» gegangen sei und sich nicht «bei pathologischer Zergliederung der Charaktere» aufgehalten habe (XXIV, 177). Man möchte diese sich im «schönen Spiel» konstituierende «gesetzlichfreie Ordnung,» die unter dem Namen der organischen Einheit bekannt und berühmt geworden ist, eine strukturalistische Einheit nennen. Aber man sieht sofort, daß sie von jenem «mutwilligen» Spielen der Phantasie noch weit entfernt ist, wie es in Schlegels Theorie der Poesie nun immer mehr zum Ausdruck kommt und sich im *Athenäum* zum Beispiel in der «Willkür des Dichters» bekundet, die «kein Gesetz über sich» leidet oder sich in jener dichterischen Haltung manifestiert, die «frei von allem realen und idealen Interesse auf den Flügeln der poetischen Reflexion in der Mitte schweben, diese Reflexion immer wieder potenzieren und wie in einer endlosen Reihe von Spiegeln vervielfachen» will (II, 182-183).

August Wilhelm Schlegel hat an dieser organischen oder strukturalistischen Konzeption der poetischen Einheit festgehalten, die er zuerst in seinem meisterhaften Aufsatz *Über Shakespeares Romeo und Julie* von 1797 entwickelte[17] und dann in den *Vorlesungen über dramatische Kunst und Literatur* als Gegensatz der «organischen Form» gegenüber der «mechanischen» weiter ausführte (VI, 157-158). Sein Begriff des ästhetischen Spiels bleibt damit auf die ausgeprägte Form und Ganzheit bezogen und resultiert in dieser Struktur. Freilich entwickelte A.W. Schlegel diesen Begriff der Kunst nicht mehr auf der Kantischen Basis einer «spielenden Tätigkeit» der Einbildungskraft und des Verstandes,[18] noch auf der Grundlage der Fichteschen «Wechsel-

---

17 August Wilhelm Schlegel, *Sämtliche Werke,* hrsg. Eduard Böcking (Leipzig: Weidmann, 1846), VII, 71-97. (Stellennachweise aus dieser Ausgabe sind direkt in den Text eingetragen.)
18 *A.W. Schlegels Vorlesungen über schöne Literatur und Kunst,* hrsg. Jacob Minor, 3 Bde., Deutsche Literaturdenkmale des 18. und 19. Jahrhunderts, 17-19 (Heilbronn: Gebr. Henninger, 1884), I, 66.

wirkung,» sondern nach den Prinzipien der Identitätsphilosophie und der von Schelling entwickelten Form der Einbildungskraft als In-eins-Bildung des Unendlichen und Endlichen.[19]

Dagegen haben Friedrich Schlegel und Novalis in den letzten Jahren des achtzehnten Jahrhunderts den absoluten Poesiebegriff entwickelt und damit das ästhetische Spiel von jeder begrenzenden Einheit und Form losgelöst und freigesetzt. Diese «Spiele der Kunst» sind für Friedrich Schlegel «ferne Nachbildungen von dem unendlichen Spiele der Welt, dem ewig sich selbst bildenden Kunstwerk» (II, 324). Die «Konstruktion des Ganzen» zeigt sich in ihnen als «diese künstlich geordnete Verwirrung, diese reizende Symmetrie von Widersprüchen, dieser wunderbare ewige Wechsel von Enthusiasmus und Ironie,» wie diese in den Dichtungen von Cervantes und Shakespeare zum Ausdruck kommen (II, 318-19). Wenn man von einem Zweck dieser Poesie sprechen will, bietet sich dafür die Formel an: «Die Musik des Lebens zu phantasieren» (II, 263; XI, 161). «Die Welt als Musik betrachtet,» heißt es bereits in einem Fragment von 1798, « ist ein ewiger Tanz aller Wesen, ein allgemeines Lied aller Lebendigen, und ein rhythmischer Strom von Geistern» (XVIII, 202). Das zentrale Wort für diese spielerische Anschauung der Welt ist für Schlegel aber die Ironie, die er bestimmt als «intellektuelle Anschauung eines ewigen Chaos, eines unendlich vollen, genialisch ewig zyklischen» (XVIII, 228).

Novalis teilt diese Ansicht von einer inneren Korrespondenz zwischen den unendlichen Spielen der Welt und denen der Kunst, wenn er zum Beispiel sagt: «Spielt Gott und die Natur nicht auch? Theorie des Spielens. *Heilige Spiele.* reine Spiellehre – *gemeine* und höhere. Angewandte Spiellehre.»[20] Die besondere Note seiner ästhetischen Spieltheorie besteht aber in sprachphilosophischen Überlegungen. Diese kommen in der *Monolog* betitelten Eintragung zum Ausdruck, die das Sprechen «um der Dinge willen» als «lächerlichen Irrtum» ansieht und das «rechte Gespräch» als «ein bloßes Wortspiel» bezeichnet (II, 672). Entsprechend ist die reine oder absolute Poesie für ihn völlig absichtslos und frei von der Sprache als «bestimmte Mitteilung,» «Ausdruck einer Absicht,» «Benennungskunst» (II, 572).

Aus dieser völligen Zweckfreiheit der «höheren» oder absoluten Poesie ergibt sich ein ganz eigentümlicher Poesiebegriff, in der die romantische Metapher von der Kunst als Spiel ihren am höchsten gesteigerten Ausdruck findet. Wenige Beispiele können dies veranschaulichen. In einem Fragment charakterisiert Novalis diese höhere Poesie als «Gemütserregungskunst,» d.h. als ein Verfahren, «innere *Stimmungen,* und Gemälde oder *Anschauungen* hervorzubringen – vielleicht auch geistige Tänze, etc.,» so daß die Poesie hier gleichsam

---

19 *A.W. Schlegels Vorlesungen über schöne Literatur und Kunst,* I, 89-90.
20 *Novalis, Schriften,* hrsg. Richard Samuel in Zusammenarbeit mit Hans-Joachim Mähl und Gerhard Schulz, Bd. 3 (Stuttgart: Kohlhammer, 1968), 320. (Stellennachweise aus dieser Ausgabe sind direkt in den Text eingetragen.)

«nur das mechanische Instrument» ist, als «innre Malerei und Musik» besondere Gemütszustände zu erzeugen (III, 639). In einer solchen Tätigkeit gebraucht der Dichter «Dinge und Worte, wie *Tasten,*» und seine «ganze Poesie beruht auf tätiger Ideenassoziation – auf selbsttätiger, absichtlicher, idealischer Zufallsproduktion.» Novalis verwendet für solche «zufällige – freie Catenation» oder Aneinanderreihung von Worten ausdrücklich den Begriff «Spiel» (III, 451).

Es versteht sich, daß die «Einheit» und sogar der «Zusammenhang» in dieser Poesie suspendiert ist. «Ein Märchen,» sagt Novalis, «ist eigentlich wie ein Traumbild – ohne Zusammenhang – ein *Ensemble* wunderbarer Dinge und Begebenheiten: z.B. eine *musikalische Phantasie.*» Und er hebt dieses völlig zweckfreie Gebilde von jeder Absichtlichkeit ab, wenn er hinzufügt: «Wird eine *Geschichte* ins Märchen gebracht, so ist dies schon eine fremde Einmischung» (III, 454). An einer anderen Stelle findet sich die bekannte Eintragung: «Erzählungen, ohne Zusammenhang, jedoch mit Assoziation, wie *Träume.* Gedichte – bloß *wohlklingend* und voll schöner Worte – aber auch ohne allen Sinn und Zusammenhang – höchstens einzelne Strophen verständlich – sie müssen, wie lauter Bruchstücke aus den verschiedenartigsten Dingen sein» (III, 572). Auf Grund dieser Merkmale seiner ästhetischen Spieltheorie – vor allem aber von Gegebenheiten wie «Selbstsprache ohne Mitteilungszweck,» «Gemütserregungskunst,» Farbe, Musik, Rhythmus und Klang – ist Novalis wohl mit Recht als Vorläufer moderner Dichtungstheorien, besonders des Symbolismus, angesehen worden.[21]

Wir brauchen aber in dieser Richtung der romantischen Metapher von der Kunst als Spiel nicht weiter fortzufahren, weil aus dem Dargelegten bereits ersichtlich ist, daß hier trotz vieler Gemeinsamkeiten nicht die Inspirationen für Nietzsches Begriff der Kunst und seiner Sehweise der Kunst als Spiel gelegen haben. Zwar hat sich Nietzsche direkt mit Novalis und den Brüdern Schlegel beschäftigt. Bereits als Schüler studierte er während der Schulferien bei einem Verwandten in Jena die Werke des Novalis, von dem er meinte, daß «dessen philosophische Gedanken mich interessieren.»[22] In Nietzsches Schriften finden sich aber nur wenige Spuren des Novalis, die sich vor allem auf dessen Annahme einer «Assoziation von Wollust, Religion und Grausamkeit» im religiösen Erleben beziehen (II, 138). Von den literarischen Theorien der Brüder

---

[21] Siehe hierzu Hugo Friedrich, *Die Struktur der modernen Lyrik,* 2. Aufl. (Hamburg: Rowohlt, 1968), S. 27-29; Werner Vordtriede, *Novalis und die französischen Symbolisten* (Stuttgart: Kohlhammer, 1963); Wolfgang Kayser, *Geschichte des deutschen Verses; für Hörer aller Fakultäten* (Bern: Francke, 1960), S. 116–17; William H. Rey, *Poesie der Antipoesie. Moderne deutsche Lyrik: Genesis, Theorie, Struktur* (Heidelberg: Stiehm, 1978), S. 75-87.

[22] Friedrich Nietzsche, *Werke in drei Bänden,* hrsg. Karl Schlechta (München: Hanser, 1956) III, 69. Siehe hierzu Carl Albrecht Bernoulli, *Franz Overbeck und Friedrich Nietzsche* (Jena: Eugen Diederichs, 1908), I, 311-12.

Schlegel interessierten Nietzsche vor allem die Ansichten dieser Kritiker über den Chor der griechischen Tragödie und das Dionysische.[23]

Nietzsches Vorstellung der zweckfreien Kunst und vom Spiel der Kunst ist nicht direkt aus der deutschen Geistesgeschichte hervorgegangen, sondern entweder von den Griechen hergeleitet oder aus Gedanken der französischen Romantik entwickelt. An die Stelle aus der Vorrede zu *Die fröhliche Wissenschaft,* welche «eine spöttische, leichte, flüchtige, göttlich unbehelligte, göttlich künstliche Kunst.... Vor allem: eine Kunst für Künstler, nur für Künstler!» fordert (III, 351), schließt sich sofort die bekannte Stelle an: «Oh diese Griechen! Sie verstanden sich darauf zu *leben:* dazu tut Not, tapfer bei der Oberfläche, der Falte, der Haut stehen zu bleiben, den Schein anzubeten, an Formen, an Töne, an Worte, an den ganzen Olymp des Scheins zu glauben! Diese Griechen waren oberflächlich – *aus Tiefe!»* (III, 352). Im Frankreich seiner Zeit und in der französischen Romantik fand Nietzsche «die Fähigkeit zu artistischen Leidenschaften, zu Hingebungen an die „Form", für welche das Wort *l'art pour l'art,* neben tausend anderen erfunden ist» und «eine Art Kammermusik der Literatur» ermöglicht hat, «welche im übrigen Europa sich suchen läßt» (V, 99). Mit dieser Konfiguration der Worte *l'art pour l'art* tritt eine zentrale Formulierung für Nietzsches Vorstellung von der Zweckfreiheit der Kunst in Erscheinung. Ohne die für ihn gleichfalls wesentliche Konzeption vom freien Spiel der Kunst zu unterminieren, kommt mit der Devise des *l'art pour l'art* ebenfalls der strenge Wille zur Form und zum Gestalten zum Ausdruck, für den Nietzsche in bezug auf die Künstler dieser Art den Begriff «Fanatiker des *Ausdrucks* „um jeden Preis'» (V, 202) geprägt hat, wobei er offenbar sich selbst in diesen Typ einbezog. Gottfried Benn hatte diesen Aspekt in Nietzsches Auffassung der Kunst im Auge, als er sagte, daß Nietzsche uns lehrte, eine Handbreit Prosa wie eine Statue zu meißeln. «Nietzsche führte uns aus dem Bildungsmäßigen, dem Gelehrten, Wissenschaftlichen, dem Familiären und und Gutmütigen ... in das gedanklich Raffinierte, in die Formulierung um des Ausdrucks willen,» so entwickelte Benn diesen Gedanken weiter: «er führte die Vorstellung der Artistik in Deutschland ein ... er sagte: Die Delikatesse in allen fünf Kunstsinnen, die Finger für Nuancen, die psychologische Morbidität, der Ernst des Mis-en-scène ...; und er krönte dies mit drei rätselhaften Worten: Olymp des Scheins.»[24]

Geht man diesem Wort *l'art pour l'art* aber genauer nach, dann stellt sich erstaunlicherweise heraus, daß es demselben Problemkreis der *Kritik der Urteilskraft* entstammt, aus dem sich die Metapher von der Kunst als Spiel in der deutschen Romantik herleitete. Während Kants Lehre von der Autonomie und

---

23 Siehe hierzu Ernst Behler, «Die Auffassung des Dionysischen durch die Brüder Schlegel und Friedrich Nietzsche,» *Nietzsche-Studien,* 12 (1983), 335–54.
24 Gottfried Benn, *Gesammelte Werke in acht Bänden,* hrsg. Dieter Wellershoff (Wiesbaden: Limes, 1968), IV, 1107.

Zweckfreiheit der Kunst in der deutschen Tradition im Bilde des Spiels der Kunst fortlebte, fand sie in Frankreich in der Bezeichnung *l'art pour l'art* Ausdruck. Nietzsche hatte deutlich «die französische Spät-Romantik der Vierziger Jahre» (v, 202) vor Augen, als er die Künstler dieses Typs mit folgenden Wendungen umschrieb: «diese Meister neuer Sprachmittel» – «diese letzten großen Suchenden» – diese «ersten Künstler von weltliterarischer Bildung» – diese «Vermittler und Vermischer der Künste und der Sinne» – «allesamt große Entdecker im Reiche des Erhabenen, auch des Häßlichen und Gräßlichen, noch größere Entdecker im Effekte, in der Schaustellung, in der Kunst der Schauläden, allesamt Talente weit über ihr Genie hinaus –, Virtuosen durch und durch, mit unheimlichen Zugängen zu Allem, was verführt, lockt, zwingt, umwirft, geborene Feinde der Logik und der geraden Linien, begehrlich nach dem Fremden, dem Exotischen, dem Ungeheuren, dem Krummen, dem Sich-Widersprechenden ...» (v, 202–203). Aber Nietzsche exemplifizierte diesen Typus auch mit Goethe, Beethoven, Heinrich Heine und Richard Wagner, also mit deutschen Repräsentanten der neuen Kunst und Romantik. Tatsächlich bilden diese beiden historischen Komponenten, deutsche und französische Romantik, grundlegende Anregungen für Nietzsches eigene Auffassung der Kunst.

Benedetto Croce hat in seiner *Ästhetik* klar gesehen, daß die Proklamierung der These *l'art pour l'art* in Frankreich unter deutschen Einflüssen von Frau von Staël ihren Ausgang genommen hatte.[25] Das heißt nicht, daß Frau von Staël selbst eine Vertreterin dieser Auffassung der Kunst gewesen wäre. In Wirklichkeit ist Frau von Staëls Konzeption der Literatur der These *l'art pour l'art* nämlich genau entgegengesetzt, da für sie die Literatur in einer Wechselwirkung mit der Gesellschaft ihrer Epoche steht und am Fortschritt der Sitten und Ideen, an der «perfectibilité» des Menschengeschlechts mitwirkt. Dennoch brachte sie diese Doktrin als eines der wichtigsten Resultate ihres Aufenthaltes in Weimar vom Winter 1803 bis zum Frühling 1804 nach Coppet zurück, von wo diese ihren Weg in die französische Romantik fand.

Bei ihrem Bestreben, sich mit der deutschen Literatur und Philosophie bekannt zu machen, war sie auf den Engländer Henry Crabb Robinson gestoßen, der damals in Jena bei Schelling Philosophie, insbesondere Ästhetik studierte und mit der Transzendentalphilosophie besser vertraut war als jeder andere der zahlreichen Besucher, die damals dieser Philosophie wegen nach Deutschland kamen. Robinson gab Frau von Staël Privatvorlesungen *On the German Aesthetics or Philosophy of Taste*, an denen ebenfalls Benjamin Constant und Vertreter des Weimarer Geisteslebens teilnahmen. Am 11. Februar 1804 dozierte Robinson über das Ideal der Schönheit und führte dabei aus, der schöne Gegenstand müsse eine «form of *intimated* design» haben: »it must have no

---

25 Zitiert nach Benedetto Croce, *Aesthetics as Science of Expression and General Linguistics* (New York: Noonday Press, [12]1968), S. 352.

object out of itself.» Dies Resultat, so fügte Robinson hinzu, das er nur kümmerlich zum Ausdruck gebracht habe und auch von Kant recht vage belassen sei, hätte zu den Lieblingsideen der modernen Kritiker, d.h. der deutschen Frühromantiker, über «pure poetry» und «pure art» geführt.[26] Benjamin Constant, der das Talent dafür besaß, komplizierte Sachverhalte in prägnante Formeln zusammenzufassen, notierte sich unter diesem Datum in seinem *Journal intime:* «L'art pour l'art, et sans but.»[27]

Hier erscheint zum erstenmal jener Ausdruck, der nach René Wellek schon bald zum «slogan» der *l'art pour l'art* Bewegung wurde und durch die Vermittlung der französischen Spätromantik, insbesondere Baudelaires, an Nietzsche gelangte.[28] Die Forderung, die Kunst um ihrer selbst willen zu betreiben, hat in der französischen Romantik um Victor Hugo, insbesondere bei Théophile Gautier, noch keineswegs die später hervortretende Konzentration auf die Form als Motiv, sondern bezieht ihren Impuls aus der Forderung, daß die Kunst zwecklos, nutzlos, von praktischen Zielen unabhängig sein soll, womit sich eine Neigung zu exotisch-phantastischen Produktionen, aber auch zum «bohème»-Stil und zu einer sich gegen Philistertum und Bürgerlichkeit gewendeten Ungezügeltheit verband. Im Vorwort zu seinem Roman *Mademoiselle Maupin* von 1835 entwickelte Gautier aber Anschauungen über das Wesen der Kunst, in der die Vollendung der Form und des Ausdrucks die vorherrschenden Eigenschaften sind und unter dem Namen des Parnassianismus bekannt wurden. Gautier kann als Vorläufer dieser Richtung angesehen werden, die über das Zeitalter der Romantik in Frankreich hinausreicht und durch Baudelaire, Flaubert, Banville, Leconte de Lisle repräsentiert ist. Anstelle des romantischen Gefühlsüberschwangs und der subjektiven Freiheiten des Künstlers steht hier der objektive, unpersönliche, beherrschte, statische Gestaltungswille (impassibilité) im Vordergrund. Gautier sagte in diesem Vorwort: «Il n'y a de vraiment beau que ce qui ne peut servir à rien: tout ce qui est utile est laid.» Gautier hat diese Kunsttheorie später in der Gedichtsammlung *Emaux et Camées* von 1852 vertieft. Emailfarben und kostbar geschnitzte Gemmen, der weiße Marmor und bleiche Statuen sollen das Schönheitsideal zum Ausdruck bringen, das durch kein außerkünstlerisches Interesse getrübt ist. Im Widerstand gegen die moralischen, politischen und sozialen Tendenzen der Romantiker, welche die Kunst in den Dienst des Fortschritts der Menschheit stellen wollten, tritt hier ein rein ästhetischer Formwille auf, der das widerstrebende Material («vers, marbre, onyx, email») zu beherrschen vermag und über der materiellen Welt, die vergeht, das Kunstwerk errichtet, das Ewigkeitswert hat.

---

26 Unveröffentlicht. Zitiert nach einer in der Sächsischen Landesbibiliothek aufbewahrten Abschrift der Vorlesungsnotizen Robinsons: «On German Aesthetics,» p. 2a.
27 Benjamin Constant, *Journaux intimes,* hrsg. Alfred Roulin und Charles Roth (Paris: Gallimard, 1952), S. 58.
28 René Wellek, «Immanuel Kant's Aesthetics and Criticism,» S. 135.

Für den hier verfolgten Zusammenhang ist dabei von Bedeutung, daß Baudelaire wenigstens zu zwei wichtigen Zeitpunkten Nietzsches Aufmerksamkeit erweckte. Baudelaire war ein Bewunderer Gautiers und hatte diesem seinen Gedichtzyklus *Les Fleurs du mal* von 1875 gewidmet, zu dem Gautier später ein Vorwort beisteuerte, das Nietzsche mit Bleistiftanstreichungen studierte.[29] Nietzsche benutzte die Ausgabe von 1882 im Frühling 1885 in Nizza, und man hat diese Lektüre mit Recht mit seiner damaligen Charakterisierung der «Fanatiker des Ausdrucks» in Zusammenhang gebracht, wie sie im Aphorismus 256 aus *Jenseits von Gut und Böse* gezeichnet sind, der die «guten Europäer» behandelt,[30] obwohl Baudelaires Name dort noch nicht erscheint. Nietzsche las zu dieser Zeit auch den Baudelaire-Aufsatz aus dem ersten Band der *Essais de psychologie contemporaine* von Paul Bourget, was ebenfalls für seine Kunstauffassung von Bedeutung war.

Die zweite Beschäftigung mit Baudelaire fand im Februar 1888 statt und gründete sich auf Baudelaires *Oeuvres posthumes et correspondances inédites*, die 1887 erschienen waren und aus denen Nietzsche zahlreiche Exzerpte in seine unveröffentlichten Schriften eintrug (XIII, 75-87, 90-92). Dieses zweite Baudelairestudium stand freilich unter einem weniger günstigen Stern als das erste. Zwar enthalten diese Exzerpte viel über Baudelaire Konzeption der «poésie pure» (XIII, 91) und seine Auffassung der Schönheit als etwas «Glühendes und Trauriges» (XIII, 79). Doch dienen diese hauptsächlich dazu, den Pessimismus der Dekadenz gleichsam «von innen her kennenzulernen durch einen, der sich selber nicht schonte» und in dessen Dekadenz «sich die zeittypische physiologische Schwäche exemplarischen Ausdruck verschafft hat.»[31] Natürlich macht es die schillernde Bedeutungsvielfalt in Nietzsches Begriff der *décadence* schwer, hier eindeutige Feststellungen zu treffen. Karl Pestalozzi erblickte sogar die besondere Spannung dieser «stummen Exzerpte» aus Baudelaire darin, daß hier «neben der unzweifelhaften Geringschätzung und Ablehnung auch eine geheime Identifikation Nietzsches mit Baudelaires irrlichtert» (S. 175).

Insofern hat auch die Parole *l'art pour l'art* für Nietzsche eine Varietät von Bedeutungen. Sie drückt nicht allein Formgestaltungs- und Schaffenswillen aus, sondern manifestiert ebenfalls «ästhetischen Pessimismus» (XII, 409), ja Nihilismus (XII, 557). Gleichzeitig begleitet eine derartige Kunst für Nietzsche auch jene Fülle an Schönheiten, die erst durch die *décadence* in die Welt gekommen ist. Das zeigt sich nirgendwo deutlicher als im Aphorismus 208 aus *Jenseits von Gut und Böse* über die «Krankheit des Willens» (Nietzsches For-

---

29 Siehe hierzu und zum folgenden den ausgezeichnet dokumentierten Aufsatz von Karl Pestalozzi, «Nietzsches Baudelaire-Rezeption,» *Nietzsche-Studien*, 7 (1978), 158-78, 165. Dem Verfasser stand Nietzsches Exemplar zur Verfügung.
30 Karl Pestalozzi, «Nietzsches Baudelaire-Rezeption,» S. 164-65.
31 Karl Pestalozzi, S. 172, 177.

mel für literarische décadence: VI, 27), der wiederum Frankreich als Schule und Schaustellung aller «Zauber der Skepsis» das «Kultur-Übergewicht über Europa» zuerkennt, weil der französische Geist «immer eine meisterhafte Geschicklichkeit gehabt hat, auch die verhängnisvollen Wendungen seines Geistes ins Reizende und Verführerische umzukehren» (V, 139). Daß Nietzsche sich hier ausdrücklich auch auf die Auffassung der Kunst als *l'art pour l'art* bezieht, geht aus der Wendung hervor: «und daß zum Beispiel das meiste von dem, was sich heute als „Objektivität", „Wissenschaftlichkeit", „l'art pour l'art", „reines willenfreies Erkennen" in die Schauläden stellt, nur ausgeputzte Skepsis und Willenslähmung ist – für diese Diagnose der europäischen Krankheit will ich einstehen» (V, 138–139).

Wie dieser Aphorismus mit dem zuvor zitierten über die «Fanatiker des *Ausdrucks* „um jeden Preis"» (V, 202) zusammenhängt, ergibt sich aus dem Aphorismus 5 in dem Abschnitt «Warum ich so klug bin» aus *Ecce Homo,* der wesentliche Gedanken des Aphorismus 256 aus *Jenseits von Gut und Böse* aufgreift, aber nun Baudelaire direkt als einen Prototyp dieser Kunst anführt. «Aber ich habe schon zur Genüge ausgesprochen,» sagt Nietzsche dort, indem er sich auf den betreffenden Aphorismus in *Jenseits von Gut und Böse*» bezieht, «wohin Wagner gehört, in dem er seine Nächstverwandten hat: es ist die französische Spät-Romantik, jene hochfliegende und hoch emporreißende Art von Künstlern wie Delacroix, wie Berlioz, mit einem *fond* von Krankheit, von Unheilbarkeit im Wesen, lauter Fanatiker des *Ausdrucks,* Virtuosen durch und durch ... Wer war der erste *intelligente* Anhänger Wagners überhaupt? Charles Baudelaire, derselbe, der zuerst Delacroix verstand, jener typische *décadent,* in dem sich ein ganzes Geschlecht von Artisten wiedererkannt hat – er war vielleicht auch der letzte...» (VI, 289). Indem er aber dies artistische Lob Wagners zurücknimmt und seine eigene Kritik an Wagner zu rechtfertigen sucht, fügte Nietzsche hinzu: «Was ich Wagner nie vergeben habe? Daß er zu den Deutschen *kondeszendierte,* – daß er reichsdeutsch wurde ... Soweit Deutschland reicht, *verdirbt* es die Kultur» (VI, 189).

Die Vieldeutigkeit des Begriffs *l'art pour l'art* zeigt sich bei Nietzsche zum Beispiel, wenn er scheinbar anerkennend über diese Haltung sagt: «Der Kampf gegen den Zweck in der Kunst ist immer der Kampf gegen die *moralisierende* Tendenz in der Kunst, gegen ihre Unterordnung unter die Moral. *L'art pour l'art* heißt: „der Teufel hole die Moral!"» Im selben Aphorismus fährt er aber mit der Überlegung fort, daß selbst wenn man «den Zweck des Moralpredigens und Menschen-Verbesserns von der Kunst ausgeschlossen hat,» daraus noch lange nicht folgt, «daß die Kunst überhaupt zwecklos, ziellos, sinnlos, kurz *l'art pour l'art* – ein Wurm, der sich in den Schwanz beißt – ist» (VI, 127). Nietzsche verfolgt dort diesen Gedanken weiter und sagt: «„Lieber gar keinen Zweck als einen moralischen Zweck!" – so redet die bloße Leidenschaft. Ein Psychologe fragt dagegen: was tut alle Kunst? lobt sie nicht? verherrlicht sie nicht? wählt sie nicht aus? Mit dem allem *stärkt* oder *schwächt* sie gewisse

Wertschätzungen» (VI, 127). Der zentrale Gedanke, der diesen Reflexionen zugrundeliegt, besteht darin, daß der «unterste Instinkt» des Künstlers nicht so sehr auf die Kunst, sondern auf das «Leben,» eine *Wünschbarkeit von Leben»* ausgerichtet ist, so daß sich das Resultat dieser Überlegung in den Satz zusammendrängt: «Die Kunst ist das große Stimulans zum Leben: wie könnte man sie als zwecklos, als ziellos, als *l'art pour l'art* verstehn?» (VI, 127).

Hier zeigt sich also bei Nietzsche ein tiefes Spannungsverhältnis, wenn nicht ein eklatanter Widerspruch, zwischen der Auffassung der Kunst als *l'art pour l'art,* die eine seiner Formeln für die Zweckfreiheit der Kunst ist, und der Sehweise der Kunst als essentiell zweckhafter, nämlich lebenserhaltender, lebensfördernder Tätigkeit. Letztlich stellt sich bei allen Formen der Kunst, selbst bei den Tragödien heraus, so ließe sich diese auf das Dasein, das «Leben» gerichtete Tendenz der Kunst umschreiben, daß sie alle «im Interesse der *Art* arbeiten, wenn sie auch glauben mögen, im Interesse Gottes und als Sendlinge Gottes zu arbeiten»: «„Es ist wert zu leben – so ruft ein Jeder von ihnen – es hat etwas auf sich mit diesem Leben, das Leben hat etwas hinter sich, unter sich, nehmt euch in Acht!"» (III, 371).

Natürlich war die Formulierung *l'art pour l'art* nur eine Version unter vielen, in denen sich für Nietzsche die romantische Kunsttheorie darstellte. Geht man auf seinen Begriff der romantischen Kunst direkt ein, dann zeigt sich eine – jedenfalls Nietzsches Worten nach – bis an den Rand der Beschimpfung gehende Ablehnung dieser Kunstperiode, mit der sich eine entschiedene Stellungnahme für die klassische Kunst verbindet. Wenige Beispiele können dies belegen. Gleichzeitig bringen diese aber auch zum Ausdruck, daß hier ein nicht weniger intensives Spannungsverhältnis zwischen romantischer und klassischer Kunst vorliegt, als dies im Gegensatz von zweckhafter, lebensfördernder Kunst und der Devise *l'art pour l'art* zum Ausdruck gekommen ist.

So wollte Nietzsche zum Beispiel eine Kunst, «wie sie aus Homer, Sophokles, Theokrit, Calderon, Racine, Goethe *ausströmt, als Überschuß* einer weisen und harmonischen Lebensführung,» und nicht «jene barbarische, wenngleich noch so entzückende Aussprudelung hitziger und bunter Dinge aus einer ungebändigten chaotischen Seele, welche wir früher als Jünglinge unter Kunst verstanden» (II, 453). In schärferer Formulierung drängt sich die Unterscheidung zwischen romantischer und klassischer Kunst für Nietzsche in die Frage zusammen: «„ist hier der Hunger oder der Überfluß schöpferisch geworden?"» (III, 621). In Beantwortung dieser Frage treten zwei gegensätzliche Typen von Künstlern hervor, «einmal die an der *Überfülle des Lebens* Leidenden, welche eine dionysische Kunst wollen und ebenso eine tragische Ansicht und Einsicht in das Leben,» also die «klassischen» Künstler; und sodann «die an der *Verarmung des Lebens* Leidenden, die Ruhe, Stille, glattes Meer, Erlösung von sich durch die Kunst und Erkenntnis suchen, oder aber den Rausch, den Krampf, die Betäubung, den Wahnsinn,» mit einem Wort die Romantiker (III, 620). Nietzsche hat keinen Zweifel daran gelassen, auf welcher Seite dieser

Dichotomie er stand, oder jedenfalls stehen wollte. Dabei ging er so weit, daß er sich zu dem strengen Zwang bekannte, «welchen sich die französischen Dramatiker auferlegten, in Hinsicht auf Einheit der Handlung, des Ortes und der Zeit, auf Stil, Vers- und Satzbau, Auswahl der Worte und Gedanken» und mit dem sie sich banden (II, 180–181). Er machte Lessing zum Vorwurf, diese Entfesselung und «Revolution in der Poesie,» welche in der Romantik ihren vollen Ausdruck fand, ausgelöst zu haben, wiederholte die klassizistischen Invektiven gegen den «großen Barbaren» Shakespeare und verwies auf Voltaires *Mahomet,* «um sich klar vor die Seele zu stellen, was durch jenen Abbruch der Tradition ein für alle Mal der europäischen Kultur verloren gegangen ist» (II, 182). Mit Genugtuung zitierte er Lord Byron, der am 15. September 1817 aus Ravenna über die Romantik an Goethe geschrieben hatte: «With regard to poetry in general, I am convinced, the more I think of it, that ... all of us ... are ... upon a wrong revolutionary poetical system, or systems, not worth a damn in itself» (II, 183).[32]

Als ob er nicht merkte, daß er damit Selbstdefinitionen vorlegte, bestimmte Nietzsche den Stil jeder literarischen *décadence* damit, «daß das Leben nicht mehr im Ganzen wohnt»: «Das Wort wird souverain und springt aus dem Satz hinaus, der Satz greift über und verdunkelt den Sinn der Seite, die Seite gewinnt Leben auf Unkosten des Ganzen – das Ganze ist kein Ganzes mehr» (VI, 27). Im selben Atemzug sagt er aber nicht nur, daß durch die Dekadenz eine Summe der attraktivsten und kostbarsten Schönheiten in die Welt gekommen sei, sondern daß er selbst «in Fragen der décadence *erfahren*» sei (VI, 265) und das Problem der *décadence* ihn in der Tat «am tiefsten beschäftigt» habe: «ich habe Gründe dazu gehabt» (VI, II). Und nachdem sich Nietzsche in *Menschliches, Allzumenschliches* so emphatisch für die Einheit und Vollendung der klassischen Kunst ausgesprochen hatte, sagte er in *Die Fröhliche Wissenschaft* über den «Reiz der Unvollkommenheit,» daß ein bestimmter Dichter «durch seine Unvollkommenheiten einen höheren Reiz ausübt, als durch alles das, was sich unter seiner Hand rundet und vollkommen gestaltet.» Ja, Nietzsche treibt diesen Preis der Unvollkommenheit so weit, daß seiner Ansicht nach sogar der Leser oder Zuhörer von einem solchen Künstler «über sein Werk und alle „Werke'» hinausgehoben wird und «so hoch» steigt, «wie Zuhörer sonst nie steigen» (III, 434–435).

Chronologisch betrachtet gibt es bei Nietzsche ferner den Gegensatz zwischen der Kunst als Schein zur Rechtfertigung des Lebens, als der «höchsten Aufgabe und der eigentlich metaphysischen Tätigkeit des Lebens» (I, 24), aus *Die Geburt der Tragödie,* und jener «Physiologie der Kunst» (XII, 284), oder physiologischer Analyse der Kunst, z.B. als «Form des Hysterismus» (VI, 27), welche ein Kapitel des geplanten, dann aber fallengelassenen «Hauptwerks» (VI, 26) sein sollte.

---

32 *The Works of Lord Byron: Letters and Journals,* hrsg. Rowland E. Prothero, A new, rev. and enl. edition (New York: Octagon Books, 1966), IV, 169.

Letztlich stellen sich diese mannigfaltigen Spannungsverhältnisse in Nietzsches Auffassung der Kunst in ein grundlegendes «Spannungsverhältnis,» oder einen fundamentalen Gegensatz, nämlich den zur Wissenschaft. Daß der eigentliche «Zweck» der Kunst lebensfördernd ist, wurde bereits gesagt. Daß die Poeten zu diesem Zweck aber lügen (IV, 110), «Kammerdiener irgend einer Moral» sind (III, 371), daß sie «zurechtfälschen, zurechtdichten» (II, 14) und ihren «Stimmungen und Zuständen» Ursachen unterschieben, «welche durchaus nicht die wahren sind» (II, 34–35), ist ein von Nietzsche häufig formulierter Gedanke, zu dessen Beleg man nur das Vierte Hauptstück «Aus der Seele der Künstler und Schriftsteller» aus *Menschliches, Allzumenschliches* heranzuziehen braucht. «Die Kunst macht den Anblick des Lebens erträglich, dadurch daß sie den Flor des unreinen Denkens über dasselbe legt» (II, 144), heißt es dort, oder: «Der Künstler hat in Hinsicht auf das Erkennen der Wahrheiten eine schwächere Moralität als der Denker; er will sich die glänzenden, tiefsinnigen Deutungen des Lebens durchaus nicht nehmen lassen und wehrt sich gegen nüchterne, schlichte Methoden und Resultate» (II, 142).

Auf diesen für Nietzsche häufig vertretenen Gegensatz von Denker und Künstler, Wissenschaft und Dichtung, Philosophie und Poesie braucht hier nicht weiter eingegangen zu werden. Sieht man sich aber die «nüchternen, schlichten Methoden und Resultate» einmal genauer an, die beim wissenschaftlichen Denken herauskommen sollen, dann treten recht erstaunliche Beobachtungen zutage. Diese bestehen zunächst darin, daß sich Nietzsches emphatische Betonung der nüchternen Wissenschaftlichkeit gegenüber den «Bildern und Gleichnissen» (II, 614) der Dichter einer metaphorischen Sprache bedient, die von vornherein den Anspruch auf Wissenschaftlichkeit unterminiert. So illustriert Nietzsche in einem «Gegen Bilder und Gleichnisse» betitelten Aphorismus das «kälteste Mißtrauen» des wissenschaftlichen Denkens durch die «kahlen Wände» der Laboratorien und Operationssäle und bezeichnet dies Mißtrauen geradezu als «Prüfstein für das Gold der Gewißheit» (II, 614). Ist er sich wohl der Paradoxie seiner gegen Bilder und Gleichnisse gerichteten «Wissenschaft» bewußt gewesen, als er den Satz formulierte, «daß kein Honig süßer als der der Erkenntnis ist» (II, 237)?

Das stärkste Indiz für dies Spannungsverhältnis, oder besser: dies Ineinanderfließen von Denken und Kunst, Wissenschaft und Dichtung, Philosophie und Poesie ist aber, daß gerade hier, im Bereich des Denkens, der Wissenschaft und der Philosophie die Metapher vom Spiel ihre zentrale Stellung in Nietzsches Schriften einnimmt, die sie im Bereich der Kunst nicht besessen hatte. Die Sehweise der Philosophie als Spiel zeigt sich bei Nietzsche zuerst in seiner Charakterisierung des Philosophen Heraklit in der frühen Schrift *Die Philosophie im tragischen Zeitalter der Griechen.* Als Mensch unter Menschen, sagt Nietzsche dort, war Heraklit «unglaublich.» Selbst wenn er nur das Spiel lärmender Kinder beobachtete, «hat er jedenfalls dabei bedacht, was nie ein Mensch bei solcher Gelegenheit bedacht hat: Das Spiel des großen Weltkinds

Zeus» (I, 834). Überhaupt war Heraklits Anschauen der Welt die Sehweise des «ästhetischen Menschen,» d.h. eines Philosophen, «der an dem Künstler und an dem Entstehen des Kunstwerks erfahren hat, wie der Streit der Vielheit doch in sich Gesetz und Ruhe tragen kann, wie der Künstler beschaulich über und wirkend in dem Kunstwerk steht, wie Notwendigkeit und Spiel, Widerstreit und Harmonie sich zur Zeugung des Kunstwerks paaren müssen» (I, 831). In derselben «Unschuld» wie das «Spiel des Künstlers und des Kindes» spielt bei Heraklit «das ewig lebendige Feuer, baut und zerstört, in Unschuld – und dieses Spiel spielt der Äon mit sich» (I, 830). Dieser Philosoph hatte ja keinen Grund, wie etwa Leibniz, nachweisen zu müssen, daß diese Welt die beste aller Welten sei: «es genügt ihm, daß sie das schöne unschuldige Spiel des Äon ist» (I, 831). Und so soll das, was Heraklit schaute, damit schließt Nietzsche diese Betrachtung ab, nämlich »*die Lehre vom Gesetz im Werden und vom Spiel in der Notwendigkeit,*« von nun an «ewig geschaut werden: er hat von diesem größten Schauspiel den Vorhang aufgezogen» (I, 385).

Wie zentral die Spielmetapher für Nietzsches Philosophie ist, zeigt sich in den Bildern des spielenden Kindes und dem jedes Lebensalter begleitenden «Märchen und Spiel» (II, 493). Sie manifestiert sich in den Worten von der «ewigen Komödie des Daseins» und den «Wellen unzähligen Gelächters,» das diese hervorruft (III, 372), ja überhaupt in der Konzeption der «fröhlichen Wissenschaft» als «la gaya scienza» (III, 343). Sie äußert sich in der Bewegung des Tanzens («Nur im Tanze weiß ich der höchsten Dinge Gleichnis zu reden» IV, 144) und in den Versen:

> Welt-Spiel, das herrische,
> Mischt Sein und Schein: –
> Das Ewig-Närrische
> Mischt *uns* – hinein! . . . (III, 639).

Die Voraussetzung für eine derartige Lektüre Nietzsches ist aber, daß keiner der sich hier auftuenden Gegensätze eliminiert oder aufgeopfert wird, indem man diese chronologisiert, hierarchisiert oder dialektisiert und damit in einen ganz gleich wie geordneten Zusammenhang bringt. Es geht also darum, Nietzsches Text in seiner vollen Widersprüchlichkeit, Gegensätzlichkeit und Spannungshaftigkeit von Wissenschaft und Leben, Kunst und Wissenschaft, Klassik und Romantik, zweckfreier und lebenserhaltender Kunst zu belassen, ohne ihn durch Systematisierungen zu entschärfen oder ihn auf Prinzipien zu reduzieren.

Dann aber zeigt sich Nietzsches Schrift selber als ein großes Spiel, das aus jedem zweckrationalen Zusammenhang, etwa dem Verkünden einer Lehre oder dem Schreiben eines Werkes, herausgetreten ist und eine ganz neue Art zu denken und zu schreiben ankündigt. Seine Schrift zeigt sich dann als «Äußerungen eines intellektuellen Spieltriebes, und unschuldig und glücklich gleich allem Spiele» (III, 470). Oder sie erscheint als Mitteilungen eines Geistes, «der naiv, das heißt ungewollt und aus überströmender Fülle und Mächtigkeit mit Allem spielt, was bisher heilig, gut, unberührbar, göttlich hieß» (III, 637).

August Wilhelm Schlegels Metamorphose des Sommernachtstraums

FRANK JOLLES, *University of Ulster*

Es wäre aufschlußreich, eine vergleichende Geschichte der Übersetzung zu entwickeln, in der der entscheidende Gesichtspunkt nicht die Rezeption des Autors oder seines Werks, sondern die Aufnahme der Übersetzung selber wäre. Das würde den Nachdruck von den bisherigen letztlich unerfüllbaren Forderungen nach Treue in der Wiedergabe von Formen und Inhalten auf die eigentliche Funktion der literarischen Übersetzung als Verbindungsglied – *interface* – zwischen zwei Kulturen verlagern. Viele, die sonst als wortgetreue Übersetzungen galten, würden diese Voraussetzung nicht erfüllen und damit hinfällig werden, andere, welche den bisherigen Kriterien nicht genügten, könnten trotzdem ihren Platz behaupten, – wenige nur dürften in beiden Hinsichten Anerkennung finden. Eine solche Geschichte der Übersetzung würde auch einen Beitrag zur Bestimmung der Zielkultur leisten: sie müßte zum Beispiel in chronologischer Folge die Gründe untersuchen, die zur Aufnahme von minderwertigen oder zur Ablehnung von hochwertigen Übersetzungen führten. Am meisten Aufschluß wäre allerdings von den Übersetzungen zu erwarten, die der dritten Kategorie angehören: von den sinngetreuen Übertragungen, welche in die Zielkultur aufgenommen wurden. Da sie günstigenfalls im Rahmen der Zielkultur als eigenständige in sich geschlossene Werke gelten, bietet sich durch den Vergleich mit dem Original ein Zugang zur Zielkultur, der durch die Untersuchung eines einheimischen Werks ohne diese äußere Vergleichsmöglichkeit nicht erreicht werden kann. Die Übersetzung läßt erst die Begrenzung der sprachlichen Ausdrucksmittel und die kulturbedingte Prägung des «neuen Autors,» d.h. des Übersetzers, deutlich erkennen.

Zu den wenigen deutschen Übersetzungen dieser Art muß August Wilhelm Schlegels Shakespeare (1797–1810) gerechnet werden. Sie ist die einzige, die sich halten konnte, aus den vielen konkurrierenden Shakespeare-Übersetzungen aus der ersten Hälfte des 19. Jahrhunderts. Sie ist es auch, die das deutsche Shakespearebild bis in unser Jahrhundert hinein geprägt hat – ein Erbe der Romantik, welches in seiner Breitenwirkung unübertroffen geblieben ist. Das lag nicht an einer größeren Genauigkeit in der Wiedergabe des englischen Texts, sondern an ihrer spezifischen Aussage. Anders ausgedrückt, Schlegel war der einzige unter den Shakespeare-Übersetzern, dem es gelang, die Stimmung der Zeit zu erfassen und sogar durch seine Übersetzung mitzuprägen. Die Eigenständigkeit seiner Arbeit wurde erst um die Mitte des 20. Jahrhunderts durch die Neuausgabe des ursprünglichen Texts bestätigt[1] – im 19. Jahrhundert wurde sie mehrfach im Interesse der «Genauigkeit» und um die Ergebnisse der neueren Shakespeare-Forschung zu verarbeiten, revidiert. Schlegel selber wehrte sich entschieden gegen solche Verbesserungsversuche:

> Ich habe kein Monopol: jedermann hat das Recht den Shakespeare zu übersetzen.
>
> Die Voße hatten das Recht; Tieck, Graf Baudissin und der oder die Ungenannte haben das Recht; Benda hat das Recht; Kaufmann hat das Recht; Ortlepp hat das Recht; Petz hat das Recht; Mügge hat das Recht; Fischer hat das Recht; die Wiener mit ihrem vaterländischen Surrogat haben das Recht; und Johann Deut, Georg Kahl, Franz Nagebein und Wilhelm Quake werden ebenfalls das Recht haben, wenn sie als meine siegreichen Nebenbuhler auftreten wollen.
>
> Auch korrigieren kann jeder meinen Shakespeare: entweder handschriftlich am Rande seines Exemplars, oder gedruckt, in Beurtheilungen usw. Aber in meine Übersetzung hineinkorrigieren, das darf Niemand ohne meine ausdrückliche Erlaubniß. ...
>
> Hierin liegt die wichtigste Bedenklichkeit gegen alle fremden Korrekturen. „Jeder hat seine eigene Manier, seine Art, die Sprache und den Vers zu brauchen. Änderungen können Fehler und Mißverständnisse tilgen, aber nicht Kolorit, Sprache und das Wesen der Arbeit selbst zu bedeutend ändern, wenn nicht zu großer Widerstreit und Ungleichheit in dem Werke selbst entstehen soll." So drückt sich Tieck in der Vorrede zum dritten Theile aus, und ich stimme ihm vollkommen bei. ...
>
> Demnach wünsche ich, wenn unter der jetzigen Sündflut von Sh. Übersetzungen etwas von der meinigen auf die Nachwelt kommen sollte, es möge ganz von meiner eignen Hand sein, und die Übersetzung möge den Titel: übers. v. Schl. mit vollem Rechte führen.[2]

Aus alledem geht hervor, daß es bei der Shakespeare-Übersetzung um 1800 nicht allein um Vermittlung ging, sondern um die Aneignung des fremden Werks aufgrund einer deutschen literarischen Situation, innerhalb der der jeweilige Übersetzer mehr oder minder bewußt operierte.

Dieser Vorgang wird begünstigt durch die eigentümliche Identifizierung mit dem Verfasser der Schauspiele,[3] die bekanntlich in der Vorstellung gipfelte, daß Shakespeare – zumindest im Geiste – ein Deutscher war. Im Aufsatz «Etwas über William Shakespeare bei Gelegenheit Wilhelm Meisters» (1796), den Schlegel in Schillers *Horen* veröffentlichte, schrieb er in diesem Sinne:

> Nein, er ist uns nicht fremd: wir brauchen keinen Schritt aus unserm Charakter herauszugehn, um ihn „ganz unser" nennen zu dürfen. ... Was er sich hie und da erlaubt, findet bei uns am leichtesten Nachsicht, weil uns eine gewisse gezierte Ängstlichkeit doch nicht natürlich ist, wenn wir sie uns auch aufschwatzen laßen; die Ausschweifungen seiner Phan-

---

1 E. Loewenthal, Hrsg., *Shakespeare, Sämtliche Werke* übers. August Wilhelm von Schlegel und Ludwig Tieck (Heidelberg: Lambert Schneider, 1939). Diese Ausgabe bringt einen Neudruck der dritten Ausgabe und Ausgabe letzter Hand (Berlin: Reimer, 1843–44).
2 «Schreiben an Herrn Buchhändler Reimer in Berlin» (1838 und 1839), *Sämmtliche Werke*, hrsg. Eduard Böcking (Leipzig, 1846; Neudr. Hildesheim: Olms, 1971 (im folgenden zitiert als: Böcking) VII, 282f.
3 Vgl. Friedrich Gundolf, *Shakespeare und der deutsche Geist* (Berlin: Bondi, 1920), S. 336.

tasie und seines Gefühls (giebt es anders dergleichen) sind gerade die, denen wir selbst am meisten ausgesetzt sind, und seine eigenthümlichen Tugenden gelten einem edlen Deutschen unter allen am höchsten.[4]

In einem Brief an Tieck vom 11. Dezember 1797 zog er die naheliegende Schlußfolgerung aus der oben zitierten Ausführung: Shakespeare müsse Deutscher gewesen sein, denn mit dem kühlen englischen Nationalcharakter habe er zu wenig gemeinsam gehabt: «Ich hoffe, Sie werden in Ihrer Schrift unter anderem beweisen, Shakespeare sei kein Engländer gewesen. Wie kam er nur unter die frostigen stupiden Seelen auf dieser brutalen Insel? Freylich müssen sie damals noch mehr menschliches Gefühl und Dichtersinn gehabt haben, als jetzt.»[5]

Aus diesem unmittelbaren Zugang zum Werk, den der junge Schlegel und seine Freunde sich zumuteten, entwickelte sich die neue deutsche Shakespearekritik, die ihrerseits eine starke Rückwirkung auf die englische – besonders durch die Vermittlung Coleridges – ausüben sollte. Es ist jedoch bemerkenswert, daß das Shakespearebild, das durch die Übersetzung und die Aufnahme Shakespearescher Gestalten in einheimische Werke in Deutschland entstand, keinen Eingang in die englische Rezeption fand. Selbst Coleridge sträubte sich dagegen. Als Tieck ihn 1817 in London besuchte, stellte er ihm in einem ausführlichen Vortrag, der von 10 Uhr abends bis 1 Uhr morgens gedauert haben soll, die Ergebnisse seiner Shakespeare-Studien dar. Ich zitiere aus den Aufzeichnungen R. Köpkes: «Am anderen Abend kam man wieder zusammen. „Ich habe", fing er (Coleridge) an, „Ihre Ansichten die ganze Nacht hindurch überlegt, und neues daraus gelernt. Ich finde, Sie haben in vielen Punkten Recht." Auf eine so unumwundene Zustimmung hatte Tieck nicht gehofft. „Dennoch", fuhr jener fort, „kann ich sie nicht annehmen!" – „Und warum nicht?" fragte Tieck überrascht. „Weil ich sie nicht annehmen will, denn sie widersprechen Allem, was man bisher in England über Shakespeare gedacht und geschrieben hat." Gegen einen so nationalen Standpunkt auch in der Kritik war nicht anzukämpfen, doch erwies sich Coleridge auch späterhin freundlich und behilflich.»[6] Die Auseinandersetzung mit dem «deutschen» Shakespeare wirkte in verschiedenen Formen bis in unser Jahrhundert fort. Noch um 1938 wehrte sich zum Beispiel der britische Editor von *A Midsummer Night's Dream,* Henry Cunningham, gegen die Verwendung von Gestalten aus diesem Stück in Goethes «Walpurgisnacht»: «The English reader will continue to rejoice in his English poet. „Robin Goodfellow" is good enough for him. He will leave to the Germans their very German „Ruprecht" and vulgar „Walpurgis-

---

4 Böcking, VII, 38.
5 Henry Lüdeke, Hrsg., *Ludwig Tieck und die Brüder Schlegel, Briefe* (Frankfurt: Baer, 1930), S. 34.
6 Rudolf Köpke, *Ludwig Tieck, Erinnerungen aus dem Leben des Dichters nach dessen mündlichen und schriftlichen Mitteilungen* (Leipzig: Brockhaus, 1855), II, 375f.

nacht's Traum", and he will decline to look at Shakespeare through the medium, as Furness would put it, of fantastic German distortions.»[7] Das alles sind Folgeerscheinungen der Metamorphose, die das Werk Shakespeares in der deutschen Überlieferung erfahren hat. Die Ursachen dafür liegen in der Verschiedenheit der Ausgangssituationen und in der inneren Konsequenz des neuen Gefüges, in dem jeder Teilaspekt gleichermaßen von der Wandlung betroffen wurde. Ich möchte im folgenden versuchen, am Beispiel des *Sommernachtstraums* den Vorgang darzustellen, durch welchen die neue Form aus der alten entstand. Die literarischen Voraussetzungen dafür habe ich an anderer Stelle behandelt:[8] hier möchte ich auf die sprachlichen näher eingehen.

Die Entstehungsgeschichte der romantischen Shakespeare-Übersetzung ist bereits im 19. Jahrhundert dokumentiert worden.[9] Der *Sommernachtstraum* war Schlegels erster Versuch; er hat ihn zweimal übersetzt: in Zusammenarbeit mit Gottfried August Bürger während seiner Studienzeit in Göttingen im Jahre 1789 und wieder 1796, als er, aus Amsterdam zurückgekehrt, sich in Jena niedergelassen hatte. In einem Brief an Schiller vom 26. Februar 1796 möchte er den Anteil Bürgers an der früheren Übersetzung auf «einige Lieder und gereimte Szenen» beschränken;[10] in einem öffentlichen «Schreiben an Herrn Buchhändler Reimer in Berlin,» im Dezember und im Januar 1838 und 1839, fügte er rückblickend hinzu: «Ich sah bald ein, daß ich die von ihm ausgearbeiteten Stücke gänzlich beiseite legen müßte, weil sonst ein schreiender Kontrast zwischen seinem und meinem Antheil entstanden wäre.»[11] Michael Bernays behauptet zwar, daß Bürger «für die Behandlung gerade der vornehmsten Bestandtheile der Dichtung den Stil festgestellt» habe.[12] Ein Vergleich von Bürgers Stellen mit den anderen Teilen der Fassung von 1789 wird Bernays Urteil kaum bestätigen können. Der Hauptunterschied der beiden Fassungen beruht auf einem Wandel in der Auffassung von der Dichtkunst; Schlegels Ablösung von Bürger ist nur eine Folge davon, nicht ihre Ursache. Die zweite Fassung stellt aber auch eine Fortentwicklung der ersten dar. Das ergibt sich schon aus Schlegels Arbeitsweise: er korrigierte die neue Fassung in die Reinschrift der alten hinein. Viele Ansätze des Stils und des Wortgebrauchs, welche in der ersten Fassung bereits vorhanden sind, aber sozusagen nebeneinander bestehen, werden systematisch ausgearbeitet und miteinander verbunden. Dadurch wirkt die Fassung von 1796 viel geschlossener und enger gefügt. Es befremdet

---

7 H. Cunningham, ed. *The Arden Shakespeare: A Midsummer Night's Dream* (London, Methuen, 1938), S. xx.
8 F. Jolles, Hrsg. *A.W. Schlegels Sommernachtstraum in der ersten Fassung vom Jahre 1789* (Göttingen: Vandenhoeck & Ruprecht, 1967), S. 13ff.
9 Vgl. Michael Bernays, *Zur Entstehungsgeschichte des Schlegelschen Shakespeare* (Leipzig: Hirzel, 1872).
10 Josef Körner & Ernst Wieneke, Hrsg., *August Wilhelm und Friedrich Schlegel im Briefwechsel mit Schiller und Goethe* (Leipzig: Insel, [1926]), S. 27.
11 Böcking, VII, 283.
12 Bernays, S. 55.

vielleicht zunächst, daß Schlegel in beiden Fällen die *Pyramus und Thisbe*-Szenen fast unverändert aus Wielands Übersetzung (1762) übernommen hat. In einem Brief an Schiller vom 1. März 1796 nannte er sie «unübertrefflich.»[13] Im Vorwort zur ersten Ausgabe 1797 rechtfertigte er sein Verfahren mit der Bemerkung: Es lag mir mehr daran, daß die von mir gelieferte Übersetzung so vollendet wie möglich, als daß sie in allen ihren Theilen neu wäre.»[14] Das deutet darauf, daß Schlegels damalige Übersetzungstheorie noch nicht die Ausschließlichkeit seiner späteren obenangeführten These von der Einmaligkeit erreicht hatte. Man könnte sie in der Terminologie seines Bruders als «progressiv» beschreiben. Friedrich Schlegel prägte diesen Begriff in seinem *Studium-Aufsatz*, um die neuere «romantische» Kunst von der antiken zu unterscheiden.[15] Jene ist seiner Auffassung nach dadurch gekennzeichnet, daß sie sich dem Ziel ihrer Vollendung ständig nähern müsse, ohne es jemals erreichen zu können – während diese auf ihrer Stufe in ihren besten Werken vollendet gewesen sei. Der *Studium-Aufsatz* erschien 1797, er wurde jedoch großenteils bereits 1795 verfaßt, und einige Bogen zirkulierten unter Freunden vom Januar 1796 ab – also gerade um die Zeit, als August Wilhelm die Übersetzung des *Sommernachtstraums* wiederaufnahm. Es liegt deshalb nahe, seine damaligen Übersetzungen aus diesem theoretischen Gesichtspunkt zu beurteilen. Der Vorgang entspricht ohnehin dem Postulat Friedrich Schlegels nach einer fortschreitenden Annäherung an ein unerreichbares Vorbild. Das Übersetzen ist demnach nicht ein Handwerk, denn das Handwerk erschöpft sich im Erreichbaren, sondern eine Kunst. Dadurch aber ist die Voraussetzung gegeben für die Metamorphose eines Kunstwerks in ein anderes: für die proteische Verwandlung also, durch welche der gleiche Inhalt in den verschiedensten sprachlichen Gestaltungen in Erscheinung treten kann.

Im semantischen Bereich lassen sich die Grenzen der Übersetzbarkeit zunächst an den Begriffsfeldern ablesen, denn, wie Jost Trier bemerkt, ist «die Geschichte der Feldeinteilung einer Einzelsprache ... die notwendige Vorarbeit für einen Vergleich zweier Sprachen im ganzen.»[16] Ich möchte zwei solche Felder näher betrachten: im sozialen Bereich die *Rangbezeichnungen* und im moralischen die Wertbegriffe im Umkreis der *Tugend*.

Die englischen Rangbezeichnungen *King* und *Queen* umfassen bei Shakespeare sowohl den weltlichen Bereich des Theseus und der Hippolyta als auch den Feenbereich Oberons und Titanias. Schlegel hingegen unterscheidet zwischen *Fürst / Fürstin* für den weltlichen und *König / Königin* für den Feenbereich:

---

13 Körner und Wieneke, S. 30.
14 A.W. Schlegel (Übers.), *Shakespeare, Dramatische Werke* (Berlin 1797–1810), I, iv.
15 «Über das Studium der Griechischen Poesie», *Kritische Friedrich-Schlegel-Ausgabe,* hrsg. von Ernst Behler (Paderborn: Schöningh), Band I (1979), S. 203–367; vgl. 255, 270, 305 u.a.
16 Jost Trier, *Der deutsche Wortschatz im Sinnbezirk des Verstandes* (Heidelberg: Winter, 1931), S. 22.

THESEUS	We will, *fair queen,* up to the mountain's top. (IV, i, 108)[17]
	Komm', *schöne Fürstin,* auf des Berges Höh'.
OBERON	Now, my Titania; wake you, *my sweet queen.* (IV, i, 74)
	Nun, *holde Königin!* wach' auf, Titania!

Sobald ein vertraulicher Ton angeschlagen wird, werden die Titel im Deutschen entweder weggelassen oder durch einen Ausdruck aus einem entsprechenden Register ersetzt:

| OBERON | ... Come *my queen,* take hands with me. (IV, I, 84) |
| | Nun komm', *Gemahlin!* Hand in Hand gefügt. |

In Grimms Wörterbuch findet sich eine ähnliche Unterscheidung der Grundbegriffe: *Fürst* ist «der erste, höchste in rang und würde,» während *König* «vater, erzeuger» bedeutet. *Fürst* bezeichnet also die Spitze der Pyramide, die von den unteren Ständen getragen wird, während *König* ein generischer Begriff ist. Die deutschen Termini sind spezifischer und an einen engeren Anwendungskreis gebunden als die englischen. Daraus ergibt sich eine Steigerung der Hauptbedeutung von *Abstand, Würde* und *Macht,* die auch in den Attributen und Zeitwörtern aus dem Umkreis des Fürsten zum Ausdruck kommen:

DEMETRIUS	.... Do you think,
	The duke was here, and *bid* us follow him? (IV, i, 193–94)
	... daß der Herzog
	Hier war, und ihm zu folgen uns *gebot?*
EGEUS	*Happy* be Theseus, our *renowned Duke!* (I, i, 20)
	Dem *großen* Theseus, unserm Herzog, *Heil!*

In der Anrede kommen die Titel hauptsächlich dort vor, wo Personen höheren Rangs angesprochen werden – im *Sommernachtstraum* beinahe ausschließlich bei Theseus und Oberon. Es handelt sich um feststehende Formeln, die ihrer Häufigkeit zufolge eine normative Wirkung ausüben. Die deutschen Formeln steigern auch hier den Abstand zwischen Fürst und Untertan:

EGEUS	.... – *My noble lord,*
	This man hath my consent to marry her. (I, i, 24–25)
	.... – *Erlauchter Herr,*
	Dem da verhieß mein Wort zum Weibe sie.

Sobald Schlegel jedoch versucht, diesen Abstand zu überbrücken, entsteht der Eindruck einer der Situation unangemessenen Vertraulichkeit:

---

17 Die Zeilenzählung richtet sich nach der *Cambridge Edition,* hrsg. von A. Quiller-Couch und J. Dover Wilson (Cambridge: Cambridge University Press, 1964); der Wortlaut des englischen Texts ist der Ausgabe entnommen, welche Schlegel selber verwendet hat: *The Plays of William Shakespeare accurately printed from the text of Mr. Malone's edition,* 10 vols. (London: Baldwin, 1786–90), vol. 1 1790. *A Midsummer Night's Dream* befindet sich im zweiten Band – vgl. auch Jolles (Anm. 8), S. 12f. Der deutsche Text stammt aus der Erstausgabe von 1797.

> PHILOSTRATUS And tragical, *my noble lord,* it is;
> For Pyramus therein doth kill himself. (v, i, 66–67)
> und tragisch ist es auch, *mein Gnädigster:*
> Denn Pyramus bringt selbst darin sich um.

Die Rangbetonung wirkt hemmend auf den Verkehr zwischen Theseus und seinem Gefolge und setzt den Herrscher ab: so entsteht aus der vorgeformten sprachlichen Gegebenheit eine strukturelle Verlagerung, die das Verhältnis der Personen zueinander verändert.

Ein weiteres Beispiel aus dem sozialen Bereich bildet die Übersetzung des Wortes *lady.* Schlegel sieht sich genötigt, es durch *Herrin, Frau, Mädchen, die Schöne, Weib, Fräulein* und *Dame* wiederzugeben. Das englisch-deutsche Wörterbuch von Bailey (1796–97) bringt kennzeichnenderweise unter *lady: Die Lady* an erster Stelle, dann: *gnädige Frau, Frau von, Dame, Gemahlin.*[18] Für die bürgerlich-empfindsamen Bedeutungen *Kind, Mädchen* reichte das englische Wort im achtzehnten Jahrhundert auch nicht mehr aus. Schlegel übersetzt *lady,* besonders *sweet lady,* häufig in diesem Sinn:

> LYSANDER ... and she, *sweet lady,* dotes,
> Devoutly dotes, dotes in idolatry. (I, i, 108–09)
> Und sie, *das holde Kind,* schwärmt nun für ihn,
> Schwärmt andachtsvoll, ja mit Abgötterey.
>
> OBERON A *sweet Athenian lady* is in love. (II, i, 260)
> Ein *holdes Mädchen* wird ...
> ... verschmäht.
>
> HELENA You would not use a *gentle lady* so. (III, ii, 152)
> So flößt' ein *armes Weib* euch Mitleid ein.

In diesen Beispielen wird als Teilaspekt des Wortes *lady* die Unmündigkeit der Frau herausgehoben. Bei *maid,* das bereits im Englischen auf Unselbständigkeit hinweist, wird dieser Aspekt darüberhinaus betont:

> THESEUS What say you Hermia? be advis'd *fair maid.* (I, i, 46)
> Was sagt ihr, Hermia? Laßt euch raten, *Kind.*

Das Epitheton *fair* entfällt, und der Nachdruck lastet auf *Kind,* welches allerdings im späten achtzehnten Jahrhundert so viel wie *junge Frau* bedeutete. Durch die Assoziierung wird nichtsdestoweniger die Unmündigkeit betont. Die Beziehung zwischen Theseus und Hermia wird dadurch um etwas verlagert, da Theseus nun bevormundend (wenn nicht gar an einigen Stellen onkelhaft) wirkt. In einem der seltenen Fälle, in denen Schlegel seine Vorlage verändert, wird ein moralisches Attribut vom Mann auf die Frau verlagert. Da die *Tugend* der Frau sich unter anderem aus ihrer unselbständigen gesellschaftlichen Stellung ableitet, paßt das Wort nicht auf einen Mann. Nach einer ermüdenden Flucht durch den nächtlichen Wald wollen die beiden Liebenden sich ausruhen. Hermia bittet Lysander, der sich neben sie legen wollte, etwas weiter wegzurücken:

---

18 Nathan Bailey, *English-German and German-English Dictionary* (Leipzig: Groß, 1796–97).

HERMIA	Such separation, as, may well be said,
	Becomes a *virtuous bachelor* and a maid,
	So far be distant, (II, ii, 66-68)
	... so weit, wie ...
	... sich, getrennt von einem Mann,
	Ein *tugendsames Mädchen* betten kann.

An diesem Beispiel läßt sich die gegenseitige Abhängigkeit der gesellschaftlichen und der moralischen Wertbegriffe erkennen.

Für die moralischen Wertbegriffe ergeben sich die folgenden Wortfelder im Englischen und in der deutschen Übersetzung:

Virtue	Tugend
Modesty	Sittsamkeit
(maiden meditation)	(sittsame Betrachtung)
Simplicity	Unschuld
(simple)	(kindisch)
Innocence	Unschuld
(childhood innocence)	(Kinderunschuld)
Obedience	kindlicher Gehorsam
Virginity	Mädchenthum

Die englischen Begriffe entsprechen bei Shakespeare einem aristokratischen Ethos, sie sind alle lateinischer Herkunft und haben im wesentlichen ihre ursprünglichen Werte beibehalten. Die deutschen sind bürgerlich, sie sind entweder Neuschöpfungen oder haben – wie *Tugend* – einen Bedeutungswandel durchgemacht, der sie Neuschöpfungen gleichsetzt. Die englischen Begriffe sind deutlich voneinander abgegrenzt und drücken eine Seinsverfassung aus, die deutschen gehen ineinander über und stellen eine bloße *dispositio* – eine Willensneigung oder moralische Gesinnung dar.[19] Einige Beispiele:

HERMIA	Nor how it may *concern my modesty*,
	In such a presence here, to plead my thoughts. (I, i, 60-61)
	Noch wie es *meiner Sittsamkeit geziemt*,
	In solcher Gegenwart das Wort zu führen;
HERMIA	So will I grow, so live, so die, my lord,
	Ere I will yield *my virgin patent* up
	Unto his lordship, whose unwished yoke. (I, i, 79-81)
	So will ich leben, gnäd'ger Herr, so sterben,
	Eh' ich *den Freyheitsbrief des Mädchenthums*
	Der Herrschaft dessen überliefern will,

Da die empfindsamen Begriffe viel direkter auf die Person bezogen sind, sieht sich Schlegel genötigt, mit besonderer Vorsicht zu übersetzen. So wird in diesem Beispiel das Personalpronomen durch den unbestimmten Artikel ersetzt, vermutlich um die zweifelhafte Wirkung von *meines Mädchenthums* zu ver-

19 Vgl. Grimms Wörterbuch zu «tugend.»

meiden. Wahrscheinlich aus einer ähnlichen Überlegung wird *enforced chastity* durch die gängige euphemistische Metapher wiedergegeben:

> TITANIA ... weeps every little flower,
> Lamenting some *enforced chastity*. (III, i, 190-91)
> ...... weint jede kleine Blume
> Um einen *wild zerrissenen Mädchenkranz.*

Wieland, der noch in einer früheren erotischen Tradition steht, nimmt sich den anakreontischen Topos der *kupplerischen Nacht* zu Hilfe, bleibt aber sonst wortgetreu:

> TITANIA ... weint jede kleine Blume
> Und klagt um irgendeine, *durch die Hülfe*
> *Der kupplerischen Nacht bezwungne Jungfernschaft.*[20]

Auch in ironischer Anwendung erhält sich der Gegensatz zwischen den englischen und deutschen Begriffen. Im dritten Akt sagt Titania zu Bottom, der in einen Esel verwandelt worden ist:

> TITANIA And *thy fair virtue's force* perforce doth move me. (III, i, 133)
> Gewaltig treibt mich *deine schöne Tugend.*

Bei Shakespeare beruht die komische Wirkung einmal auf der aristokratischen Redewendung, die auf einen Esel nicht paßt, und zum andern natürlich auf der Zweideutigkeit des Ausdrucks *thy fair virtue's force*. Im Deutschen beruht sie auf dem moralischen Stellenwert des Wortes *Tugend,* das der Situation unangemessen ist. Man kann einwenden, daß *Tugend* im gleichen Verhältnis zu mhd. *tugent* steht wie *virtue* zum lat. *virtus* und daß beide unter Umständen *Manneskraft, Potenz* bedeuten konnten. Es bleibt jedoch zweifelhaft, ob Schlegels Leser diesen Zusammenhang erkannt haben, wogegen der andere sich wohl aufgedrängt haben wird. – Die männlichen Tugenden machen eine ähnliche Entwicklung ins Bürgerliche durch:

> HELENA I thought you lord of more true *gentleness*. (II, iii, 140)
> Ich glaubt' in euch mehr *Edelmuth* zu sehen.
> HELENA If you were *civil,* and knew *courtesy*. (III, ii, 147)
> Wär' *Sitt'* und *Edelmuth* in euch Verwegnen.
> LYSANDER You are *unkind,* Demetrius; be not so. (III, ii, 162)
> Demetrius, du bist *nicht bieder:* sey's!

Die Tugendbegriffe werden fast ausschließlich von Helena, Hermia, Demetrius und Lysander und von Hermias Vater Egeus verwendet. Das ist der Personenkreis, der das Gefolge des Theseus bildet. Bei Shakespeare sind es junge Edelleute, die eine höfische Sprache sprechen. Die Übernahme des bürgerlich-empfindsamen Wertsystems bindet diese Personen enger aneinander und setzt

---

20 *Shakespears Theatralische Werke,* 8 vols. (Zürich: Orell, Füeßli, 1762-66).

sie stärker ab von dem Fürsten und seiner Gemahlin. Es ist bemerkenswert, daß eine solche Verschiebung stattfinden kann, obgleich keine anderen Begriffe als diese Schlegel zur Verfügung standen und man deshalb meinen würde, daß der gleiche Gesinnungswandel das ganze Stück erfassen müßte. Das ist nicht der Fall, weil der Wortgebrauch der verschiedenen Gruppen innerhalb des Stücks sehr unterschiedlich ist.

Die Untersuchung der Wortfelder hat den Vergleich geliefert zwischen den Sprachstrukturen, welche dem Übersetzer zur Verfügung standen, und denen seiner Vorlage. Die Untersuchung des Stils, die nun folgt, soll den Vergleich auf die literarischen und geistesgeschichtlichen Voraussetzungen erweitern. Auch hier handelt der Übersetzer keineswegs als freies Agens, aber sein Ermessensraum ist viel größer. Er kann die Konventionen seiner Zeit erweitern, und er muß vor allem Entscheidungen treffen. Ein Übersetzer von einer unflektierten in eine flektierte Sprache steht zum Beispiel immer unter dem Zwang, Wörter auszusparen, sofern er das gleiche Versmaß anstrebt: welche er ausläßt, muß er selber bestimmen. Es müssen also neben den Metaphern, Steigerungen von Beiwörtern und Zeitwörtern, Wortspielen und den Spezialsprachen bestimmter Gruppen innerhalb des Stücks auch Auslassungen und Hinzufügungen untersucht werden. Die Veränderungen sind oft komplex: man vergleiche die Übersetzung des einfachen Bilds *pelting river* im folgenden Beispiel:

> TITANIA   Contagious fogs; which falling in the land,
> Have every *pelting river* made so proud,
> That they have overborne their continents. (II, i, 90–92)
> ... die fielen auf das Land,
> Und machten jeden *winz'gen Bach* so stolz,
> Daß er des Bettes Dämme niederriß.

Das Wort *pelting* wurde zu Shakespeares Zeit sehr häufig verwendet. Es bedeutete: «paltry, petty trumpery, inconsiderable; worthless.» Es enthielt eine Wertung im Sinne von «verächtlich.» Da *river* einen eher größeren Fluß bezeichnet, besteht eine Diskrepanz zwischen Adjektiv und Substantiv, die für die höfische Ausdrucksweise Titanias kennzeichnend ist und dem Inhalt dieser Verse entspricht, in denen Titania ihren Ärger über Oberon auf die äußere Natur überträgt. Das geht in der Übersetzung verloren, ersetzt wird es durch eine charakteristische Verdoppelung und daher Steigerung des Kleinen. Shakespeares Titania redet geziert, Schlegels zierlich.

Manchmal lassen sich solche Änderungen auf Schlegels Hilfsmittel zurückführen. Im folgenden Beispiel entsteht ebenfalls eine Steigerung, aber diesmal durch die Verwendung eines unspezifischen Begriffs:

> TITANIA   That rheumatic diseases do abound:
> And thorough this *distemperature,* we see
> The seasons alter. (II, i, 105–7)
> Und fieberhafte Flüsse viel erzeugt.

> Durch eben die *Zerrüttung* wandeln sich
> Die Jahreszeiten.

Distemperature bleibt bei Shakespeare im Bilde mit *rheumatic diseases*, bezieht sich aber auf die Witterung: «a condition of the air or elements not properly tempered for human health and comfort» – in diesem Sinn ab 1531 belegt. Arnolds Wörterbuch (1790), welches Schlegel verwendet hat, gibt nur *eine Unpäßlichkeit*.[21] In einer Anmerkung, die auch in der Shakespeare-Ausgabe von 1790, die Schlegel vorlag, abgedruckt ist, schrieb Steevens: «*distemperature*, is *perturbation* of the elements.» Unter *perturbation* fand Schlegel im Arnold: *die Verstöhrung, Beunruhigung*, woraus er dann die Steigerung *Zerrüttung* machte.

Metaphern sind in Shakespeares *Midsummer Night's Dream* weitgehend Teil des höfischen Idioms. Die unzähligen bildlichen Redensarten, die fast schon zur aristokratischen Umgangssprache gehörten, werden in der Übersetzung meistens aufgelöst:

THESEUS	I have some *private schooling* for you both. (I, i, 116)
	... weil ich mit euch
	Verschiednes insgeheim verhandeln will.
LYSANDER	That, *in a spleen*, unfolds both heaven and earth. (I, i, 146)
	In einem Winke Himmel und Erde, entfaltet.
HELENA	... and *your tongue's* sweet *air*
	More tuneable than lark to shepherd's ear. (I, 183–84)
	... *die Töne*
	Der Lippe süßer, als der Lerche Lied.
DEMETRIUS	*Lay breath so bitter* on your bitter foe. (III, ii, 44)
	Den Todfeind solltet ihr *so tödlich quälen!*
PUCK	Follow my voice; *we'll try no manhood* here. (III, ii, 412)
	Folg' meinem Ruf, *zum Kampf* ist dieß *kein Ort*.

Auch sogenannte *euphuisms*, die im englischen Text oft mit der Leidenschaftlichkeit des Ausdrucks und der Situation im Gegensatz stehen und dadurch eine Spannung in die Rede hineintragen, werden bei Schlegel aufgelöst:

LYSANDER	I swear *by that which I will lose for thee*,
	To prove him false, that says I love thee not. (III, ii, 252–53)
	Ich liebe dich, *und will dieß Leben wagen*,
	Der Lüge den zu zeihn, der widerspricht.
TITANIA	And never, since *the middle summer's spring*. (II, i, 82)
	Und nie, seit *jenem Sommer*, trafen wir.

Die auffallenden komplexen Bilder Shakespeares versucht Schlegel soweit möglich nachzubilden, wobei im zweiten Beispiel das Wortspiel doch verloren geht:

---

21 Theodor Arnold, *A Compleat Vocabulary, English and German*... insonderheit für Anfänger und Reisende (Leipzig: Groß, 1790). Im Versteigerungskatalog von Schlegels nachgelassener Büchersammlung unter Nr. 1090 verzeichnet.

TITANIA	... and the green corn
	Hath rotted, *ere his youth attain'd a beard.* (II, i, 94-95)
	... das grüne Korn
	Verfault, *eh' seine Jugend Bart gewinnt.*
THESEUS	The *iron tongue* of midnight *hath told* twelve. (V, i, 361)
	Die Mitternacht *rief* Zwölf *mit eh'rner Zunge.*

Ebenso oft werden sie jedoch umschrieben:

HERMIA	Keep thy word, Lysander: we must *starve our sight* (I, i, 222-23)
	From lovers' food, 'till morrow deep midnight.
	Lysander, halte Wort! – *Was Lieb' erquickt,*
	Wird unserm Blick bis morgen Nacht *entrückt.*

Gleiches gilt auch von den *concetti* und den Bildern, die einen inneren Widerspruch enthalten:

THESEUS	Sees Helen's beauty *in a brow of Egypt.* (V, i, 11)
	... die Schönheit Helena's
	Auf einer Äthiopisch braunen Stirn.
THESEUS	Whether ...
	You can endure the *livery of a nun.* (I, i, 70-71)
	Ob ihr die *Nonnentracht* ertragen könnt.
HELENA	But herein mean I to *enrich my pain.* (I, i, 250)
	Doch will ich, *mich für meine Müh' zu laben.*

Die Nachbildung der Wortspiele mehr noch als die der Metaphern ist vom Zufall der Sprache abhängig. Wieland hat sie abgelehnt und ausgelassen, Herder erkannte zwar ihre Bedeutung, betrachtete sie aber als unübersetzbar, als «Früchte, die nicht in ein anderes Clima entführt werden können. Der Dichter wußte den Eigensinn der Sprache so mit dem Eigensinn seines Witzes zu paaren, daß sie für einander zu seyn scheinen...»[22] Man unterscheidet zwischen homonymen Wortspielen, semantischen Wortspielen und Wortentstellungen. Homonyme Wortspiele gehörten zum Inventar der aristokratischen Umgangsform, sie lassen sich nur ausnahmsweise übersetzen. Schlegel überträgt nur eines und ersetzt zwei weitere durch semantische Wortspiele. Die Wortentstellungen hingegen kommen alle in den Handwerkerszenen vor, sie werden entweder übersetzt oder durch ähnliche ersetzt. Die semantischen Wortspiele entsprechen keiner sozialen Schicht, sie werden teilweise wiedergegeben. Es ergibt sich folgende Verteilung:

---

22 Bernard Suphan, Hrsg., *Herders Sämmtliche Werke* (Berlin: Weidmann, 1877-1913), II, 45.

Schlegels Metamorphose des Sommernachtstraums 41

Wortspielart	bei Shakesp.	wieder-gegeben	ersetzt	nicht wieder-gegeben
1. *Sommernachtstraum*				
Homonyme Ws	10	1	2	7
Semantische Ws	9	6	–	3
Wortentstellungen	7	7	–	–
2. *Alle Komödien*[23]				
Homonyme Ws	207	20	50	137
Semantische Ws	161	67	6	88
Wortentstellungen	24	23	–	1

Weitgehend aufgrund der sprachlichen Voraussetzungen entfallen vorzüglich jene Wortspiele, welche der Sprache der aristokratischen Gesellschaft angehören. Unter dem Druck, Silben zu sparen, ließ Schlegel vor allem solche Wörter und Wendungen aus, die nicht eigentliche Sinnträger sind. Daher kommt es, daß gerade die rhetorischen Stilelemente der Sprache Shakespeares am stärksten von den Auslassungen betroffen werden. In diesem Zusammenhang spielen die Epitheta eine wichtige Rolle, denn sie durchziehen den ganzen Text. So kommt zum Beispiel *sweet* als Epitheton 20mal vor, wird jedoch nur 8mal übersetzt. Diese Tendenz ist durchgehend:

OBERON   Upon the next *live* creature that it sees. (II, i, 72)
         ... in jede Kreatur,
         Die sie zunächst erblicken ...
HELENA   How came her eyes so bright? Not with *salt* tears. (II, ii, 100)
         Wie wurden sie so hell? Durch Thränen? Nein!
HERMIA   To pluck this *crawling* serpent from my breast! (II, ii, 154)
         Die Schlange, die den Busen mir umflicht?
TITANIA And light them at the *fiery* glow-worm's eyes. (III, i, 161)
         Und steckt es an bey eines Glühwurms Schein.
HERMIA   *Dark* night, that from the eye his function takes. (III, ii, 177)
         Die Nacht, die uns der Augen Dienst entzieht.

Rhetorische Wiederholungen, Epizeuxis, besonders von Personennamen, werden ebenfalls ausgespart:

LYSANDER She sees not *Hermia:* – *Hermia,* sleep thou there, (II, ii, 143)
         Sie siehet *Hermia* nicht. – So schlaf' nur immer,

auch Wendungen und Klischees wie *faithful lovers, so it came to pass* und *that is finished too:*

PUCK   When in that moment *(so it came to pass)*
         Titania wak'd, and straightway loved an ass. (III, ii, 33-34)

---

[23] Vgl. P.H. Düssel, «Wortspiele und ihre Übersetzung in Shakespeares Komödien,» Staatsexamensarbeit (Köln 1955) (Maschinenschrift).

> Gleich mußte nun Titania erwachen,
> Und aus dem Langohr ihren Liebling machen.

In diesem Beispiel ersetzt Schlegel das Klischee durch eine ausmalende Alliteration und steigende Klangmalerei des Erwachens und Verliebens: m*u*ßte: n*u*n – Tit*a*nia – erw*a*chen, L*a*ngohr *i*hren – L*ie*bling – m*a*chen. Die Entfernung der rhetorischen Stilmerkmale übt eine auflockernde Wirkung auf den Text aus. Es gehen Wiederholungen verloren, die eine statisch-bindende Funktion haben. Es kommt hinzu, daß Schlegel häufig durch Steigerungen einen dynamischen Effekt erzielt. Das ist besonders bemerkbar bei seiner Wahl der Zeitwörter:

> LYSANDER Or I will *shake* thee from me, like a serpent. (III, ii, 261)
> Sonst *schleudr'* ich dich wie eine Natter weg
> PUCK I jest to Oberon, and make him *smile*. (II, i, 44)
> Oft *lacht* bei meinen Scherzen Oberon.
> PUCK That *work* for bread upon Athenian stalls. (III, ii, 10)
> Die *mühsam kaum* ihr täglich Brot *erbeuten*.

Manchmal greift er selber zu rhetorischen Mitteln, um eine Steigerung zu bewirken:

> THESEUS The poet's eye, in a fine frenzy rolling,
> Doth *glance* from heaven to earth, from earth to heaven. (V, i, 12–13)
> Des Dichters Aug', in schönem Wahnsinn rollend,
> *Blitzt* auf zum Himmel, *blitzt* zur Erd' hinab.

Öfters fügt er auch Ausrufe ein, sogar solche, die im Original gar nicht vorhanden sind:

> LYSANDER So thou, *my surfeit, and my heresy,*
> Of all be hated; but the most of me! (II, ii, 149–50)
> *Mein Übermaß! mein Wahn!* so flieh' ich dich;
> Dich hasse jeder, doch am meisten ich, –
> LYSANDER If thou say so, withdraw, and prove it too. (III, ii, 255)
> *Ha!* sagst du das, so komm', beweis es auch!

Änderungen mit «romantischer» Tendenz befinden sich hauptsächlich an lyrisch-beschreibenden Stellen wie in den großen Reden Titanias im zweiten Akt. Dort werden manche Bilder, die Shakespeare klar umrissen und naturgetreu gezeichnet hat, unbestimmt, verschwommen und sogar unheimlich:

> TITANIA Therefore the winds, piping to us in vain,
> As in revenge *have suck'd up from the sea*
> *Contagious fogs.* (II, i, 88–90)
> Drum sog der Wind, der uns vergeblich pfiff,
> Als wie zur Rache, *böse Nebel auf*
> *Vom Grund des Meers.*

Contagious fogs: ansteckende, Krankheit bringende Nebel sind als solche klar definiert, während *böse Nebel* über «schädlich» und «schlimm» hinaus eine

Konnotation des Bösen trägt und deshalb unheimlich wirkt. Das ist umso mehr der Fall, da bei Schlegel das ganze Bild ins Irrationale verzogen ist durch die Vorstellung, daß die Nebel *vom Grund* des Meers emporgesogen werden. Ein weiteres Beispiel mit ähnlicher Tendenz: nachdem Hermia und Helena, Lysander und Demetrius am Morgen erwacht sind, denken sie mit Verwunderung an die verworrenen Begebenheiten der Nacht zurück; Demetrius spricht:

> DEMETRIUS   These things seem small, and undistinguishable,
> Like far-off mountains turned into clouds. (IV, i, 186–87)
> Dieß alles scheint so klein und unerkennbar,
> Wie ferne Berge, schwindend im Gewölk.

Der Unterschied beruht zunächst auf einer Verlagerung des Nachdrucks. Bei Shakespeare liegt die Betonung auf *small, and undistinguishable,*[24] bei Schlegel auf dem romantischen Bild der fernen Berge, die im Gewölk verschwinden. Shakespeares Gleichnis bezieht sich unmittelbar auf die Begebenheiten der Nacht, die wie Berge schienen, aber jetzt so weit entrückt sind, daß sie sich in bestandlose Wolken auflösen. So hat Eschenburg diesen Vers auch aufgefaßt.

> Dieß alles, was uns hier begegnet ist,
> Scheint klein und unerkennbar, gleich entfernten
> Gebirgen, die für uns zu Wolken werden.[25]

Schlegels Vers weist auf die Ferne hin, die die Dinge verschleiert und ihnen den Reiz der Unwirklichkeit verleiht. Als Theseus in Hinsicht auf die gleichen Geschehnisse seine ungewollt tiefsinnige, aber letzten Endes abwertende Ästhetik entwickelt, rettet Schlegel die Sache der Kunst:

> THESEUS   Such tricks hath strong imagination,
> That, if it would but apprehend some joy,
> It comprehends some bringer of that joy. (V, i, 18–20)
> So gaukelt die gewalt'ge Einbildung;
> Empfindet sie nur irgend eine Freude,
> Sie ahndet einen Bringer dieser Freude.

Das hintergründige *gaukelt,* die Steigerung von *strong* auf *gewalt'ge* und die Alliteration erheben die *Einbildung* zu einem übergeordneten Prinzip. Das weitere folgt daraus: bei Shakespeare wird der Mechanismus der Selbsttäuschung beschrieben: «wünscht sich die Einbildung eine Freude, so schafft sie sich einen Überbringer dieser Freude.» *Comprehend* steht im Sinne von «to lay hold of» (bis ca. 1650) und *apprehend* im Sinne von «to feel» (bis ca. 1670).

---

24 Vgl. H. Stahl, «Schöpferische Wortbildung bei Shakespeare,» *Shakespeare Jahrbuch,* 90 (1954), 273, für eine kennzeichnende Nachwirkung der Romantik in der deutschen Shakespearerezeption. Für sie ist das an sich nüchterne englische *undistinguishable* ein «atmosphäreschaffendes Wort,» welches «romantischen Stimmungswert» hat.

25 J.J. Eschenburg, (Übers.), *William Shakespeares Schauspiele,* 13 vols. (Zürich: Orell, Füeßli, 1775–82), I, 209.

Das Exempel zu diesem Täuschungsmanöver wird in den beiden nächsten Versen erbracht:

> Or in the night, imagining some fear,
> How easy is a bush supposed a bear!

Schlegel scheint dagegen auf einen göttlichen Ursprung der Fantasie und ihren Eingebungen anzuspielen: «sobald die Einbildung eine Freude fühlt, empfindet sie dunkel einen Bringer dieser Freude.» Die Freude oder Angst entsteht nicht mehr in der Einbildung, sondern sie wird von außen an sie herangetragen. Diese Umdeutung wird durch die Abwandlung von *would apprehend* in *empfindet* und die Verwendung von *ahndet* für *comprehend* ermöglicht.

Solche Verlagerungen – Vieldeutigkeit, wo Eindeutigkeit war, irrationale und stimmungsgeladene Bilder, Aufwertung der Einbildung – eröffnen dem Numinosen einen Zugang zur Menschenwelt des Theseus und seines Gefolges. Sie bewirken auch, daß in der Übersetzung mehr als im Original die Stimme des Autors beziehungsweise des Übersetzers vernehmbar wird. Das geschieht, weil an den entsprechenden Stellen die Aussagen nicht mehr ganz mit den Charakteren im Einklang sind.

Die drei Bereiche des *Sommernachtstraums:* Elfen, Hof und Handwerker unterscheiden sich auch in ihrem jeweiligen Sprachgebrauch. Die Norm stellen Theseus und sein Gefolge dar. Sie sind die Träger der Haupthandlung und stehen im Mittelpunkt des Interesses. Die Elfen heben sich von der Norm durch ihre lyrische Sprache ab, die alle Szenen, in denen Oberon, Puck, Titania und ihr Gefolge auftreten, durchzieht. Sie entspricht dem vergeistigten, weniger materiellen Wesen der Elfen in der Kette des Daseins. Die standesbedingte Sprache der Handwerker am anderen Ende der Skala hebt sich von der Norm durch die mangelnde Verarbeitung der kulturellen Tradition ihrer Zeit ab. Die Sprecher verwechseln ständig Fremdwörter und liefern eine ungewollte Parodie der *Pyramus und Thisbe*-Tragödie.

In der Übersetzung erfährt die Sprache der Elfen eine eigene Entwicklung, von der zwei Bereiche besonders betroffen werden: die Geister- und Gräberbeschreibungen – ein eigentlicher Topos des achtzehnten Jahrhunderts – und das Kleine überhaupt, das in der Verniedlichung des Elfenwesens zum Ausdruck kommt. Im folgenden Abschnitt wird eine fast sachliche Darstellung Shakespeares in eine «schauerliche» verwandelt:

> PUCK And yonder *shines* Aurora's harbinger;
>   At whose approach, *ghosts, wandering here and there,*
>   *Troop home to church-yards: damned spirits all,*
>   That in cross-ways and floods have burial,
>   Already to their wormy beds are gone. (III, ii, 380–84)
>   Auch *schimmert* schon Auroras Herold dort,
>   Und seine Näh' *scheucht irre Geister fort*
>   *Zum Todtenacker; banger Seelen Heere,*
>   Am Scheideweg' begraben und im Meere;
>   Man sieht ins wurmbenagte Bett sie gehn.

Shakespeare unterscheidet zwischen *ghosts,* die erst im Morgenrot zu den Friedhöfen zurückkehren, und den besonders lichtscheuen *damned spirits,* die schon weit früher in ihre Gräber auf ungeweihtem Boden gehen müssen. Shakespeares Geister *wander here and there,* sie gehen umher, *troop home,* kehren scharenweise nach Hause zurück zu *church-yards,* Friedhöfen. Schlegels *irre Geister* werden zum *Todtenacker gescheucht.* Für *irre* hat Bailey's Wörterbuch «*astray, irreseyn* to be out, perplexed, got out of the way, to be mistaken.» Sie haben sich offenbar «verirrt» oder sind «irre» (= fehl am Platz) im Morgenrot. Die *damned spirits all, banger Seelen Heere* – eine bemerkenswerte Steigerung – verziehen sich zur gleichen Zeit. Shakespeares Darstellung entspricht dem Volksglauben, während Schlegels auf literarische Vorbilder zurückgreift, deren Funktion es war, eine gruselige Stimmung zu erwecken. Das folgende Beispiel läßt die sprachliche Grundlage der Umgestaltung deutlich erkennen:

> PUCK Now it is the time of night,
> That the *graves,* all gaping wide,
> Every one *lets forth* his sprite,
> In the church-way paths to *glide.* (v, i, 377-79)
> Jetzo gähnt *Gewölb' und Grab,*
> Und, *entschlüpft* den *kalten Mauern,*
> Sieht man Geister auf und ab,
> Sieht am Kirchhofszaun sie *lauern.*

Die hergebrachte Einleitung *Now it is the time of night* wird zugunsten der Verdoppelung *Gewölb' und Grab* und der Zufügung *kalte Mauern* auf *jetzo* verkürzt. Die Zeitwörter sind auch beteiligt: *lets forth* wird zu *entschlüpft* und *glide* zu einem bedrohlichen *lauern* gesteigert, das sich auch auf die elliptische Konstruktion des dritten Verses erweitert. Dagegen werden die Elfengestalten selber durchgehend verharmlost. Im folgenden Vers spricht eine der Elfen Puck an mit:

> FAIRY   ... are you not he,
> That *frights* the maidens of the villagery. (II, i, 34-35)
> Der auf dem Dorf' die Dirnen *zu erhaschen,*
> *Zu necken* pflegt.

und am Ende der verzauberten Nacht nach seiner Versöhnung mit Titania ruft Oberon:

> OBERON ... Come, my queen take hands with me,
> And *rock the ground* whereon these sleepers be. (v, i, 84-85)
> Nun komm, Gemahlin! Hand in Hand gefügt,
> Und dieser Schläfer *Ruheplatz gewiegt!*

Rock the ground wird von den englischen Herausgebern allgemein im Sinn von «den Boden erschüttern» gedeutet, denn die Elfen zu Shakespeares Zeit konnten stampfen: man vergleiche Malones Anmerkung zu *stamp* (III, ii, 25) in der Ausgabe von 1790 und den dort zitierten Ausruf Pucks aus Reginald Scotts

Discoverie of Witchcraft (1584) «Hemton hamten, here will I never more tread, nor stampen.» Eschenburg folgt den englischen Kommentatoren und übersetzt:

> ... wo diese Schläfer sich
> Ausstrecken, komm, hier stampfen du und ich
> Im Tanz den grünen Boden feyerlich! (I, 205)

Alle Spuren der elementaren, furchterregenden Macht der Elfenwesen, die bei Shakespeare noch erhalten sind, schwinden in der Übersetzung.[26] Die allgemeine Verniedlichung erreicht bei den Nebengestalten ihren Höhepunkt:

> PUCK   And we fairies, that do *run*
> By the triple Hecate's team,
> From the presence of the sun,
> *Following* darkness like a dream,
> Now *are frolick;* (v, i, 381-85)
> Und wir Elfen, die *mit Tanz*
> Hekate's Gespann *umhüpfen,*
> Und *gescheucht* vom Sonnenglanz,
> Träumen gleich ins Dunkel *schlüpfen,*
> *Schwärmen* jetzo;

Die anthropomorphen Gestalten Shakespeares spiegeln die menschliche Welt auf übergeordneter Ebene wider, während die entmachteten und verniedlichten Wesen Schlegels eher in einer Nebenwelt der Naturerscheinungen beheimatet sind. Das ist eine Tendenz, die deutlich zum Ausdruck kommt: sie hat zur Folge, daß im Bau des Stücks die gegenseitige Beziehung der Elfen und Menschen in der Übersetzung gestört wird.

Die Sprache der Handwerker ist auf zwei Ebenen vertreten: im *Pyramus und Thisbe*-Stück und in den Prosaszenen. Im ersteren parodiert Shakespeare den bombastischen Stil seiner unmittelbaren Vorgänger. Schlegel entnimmt diesen Teil unverändert der Wielandschen Übersetzung. In beiden Fällen also, im Original und in der Übersetzung, wird das Stück im Stück durch eine historische Stilverschiebung vom übrigen Text abgesetzt. Bei Schlegel wird die komische Wirkung durch die Altertümlichkeit des Ausdrucks gesteigert, und die steifen Alexandriner erinnern auch an einen allerdings viel weiter als bei Shakespeare zurückliegenden dramatischen Stil. Es besteht jedoch ein wesentlicher Unterschied: Shakespeares Handwerker sind überholt, sie befinden sich nicht auf dem letzten Stand in der Wahl ihres Stücks, geschweige denn in der Bearbeitung. Sie wirken deshalb auf eine übertriebene, aber immer noch glaubwürdige Weise lächerlich. Schlegels Handwerker hingegen haben über-

---

26 Vgl. auch I. Candidus und E. Roller, «Der Sommernachtstraum von Wieland bis Flatter,» *Shakespeare Jahrbuch,* 92 (1956), 133.

haupt keinen Bezug zur Gegenwart. Ihre Sprache gehört einem längst überwundenen historischen Stil an. Sie sind durch und durch literarisch geprägt. Der gleiche Gegensatz besteht auch in den Prosaszenen. Hier hat Schlegel den Text Wielands häufig geändert und auch einige Varianten Eschenburgs übernommen. Der erste Auftritt der Handwerker hebt mit den folgenden Sätzen an:

BOTTOM Are we all met?
QUINCE Pat, pat; and here's a marvellous convenient place for our rehearsal. (III, i, 1-2)

Wieland: –

ZETTEL Sind wir alle beysammen?
SQUENZ Recht gut! Recht gut! Das ist ein unvergleichlicher Platz zu unserer Probe.

Eschenburg: –

ZETTEL Sind wir alle beysammen?
SQUENZ Ja doch, ja doch; und hier ist ein unvergleichlicher Platz zu unserer Probe.

Schlegel: –

ZETTEL Sind wir alle beysammen?
SQUENZ Aufs Haar; und hier ist ein prächtig bequemer Platz zu unsrer Probe.

Vielleicht hat Schlegel ein Wortspiel zwischen *pat* (adv) «ganz genau» und *pat* (vt) «streicheln» vermutet und deshalb *Aufs Haar* gesetzt. Wie dem auch sei, die Übersetzung wirkt literarisch, denn kein Handwerker würde so antworten. Bei Shakespeare beruht die Komik häufig auf einer falschen Verwendung von Fremdwörtern. Der angeberische Bottom wird dadurch charakterisiert, die anderen ahmen ihn nach. Wieland behält die Fremdwörter bei, Schlegel ersetzt sie durch deutsche:

BOTTOM We will meet; and there we will rehearse more *obscenely*, and *courageously*. (I, ii, 99-100)

Wieland: –

ZETTEL Wir wollen kommen! Der Einfall ist gut; wir können im Wald *obscener* und *herzhafter* probieren.

Schlegel: –

ZETTEL Wir wollen kommen, und da können wir recht *unverschämt* und *herzhaft* probiren.

Bei Schlegel beruht die komische Wirkung nicht auf der Verwechslung, sondern auf der Unglaubwürdigkeit des Wortes *unverschämt* in diesem Zusammenhang. In einem vereinzelten Fall setzt Schlegel auch Fremdwörter in den deutschen Text. Quince spricht über Bottom:

QUINCE	Yea, and the best person too; and he is a very *paramour,* for a sweet voice.
FLUTE	You must say *paragon: A paramour* is, God bless us! a thing of nought. (IV, ii, 11–13)
SQUENZ	Ja, der Tausend! Und die beste Person dazu. Und was eine süße Stimme betrifft, da ist er ein rechtes *Phänomen.*
FLAUT	Ein *Phönix* müßt ihr sagen. Ein *Phänomen* (Gott behüte uns!) ist ein garstiges Ding.

Die Verwechselung von *paragon* und *paramour,* die bei Shakespeare den Anstoß zur Komik gibt, lag nach der Überflutung der englischen Sprache mit Fremdwörtern im sechzehnten Jahrhundert im Bereich des Möglichen. Flauts Erwiderung in Schlegels Fassung erzielt ihren Effekt aufgrund der entgegengesetzten Wirkung: nämlich der Unmöglichkeit einer ähnlichen Verwechselung von *Phönix* und *Phänomen.* Durch solche Stilmittel in der Darstellung erreicht Schlegel einen Verfremdungseffekt: die Handwerker verlieren ihre Unmittelbarkeit, und das Stück, das sie aufführen, gewinnt an sinnbildlicher Bedeutung – etwa einem Marionettenspiel vergleichbar. Durch den Realitätsverlust entfernen sie sich etwas mehr von der Norm, die durch die Welt des Theseus und seines Gefolges gesetzt wird. In der Konstruktion des Schauspiels wird die Stellung der Handwerker nun analog zu der der Elfen. Die beiden Bereiche werden schließlich überbrückt in der Szene, in der sich Titania in den in einen Esel verwandelten Bottom verliebt.

Über Notwendigkeit und Beschaffenheit einer metrischen Übersetzung hat sich Schlegel an mehreren Stellen geäußert. Durch sie «würde es erlaubt seyn, sich dem Dichter in seiner Gedrungenheit, seinen Auslassungen, seinen kühnen und nachdrücklichen Wendungen und Stellungen weit näher anzuschmiegen,» als in einer Prosaübersetzung möglich sei.[27] Er erkannte die grundsätzliche Übereinstimmung von metrischer und syntaktischer Einheit des englischen Blankverses und folgerte daraus, daß der Übersetzer mit der gleichen Zahl der Verse wie das Original auskommen müsse:

> Dieß ist sehr wichtig, denn geht er in einem Verse über das Maß hinaus, so muß er es auch in den folgenden, bis er sich wieder in gleichen Schritt gesetzt hat. Dadurch werden dann Sätze, welche im englischen eine Zeile mit schöner Rundung umschließt, zwei aus einander gerissen, und die bedeutenden Schlüße der Verse, worauf bei ihrem harmonischen Falle so viel beruht, verändert.[28]

Durch die Flektionen der deutschen Sprache ergibt sich eine größere Regelmäßgkeit der Hebungen und Senkungen als im englischen Blankvers, in welchem das Metrum weitgehend durch den Satzrhythmus modifiziert wird. Das läßt sich am folgenden Beispiel erkennen:

---

27 «Etwas über William Shakespeare bei Gelegenheit Wilhelm Meisters,» Böcking, VII, 62.
28 Ibid.

PUCK	Near to her close and consecrated bower,
	While she was in her dull and sleeping hour, (III, ii, 7–8)
	Sie lag im Schlaf versunken auf dem Moos,
	In ihrer heil'gen Laube dunklem Schooß.

Der Neigung zur «Schwerfälligkeit,» die daraus entsteht, müsse der Übersetzer entgegenwirken. Schlegel tut das u.a. durch die Verwendung von weiblichen Endungen, welche bei Shakespeare im *Sommernachtstraum* nur sehr selten vorkommen:

> Auf den Bau der reimlosen Jamben habe ich vielen Fleiß verwandt: wie finden Sie ihn? die weiblichen Endungen sind unentbehrlich, und ohne sie würden die Jamben auch zu steif werden; aber mich däucht, man müsse sich hüten, ihrer zu viele aufeinander folgen zu lassen, wenigstens alsdann männliche Abschnitte in die Mitte bringen, sonst wird der Vers schleppend.[29]

In der Tat läßt sich feststellen, daß von den ungereimten Versen etwas weniger als ein Drittel und von den gereimten beinahe die Hälfte weiblich ist, bei den letzteren findet sich oft ein regelmäßiger Wechsel zwischen männlichen und weiblichen Reimen.

Zwischen Schlegels Prinzip eines dynamischen, abwechslungsreichen Versbaus und dem «harmonischen Falle» der englischen Verse besteht ein Widerspruch, der sich an vielen Einzelheiten nachweisen läßt. Besonders in den lyrischen Stellen durchbricht in der Übersetzung der bewegte Fluß der Rede die syntaktische Einheit der Verse. Im folgenden längeren Abschnitt scheint Schlegel absichtlich die Enjambements *weiß / Die Zeit, Feenland / Geschlichen, Corydon / Gesessen, Phyllida / Gesungen* herbeizuführen und die stehende Formel *Heil / Und Segen* zu trennen. Dadurch und durch die unregelmäßigen Zäsuren wird eine leidenschaftliche Bewegung in die Schmährede Titanias hineingetragen:

TITANIA	Then I must be thy lady: But I know
	When thou hast stol'n away from fairy land
	And in the shape of Corin sate all day,
	Playing on pipes of corn, and versing love
	To amorous Phillida. Why art thou here,
	Come from the farthest steep of India?
	But that, forsooth, the bouncing Amazon,
	Your buskin'd mistress, and your warrior love,
	To Theseus must be wedded; and you come
	To give their bed joy and prosperity. (II, i, 64–73)

So muß ich wohl dein Weib seyn; doch ich weiß
Die Zeit, daß du dich aus dem Feenland'
Geschlichen, Tage lang als Corydon
Gesessen, spielend auf dem Haberrohr,

---

29 Körner und Wieneke, A.W. Schlegel an Schiller 1.3.1796, S. 29.

Und Minne der verliebten Phyllida
Gesungen hast. – Und warum kommst du jetzt
Von Indiens entferntestem Gebirg',
Als weil – ey denkt doch! – weil die Amazone,
Die strotzende, hochaufgeschürzte Dame,
Dein Heldenliebchen, sich vermählen will?
Da kommst du denn, um ihrem Bette Heil
Und Segen zu verleihn.

Die unregelmäßige Verteilung der Zäsuren, beziehungsweise der syntaktischen Unterteilungen der Verse kann die Gesamtstruktur auch dort auflockern, wo die Verseinheiten mehr oder weniger dem Satzrhythmus entsprechen:

HIPPOLYTA	'Tis strange, my Theseus, / that these lovers speak of.	5/6
THESEUS	More strange than true. / I never may believe	4/6
	These antique fables, / nor these fairy toys.	5/5
	Lovers, and madmen, / have such seething brains,	5/5
	Such shaping fantasies, / that apprehend	6/4
	More than cool reason / ever comprehends. (v, i, 1ff.)	5/5
HIPPOLYTA	Was diese Liebenden erzählen, / mein Gemahl	9/3
	Ist wundervoll. /	
THESEUS	Mehr wundervoll, wie wahr	4/6
	Ich glaubte nie / an diese Feenpossen	4/7
	Und Fabeley'n / Verliebte und Verrückte	4/7
	Sind beyde / von so brausendem Gehirn,	3/7
	So bildungsreicher Fantasie, / die wahrnimmt,	8/3
	Was nie die kühlere Vernunft begreift.	–

Eine solche Auflockerung läßt sich häufig nachweisen. Sie bewirkt, daß die statischen Strukturen, auf denen das Gleichgewicht von Shakespeares Versbau beruht, aufgehoben werden und einem unruhigeren, bewegteren Gang Platz machen. Man kann behaupten, daß die charakteristischen Eigenschaften der Schlegelschen Verskunst den neuen Inhalten entsprechen und daß die aufgelockerte Form besonders der Tendenz zur ungrammatikalischen Sprachfügung, auf die sich Schlegel selber beruft, entgegenkommt: «Hart möchte die Treue des Übersetzers zuweilen sein, und er müßte sich den freiesten Gebrauch unsrer Sprache in ihrem ganzen Umfange (eine alte Gerechtsame der Dichter, was auch Grammatiker einwenden mögen) nicht vorwerfen lassen; aber nie dürfte sie schwerfällig werden.»[30]

Die Tendenzen und Verlagerungen, die sich an Schlegels *Sommernachtstraum* feststellen lassen, stehen alle im Rahmen einer erstaunlich genauen Übersetzung. Einzeln für sich genommen, kann ihnen nur wenig Bedeutung beigemessen werden. Da sie jedoch wiederholt und folgerichtig auftreten und sich gegenseitig unterstützen, bewirken sie eine Veränderung der inneren Konstruktion des Stücks. Der Ausgangspunkt ist die hierarchische Anordnung bei

30 Böcking, VII, 62.

Shakespeare, in der die Elfen in ähnlicher Weise dem Adel übergeordnet sind wie der Adel den Handwerkern:

Elfen ——————— Adel ——————— Handwerker

Durch die Steigerung der Rangbezeichnungen einerseits und die Verbürgerlichung der moralischen Wertbegriffe und die Auflösung der aristokratischen Sprache andererseits wird die mittlere Gruppe in zwei unterteilt. Der Fürst und seine Gemahlin bleiben aristokratisch, während die Liebespaare verbürgerlicht werden, – das entspricht einem Wandel in der Sozialstruktur des Stücks:

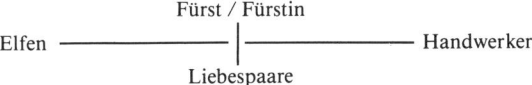

Die Elfen werden entweder verniedlicht oder durch Steigerung von Ausdruck und Bildern mythisiert. Sie sind in beiden Fällen weniger anthropomorph und deshalb von den Menschen abgesetzt. Die Spaltung der Herrschaftsbegriffe in ein *Fürstentum* für die Menschen und ein *Königreich* für die Elfen verstärkt diese Tendenz. Es entsteht eine Kluft zwischen den übernatürlich-irrationalen Naturmächten und der Menschenwelt:

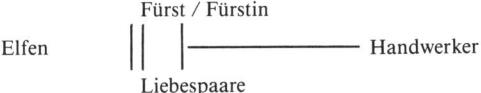

Die Handwerker ihrerseits werden «entwurzelt» und ebenfalls als «Naturwesen» – allerdings literarischer Prägung – dargestellt. Man kann sie als analog zu den Elfen betrachten, aber auf niederer Ebene. Der unmittelbare Bezug zwischen den beiden Bereichen wird durch die Verbindung von Bottom mit Titania geknüpft, die nun über ihre parodistische Funktion hinaus eine mythische Komponente gewinnt. Daraus ergibt sich folgende Konstruktion:

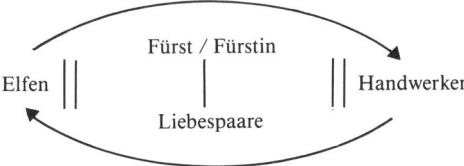

Die Renaissance-Auffassung, in der das Menschliche als Glied einer Kette zwischen übergeordneten und untergeordneten Kräften seinen bestimmten Platz behauptete, weicht einer Situation, in der das Menschliche von irrationalen Mächten umgeben ist. Dieser Deutung nach würde die Handlung des *Sommernachtstraums* einem Einbruch des Irrationalen in die Menschenwelt entsprechen. Da es sich überall um Tendenzen und Andeutungen handelt, bleibt die ursprüngliche Bedeutung des Lustspiels zumindest vordergründig erhalten. Es gewinnt jedoch eine unterschwellige Gegenkonstruktion, welche die

Heiterkeit der Handlung verleugnet. Das Bewußtsein von der ungesicherten Grundlage des menschlichen Daseins, – der allgemeinen Gefährdung, die im «Wahnwitzigen, Poeten und Verliebten» zum Durchbruch kommt, macht, daß ein Schatten der Bedrohung die Verirrungen der Liebenden begleitet. Es ist diese Hintergründigkeit und die Ironie, die ihr entspringt, die den Schlegelschen *Sommernachtstraum* als Frühwerk der Romantik kennzeichnet. Im Vergleich zwischen dem Ausgangspunkt, Shakespeares *Midsummer Night's Dream,* und der Übersetzung lassen sich alle Einzelheiten feststellen, die als System zusammengeschlossen jene neu entstehende, umfassende, in der Terminologie Schlegels «enzyklopädische» Ganzheit der romantischen Weltanschauung bilden.

«Hüte dich, das wilde Tier zu wecken» (Eichendorff). Beobachtungen zum Verhältnis Mensch–Tier in der Literatur des 19. Jahrhunderts

FRIEDRICH GAEDE, *Dalhousie University*

In seinem Roman *Le Père Goriot* beschreibt Balzac die Wirtin der schmutzigen Pension Vauquer mit folgenden Worten: «Ihr ältliches, schwammiges Gesicht, in dessen Mitte eine Papageiennase hervorspringt; ihre kleinen fetten Hände; ihre Gestalt, die vollgefressen wie eine Pfarrhausratte ist ... Die bleifahle Fettleibigkeit der kleinen Frau ist das Ergebnis ihrer Lebensweise.»[1] Balzac läßt nicht nur die Wirtin einer Ratte gleichen, sondern auch die Gäste der Pension Vauquer werden auf charakterisierende Tiere bezogen, sie erscheinen als Grille, Truthahn oder verwundete Taube. Diese Vergleiche sind nicht zufällig, sondern Ausdruck des Systems, das Balzac seiner ganzen *Comédie humaine* zugrundelegt und im Vorwort von 1842 beschreibt und begründet. Ausgehend von der Annahme, «daß das Tierische in einem ungeheuren Lebensstrom hinüberspielt ins Menschliche,» sagt Balzac: «Das Tier ist ein Grundwesen, das seine äußere Gestalt oder, genauer, die Unterschiede seiner Gestalt in den Umgebungen annimmt, in denen es sich zu entwickeln berufen wird. Aus diesen Unterschieden ergeben sich die zoologischen Arten ... Da ich von diesem System durchdrungen war, ... erkannte ich, daß die Gesellschaft in dieser Hinsicht der Natur glich ... Die Unterschiede zwischen einem Soldaten, einem Arbeiter, einem Beamten, ... einem Bettler und einem Priester sind ... nicht minder beträchtlich als jene, die den Wolf, den Löwen, den Esel, die Krähe, den Hai, die Meerkuh, das Schaf und andere unterscheiden.»[2] Balzacs Versuch, die menschliche Gesellschaft nach dem Vorbild des zoologischen Systems darzustellen, ist nur in seinem Totalitätsanspruch ein Novum, denn der Vergleich von Menschlichem und Tierischem ist so alt wie die erzählende Kunst überhaupt. Bevor geprüft wird, welches besondere Gewicht die Mensch–Tier-Gleichung für das 19. Jahrhundert hat, ist ein kurzer Blick auf die vorangehende Tradition zu werfen.

In der Welt der Märchen sprechen die Tiere nicht nur mit den Menschen und darum wie die Menschen, sie sind zuweilen auch ineinander verwandelt: der Frosch kann ebenso Prinz werden wie der Prinz ein Esel. Doch schon in dieser

---

1 Honoré de Balzac, *Vater Goriot*, übers. v. E. Sander (München: Goldmann, o.J.), S.12f.
2 Honoré de Balzac, «Vorrede,» *Menschliche Komödie* (Leipzig: Insel, 1925), Bd. 1, 222.

Welt märchenhaft beseelter Natur, in der keine Naturgesetze gelten, ist die Verwandlung des Menschen in ein Tier entweder eine Strafe für eine böse Tat oder, wenn es einen Unschuldigen trifft, eine böse Tat selbst. Die märchenhafte Rückverwandlung in menschliche Gestalt bedeutet deshalb immer eine Erlösung. In dieser Erlösung verrät sich mit der Anthropomorphisierung aller Natur die Funktion, die das Tier schon im Märchen hat: da es sich der menschlichen Sprache bedient und zur menschlichen Existenz erlöst wird, ist das Menschliche sein Maßstab, der sowohl die Bedingtheit des Tieres als auch – durch den Gegensatz – menschliche Freiheit und Würde deutlich macht. Diese im Märchen erscheinende Doppelrolle des Tieres, sowohl menschlich reden zu können, als auch wegen seiner Animalität aufzutreten, vereinzelt dann zu zwei verschiedenen Traditionen, die beide nicht mehr wie das Märchen Ausdruck des mythischen Weltzustands oder naiver Naturbeseelung, sondern des bewußt gestaltenden poetischen Geistes sind: einerseits dem Tierepos und besonders der Tierfabel und andererseits dem Motiv des kreatürlichen Tieres, dessen bloße Animalität zur Kontrastfolie des Humanen wird. Ist in der Fabeltradition das Tier als Maske des Menschlichen nur noch leere Form, so ist im Gegensatz dazu im kreatürlichen Tiermotiv das Tier wegen seines Vernunftmangels und wegen seines Trieb- und Instinktmechanismus genannt. Beide Möglichkeiten beherrschen die Dichtung seit Ende des Mittelalters in verstärktem Maße. In dieser Zeit entsteht nicht nur eine aktive Fabeldichtung. Seit der Renaissance wird der Dualismus von Kreatürlichem und Geistigem, von Physis und Affekten einerseits und Ratio andererseits zum Gegensatz, der als Zwiespalt von Animalität und Geistigkeit den Menschen bestimmt.

Der christliche Platonismus der Renaissance kann mit seiner Fassung dieses Zwiespalts auf Plato zurückgreifen. Plato schildert im IX. Buch von *Politeia* den Menschen als einen Behälter, in dem der «innere Mensch,» ein Löwe und ein vielgestaltiges Ungeheuer miteinander konkurrieren. Für Plato ist darum das Edle das, «wodurch das Tierische in der Natur unter den Menschen oder vielmehr unter das Göttliche gebracht wird.»[3] Entsprechend läßt der Neoplatoniker Pico della Mirandola in seiner Rede *De hominis dignitate* Gott den Menschen auffordern, sich als sein «eigener, vollkommen frei schaltender Bildhauer und Dichter» selbst die Lebensform zu bestimmen: «Es steht dir frei, in die Unterwelt des Viehes zu entarten. Es steht dir ebenso frei, in die höhere Welt des Göttlichen dich durch den Entschluß deines eigenen Geistes zu erheben.»[4] Freiheit als geistige Selbstverwirklichung bedeutet für Pico Distanz zum Sinnlich-Kreatürlichen. Da dieser Bereich der des Instinkts und der Triebgebundenheit ist, gibt die Freiheit, die sich für das Sinnliche entscheidet, sich selbst auf. Seit der Renaissance wird in Philosophie und Literatur der

---

3 Platon, *Sämtliche Werke,* Bd. 3, hrsg. W.F. Otto u.a. (Hamburg: Rowohlt, 1958), 284ff.
4 Giovanni Pico della Mirandola, *Die Würde des Menschen,* übers. u. hrsg. H.W. Rüssel (Fribourg: Parthenon, o.J.), S. 52f.

Dualismus von Kreatürlichem und Geistigem, von Natur und Kunst und entsprechend von Immanenz und Transzendenz verschärft und das Tier zum Inbegriff des nur Physischen, Mechanistischen und Unfreien gemacht. Es wird im 17. Jahrhundert zum Sinnbild der depotenzierten Natur.[5] Für Descartes ist das Tier ein seelenloser Mechanismus, und für Hobbes wird es zum Repräsentanten des «status naturalis,» der vom «status civilis» zu überwinden ist.[6] Im 18. Jahrhundert wird das Thema fortgesetzt. Schnabels *Insel Felsenburg* ist das literarische Paradigma der depotenzierten Natur, in der sich auf bloße Nützlichkeit reduzierte Insellandschaft und von allen Lastern gereinigtes Innenleben der Inselbewohner entsprechen. An den Affen der Insel wird das Prinzip der inneren und äußeren Naturbeherrschung explizit gemacht: die Tiere werden bekämpft, dezimiert, geprügelt und dem Haushalt nützlich gemacht. Auch für Goethe sind die Tiere «durch eine unendliche Kluft von uns getrennt und in das Reich der Notwendigkeit verwiesen.»[7] In seiner Alterserzählung *Novelle* zeigt Goethe jedoch, wie die bisherige Art der Naturbeherrschung, für die die Behandlung der Affen auf der Insel Felsenburg charakteristisch ist, durch eine höhere Form der Versöhnung von Natur und Geist übertroffen werden kann. Ein Tiger und ein Löwe sind in einer Stadt während einer Feuersbrunst ausgebrochen. Der Tiger wird im Sinne bisheriger Problemlösung von einem Adligen getötet, der Löwe hingegen durch ein musizierendes und singendes Kind bewogen, in den Käfig zurückzukehren. Damit ist die «unendliche Kluft,» von der Goethe an anderer Stelle gesprochen hat, für den menschlichen Geist dann überwindbar, wenn dieser Geist das naive Vertrauen und die gläubige Selbst- und Weltgewißheit des künstlerischen Kindes hat. Die Überwindung der Kluft ist nur einem früheren Bewußtseinsstand, einem kindlichen Weltalter möglich, dem das Märchen entspricht. Wie das Irreale eines Märchens gerade dadurch deutlich wird, daß hier alles seinen gerechten Lauf nimmt, so erweist sich das Unwirkliche von Goethes märchenhafter Lösung an ihrem Widerspruch zur gleichzeitigen empirischen Situation: statt Versöhnung wächst, als die Novelle geschrieben wird, der Zwiespalt, und statt der Zähmung brutaler Natur durch den Geist beginnt noch zur Zeit der Romantik der Triumph der Brutalität.[8]

Im Jahr 1837 beschließt Eichendorff seine Erzählung *Das Schloß Dürande* mit der Warnung: «Du aber hüte dich, das wilde Tier zu wecken in der Brust,

---

5 Siehe Friedrich Gaede, «Homo homini lupus et ludius est – Zu Grimmelshausens *Der seltzame Springinsfeld*,» *DVjs*, 57 (1983), 240–58.
6 Siehe Ulrich Weiß, *Das philosophische System von Thomas Hobbes* (Stuttgart-Bad Cannstatt: Frommann-Holzboog, 1980)
7 J.W. v. Goethe, *Dichtung und Wahrheit*, IV. Teil, 16. Buch.
8 Siehe E.T.A. Hoffmann, *Die Elixiere des Teufels*, und H. v. Kleist, *Penthesilea;* zu letzterem: Peter Michelsen, «Der Imperativ des Unmöglichen – Über Heinrich von Kleists *Penthesilea*,» *Antike Tradition und Neuere Philologien* (Festschrift Sühnel), hrsg. H.-J. Zimmermann (Heidelberg: Winter, 1984), S. 127–50.

daß es nicht plötzlich ausbricht und dich selbst zerreißt.» Hans Eichner hat in seiner Darstellung Eichendorffs auf dessen Wiederholung der Warnung, die sich auf Kleist bezieht, hingewiesen: «Hüte jeder das wilde Tier in seiner Brust, daß es nicht plötzlich ausbricht und ihn selbst zerreißt! Denn das war Kleists Unglück und schwer gebüßte Schuld, daß er diese keinem Dichter fremde dämonische Gewalt nicht bändigen konnte oder wollte.»[9] Als diese Warnung ausgesprochen wird, ist das Tier bereits los; es hatte nicht nur bei Kleist zum Sprung über die Kluft angesetzt, die laut Goethe Mensch und Tier trennt, und es beweist im Laufe des 19. Jahrhunderts mit seinem erfolgreichen Sprung, daß diese Kluft keinesfalls unendlich ist, wie Goethe noch zu Anfang des Jahrhunderts angenommen hat. Gleichzeitig mit Balzac dokumentiert Georg Büchner diesen Sprung. Annette von Droste-Hülshoff, Gottfried Keller und Theodor Storm folgen. Die im 17. und 18. Jahrhundert depotenzierte Natur beginnt sich zu «befreien,» indem sie den Geist und damit den Menschen entmachtet. Das Scheitern der naturverfallenen Menschen ist darum eines der großen Themen der Literatur des 19. Jahrhunderts und das Tier das Mittel, diesen Vorgang deutlich zu machen. So demonstriert Büchner in *Woyzeck* auf sarkastische Weise die «viehische Vernünftigkeit» eines Pferdes, um die Vernunft als solche bloßzustellen. Das wegen seiner «Intelligenz» auf dem Jahrmarkt ausgestellte Tier benimmt sich plötzlich, wie es heißt, «ungebührlich.» Indem das scheinbar kluge Pferd der Notwendigkeit seiner Natur folgen muß, relativiert es den Begriff der vernunftbestimmten oder idealen Natur und spiegelt damit den in unausweichliche Notwendigkeiten gestellten Menschen Woyzeck, der die Freiheit, von der Pico oder Goethe sprechen, nicht mehr kennt und an den Zwängen, denen er ausgeliefert ist, zerbricht. Zwanghaft ist auch das Verhalten von Büchners Lenz. Auch in seinem Falle wird der Vernunftverlust durch die Konfrontation mit einem Tier, hier einer Katze, ausgedrückt. Büchner schreibt: «Einst saß Lenz neben Oberlin, die Katze lag gegenüber auf einem Stuhl. Plötzlich wurden seine Augen starr, er hielt sie unverrückt auf das Tier gerichtet; dann glitt er langsam vom Stuhl herunter, die Katze ebenfalls: sie war wie bezaubert von seinem Blick, sie geriet in ungeheure Angst, sie sträubte sich scheu; Lenz mit den nämlichen Tönen, mit fürchterlich entstelltem Gesicht; wie in Verzweiflung stürzten beide aufeinander los.»[10] Die Reduktion auf das Animalische bringt die «entsetzliche Gleichheit in der Menschennatur» zutage, die Büchner immer wieder ausspricht und gestaltet und die mit dem in *Dantons Tod* betonten Satz «Es gibt keinen Gott» zusammenhängt.[11] Lenz ist «auf die Katze gekommen,» nachdem ihn der Atheismus ergriffen und «ihn ganz sicher ruhig und fest» erfaßt hat.

---

9 Hans Eichner, «Joseph von Eichendorff,» *Handbuch der deutschen Erzählung,* hrsg. Karl Konrad Polheim (Düsseldorf: Bagel, 1981), S. 580.
10 Georg Büchner, *Sämtliche Werke und Briefe,* hrsg. Werner R. Lehmann (München: Hanser, ³1979), I, 98.
11 Siehe Friedrich Gaede, «Büchners Widerspruch – Zur Funktion des type primitif,» *JbIG,* 11: 2 (1979), 42–52.

Annette von Droste-Hülshoff bestätigt den Zusammenhang von Naturverfallenheit und religiöser Not. In ihrem Gedicht *Die ächzende Kreatur* (1846) erklärt sie die kreatürliche Unerlöstheit der Natur aus dem Verhältnis des Menschen zu Gott. Sie schildert, wie «Gottes hartgeprüftes Kind,» selbst innerlich bedrängt, die Angst der Tiere, des Vogels, der Grille, des Käfers beobachtet. Auf die Beobachtung folgt die Reflexion über die Gründe der inneren und äußeren Not aller Naturwesen. Diese Not begann «mit dem Fluch, den erwarb der Erden Fürst im Paradies,» der «sein gesegnet Reich verdarb.» Was war Adams Schuld, die zur Erbschuld wurde und sich als Naturverfallenheit äußert? Droste-Hülshoffs Antwort auf diese Frage legt die Voraussetzung des Problems mit einer Hellsicht bloß, die das Gedicht *Die ächzende Kreatur* zu einem bedeutenden, auch für die Gegenwart wesentlichen Dokument macht. Die Schuld an der mit Adam beginnenden Naturverfallenheit aller Kreatur liegt im Sündenfall, also im Essen vom Baum der Erkenntnis. Zur Schuld Adams, zum Verstoß gegen Gottes Gebot wurde nicht das Erkenntnisstreben schlechthin, sondern dessen besondere Art. Im Sündenfall sind das unterscheidende, zerlegende und fixierende Denken einerseits und das Böse andererseits eine feste Verbindung eingegangen. Zu wissen, was gut und böse ist, heißt abstrahieren können. Im Sündenfall wird die Fähigkeit zur Abstraktion gewonnen, zum Verstandesdenken, das analytisch verfährt und darum stets einseitig ist. Abstraktion bedeutet die im analytischen Vorgehen begründete Reduktion und Manipulierbarkeit des Erkenntnisobjekts. «Anbruch einer Willkürherrschaft über Dinge» hat darum W. Benjamin diesen Aspekt des Sündenfalls genannt.[12] J. Bernarts Argumentation geht in die gleiche Richtung, wenn er davon spricht, daß «die Feindschaftsetzung zwischen Mensch und Tier» Folge des Sündenfalls ist.[13] Mit dem Essen vom Baum der Erkenntnis sind Mensch und Natur in den Gegensatz geraten. Das erklärt den Zusammenhang, der zwischen der ächzenden Kreatur, der Rolle Adams und der bedeutsamen Schlußstrophe des Gedichts besteht, mit der das Thema der Schuld noch einmal erweitert wird:

Das ist die Schuld des Mordes an
Der Erde Lieblichkeit und Huld,
An des Getieres dumpfem Bann
Ist es die tiefe, schwere Schuld,
Und an dem Grimm, den es beseelt,
Und an der List, die es befleckt,
Und an dem Schmerze, den es quält,
Und an dem Moder, der es deckt.[14]

---

12 Walter Benjamin, *Schriften*, hrsg. Th. u. G. Adorno (Frankfurt: Suhrkamp, 1955), I, 359.
13 Joseph Bernart, *Die unbeweinte Kreatur – Reflexionen über das Tier* (München: Kösel, 1961), S. 27.
14 Annette von Droste-Hülshoff, *Sämtliche Werke*, hrsg. Clemens Heselhaus (Darmstadt: Wissenschaftliche Buchgesellschaft, 1960), S. 628.

Der Mensch zerstört die Natur, solange er sie nur analysiert, d.h. in ihre Teile zerlegt und verbraucht und damit die Einheit der Natur aufhebt. Droste-Hülshoff hat in ihrer Erzählung *Die Judenbuche* beschrieben, wie der Wald von Holzfrevlern des Profits wegen radikal abgeholzt oder zerstört wird. Der in der *Judenbuche* beschriebene Mord an der Natur steht im unmittelbaren Zusammenhang mit dem in der Erzählung gezeigten Mord am Menschen. Dadurch gewinnt die Schuld- oder Sündhaftigkeit der Holzfrevler erst ihre eigene, unentschuldbare Dimension. «Schuld des Mordes an der Erde Lieblichkeit und Huld» folgt aus dem mit dem Sündenfall gesetzten Denken und der damit gegebenen Willkürherrschaft über die Natur. Der Mensch macht mit der Natur sich selbst zum zerstörbaren Objekt, die Natur zerstörend, verfällt er ihr. Am Ende der Novelle *Die Judenbuche* hängt die Hauptfigur, der Hauptschuldige als verwesende Leiche im Baum: ein eindringliches Bild, das die Naturverfallenheit des Menschen mit seiner unerlösten Sündhaftigkeit gleichsetzt und begründet. Die Forschung hat im Gedicht *Die ächzende Kreatur* die Gedanken des 8. Kapitels des Römerbriefes erkannt.[15] Dort heißt es u.a.: «Denn wo ihr nach dem Fleisch lebet, so werdet ihr sterben müssen, wo ihr aber durch den Geist des Fleisches Geschäfte tötet, so werdet ihr leben.» Die Tiere oder die Kreatur, wie es in Gedicht und Bibel heißt, können nur gemäß ihren physischen Notwendigkeiten leben, sie sind, wie im Römerbrief gesagt wird, der Eitelkeit unterworfen, – ohne Offenbarung – und darum auch der Angst ausgesetzt. Die Kreatur wird deshalb in dem Augenblick zum Spiegel menschlicher Angst, in dem der Mensch nur noch «nach dem Fleisch» lebt. Achtzig Jahre später greift Brecht dieses Thema in *Aufstieg und Fall der Stadt Mahagonny* auf und setzt den Teil der Weisung aus dem Römerbrief, der das Sterbenmüssen betrifft, unmittelbar in Handlung um. Die Hauptfigur erkennt kurz vor ihrem Tod die Ursache ihres Untergangs und sagt: «Ich aß und wurde nicht satt, ich trank und wurde durstig ... Jetzt sitze ich hier und habe doch nichts gehabt. Ich war es, der sagte: jeder muß sich sein Stück Fleisch herausschneiden ... Da war das Fleisch faul!»[16]

Zum «erstickten heisern Gekrächze» wird das «Ächzen der Natur» in einer der merkwürdigsten Figuren, die in der Literatur des 19. Jahrhunderts nur «nach dem Fleisch lebt» und darum als Opfer ihrer Tiere zu einem ewigen Sterben verurteilt wird. In seiner Erzählung *Bulemanns Haus* (1864) schildert Theodor Storm, wie der Pfandleiher Bulemann, nur von seiner alten Magd und zwei Katzen umgeben, ganz seinem Besitz lebt. Bulemanns Geld- und Profitgier zerstört seine letzten menschlichen Bindungen, so daß er schließlich nur noch seine Katzen um sich hat. Diese beginnen zu wachsen, und je größer Bulemanns Einsamkeit wird, desto riesiger erscheinen ihm die Tiere, bis sie ihn

---

15 Gottfried Hasenkamp, «Das verlorene Paradies der Tiere,» *Jahrbuch der Droste-Gesellschaft*, 9 (1962), 18–30.
16 Bertolt Brecht, *Aufstieg und Fall der Stadt Mahagonny* (Berlin: Suhrkamp, 1959), S. 97.

ganz beherrschen und ihm nicht mehr erlauben, Kontakt mit der Außenwelt zu haben. Wörtlich heißt es bei Storm: «Das waren keine Katzen mehr, das waren zwei furchtbare, namenlose Raubtiere. Die stellten sich gegen ihn, sahen ihn mit ihren glimmenden Augen an und stießen ein heiseres Geheul aus.» Bulemann «wollte an ihnen vorbei, aber ein Schlag mit der Tatze ... trieb ihn zurück. Er lief ins Zimmer, wollte ein Fenster aufreißen, um die Menschen auf der Gasse anzurufen, aber die Katzen sprangen hintendrein und kamen ihm zuvor.»[17] Der gefangene Bulemann schrumpft zu einer Mumie zusammen. Am Ende herrscht nur noch das Chaos der Tiere in dem verlassenen Haus: Von außen hörte man «ein Gequieke wie von unzähligen Mäusen,» jemand behauptet sogar, «er habe drinnen auf den Treppen ganz deutlich das Springen großer Tiere gehört.» Bulemann selbst, der eingeschrumpfte Mensch, kann jedoch nicht völlig sterben, d.h. keine Ruhe finden, er bleibt zu einem unaufhörlichen, einsamen Warten verdammt, ein ewig Ruheloser. Der Eingeschrumpfte schaut damals – und jetzt immer noch, wie Storm schreibt, – «in den leeren Nachthimmel hinauf» und «erwartet die Barmherzigkeit Gottes» – ein unendliches und deshalb hoffnungsloses Warten, wenn der Himmel leer ist. Mit dem Größerwerden der Katzen wächst nicht nur Bulemanns Unfreiheit, sondern auch seine Gottferne und damit die absolute Sinn- und Hoffnungslosigkeit seiner Existenz.

Die metaphysische Dimension, die die Machtergreifung des Tieres bei Storm wie bei Büchner oder Balzac hat, tritt zum Ende des Jahrhunderts in Hofmannsthals Weise, das Motiv zu gestalten, zugunsten einer politischsozialen Dimension in den Hintergrund. Damit werden die auf Europa zukommenden revolutionären Änderungen seismographisch angezeigt und gedeutet. In seiner *Reitergeschichte* (1898) gestaltet Hofmannsthal ein tierisches Pandämonium, um das Zugrundegehen eines Wachtmeisters zu zeigen, dessen physischer Tod in seinem Verfallen an das Unbewußt-Bestialische gründet. Hofmannsthals Wachtmeister wird am Ende der Erzählung von seinem Offizier erschossen, da er dessen Befehl nicht nachkommt. Diese Insubordination wird in der Erzählung als die allmählich durchbrechende kreatürliche oder animalische Anarchie des Wachtmeisters gezeigt, die der Welt des Geistes, des Schönen und der Ordnung, auch der militärischen Ordnung, entgegengesetzt ist. Die zunehmende Anarchie des Wachtmeisters kommt in einer traumartigen Begegnung mit einem Dorf zum Ausdruck, das durch seine widerwärtigen und grotesken Tiere gekennzeichnet ist. So heißt es: Des Wachtmeisters «Pferd ging schwer und schob die Hinterbeine mühsam unter, wie wenn sie von Blei wären ... Unter einer Türschwelle zur Linken rollten zwei ineinander verbissene blutende Ratten in die Mitte der Strasse ... Aus dem nächsten Hause lief eilfertig mit gehobenem Kopfe ein Hund heraus, ließ einen Knochen in der

---

17 Theodor Storm, *Werke*, hrsg. G. Honnefelder (Frankfurt: Insel, ²1977), I, 256.

Mitte der Strasse fallen und versuchte, ihn in einer Fuge des Pflasters zu verscharren. Es war eine weisse unreine Hündin mit hängenden Zitzen.»[18] Mehr deformierte Hunde kommen, mager, gierig, krank und scheußlich. Eine Kuh versperrt dem Reiter den Weg, sie läßt sich nicht weiterziehen, weil sie den Blutgeruch der Gegend scheut. In der krankhaften Lebensgier der deformierten, ekelhaften Natur offenbart sich deren Todesverfallenheit. Die Begegnung des Wachtmeisters mit dieser Art Natur antizipiert seinen eigenen Tod, denn in ihm begehrt anschließend etwas «Gedrücktes, Hündisches» auf, und es entsteht in ihm, wie es heißt, ein «bestialischer» Zorn gegen seinen Vorgesetzten, der ihn zur Gehorsamsverweigerung und so in den Tod treibt. Das Ende des Wachtmeisters kennzeichnet das vorrevolutionäre Europa der Jahrhundertwende. Sein «bestialischer Zorn» wird wenige Jahre später nicht ihn, sondern die vernichten, die nicht mehr wie Hofmannsthals Offizier die Kraft haben, sich gegen ihn zu stellen.

Daß die erwähnten literarischen Beispiele, in denen sich Vernunftverlust, triumphus animalis und menschlicher Untergang verbinden, keine zufällige Auswahl darstellen, zeigt ihr Zusammenhang mit der gleichzeitigen Philosophie. Diese macht die sich im 19. Jahrhundert vollziehende Zerstörung oder Selbstaufgabe der Vernunft als der alles Seiende bestimmenden oder ordnenden Kraft zum expliziten Thema und schafft damit den prinzipiellen Grund für die von den Dichtern an warnenden Beispielen deutlich gemachte Krise.[19] So ist für Schopenhauers metaphysischen Naturalismus das Denken nur noch die Vorstellungsquelle, die das vom Naturwillen Bewirkte als empirische Erscheinung faßt. Solcher Einschätzung des Geistes ist die Differenz von Mensch und Tier peripher geworden: «Man muß an allen Sinnen blind sein, um nicht einzusehn, daß das Tier im wesentlichen und in der Hauptsache durchaus dasselbe ist, was wir sind, und daß der Unterschied bloß im Akzidenz, dem Intellekt, liegt, nicht in der Substanz, welche der Wille ist.»[20] Die Tatsache, daß Schopenhauer den menschlichen Geist als das nur Akzidentielle faßt, entspricht der Weise, wie Büchner Rolle und Funktion des Verstandes einschätzt. Wenn Büchner im Jahre 1834 schreibt: «Der Verstand nun gar ist nur eine sehr geringe Seite unseres geistigen Wesens und die Bildung nur eine sehr zufällige Form desselben,»[21] dann ist es keineswegs zufällig, daß Schopenhauer zur fast gleichen Zeit schreibt, «daß das Wesentliche und Hauptsächliche im Tiere und im Menschen dasselbe ist und daß, was beide unterscheidet, nicht im Primären, im Prinzip ... beider Erscheinungen liegt, ... sondern allein im Sekundären, im Intellekt.»[22] Radikaler läßt sich die

---

18 Hugo v. Hofmannsthal, *Die Erzählungen,* hrsg. H. Steiner (Frankfurt: Fischer, 1968), S. 55f.
19 Dazu Martin Heidegger, «Der europäische Nihilismus,» *Nietzsche* (Pfullingen: Neske, ³1961), II, 31ff.
20 Arthur Schopenhauer, *Paralipomena,* #177.
21 Georg Büchner, II (1972), 422.
22 Arthur Schopenhauer, *Über die Grundlage der Moral,* Abschnitt 19.

Mensch–Tier-Gleichung und die Selbstentmündigung des Geistes nicht formulieren. In Schopenhauers Position sind Aufklärung und Idealismus im Sinne der Kant'schen Definition «Aufklärung ist der Ausgang des Menschen aus seiner selbstverschuldeten Unmündigkeit» zurückgenommen. Nietzsche folgt ihm darin und schreibt: «das meist bewußte Denken eines Philosophen ist durch seine Instinkte heimlich geführt und in bestimmte Bahnen gezwungen. Auch hinter aller Logik und ihrer anscheinenden Selbstherrlichkeit ... stehen ... physiologische Forderungen zur Erhaltung einer bestimmten Art von Leben.»[23] Es ist darum konsequent, daß auch Nietzsche auf die Mensch–Tier-Gleichung kommt und im Jahre 1883 feststellt:

> Wir leiten den Menschen nicht mehr vom Geist, von der „Gottheit" ab, wir haben ihn unter die Tiere zurückgestellt. Er gilt uns als das stärkste Tier, weil er das listigste ist. Wir wehren uns andrerseits gegen eine Eitelkeit, die auch hier wieder laut werden möchte: wie als ob der Mensch die große Hinterabsicht der tierischen Entwicklung gewesen sei. Er ist durchaus keine Krone der Schöpfung: jedes Wesen ist, neben ihm, auf einer gleichen Stufe der Vollkommenheit ... Und indem wir das behaupten, behaupten wir noch zuviel: der Mensch ist, relativ genommen, das mißratenste Tier, das krankhafteste, das von seinen Instinkten am gefährlichsten abgeirrte – freilich, mit alledem, auch das interessanteste! Was die Tiere betrifft, so hat zuerst Descartes mit verehrungswürdiger Kühnheit den Gedanken gewagt, das Tier als machina zu verstehen: unsere ganze Physiologie bemüht sich um den Beweis des Satzes.»[24]

Während die Philosophen die Regression proklamieren und darum mitverantworten, haben die Dichter die Regression in ihrer Fragwürdigkeit dargestellt und damit erneut bewiesen, daß Literatur nicht nur das jeweils Zeittypische zum Ausdruck bringt, sondern es in kritischem Licht zeigt. Die Dichter haben mit der Weise, wie sie die Mensch–Tier-Beziehung gestalten, die Warnungen fortgesetzt, die schon in Picos Schrift über *Die Würde des Menschen* formuliert sind. Für den Renaissancehumanisten erfordert der Doppelcharakter des menschlichen Wesens, seine tierische und seine göttliche Inklination, den Sieg über das Tierische. Da die bloße Natur, wie Pico in Anlehnung an Heraklit schreibt, aus dem Krieg entstanden ist, «kann man in ihr keine wahre Ruhe und keinen festen Frieden finden» ... nur, wenn «in uns der tierische Teil tödlich getroffen ist,» wird es «zwischen dem Fleisch und dem Geist ein unverletzbares Friedensbündnis» geben. Nur dann werden, wie Pico in Anspielung auf das in der Bibel genannte siebenköpfige Tier der Lästerung schreibt, «die zügellosen Anfälle des vielgestaltigen Tieres, die Streitsucht, der Zorn und die Wut des Löwen in uns besänftigt.»[25] Die Literatur des 19. Jahrhunderts zeigt, wie das von Pico beschworene Bündnis zwischen dem geistigen und dem sinnlichen Teil des menschlichen Wesens zerbrochen ist, und jetzt nicht mehr der tierische, wie Pico fordert, sondern der geistige Teil der tödlich getroffene ist

---

23 Friedrich Nietzsche, *Jenseits von Gut und Böse,* Erstes Hauptstück, 3.
24 Friedrich Nietzsche, *Der Antichrist,* 14.
25 G.P. della Mirandola, *Die Würde des Menschen,* S. 63.

und damit die Natur, die friedlos per se ist, freisetzt. In Umkehrung der Kant'schen Formel läßt sich darum sagen: der Naturalismus ist der Eingang des Menschen in seine selbstverschuldete Unmündigkeit.[26] Die Folgen der Hingabe an den Naturalismus sind bekannt, sie haben den Lauf unseres Jahrhunderts bestimmt.

---

26 Der Begriff Naturalismus wird hier nicht im literaturhistorischen sondern im philosophischen Sinn gebraucht; siehe hierzu Robert Spaemann, «Natur,» *Handbuch philosophischer Grundbegriffe,* IV (München: Kösel, 1973), 956–69.

Mörike's *Maler Nolten* as a Romantic Novel: The Problem of Unity

RAYMOND IMMERWAHR, *University of Western Ontario*

In Kosch's *Deutsches Literatur-Lexikon* we read: «Das Erstlingswerk, den von ihm nur „Novelle" genannten Künstlerroman „Maler Nolten" in der Reihe der großen deutschen Erziehungsromane, arbeitete M. später wegen seiner Formlosigkeiten teilweise um, ohne zu einem Abschluß zu gelangen.»[1] But Mörike's later revision, completed for the first half of the work, despite significant changes in characterization and in some elements of the action, clearer motivation, and a more direct and lucid style,[2] did not aim at radical changes in form or structure. If the first version suffers from a plurality of «Formlosigkeiten,» this would have been scarcely less true of the second one, had the author completed it.

Mörike himself called the original version a «Novelle» but soon began referring to it in correspondence as a «Roman» and decided that the revised version was to be so designated.[3] There is some consensus in the critical literature that the work was first conceived as a Romantic novella of fate centred on the figure of the gypsy girl Elisabeth, the personification of a demonic power inexorably destroying the other principal characters and pursuing the hero even beyond death. But in the course of writing, the accretion of minor characters and episodic interpolations made what the author had called a *Novelle* something like what Friedrich Schlegel had meant by the term *Roman,* an example of «progressive Universalpoesie.»[4] In the eyes of some critics these interpolations detract from the unity of the work, unnecessarily retard the action and make

---

1 Wilhelm Kosch, *Deutsches Literatur-Lexikon,* bearb. Bruno Berger (Bern: Francke, 1963), p. 278.
2 See Mörike's letter to Ferdinand Weibert, 17 December 1870, cited by Herbert Meyer, «Stufen der Umgestaltung des *Maler Nolten,*» *Eduard Mörike,* ed. Viktor Doerksen, Wege der Forschung, 446 (Darmstadt: Wissenschaftliche Buchgesellschaft, 1975), p. 224. Cf. also Ernst Arno Drawert, «Mörikes Maler Nolten in seiner ersten und zweiten Fassung» (Diss., Jena 1935). These and all other works will be cited hereafter by the name of the author, with short titles added where necessary.
3 Meyer, «Stufen der Umgestaltung,» p. 215f.
4 Cf. Friedrich Schlegel, *Athenäum*-Fragment 116, *Kritische Friedrich-Schlegel-Ausgabe,* II *(Charakteristiken und Kritiken I),* hrsg. Hans Eichner (Paderborn: Schöningh, 1967), 182, and the «Brief über den Roman,» ibid., 329-38. This edition will hereafter be cited as *KA.*

the tragic outcome less plausible.[5] Even Benno von Wiese shares something of this view. In his attempt to interpret «den Kern des Romans, den tragischen Schicksalsgedanken,» he deliberately excludes from consideration in his chapter on *Nolten* «die arabeskenhaften Einlagen...: den „Letzten König von Orplid," die Peregrina-Lieder oder die Legende von Jung Volker.»[6] However, Mörike himself was satisfied with the basic structure of the work. In his letter thanking Gustav Schwab for a generally favourable review he defended «die durch die Episoden beabsichtigte Mannigfaltigkeit, wodurch die Hauptbegebenheiten so lange auseinandergehalten werden, als nötig schien, damit das Gemüt des Lesers sich nicht ermüde und für Kapitalschläge empfänglich bleibe...»[7] I shall attempt to demonstrate here that this is not their sole or most important function.

We have already noted the application to *Maler Nolten* by literary critics of terms used by Friedrich Schlegel to enunciate his concept of the Romantic novel: «progressive Universalpoesie» and «Arabeske.» Another attribute of the Romantic novel for Schlegel is found in the following sentence of his «Brief über den Roman»: «Ja ich kann mir einen Roman kaum anders denken, als gemischt aus Erzählung, Gesang und andern Formen.»[8] A further attribute stressed by Schlegel, to be sure, does not permeate Mörike's novel as a whole but is concentrated in the figure of Larkens, self-reflective irony.[9] When we compare *Maler Nolten* with earlier novels of German Romanticism we find few of those actually completed that achieve a comparable integration of their lyric, narrative, dramatic, or «musical» digressions. In this as well as in other respects, the precursors most closely anticipating Mörike's novel are Eichendorff's *Ahnung und Gegenwart* and *Dichter und ihre Gesellen.*

Some critics who compare *Maler Nolten* with *Mozart auf der Reise nach Prag* deny any significant role in the novel to Nolten's creativity as a painter.[10]

---

5 Cf. especially Rudolf Völk, *Die Kunstform des «Maler Nolten» von Eduard Mörike,* Germanische Studien, 82 (Berlin: Ebering, 1930), p. 12f., 29ff., 43ff., and Wilhelm Weischedel, «Mörikes *Maler Nolten,*», *DU,* 11 (1959), 53. Margaret Mare, *Eduard Mörike* (London: Methuen, 1957) accepts the inclusion of some tales and poems as a convention of the time but regards the Peregrina cycle and the poems «An L.» as «unjustifiable additions» (p. 94f.).
6 Benno von Wiese, *Eduard Mörike* (Tübingen/Stuttgart: Rainer Wunderlich / Hermann Leins, 1950), p. 181.
7 Eduard Mörike, *Sämtliche Werke,* hrsg. Gerhart Baumann in Verbindung mit Siegfried Grosse, III, *Briefe* (Stuttgart: Cotta, 1959), 370, letter dated Ochsenwang, 17 February 1833. This volume will hereafter be cited as *Briefe,* other volumes as *SW.*
8 *KA* II, 336.
9 See especially *Athenäum*-Fragment 116, *KA,* II, 182f.
10 Cf. Völk, p. 41, and Ruth Bachert, *Mörikes Maler Nolten,* Von deutscher Poeterey, 1 (Leipzig: Weber, 1928), 37, who argues that the problem of art and the artist, which was focal to Heinse's *Ardinghello* and to *Wilhelm Meisters Lehrjahre,* is mere «Staffage» in *Nolten.* But Gerhard Storz, *Eduard Mörike* (Stuttgart: Klett, 1967), p. 144, maintains that the connection with art is less obvious only because it lies in the very nucleus of the work. Elsewhere (p. 153) he mentions Larkens's radical doubts concerning the absolute validity of art as prophetic of the modern artist.

Benno von Wiese[11] omits any mention whatsoever of the paintings by Nolten described at the beginning of the novel: the satyr who has brought a fearful boy to the waiting arms of a mermaid and the spectral organist accompanying the dance of death in a cemetery,[12] creations not only prophetic of the novel's ending but relevant to its central theme. As a novel of artistic creation, *Maler Nolten* suffers from the division of creativity between the painter Nolten and the actor-poet Larkens. After these first pages the novel is concerned with Nolten's career more than with his work, and apart from the joint project of the «phantasmagorical» shadow-play, the artistic creations presented are largely those of Larkens.[13] Nevertheless, Nolten manifests an imaginative sensitivity resembling that of Mörike himself, even to the point of expressing itself lyrically.[14]

But even though art is less prominent in *Maler Nolten* than music in *Mozart auf der Reise nach Prag,* a comparison can illuminate both works. In his musical creation Mozart transfigures the cultural and artistic ideals of the fragile Rococo age as he himself maintains a precarious balance constantly threatened by poverty, limited appreciation from his contemporaries, and his own human frailties. As a genius consumed by his own creativity, Mozart is reflected in his musical characterization of Don Juan. Like Don Juan, Mozart is consumed both by the intensity of his genius and by his human failings, including one that the novella only touches lightly in the case of Mozart himself, but which assumes titanic dimensions in his Don Juan, the consuming fire of erotic passion. It is this that evokes the apocalyptic chords at the tomb of the Commander, foretelling in the opera the fate of Don Juan,[15] in the novella the approaching death of Mozart.

Theobald Nolten is a fictitious painter living in a society declining from its cultural prime. (These cultural and social implications, to be sure, come out primarily in the shadow-play «Der letzte König von Orplid» and in the events of the main action related to it,[16] the imprisonment of Nolten and Larkens.) Unlike Mozart, who achieves supreme greatness in his musical creation and an unstable equilibrium in his brief personal life, Nolten's promising career and

---

11 In his chapter on *Malter Nolten,* «Das Schicksal,» p. 170–210.
12 Eduard Mörike, *Werke und Briefe, Historisch-kritische Gesamtausgabe* (Stuttgart: Klett, 1976 – III, 13–16). Hereafter references to the first version of *Maler Nolten* will be cited in the text by page numbers only, references to the incomplete revised version by volume (IV) and page numbers.
13 Drawert (p. 68f.) points out the considerably greater emphasis on Nolten's artistic creativity and the mention of several other sketches and projects in the second version.
14 As in «Hier lieg' ich auf dem Frühlingshügel,» p. 263f., in which, to be sure, the narrator admits to some assistance.
15 See my article «Apocalyptic Trumpets: The Inception of *Mozart auf der Reise nach Prag,*» *PMLA,* 70 (1955), 390–407.
16 In the revised version the Countess Constanze manifests a decided preference for Rococo over contemporary early nineteenth-century art, a nostalgic «Zärtlichkeit für Alles was nur *du siècle passé* sei» (IV, 31–35, quotation from p. 35).

his plans for personal fulfilment are wrecked by his individual destiny, embodied in the gypsy girl Elisabeth, who appears in Nolten's painting as the organist of death. The critical literature generally takes the theme of the central plot as the irrational demonic forces personified in this figure, which are inexorably fated to destroy Nolten and the other principal characters. But if we view the work as a whole in the light of Mörike's *Mozart,* the theme may be expressed in terms that are at once broader and more explicit. The sensitive creative artist, at home only in a realm of ideal harmony and beauty, is doomed to a temporal existence involving consuming passion, guilt, remorse, foreboding, and death, but the very irrational forces which consume him as a human personality are the inspiration of his work. In *Mozart auf der Reise nach Prag* the elements of erotic passion and guilt are in large measure presented indirectly, through the figure of Don Juan, while Mozart is shown being consumed by his own creative genius and his experience of temporality.[17] In *Maler Nolten* consuming passion and guilt are also presented for the most part indirectly, through the songs of the one innocent major character, Agnes, shortly before her death and through other episodic lyrics, ballads, and legends. Nolten is not destroyed, like Mozart, by the process of his creative inspiration, but rather by its source, the intense erotic feeling awakened early in his life by Elisabeth. Nolten, even though for a time he allows such feeling to be directed at another object, Constanze, attempts to banish it in its original incarnation, Elisabeth, from his life. He is torn between the chaste love of angelic, childlike innocence, which he and Larkens have projected upon Agnes, and his erotic passion for Constanze, but his destruction manifests itself as the work of the now unloved Elisabeth.

There is also a religious dimension to this conflict between chaste and sinful love, even though it is obscured in the characterization of Nolten and Larkens. It seems rather to be taken for granted that both of them, like Mörike himself, have been inculcated in their youth with ideals of chaste Christian love and marriage, and they clearly feel guilt over their departure from these ideals as adults. But the linkage of intense erotic passion with religious guilt is much more strikingly evident in the episodic ballads, lyrics, and legends – the relevance of which is denied or minimized by many critics –[18] especially those

17 Cf. Wolfgang Taraba, «Die Rolle der „Zeit" und des „Schicksals" in Eduard Mörikes *Maler Nolten,*» *Euphorion,* 50 (1956), 405–27.
18 Among the exceptions: Bernhard Seuffert, *Mörikes Nolten und Mozart* (Graz: Leuscher & Lubensky, 1925) presents so many detailed and in part trivial parallels that their significance is obscured. Hildegard Emmel, *Mörikes Peregrinadichtung und ihre Beziehung zum Notenroman* (Weimar: Böhlau, 1952) treats all the lyrics in the novel as relevant, demonstrating this most cogently in the case of Agnes's song, «Rosenzeit, wie schnell vorbei» (Emmel, p. 36ff.), but she concentrates on the later version, including the part completed only by Klaiber. Gerhart von Graevenitz, *Eduard Mörike: Die Kunst der Sünde; Zur Geschichte des literarischen Individuums* (Tübingen: Niemeyer, 1978) treats the element of erotic guilt in the episodic poems and narratives primarily as a literary tradition and omits consideration of the Legend of St. Alexis' Well.

associated with Jung Volker and the Well of St. Agnes. It is these with which we shall be primarily concerned here, referring only tangentially to the shadow-play and the «Peregrina» cycle, both of which have been thoroughly treated in the literature.[19]

The theme of Mörike's ballad «Der Feuerreiter» is not eroticism as such but an obsessive fascination by all-consuming elemental power. Nevertheless, its presentation between the two first appearances of Elisabeth in the mask of a nightwatchman at a New Year's Eve party associates the Fire Rider's fatal obsession with the compulsive eroticism embodied in the gypsy girl.[20] The ballad is introduced by a leisurely prose narration «aus dem Munde eines jungen hübschen Burschen» (p. 35), but at the urging of a companion he switches over to song. The eccentric rider with the red cap, first seen pacing back and forth behind his window, dashes out furiously on his «rippendürren» nag to the mill, where a fire has broken out. Afterwards he is found on his mare as an ashen image on the wall: «Husch! da fällt's in Asche ab –» (p. 36f.). The skeletal horse associates the Fire Rider with the image of death familiar from Dürer's «Ritter, Tod und Teufel.» The intended association with Elisabeth in the original version of the novel is clear from the following: «Schon vor dem Schlusse des Gesanges öffnete sich die Thür und leise trat die Gestalt des *Nachtwächters* herein. Er blieb unbeweglich an der Wand hingepflanzt stehen, während der erschrockene Sänger, im Begriff abzubrechen, auf einen Wink des Larkens mit der letzten Strophe fortfuhr...» (p. 37, emphasis in source).

In the second strophe of the ballad we read: «Durch den Qualm und durch die Schwüle / Rennt er schon wie Windesbraut...» (p. 37). The image «Windesbraut,» which does not occur here in the later version of the novel (IV, 43) or in Mörike's editions of his poems, links the Fire Rider with two more episodic figures, the fiercely independent minstrel, fiddler, and robber captain Jung Volker and his mother, the Bride of the Wind:

> ... Und die mich trug in Mutterleib,
> Die durft' ich niemals schauen,
> Sie war ein schön, frech, braunes Weib,
> Wollt' keinem Manne trauen.

---

19 Taraba's essay is particularly valuable for the shadow-play. Beatrice Funk-Schoellkopf, *Eduard Mörike «Der letzte König von Orplid»* ([Diss.] Zürich: Juris, 1980) interprets Ulmon as «das traditionelle geistige Prinzip, das nicht sterben kann und darum erstarrt ist» (p. 138). Hildegard Emmel's dating of the «Peregrina» cycle is corrected by Adolf Beck, «Forschungsbericht: Peregrina. Zur Berichtigung und Ergänzung des Buches von Hildegard Emmel: Mörikes Peregrinadichtung...,» *Euphorion,* 47 (1953), 194–217, reprinted in Beck, *Forschung und Deutung* (Frankfurt/Bonn: Athenäum, 1966), p. 311–45. Heinz Gockel, «Venus-Libitina: Mythologische Anmerkungen zu Mörikes Peregrina-Zyklus,» *WW,* 24 (1974), 46–56, compares Peregrina as Venus with similar figures in Eichendorff and attributes the element of «Betrug» to the distortion resulting from Mörike's Christian perspective.

20 This connection is recognized by von Graevenitz (p. 79ff.) and Emmel (p. 21f.). In the revised version Larkens recites the ballad himself and has an opera singer instead of Elisabeth play the role of the Nightwatchman, and her appearances are less closely tied to the ballad (IV, 40ff.).

> Und lachte hell und scherzte laut:
> Ei, laßt mich gehn und stehen!
> Möcht' lieber seyn des Windes Braut,
> Denn in die Ehe gehen.
>
> Da kam der Wind, da nahm der Wind
> Als Buhle sie gefangen,
> Von dem hat sie ein lustig Kind
> In ihren Schoos empfangen. (P. 299)

The cycle of ballads and narrative legends on Jung Volker is presented by several minor characters during an outing with Nolten and Agnes to a hill named «Geigenspiel» in allusion to Volker. Another friend, the sculptor Raymund, makes a surprise appearance from behind a linden tree after they have heard him singing:

> Jung Volker das ist der Räuberhauptmann
> Mit Fidel und mit Flinte,
> Damit er geigen und schießen kann
> Nachdem just Wetter und Winde,
>   ja Winde! ...» (P. 300f.)

Raymund is the lover of his model Henriette, who happens also to be the daughter of the warden of the prison where Nolten was confined in punishment for the production of the shadow-play with its alleged political allusions. During his imprisonment Nolten had heard her singing the song of a deserted maiden awakening from a dream of her faithless lover: «Früh, wenn die Hähne krähn ...» Hearing this song in illness after restless dreams of Constanze and Agnes, Nolten imagines a wonderful similarity to the voice of Agnes and gives himself over to tears, «ganz der Süßigkeit eines – dennoch so bittern! Schmerzens genießend» (p. 183). But Henriette's relationship to her lover Raymund is altogether different from that of Agnes to Nolten. After a brief estrangement, Raymund forces her to accept a love without civil or religious sanction. When Nolten's friend, the pastor Amandus, asks Raymund whether he is heathen, he replies, «Und zwar ein frommer!» – an exchange not surprisingly upsetting to Agnes (p. 303ff.).

Although Jung Volker himself is untouched by love, he and his mother resemble Raymund in the complete freedom of their lives from religious or social constraints. But it turns out that, unlike Raymund, Volker cannot go on leading a life guided by impulse alone without remorse or retribution. When he wantonly destroys another symbol of freedom, a white dove with a cross on its back, sacred to the Virgin Mary, Volker sees that he has «mich freventlich vergriffen an eim eigenthumb der muetter Gottes selbs» and pledges henceforth «ein frumm leben» (p. 298). But we also are presented with a variant legend according to which, while on the way to Jerusalem, he is abducted by his sorceress mother (p. 299). The pagan Raymund can love after his own fashion without punishment or remorse, but the redemption of the convert Volker is left in doubt.

Henriette's song of the deserted maiden anticipates one sung by Agnes shortly after Nolten's return to her, just before the excursion to the «Geigenspiel»:

> Rosenzeit! wie schnell vorbei,
>   Schnell vorbei,
> Bist du doch gegangen!
> Wär' mein Lieb nur blieben treu,
>   Blieben treu,
> Sollte mir nicht bangen.
>
> In der Ernte wohlgemuth,
>   Wohlgemuth,
> Schnitterinnen singen;
> Aber ach, mir kranken Blut,
>   Mir kranken Blut,
> Will Nichts mehr gelingen.
>
> Schleiche so durch's Wiesenthal
>   So durch's Thal,
> Als im Traum verloren,
> Nach dem Berg, da tausend Mal,
>   Tausend Mal,
> Er mir Treu' geschworen.
>
> Oben auf des Hügels Rand,
>   Abgewandt,
> Wein' ich bei der Linde:
> An dem Hut mein Rosenband,
>   Von seiner Hand,
> Spielet in dem Winde.
>
> Agnesen hatte der Ton zuletzt vor Bewegung fast versagt; jezt warf sie das Instrument weg und stürzte heftig an die Brust des Geliebten. „Treu! Treu!" stammelte sie unter unendlichen Thränen, indem ihr ganzer Leib zuckte und zitterte, „du bist mir's, ich bin dir's geblieben!" – „Ich bleibe dir's!" mehr konnte Theobald, mehr durfte er nicht sagen. (P. 287f.).

Lyric interludes like this do not «retard» the action, nor do they distract our attention from the central plot; they are signposts pointing ahead towards the tragic destination.[21]

The episodic digression most closely linked to the central theme of the novel is the legend of the Well of Alexis,[22] narrated to Agnes by the blind youth

---

21 Cf. Emmel, p. 37: «Daß die Verse Agnesen so stark erregen, zeigt, daß sie dem ihr auferlegten Leid schon ausgeliefert ist, ehe es sich verwirklicht.»
22 Cf. Herbert Meyer, «Mörikes Legende vom Alexisbrunnen,» *DVjs,* 26 (1952), 225–36. Meyer demonstrates its relevance (as he sees it, a note of affirmation softening the impact of the novel's tragic ending) by contrasting it with its probable inspiration, the traditional legend of St. Alexis, as narrated to Goethe by a pious hostess in the high Alps, in *Briefe aus der Schweiz,*

Henni shortly before she takes her life in that same well. But we must first consider it in its context. It follows directly upon the cycle of six poems «An L.,» the first five of which are sonnets. The cycle is attributed in the narrative to Larkens, inspired by his early love for a pastor's daughter, who had died «in der schönsten Jugend»(p. 360). But Agnes believes Theobald has written them to her, because one of her given names is Luise (p. 389). They were in actuality written by Eduard Mörike to Luise Rau, who was, unlike Agnes, the daughter of a pastor. And it is not only the deranged Agnes who suffers from a confusion of personalities. While working on the novel Mörike was likewise confusing his actual fiancée Luise with his fictive creation Agnes, suggesting that Luise as well suffered from a precariously delicate psychological constitution.[23]

A common denominator of this whole cycle might be perceived in the shifting views of nature expressed by the persona in a variety of moods and situations, but we shall be concentrating upon the first four sonnets, which are more closely linked. We need only briefly mention the last two poems: In the fifth the poet escapes from the uncongenial «Fratzen der Gesellschaft» to the edge of the forest, where he can delight in his facile weaving of sonnets. The final poem, «In der Char-Woche,» implores nature to attune itself to the mournful spirit of the observance, but expresses the persona's wish that his beloved in her adoration of Christ will also remember him. The first four sonnets and this last poem[24] are more closely unified: they express an intense personal love striving for spiritual unity with both its human object and the divinely created universe. The first sonnet contrasts that loving, harmonious unity achieved by the physical landscape («die starre Welt») in the light of spring with the conflicting emotions, at once bitter and sweet, of the persona under love's spell. He invokes the aid, first of Love, then of Spring, to break the spell and curb his passion. He finally asks the daylight to extinguish itself so that, cooled by the stars of night, he can descend «zum Abgrund der Betrachtung» and so recover, for it appears that the depth of insight needed to resolve the conflict and turmoil aroused by his love is only attainable through the intuitive depth as-

2. Abteilung, 11. Nov. 1779. Here Alexis sacrifices his marriage to keep a vow of chastity. Although I agree with Meyer on Mörike's desire for a conciliatory treatment of the relation between sexual love and Christian faith just before the tragic end of the novel, I am more inclined to emphasize the ironic bearing of Mörike's Alexis legend and the immediately preceding songs «An L.» upon the plot of the novel, at all events for the twentieth-century reader. Cf. my earlier article, «The Loves of Maler Nolten,» *Studies in German in Memory of Robert L. Kahn,* Rice University Studies, 57 (1971), No. 4, p. 82 and note 24 (p. 87).

23 «Weißt Du nicht, daß Du mein krankes Kindchen bist ...? Hast Du mir nicht selber ehrlich heraus gesagt, welchen Unfall Du noch neulich mit Deinen Nerven hattest? ... Du mußt Dich *auf alle Weise* schonen» (20 May 1830, *Werke und Briefe,* xi, lllf.).

24 In the collected poems this one appears before and apart from the cycle with important revisions that make the setting expressly Catholic and have the girl mourning her dead bridegroom. Although the poem resumes its original place in the later version of the novel (IV, 360), the incorporation of these same variants severs its connection with the first four sonnets.

sociated with night.[25] But in the second sonnet this resolution must still be attained. Away from the beloved «ein irrer, ungeduld'ger Sinn» pursues him, but even in her arms «die alte Wehmuth» stirs until he faints in intoxication. So he feels that «dieß schnell bewegte Herz» will never come to rest on earth: «Im ew'gen Lichte löst sich jeder Schmerz, / Und all' die schwülen Leidenschaften fließen / Wie ros'ge Wolken, träumend, uns zu Füßen» (p. 390). Clearly the persona cannot be fully reconciled to his love until the elements of passionate eroticism – «all' die schwülen Leidenschaften» – have melted away. He is troubled not merely by the intensity of his passion but by its erotic sensuality, which he somehow feels to be shameful. Mörike's desire not to admit to this kind of eroticism in his love for Luise Rau may well explain his deletion of this sonnet from his collected poems.

The third sonnet finally resolves the spiritual conflict through a mystic experience of the sanctity of his beloved, even to the point that he hears the breath of the angel concealed within her. In a smile of mixed bliss and wonder his lips pose the question, «ob mich kein Traum betrüge, / Daß nun in dir, zu himmlischer Genüge, / Mein kühnster Wunsch, mein einz'ger sich erfüllt.» The concluding tercets make it plain what this bold wish is: the complete reconciliation of earthly erotic love and heavenly grace:

> Von Tiefe dann zu Tiefen stürzt mein Sinn,
> Ich höre aus der Gottheit nächt'ger Ferne
> Die Quellen des Geschicks melodisch rauschen;
>
> Betäubt kehr' ich den Blick nach oben hin,
> Zum Himmel auf: da lächeln alle Sterne!
> Ich kniee, ihrem Lichtgesang zu lauschen. (P. 390)

But how are we to interpret this happy resolution, the divine sanction accorded an intensely passionate erotic love, in the context of the novel? The whole cycle is the creation of Larkens who, before Nolten finds it, has taken his own life. This event has been interpreted by Agnes «als die gewisse Erfüllung eines ungewissen Vorgefühls,» as an actual catastrophe foreshadowing the threatened one still awaiting her (p. 337). And the resolution of the conflict within these sonnets is no more plausible than was Larkens' anticipation of the mature Nolten's return to his untroubled youthful love of an angelic child. In the context of the novel we cannot avoid associating «die Quellen des Geschicks» with that «lebhafter Quell'» pouring forth at the feet of the organist of death in Nolten's painting (p. 14f.). In this novel the «springs of fate» most certainly do not originate with the divine (in any Christian sense), nor do the heavenly stars shine on them.

---

25 Gerhard Storz, «Eduard Mörike – der Dichter zwischen den Zeiten,» *JbDSG,* 20 (1976), 495, attributes the mythic quality of Mörike's early lyric poetry to its origin in nocturnal dreams. This article will be cited hereafter as «Storz,» *JbDSG.*

The question posed by the fourth sonnet is more modest: not whether this springtime love is divinely sanctioned but whether it will last. The lovers must follow the examples of the rose blooming in the morning dew without thought of withering, of the eagle soaring up without fear of striking its head on the vault of heaven:

> Mag einst der Jugend Blume uns verbleichen,
> So war die Täuschung doch so himmlisch süße,
> Wir wollen ihr vorzeitig nicht entsagen.
>
> Und unsre Liebe mag dem Adler gleichen:
> Ob Alles, was die Welt gab, uns verließe –
> Die Liebe darf den Flug in's Ew'ge wagen. (P. 390f., quotation from p. 391)

Is the heavenly sweet illusion the endurance of youthful beauty or of love itself? Is the «Flug in's Ewige» now to be ventured the mystic certainty already achieved in the third sonnet, or simply a wager that human love can outlast the bloom of youth? From what the reader already knows at this point in the novel about the destiny of Theobald's and Agnes's love, such questions are worse than futile; they are tragically ironic.

In the paragraph immediately following this lyric cycle we find Agnes walking out over the fields with the blind youth Henni, the one character in the novel manifesting a secure religious faith, to an old, crumbling well, the «Alexis-Brunn.» Here he narrates the legend associated with this name (p. 393–96); before the region was converted to Christianity, two noblemen betrothed their children, Alexis and Belsore, to each other: «Diese liebten einander treulich und rein» (p. 393). On a journey to Constantinople, Alexis and his father are converted to Christianity and baptized; the father orders a pair of wedding rings with the cross engraved on them in precious stones. On his return Alexis converts Belsore; they secretly exchange these rings and pledge faithfulness to death, but Belsore's pagan father will not consent to the marriage unless Alexis renounces his faith. Despite his conversion of many others, Alexis himself is at times beset by doubts that Christ is indeed the Son of God. Coming to a spring, he prays to God for a sign: if a completely withered rose-bush on which he places his ring still bears it and is blooming on his return a year later, his faith and love will be confirmed. The blossoms he finds on the bush when he returns confirm Alexis' faith, but the seeming absence of the ring makes him doubt that his love for Belsore is pleasing to Heaven. In despair he uproots the bush and casts it down into the rocky chasm from which he had drunk the waters of the spring. He goes home for another year, wracked by doubts concerning the sanctity of his love. On a third pilgrimage to the spring he finds nothing at first, but at night he notices a gleam of gold and rose colours flickering in the water. Climbing down in the morning, he finds the rose-bush rooted in the rocks, blossoming, with the gold of the ring, which he had failed to see the year before, visible inside the bark. He returns home to marry Belsore. According to local legend a roseate glow may still be seen at the bottom of the well in Holy Week.

After Henni has narrated this legend, he and Agnes climb a hill together and she sings a song to the Wind, asking «wo der Liebe Heimath ist.» The reply:

> ... Lieb ist wie Wind,
> Rasch und lebendig,
> Ruhet nie,
> Ewig ist sie,
> Aber nicht immer beständig. (P. 397)

This is in direct contradiction to the third and fourth sonnets «An L.» and to the legend of Alexis' Well as far as Agnes is concerned. She cannot hope for a human love that will be constant throughout life and enjoy divine sanction. Soon afterwards, during an absence of Nolten recommended by their friends, the latter notice that Agnes is no longer wearing her engagement ring. She explains that her mother (long since deceased) has taken it from her but that she knows where it is and will go to fetch it. Then she explains Nolten's absence to them by his natural unwillingness to marry a mad woman and expresses her own relief that she can die a virgin: «Nun mag es enden wann es will, mir ist doch mein Mädchenkranz sicher, ich nehm' ihn in's Grab –... ich habe mir immer gewünscht, so und nicht anders in den Himmel zu kommen. Aber den Ring muß ich erst haben, ich muß ihn vorweisen können» (p. 400).

One more lyrical interlude precedes the suicide of Agnes in Alexis' Well. She and Henni are found singing to his organ accompaniment eight short lines in Latin and five quatrains in German with the common theme of a wanting faith in Christ. As Mörike explains in a footnote, to which he appends his own free translation, he had found the hymn in an old prayer-book. (At his request, his brother Karl composed a musical setting for it, which was incorporated into the first edition of the novel.)[26]

> JESU, BENIGNE!
> A CUJUS IGNE
> OPTO FLAGRARE,
> ET TE AMARE; –
>
> CUR NON FLAGRAVI?
> CUR NON AMAVI
> TE, JESU CHRISTE?
> – O FRIGUS TRISTE!

Mörike's translation:

---

26 The musical setting is reproduced in *Werke und Briefe*, v, 271–72.

> Dein Liebesfeuer,
> Ach Herr! wie theuer
> Wollt' ich es hegen,
> Wollt' ich es pflegen –
> Hab's nicht geheget,
> Und nicht gepfleget,
> War Eis im Herzen,
> – O Höllenschmerzen![27]

Here the spiritual frigidity responsible for the failure to nurture the flame of Christ's love brings with it the torments of Hell. The second, German hymn that follows (Mörike's own), sung by Agnes to Henni's accompaniment, contrasts two kinds of love: the never-failing Divine love of Christ and evil human desire. The persona, in whom the second of these has triumphed, is left writhing in fear, to cry out in the last three stanzas an agonized prayer for redemption:

> Und was ist's, daß ich doch traurig bin?
> Daß ich angstvoll mich am Boden winde?
> Frage: Hüter, ist die Nacht bald hin?
> Und: was rettet mich von Tod und Sünde?
>
> Arges Herze! ja gesteh' es nur,
> Du hast wieder böse Lust empfangen;
> Frommer Liebe, alter Treue Spur –
> Ach, das ist auf lange nun vergangen!
>
> Darum ist's auch, daß ich traurig bin,
> Daß ich angstvoll mich am Boden winde –
> Hüter! Hüter! ist die Nacht bald hin?
> Und was rettet mich von Tod und Sünde? (P. 401f.)

The next morning Agnes is missing, and late the following night her body is brought back from St. Alexis' Well (p. 402ff.). Her death thus results from a failure to realize that harmonizing union of divine and human love celebrated in the third sonnet «An L.» and confirmed for Alexis by the ring in the bark of the miraculously blooming rose bush. Agnes dies because no such divinely sanctioned, constant human love free of sinful passion could be achieved between her and Nolten. To be sure, it is not Agnes herself but Nolten – along with Constanze and Larkens – who has experienced sinful passion at first hand. The theme running through these lyrical and narrative interludes near the end of the novel is applicable only indirectly and peripherally to Agnes, who dies inviolate and has no reason either for feelings of guilt or for doubt in her Christian redemption. But we have learned early in the novel, even before

---

27 In his letters of 22 February 1832 to Karl Mörike and 26 February 1832 to Friedrich Theodor Vischer (*Briefe,* p. 300ff. and 311f.) we learn that Mörike had a considerable struggle with the translation, also that he had found the prayer book in a village tavern between Nürtingen and Tübingen (*Werke und Briefe,* XI, 253ff., 267).

Elisabeth exerted her baneful influence, that Agnes's emotional constitution was too delicate and unstable to integrate intense erotic emotion. Perhaps it is even out of fear of the potential intensity of her love for her fiancé Theobald that, after her first emotional breakdown, she indulges the more superficial erotic feelings aroused in her by her cousin Otto.

Agnes's inability to accept fervent erotic passion and the resulting inner conflict are strikingly manifested in an incident a short time before her death. Just after her song to the wind she asks to see Nolten in her room. As he sits beside her on her bed, her expression changes:

> Aber heißer, schmelzender wird ihr Blick, ihr Athem steigt, es hebt sich ihre Brust, und jezt – indem sie mit der Linken sich beide Augen zuhält – streckt sie den rechten Arm entschlossen gegen ihn, faßt leidenschaftlich seine Hand und drückt sie fest an ihren Busen; der Maler liegt, eh' er sich's selbst versieht, an ihrem Halse und saugt von ihren Lippen eine Gluth, die von der Angst des Moments eine schaudernde Würze erhält; der Wahnsinn funkelt frohlockend aus ihren Augen...» (P. 397f.)

But she quickly becomes restless and with the words «du tückischer Satan» orders Nolten away. Throughout her final period of insanity, except for this last brief moment, she has taken Nolten for a diabolical monster in the guise of her fiancé, and this delusion now returns: «Der Lügner wird hingehn, mich zu beschimpfen bei meinem Geliebten, als wär' ich kein ehrliches Mädchen, als hätt' ich mit Wissen und Willen dieß Scheusal geküßt – O Theobald! wärest du hier, daß ich dir Alles sagte'...» (p. 398).

There is truth concealed in this madness: The person whom Agnes has just ardently embraced is no longer the idol of her innocent childhood adoration but a mature man who has known passionate love for another woman. From the perspective of her attempt to restore her pre-adolescent love he may well appear to be a repulsive monster. The real object of her love is another, albeit imaginary person, the innocent Nolten untainted by passion whom Larkens re-created for her in his forgery. Mörike's brilliant and prescient depiction of a case history of mental illness has often been praised. But more than that, once we remove the obscuring shroud of angelic innocence cast over Agnes by Larkens's forgery, we can recognize her as the one thoroughly convincing characterization in the entire novel: a sensitive girl with a frail psychological constitution, who is unable to face emotional maturity (outwardly manifested by the darkening of her hair and a newly awakened musical expressiveness) and is utterly shattered by the revelation that her idealized image of her fiancé and their mutual love has become a forgery. For all its sinister influence, there is a truth in Elisabeth's prophecy which Agnes would have done well to recognize: that as a mature young woman she should accept erotic love for someone she can understand and accept as he is, rather than for one whom her idolizing imagination has placed on an exalted moral and spiritual pedestal.

I have attempted to interpret the other three principal characters on the basis of certain assumptions of twentieth-century depth psychology in the earlier paper cited in note 22, to which this one may be considered a sequel. I shall consider these characters here only from the standpoint of their intrinsic plausibility. Mörike's intuitive anticipation of depth psychology has been aptly described by Herbert Meyer:

> Die Verwandlungsfähigkeit Mörikes wurzelt in dem gleichen Boden wie das ihn nie verlassende Gefühl der Spaltung seiner Persönlichkeit in ein dem Bewußtsein und Intellekt verhaftetes und ein in den Bereichen des Unbewußten und des Instinkts beheimatetes Ich...
>
> Es bedeutet im Grunde nichts anderes, wenn . . . es von Nolten an einem entscheidenden Wendepunkt seines Lebens heißt, der „unterirdische Strom seines Daseins" breche plötzlich „laut rauschend zu seinen Füßen hervor aus der Tiefe." Als Dichter und Mensch des frühen 19. Jahrhunderts umschreibt Mörike hier in Gleichnissen und Bildern seelische Phänomene, die erst wesentlich später die Psychoanalyse und die Tiefenpsychologie aus dem Dunkel tastender Ahnung in das helle Licht begrifflicher Fixierung gerückt haben.[28]

In the earlier paper just mentioned I approached the three loves of Theobald Nolten in essentially Freudian terms: The one who objectifies his subconscious erotic drives (Elisabeth), the one whom the ideals inculcated by his upbringing and reinforced by the intervention of Larkens tell him he ought to love (Agnes), and the one capable of integrating his erotic feelings with the values of his maturity (Constanze).[29] But some twentieth-century concepts of myth deriving in large measure from Jung may also be relevant to this novel, the more so as its narrator himself applies the term «mythic composition» to a major episodic interpolation, the «Peregrina» cycle (p. 361). I should like to quote here from a book dealing with Jungian concepts by an author who may never have heard of *Maler Nolten*; it concerns «anima» figures in literature: «Another favourite anima figure in novels is that of the gypsy girl: Esmeralda in Victor Hugo's *Notre Dame de Paris*, Mirabell in [Hugh Seymour] Walpole's *Rogue Herries* [1930] – strange, elusive, half-unreal figures to whom men are bound as if by a spell.»[30] Here we immediately recognize Elisabeth.

The «decisive turning-point» in Theobald Nolten's life to which Herbert Meyer refers in the passage quoted two paragraphs above is his first encounter

---

28 Herbert Meyer, *Eduard Mörike* (Stuttgart: Steinkopf, 1950), p. 34f. Cf. also Liselotte Dieckmann, «Mörike's Presentation of the Creative Process,» *JEGP*, 53 (1954), 291–305.

29 Similar conclusions regarding Nolten, Larkens, Elisabeth and Agnes had already been reached by Jeffrey L. Sammons, «Fate and Psychology: Another Look at Mörike's *Maler Nolten*,» in *Lebendige Form: Interpretationen der deutschen Literatur; Festschrift für Heinrich E.K. Henel*, hrsg. J.L. Sammons und Ernst Schürer (München: Fink, 1970), p. 219, 222, 226.

30 P.W. Martin, *Experiment in Depth. A Study of the Work of Jung, Eliot and Toynbee* (London: Routledge & Kegan Paul, 1955; paperback edition 1976), p. 81. Another passage mentions a typical «Shadow-figure,» this time occurring in the dream of an unidentified individual; it calls to mind Wispel: «the shadow in its unacceptable aspect: a dark, disreputable tramp-like fellow, sometimes shabbily, sometimes flashily dressed. He is untrustworthy, thoroughly dislikable . . .» (p. 73f., quotation from p. 74). On Wispel cf. my article «The Loves of Maler Nolten» (note 22 above), p. 84.

with this gypsy girl, whose image he has known from childhood in a portrait, which he now learns was that of her mother Loskine, the gypsy bride of his uncle. The pertinent passage of the novel merits quotation here:

> Wenn er seit seinen Kinderjahren ... so manchen verstohlenen Augenblick mit der Betrachtung jenes unwiderstehlichen Bildes zugebracht hatte, wenn sich hieraus allmählig ein schwärmerisch religiöser Umgang wie mit dem geliebten Idol eines Schutzgeists entspann ... so mußte der Moment, worin das Wunderbild ihm lebendig entgegentrat, ein ungeheurer und unauslöschlicher seyn. Es war, als erleuchtete ein zauberhaftes Licht die hintersten Schachten seiner inneren Welt, als brächte der unterirdische Strom seines Daseyns plötzlich lautrauschend zu seinen Füßen hervor aus der Tiefe ... (P. 216f.)

This passage, coming after Theobald has learned the identity of Elisabeth and her relationship to the subject of the portrait, should be compared with the earlier one explaining his immediate reaction to the first sight of Elisabeth:

> Seht nur ... als ich Euch ansah, da war es, als versänk' ich tief in mich selbst, wie in einen Abgrund, als schwindelte ich, von Tiefe zu Tiefe stürzend, durch alle die Nächte hindurch, wo ich Euch in hundert Träumen gesehen habe, so, wie Ihr da vor mir stehet; ich flog im Wirbel herunter durch alle die Zeiträume meines Lebens und sah mich als Knaben und sah mich als Kind neben Eurer Gestalt ...; ja ich kam bis an die Dunkelheit, wo meine Wiege stand, und sah Euch den Schleier halten, welcher mich bedeckte: da verging das Bewußtseyn mir ... aber wie sich meine Augen aufhoben von selber, schaut' ich in die Eurigen, als in einen unendlichen Brunnen, darin das Räthsel meines Lebens lag. (P. 195)

In twentieth-century terms, Elisabeth objectifies latent sexual feelings and an image of feminine beauty – an «anima» – that have been part of Theobald's subconscious life since early childhood.[31] For Theobald these had been associated with the unidentified portrait of Elisabeth's mother, which he had idolized as a kind of guardian angel. Here we can see the young Mörike's own proclivity for blending religious idealism with erotic passion, the theme of the first three sonnets «An L.» and also an important element of the «Peregrina» cycle. Maria Meyer, despite her vagrancy and free sexual life, had for a time been an adherent of the wandering preacher Baroness von Krüdener, was reported to have sung hymns with a strange intonation, suffered periodic spells of insanity as well as epileptic seizures, was herself somnambulant, and shared Mörike's interest in the occult.[32] Strongly impressed by the pietistic and mystical aspects of her personality, Mörike managed for a time to attribute an almost saintly religiosity to Maria. The shattering effect of the inevitable disil-

---

31 Cf. Heide Eilert, «Eduard Mörike: *Maler Nolten*» in *Romane und Erzählungen: Zwischen Romantik und Realismus,* ed. P.M. Lützeler (Stuttgart: Reclam, 1983), p. 165–82: »Elisabeth erscheint Nolten hier ganz im Sinne der tiefenpsychologischen Erkenntnisse C.G. Jungs als die „Führerin nach Innen" die dem Ich „die lebenswichtigen Botschaften des Selbst" übermittelt» (p. 168).
32 Cf. Paul Corrodi, *Das Urbild von Mörikes Peregrina* (Kirchheim/Teck: Jürgen Schweier, 1976), especially p. 8ff., 21ff., 27ff., 32.

lusionment,[33] the sudden transformation of the sacred into the sinful, finds poetic expression in two of the «Peregrina» poems, «Warnung» and «Scheiden von Ihr»:

> Der Spiegel dieser treuen braunen Augen
> Ist wie von innrem Gold ein Widerschein;
> Tief aus dem Busen scheint er's anzusaugen,
> Dort mag solch' Gold in heil'gem Gram gedeihn.
> In diese Nacht des Blickes mich zu tauchen,
> Unschuldig Kind, du selber lädst mich ein, –
> Willst, ich soll kecklich dich und mich entzünden –
> Reichst lächelnd mir den Tod im Kelch der Sünden![34]
>
> Ein Irrsal kam in die Mondscheinsgärten
> Einer einst heiligen Liebe,
> Schaudernd entdeckt' ich verjährten Betrug;
> Und mit weinendem Blick, doch grausam
> Hieß ich das schlanke,
> Zauberhafte Mädchen
> Ferne gehen von mir ... (P. 363)

The complete emotional and nervous collapse of the young student Mörike following upon this disillusionment and his final rejection of Maria Meyer may be explained by two factors: first, the inculcation throughout his boyhood of the pietistic Protestant values of personal chastity and of human love in harmony with the love of Christ; second, Mörike's lifelong inability to endure intense emotional experience of any kind, reflected in the second strophe of his famous lyric «Gebet»:

> Wollest mit Freuden
> Und wollest mit Leiden
> Mich nicht überschütten!
> Doch in der Mitten
> Liegt holdes Bescheiden. (*SW,* I, 135)

Mörike most assuredly did not reject erotic feeling, but its intensity had to be within limits he could tolerate, and it also had to be compatible with other values: in his youth with Christianity, in his maturity with the playful grace of classical antiquity, notably the Anacreontic poets whom he translated. Even shortly before the love for Luise Rau and the conception of *Maler Nolten,*

---

33 Storz, *JdDSG,* 20, 496, explains the germination of the cycle from the emotional conflict incited by Maria Meyer as follows: «Leidenschaft, erotisches Verlangen, andererseits Berührungsscheu, auch Angst vor dem in der pietistischen Umwelt dämonisierten Sexus, – das alles mag ineinander gewirkt, seltsame Verwirrung gezeitigt haben, aus der aber kostbare Dichtung entsprang.»
34 Storz, *Eduard Mörike,* p. 171, points out the antithetical connotations of «Kelch der Sünden» as «communio sacrilega. Der lächelnd dargereichte Kelch ist freilich das Gegenbild zum heiligen Kelch ... Von ihm geht nicht Erneuerung, sondern Verzauberung aus, nicht ewiges Leben, sondern selig-unseliger Tod.»

Mörike was able to express a playful eroticism in a few poems apparently inspired by a Catholic girl encountered during a brief visit with his brother Karl in the village of Scheer, and in one of these, whose title «Josephine» supplied Constanze von Armond with a middle name,[35] the persona touches the girl's dress «in unschuldsvoller Lust» as she sings in the choir at mass.

This digression into the young Mörike's emotional biography was necessary for us to appraise his transformation of personal experience into objective characters, Nolten and Larkens, with a plausible life of their own. In a review of the novel in 1833, Mörike's friend Gustav Schwab introduced the concept of «double motivation» to criticism of this novel: everything is explicable on the one hand in terms of an irrational force, the fateful bond between Elisabeth and Nolten, on the other hand in terms of the psychological motivation of the characters.[36] We would not today seek psychological character motivation in the sense of nineteenth-century English, French or Russian novels in the work of Mörike; his special strength lies not in rational nineteenth-century psychology but rather in his anticipation of the depth psychology of our own time. In my view this depth psychology and its mythical objectification are manifest in the plot of the novel as a whole, but they are not sufficiently evident in the individual characterization of Nolten and Larkens to make their conduct entirely plausible.[37] We can understand why Nolten comes to hate Elisabeth after he has observed the baneful effects of her prophecy and subsequent appearances upon Agnes, but there is nothing to explain how, even before the start of the action, he has forgotten his betrothal to the gypsy girl. Mörike could project the transformation of idealizing passion into rejection in superb lyrical poetry, but the experience seems to have been too intimately personal to be projected into prose fiction. The author does take considerable pains to account for the break with Constanze, but after this Nolten makes a well-considered decision to devote all his energies to art, and his explanation of this to Larkens (p. 226ff.) convinces the reader that here at last he has found his true destiny. It is at this point that Larkens' revelation of the forgery, in a farewell letter left behind with the packet of love letters (between Agnes and Lar-

---

35 See «The Loves of Maler Nolten» (note 22 above), p. 77f., and Harry Maync, *Eduard Mörike. Sein Leben und Dichten* (Stuttgart: Cotta, 1913), p. 104f. The girl in question is frequently mentioned by subsequent critics without anything substantial being known about her. The name Josephine occurs in the prophecy by Elisabeth in Constanze's dream: «*Constanze Josephine Armond wird auch bald die Orgel mit uns spielen*» (p. 70, emphasis in source).
36 See Storz, *Eduard Mörike*, p. 163 and the accompanying footnote 48. Cf. also von Wiese, p. 179: «Aber diese [dämonischen] Mächte ... werden ... vom Erzähler nachträglich natürlich erklärt und psychologisch begründet.»
37 That this may also be asserted of Constanze, a rather lightly sketched figure, is less important, but one wonders how this mature and cultivated woman can believe that Nolten will find happiness in the arms of a childlike angel, as she writes in her farewell letter to him (p. 262).

kens in the guise of Nolten), has its fatal effect.[38] Nolten reads these letters in a weakened state, while convalescing from the illness contracted during his imprisonment, and we can understand their impact on him at this moment, but it is still hard to see how this hitherto balanced, circumspect, and mature hero willingly becomes party to the forged revival of a dead love, why he returns to a fiancée loved in his youth primarily for her childlike innocence and purity, whom he now knows to be mentally unstable. What is more, his mood on reading the packet is ambivalent, even ironic:

> ... Und was ist's denn weiter? wie, darf diese Entdeckung so ganz mich vernichten? was ist mir denn verloren, seit ich das Alles weiß? genau besehen – Nichts, gewonnen – Nichts – ei ja doch, ein Mädchen, von dem mir Jemand schreibt, sie sey ein wahres Gotteslamm, ein SANSPAREIL, ein ANGELUS! (P. 242)

Even the narrator expresses ambivalence as he describes the crucial turning-point where Nolten gives in and accepts participation in the forgery. While reading the letters at an inn he sees an etching depicting a kneeling figure, beneath which are some religious verses he has heard in childhood from his deceased mother. His reaction is comparable to that of Faust hearing the Easter music:

> ... so war Noltens Innerstes auf Einmal aufgebrochen und schmolz und strömte in einer unbeschreiblich süßen Fluth von Schmerz dahin ... Die Vergangenheit steht vor ihm, Agnes schwebt heran, ein Schauer ihres Wesens berührt ihn, er fühlt, daß das Unmögliche möglich, daß Altes neu werden könne.
>
> Dieß sind die Augenblicke, wo der Mensch willig darauf verzichtet, sich selber zu begreifen, sich mit den bekannten Gesetzen seines bisherigen Seyns und Empfindens übereinstimmend zu vergleichen; man überläßt sich getrost dem göttlichen Elemente, das uns trägt, und ist gewiß, man werde wohlbehalten an ein bestimmtes Ziel gelangen. (P. 245)

This may well be a candid expression of Eduard Mörike's own subjective temperament,[39] but is it Theobald Nolten as we have known him up to now? Even if we waive the question as to why he goes through with a decision contrary «to the laws of his previous being and feeling,» we cannot overlook the irony of this passage. The reader who has finished the novel – like the narrator, who knows how it will end – must be aware that it is no «divine element» that carries Nolten along at this point, but a tragic error. The impossible cannot become possible; what is past cannot be renewed.

The conduct of Larkens is hardly more plausible, whether or not we view him as in some sense a Romantic «Doppelgänger» of the hero. We are given to

---

38 Cf. Storz, Eduard Mörike, p. 150: «In diese erste Sicht eines neuen und zugleich des eigenen Weges drängt Larkens seinen Entwurf von der Zukunft des Freundes – mit Agnes – und verdunkelt dadurch die Klarheit, zu der Nolten während Krankheit und Haft durchgedrungen ist. Nur von diesem Punkt aus ... wird die tragische Fatalität der Mentorschaft, die Larkens hingebungsvoll ausübt, völlig sichtbar ...»

39 Cf. the psychological portrait depicted throughout Herbert Meyer's *Eduard Mörike,* particularly the chapter «Der Abgrund der Betrachtung,» p. 52–73.

understand that he had been enmeshed by a guilty passion into a degenerate personal life and that the remorse over his own past makes him exalt all the more the ideal of angelic innocence he sees in Agnes, perhaps even fall in love with her himself. But we learn too little about Larkens' early life for this drastic and belated reaction to his fall from innocence – a virtual attempt to regain virginity by proxy – to be credible. Whatever problems he might see in Nolten's love for Constanze,[40] he ought to realize that his friend could never find lasting fulfillment in the return to an adolescent past. Larkens' authorship of the «Peregrina» poems is even more problematical. How are we to regard these poems as a self-projection by Larkens into the feelings of Theobald Nolten for Elisabeth, when, so far as the reader can know, Theobald's love for Elisabeth was never consummated and there has been no evidence – prior to his reading of these very poems[41] – that he ever felt remorse over rejecting her? It seems as though Larkens, as the fictive creator of these poems, is projecting himself into the imagination of their actual creator, Eduard Mörike. The latter has thus come perilously close to making himself, like Brentano-Maria in *Godwi,* a character in his own novel, but – unlike Brentano-Maria – without due regard for the narrative implications. Although Larkens exemplifies considerable elements of «Romantic irony,» for example in his reported production of Tieck's *Verkehrte Welt,* into which he injected himself as spectator-character (p. 338ff.), this particular manifestation of irony is neither suited for *Maler Nolten* nor intended by the author. On a deeper level, as a confession by Eduard Mörike, the «Peregrina» cycle is pertinent to the underlying meaning of the novel, but not as a reflection of its characters.

Larkens' forgery, to which Nolten, despite misgivings, becomes an accomplice, is nothing less than the delusion that a mature man can return to his adolescence, «daß das Unmögliche möglich, daß Altes neu werden könne.» An adequate explanation for this deliberate self-deception is not provided by the main action of the novel but only by the episodic materials considered earlier in this paper. The self-deception results from a futile striving to integrate elemental – hence essentially pagan – erotic love with pietistic Christian ideals of chaste love and marriage. Theobald Nolten can never realize the miracle vouchsafed for Alexis and Belsore by the golden ring in the bark of the blooming rose bush. Erotic passion as a fatal destiny is personified for Theobald in the figure of Elisabeth,[42] whom he no longer loves, who has become

---

40 Even in the first version of the novel there is no suggestion of insurmountable obstacles to a lasting union between the two lovers. Mörike's later revision details a plan by Constanze to obtain the necessary title and rank for Nolten to make her marriage to him possible (IV, 148f.).
41 At this point, too, the narrator's effort to relate the poems to Nolten's own subjective experience seems somewhat feeble: «Wie sonderbar ist Nolten von dieser Schilderung ergriffen! wie lebhaft erkennt er sich und Elisabeth selbst noch in einem so bunt ausschweifenden Gemälde! und diese Wehmut der Vergangenheit, wie vielfach ist sie bei ihm gemischt» (p. 365).
42 This is also the view of Heide Eilert (note 31 above).

more a demonic force than a human being. After his first encounter with her at puberty, the adolescent Theobald had been able to convince himself for a time that he could love the image of angelic innocence he projected upon Agnes, but this love had been shaken by the report that erotic feeling, directed toward another man, had awakened in Agnes herself. Nolten can then, for a time with minimal feelings of guilt, indulge a passionate relationship with the cultivated aristocratic widow Constanze von Armond. But the conviction that his mature love has been sinful and that he must go back to his youthful ideal of childlike innocence is forced upon him by Larkens's forgery. The return to Agnes, no longer the seemingly unproblematic child to whom Nolten had betrothed himself, but an unstable young woman, herself unable to cope with erotic emotion, results in the destruction of them both.

This interpretation of the mythic significance of Elisabeth and of her and Larkens' respective roles in the tragic outcome of the novel does not invalidate the consensus of prior criticism that she personifies Mörike's sense of the demonic, irrational forces to which human existence falls prey. It merely emphasizes that for Mörike the focus of these forces lies in erotic passion as a source of guilt and death, a focus made clear within the novel by the narrative and lyric interpolations. This focus clarifies the special sense in which we may take the plot of the novel as a «poetic confession.» It is the fictional expression of a personal myth.[43] Underlying its conception was an attempt by Mörike to project the innocent boyhood love for his cousin Klärchen Neuffer upon a mature young woman, Luise Rau.[44] In this love for Luise, which he hoped could reconcile erotic passion with his Protestant Christian ideals, he was in a sense «returning» to his earlier boyhood love, even «forging» a love which was no longer attainable for him. In Mörike's own life, however, the encounter with a personal embodiment of elemental erotic passion took place between the first love of childlike innocence (Klärchen) and the attempt to «forge» its revival (Luise). With uncanny psychological insight, the personal myth as it is projected into the novel shifts the hero's initiation into intense erotic awareness back to the threshold of adolescence. And because the initiator, within the action of the novel, has taken on broader significance as an embodiment of tragic destiny, the hero's erotic passion is transposed to a distinct character, Constanze. Mörike's own Protestant conscience (represented in the novel by Larkens) forces the attempt to reconcile erotic passion with Christian ideals in the person of Luise, but memories of the guilt-ridden passion for Maria Meyer doom this effort to failure. A crisis of faith apparently suffered by Mörike dur-

---

43 See «The Loves of Maler Nolten» (note 22 above), p. 73ff.
44 In letters to Luise, Mörike repeatedly addresses her as «Kind,» often as «Engel.» At the close of a letter to her from Owen in March of 1830 he writes: «Schlaf wohl *Engelskind!*» [emphasis in the source], and in a letter of 23 July 1830 to Hartlaub he calls her both «mein Kind» and «ein einfaches, heilig unschuldiges Wesen» (*Werke und Briefe,* XI, 97, 132).

ing the time *Maler Nolten* was being conceived[45] may have contributed that specifically religious colouring of the underlying spiritual struggle which comes out so clearly in the last songs of Agnes.

In *Maler Nolten* the seeming digressions from the main plot are no mere «arabesque» embellishments as in some earlier novels of German Romanticism. It is precisely such episodic interpolations – often considered detrimental to the form of Romantic novels – that save the thematic unity of *Maler Nolten*. From the standpoint of its unifying theme, this novel continues a tradition that runs from Tieck through Brentano, Arnim, and Eichendorff: the conflict of pagan and Christian love. The precursors most closely anticipating *Maler Nolten* are Eichendorff's two novels *Ahnung und Gegenwart* and *Dichter und ihre Gesellen*.[46] Eichendorff's principal male characters, Friedrich and Leontin in *Ahnung und Gegenwart*, Viktor in *Dichter und ihre Gesellen*, are stronger than Theobald Nolten; they can recognize and cope successfully with pagan eroticism, which destroys only weaker male figures (like Rudolf in *Ahnung und Gegenwart*, Otto in *Dichter und ihre Gesellen*) and the demonic women through whom it is primarily exerted.[47] Although the unity of Eichendorff's two novels is strained by the looser integration of episodic materials and by the plurality of male–female couples, they bring out the central problem more clearly than *Maler Nolten* with its tightly knit plot, perhaps because their author – unlike Eduard Mörike at this stage of his development – had mastered it in his own emotional life.

---

45 Herbert Meyer, *Eduard Mörike*, p. 48, quotes the «Gretchenfrage of Mörike's dying sister Luise in 1827: «Hast Du auch einen Glauben an den Heiland, E.[duard]?» which Mörike could not readily answer (letter to Charlotte Späth, 3 April 1827, *Werke und Briefe*, X, 147).
46 The first of these novels is also strongly concerned with the broader social, ethical, and political crisis of Germany at this period, a theme found only on the periphery of *Maler Nolten*.
47 Cf. the trenchant discussion of the female characters of *Ahnung und Gegenwart* by Egon Schwarz in «Joseph von Eichendorff: *Ahnung und Gegenwart*» in *Romane und Erzählungen der deutschen Romantik*, ed. Paul Michael Lützeler (Stuttgart: Reclam, 1982), p. 311f.

Double-Dealing:
Irony in Kleist's *Die Marquise von O . . .*

«Und gleichwohl muß es doch notwendig
eins oder das andere gewesen sein.»

LILIAN R. FURST, *University of North Carolina*

To students of irony Kleist's *Die Marquise von O...* has a peculiar fascination. Within the compact form of a quite short *Novelle* it encompasses an astonishing range of ironies intertwined into a tight web. Kleists draws largely on the traditional devices and strategies of irony, but he does so with such virtuosity and subtlety as to intensify the possibilities of ironic narration into a vexatory metaphor of his perplexed vision of the universe. The figural means of representation become an allegory of the world represented. There is no surer way to experience the complexities of Kleist and of his characters than to wrestle as a reader with the ironic mobility of his text.

Much of the irony in *Die Marquise von O...* hinges on the reader's capacity to work out the situation long before the protagonists are able to do so. Kleist deliberately manipulates the element of surprise so that *Die Marquise von O...* can be read at one level as a detective story. In the opening sentence the reader has the shock of discovering the body, so to speak. This is followed by an extended retrospective account of the circumstances leading up to this point: the storming of the citadel, the Count's sudden marriage proposal, the diagnosis of the Marquise's pregnancy, her conflict with her family, and her retreat with her children to her country estate. It is not until three-fifths of the way through the story that we return to the present time of narration, to «jene sonderbare Aufforderung» in the newspapers of M... «die man am Eingang dieser Erzählung gelesen hat.»[1] This lengthy excursus from the starting-point into the past heightens the tension by delaying the eventual solution to the enigma in the response to the advertisement. However, it also serves another purpose: by giving the reader access to the Marquise's immediate past it enables him to see through the situation, as it were, from an early moment on. The entire disposition of the narrative is therefore designed to permit the maximum latitude for the exercise of those kinds of irony which devolve from the reader's possession of an understanding superior to that of the duped protagonists. Or rather, as he later discovers, from the reader's belief that he is in

---

1 Heinrich von Kleist, *Sämtliche Werke,* ed. Helmut Sembdner, 2nd rev. ed. (München: Hanser, 1961), II, 127. All subsequent references are to this edition.

possession of such superior understanding. For that belief in turn is ultimately undercut by an irony of a different dimension from that which dominates the first half of the narrative. The reader finds himself the victim of double-dealing: he has been dealt a set of cards with which he has engaged in a game with whose rules he is conversant; only gradually does it dawn on him that another game is simultaneously being played in which he is as much at a loss as the protagonists. From the role of ironic observer, which he assumes through most of the narrative, he is demoted to that of ironic victim. In the jolt of this fall he experiences the full impact of the Kleistian vision of the universe.

The reader attains his position as an ironic observer by virtue of the acuteness of his detective capacity. His awareness of the irony of the situation being enacted depends entirely on his ability to decipher the puzzle of the Marquise's pregnancy in advance of her and her family. The reader's insight becomes the organizing centre of his interpretation of the narrative in progress as an ironic plot. What is more, his increasing assurance of his own reading creates the pride that precedes the fall.

How soon then is the reader able to solve the «whodunit?» aspect of *Die Marquise von O...*? It has recently been asserted that modern students are «alerted to the true state of affairs after only a few paragraphs.»[2] That may be so, but mainly because Kleist's paragraphs are exceptionally long. There are in fact surprisingly few of those stylistic signals of an ironic intent that occur at the beginning of such works as *Pride and Prejudice* and *Don Juan* by Kleist's contemporaries, Jane Austen and Byron. The opening sentence is startling in its disruption of our expectations of the behaviour of a woman of that class and of that moral standing at that time. It is rife with ironies of situation in the discrepancy between the Marquise's impeccably virtuous past and her present position and action, and also in her strange decision to publicize her dilemma and to marry «aus Familienrücksichten» (p. 104), when those very considerations might have dictated the diametrically opposite course of discreet secrecy. Yet there is nothing either in that sentence or in the subsequent rapid narration of the attack on the citadel to warrant the assumption that this text is meant to be read in any sense divergent from its overt surface. The narrator's tone is that of the detached chronicler, and the language is devoid of ambiguity. It is only after the notorious gap, denoted by a dash which has aptly been likened to «einer spanischen Wand, hinter der der Erzähler erst hervorkommt, als „die erschrockenen Frauen" der Marquise erscheinen,»[3] that the timbre of the narration modulates, as perceptible clues insinuate the presence of irony. The word *Umstände,* which crops up no fewer than sixteen times in

---

2 Erika Swales, «The Beleaguered Citadel: A Study of Kleist's *Die Marquise von O...,*» *DVjs,* 51 (1977), 129.
3 Michael Moehring, *Witz und Ironie in der Prosa Heinrich von Kleists* (München: Fink, 1972), p. 153.

this relatively brief story, creates an ingenious verbal and ideational link between the Marquise and the Count. Both have recourse to that conveniently capacious term to characterize the duress prompting their actions. The imperative of the Marquise's «andere Umstände» (p. 104) is echoed by the Count's constraint «daß er sich der Frau Marquise unter diesen Umständen gehorsamst empfehlen müsse» (p. 108); similarly, the pressures exerted by her recognition «daß sie in gesegneten Leibesumständen wäre» (p. 109) are countered by his concession that he is «durch die Umstände gezwungen» (p. 110). Such stealthy lexical indicators reinforce the suspicions aroused in the reader's mind by the Count's bizarre conduct and by the urgency not just of his proposal but of his wish for an instantaneous marriage.

The conjecture of an ironic subtext is corroborated by a striking and curious phrase in the conversation between the Marquise's father and the Count when the latter is pressing his precipitate suit. To the Count's assurances about his integrity, veracity, etc.: « – Der Kommandant erwiderte, indem er ein wenig, obschon ohne Ironie, lächelte, daß er alle diese Äußerungen unterschreibe» (p. 112). The parenthetically inserted «obschon ohne Ironie» is conspicuous as one of the very few interpretative comments regarding a character's inner attitude in a story where it is the notation of external, often physical responses such as gestures, blushing, fainting, or silence that predominates. Given both the economy and the deliberate ambiguity of the narration in *Die Marquise von O...*, this overt reference to irony can hardly be accidental. It seems as if Kleist specifically names the trope in order to confirm the idea in the reader's mind. Its posited absence suggests per contrariam its possible presence. The context of the phrase bears out this hypothesis for it comes at the moment when the Count is making the most grossly ironic assertions of his rectitude. To which the Marquise's father replies with that non-ironic smile and the confident statement: «Noch hätte er keines jungen Mannes Bekanntschaft gemacht, der in so kurzer Zeit so viele vortreffliche Eigenschaften des Charakters entwickelt hätte» (p. 112). That this peerless young man had in an equally short time demonstrated the opposite by violating his daughter is patently the last thought that would cross his mind. Hence his lack of any sense of the ironic implications of either his own bearing or the Count's, or indeed of any alternative interpretation of the situation. To the reader, however, to whom that alternative has already occurred, the evocation of «Ironie» at this point acts as an endorsement of his increasingly probable surmise. Kleist has here introduced a phrase into his narration that is of no more than marginal significance for the progress of the narrative, but that is of crucial importance for its reading.

The reader's growing confidence in the validity of his inferences brings a pronounced dramatic irony into play. The audience commands knowledge denied to the protagonists. This is underscored by the repeated insistence on the family's utter bewilderment: «Die Familie wußte nicht, was sie zu dieser Äußerung sagen sollte» (p. 113); «Als er das Zimmer verlassen, wußte die Familie nicht, was sie aus dieser Erscheinung machen solle» (p. 113-4); «Inzwischen war die Familie in der lebhaftesten Unruhe. ... Der Kommandant sagte, daß er von der Sache nichts verstehe» (p. 115). The unknowing actors are contrasted with the knowing reader who is able to assess things from the vantage of his superior insight. The irony is therefore at the expense of the characters as they grope towards an understanding already attained by the audience. The disparity between the internal and the external interpreters of the situation is most flagrant in the scene following the Count's surprising return after his reported death and his abrupt proposal of marriage (p. 109-19). To the initiated reader the discussion among the members of the family has a tragi-comic undertone.

As the reader becomes ever more convinced of the appropriateness of his construction, the dramatic irony intensifies to a pitch where it begins to create a problem of credibility. It is hard for modern readers to accept the characters' protracted blindness, even within the framework of early nineteenth-century trust in the conduct proper to a gentleman. There is evidence to support the argument – an argument made, incidentally, more often by women critics[4] than by men – that the Marquise, and indeed her mother, have begun to have a shrewd inkling of the culprit's identity considerably before the actual denouement. In the last resort, however, such a pseudo-realistic question as «when does she begin to know?» is beside the point in the most literal sense of the word. For the point of *Die Marquise von O. . .* is not so much «when?» or even «what?» do the characters know, as how can they deal with the knowledge they have acquired, how can they accommodate it to their accustomed world view. So the Marquise's lasting ignorance can be seen as a form of denial. Even more important, with this displacement of interest, the dramatic irony loses its momentum. The distance between the reader and the characters is suddenly and drastically foreshortened. The superior insight on which the reader has relied proves to be of limited worth. In an irony of reversal the tables have been turned on him; he is ousted from his privileged observation tower and thrown into the maelstrom of uncertainty.

This ironic manipulation of the dramatic irony is paradigmatic of the shifting nature of the irony in *Die Marquise von O. . . .* Through Kleist's use of many devices traditional to irony, the reader is encouraged to develop certain consistent patterns of reading which derive from the established strategies for recognizing and constructing ironies. However, this primary level of seemingly stable irony is itself subject to ironic subversion through other narrative tactics which undermine the authority of the constructed meaning. So the characteristic dualities of irony are sharpened in *Die Marquise von O. . .* into duplici-

---

4 See notably Dorrit Cohn, «Kleist's *Die Marquise von O . . .*: The Problem of Knowledge,» *Monatshefte,* 67 (1975), and Swales (note 2).

ties that thwart the reading process and that leave the reader in a dilemma parallel to that of the characters.

A good example of this complicated double-dealing is the handling of verbal irony. The extraordinarily dense linguistic texture of *Die Marquise von O...* is a major source of its ironies. It is through his distinctive use of words that Kleist opens up an ironic aperture, and he does so by the rhetorical means generally associated with ironic discourse. His favourite procedure is the simplest and most common device of irony, *double entendre,* which he exploits with the utmost inventiveness. Innocuous words and phrases such as «Folgen,» «verbindlich,» «empfangen,» «ergeben,» «nähere Bekanntschaft» are given an ambiguous aspect through the context of dramatic irony in which they are embedded. It is an outcome of this practice «daß keine Bemerkung unverfänglich bleibt, daß jede neben dem gemeinten noch einen zweiten Sinn erhält, der zwar dem Sprechenden verborgen bleibt – dafür aber Autor und Leser um so größeres Vergnügen bereitet.»[5] Often Kleist has recourse to variants on the ironic *double entendre.* What is said, far from being the opposite to what is meant is exactly what is meant, at least in the mind of the speaker, but is not understood as such. The Count's statements are frequently the object of a failure to understand on the hearer's part. When he tells the family of his need «über eine notwendige Forderung seiner Seele ins Reine zu sein» (p. 111), when he claims to have decisive («Entscheidende!» [p. 115]) reasons for his decisions, and finally when he declares, «es würde ein Tag kommen, wo sie ihn verstehen würde!» (p. 119): in all these instances he is in fact speaking without any ironic intent. The irony arises, contrary to his purpose, through the listener's refusal to take his words at their face value. There is then a further layer of irony in the disparity between the responses of the fictional hearers within the text and those of the readers outside the text who can see the literal meaning. The Marquise's misperception of her name «Julietta!» on the Count's lips as referring to some unfortunate «Namensschwester» (p. 108) is a further instance of such misinterpretation. Another kind of *double entendre* occurs when a protagonist speaks with ironic intent, yet – ironically – hits the nail on the head without realizing it. The most prominent occurrence of such unconscious irony is the father's dictum: «Sie hat es im Schlaf getan» (p. 131) which is put forward as a scathing sarcasm, but is nearer to the facts than the speaker believes. The Marquise's mother too makes comments that come unwittingly close to the heart of the matter: «Sein heftiger, auf einen Punkt hintreibender Wille, meinte sie, scheine ihr einer solchen Tat fähig» (p. 114); «ob er nicht kommen, seine leichtsinnige Tat bereuen und wieder gutmachen werde» (p. 115); «ein unerhörtes Spiel des Schicksals» (p. 132); «ein junger, sonst wohlerzogener Mensch, dem wir eine solche Nichtswürdigkeit niemals

---

5 Moehring, *Witz und Ironie,* p. 239.

zugetraut hätten» (p. 134). In these numerous cases of *double entendre* irony appears in its characteristic guise as «a form of utterance that postulates a double audience, consisting of one party that hearing shall hear and shall not understand, and another party that when more is meant than meets the ear, is aware both of that more and of the outsiders' incomprehension.»⁶

There is another rather more subtle type of *double entendre* that also plays an important part in *Die Marquise von O...* Words are introduced which, either in themselves or in the combination in which they are placed, have pronounced associative overtones. In itself this is so familiar a feature of any poetic discourse as to warrant no special mention. What distinguishes it in *Die Marquise von O...* is the consistent referent and position of such connotative language. The connotation is invariably sexual, and its focus is the Count. He addresses the Marquise «mit einer aufflammenden Freude» (p. 110); he had thought of her constantly after he had been wounded, and he tells her «daß er die Lust und den Schmerz nicht beschreiben könnte, die sich in dieser Vorstellung umarmt hätten, daß er endlich nach seiner Wiederherstellung wieder zur Armee gegangen wäre; daß er daselbst die lebhafteste Unruhe empfunden hätte» (p. 110-11). His boyhood memories of the swan whom he had tried in vain «an sich zu locken» after besmirching her with mud, come to him «in der Hitze des Wundfiebers» (p. 116) when he confuses the Marquise with the swan. The subliminal resonance of the prevalent phrase «in der Hitze des Gefechts» clearly suggests the parallel between the Count's behaviour towards the swan and towards the Marquise. The unmistakable sexual colouring of the Count's speech is a pointer to the powerful, barely repressed erotic undertow of his personality which breaks out in his crucial deed. His penchant for such diction represents an ironic inversion of the highly stylized discourse of his class and time; his ritualistic «untertänigst» (p. 114) and «gefälligst» (p. 115) are contravened by his instinctive and instinctual vocabulary.

The evidence of the rhetoric therefore suggests that *Die Marquise von O...* is governed by a web of literary ironies which are relatively transparent to the reader once he has grasped the fundamental situation. The ambiguities of the language seem to be the appropriate expression for the discrepancy between the masking appearance and the ulterior reality. Seen in this light, *Die Marquise von O...* conforms to the classical paradigm of irony. But in a characteristic double-dealing there is still another dimension, where this legible irony is severely undercut. The cutting instrument in the case of the rhetoric is indirect discourse, which produces a distinctively dualistic effect. On the one hand, it serves to lend credibility to the characters' utterances. In page after page of reported speech the narrator presents their words and thoughts from their point of view. The tone is cool and detached; the narrating voice refrains

---

6 H.W. Fowler, *A Dictionary of English Usage* (Oxford: Oxford University Press, 1965), p. 305-06.

from explicit comment or ostensible interpretation. What Wolfgang Kayser has noted of a passage in *Das Erdbeben in Chili* holds true for *Die Marquise von O...* too: «Der Erzähler hat sich mit der Wendung ganz auf die Gestalt, von der er spricht, eingestellt, er wertet aus ihrer Perspektive.»[7] Kayser later elaborates on his argument: «Er wertet hier – soll man sagen: wie einer oder als einer, der das Vorhergehende nicht kennt und nun vor den Mandaten steht.»[8] This very aptly describes the posture of the Kleistian narrator. Maintaining his aesthetic distance through an austere non-involvement, he assumes the role of the neutral, factual chronicler whose function is solely to report. He retreats behind the events narrated, speaking indeed as if his back were turned to the audience.[9] Yet the air of authenticity that is created thereby is in itself more questionable than first appears. Kleist – long before Flaubert – explored the ironic potential of indirect discourse as a mode of narration. What is reported is, notwithstanding its semblance of veracity, after all nothing other than the subjective perceptions of the various characters. The wide range of their views of the predicament suggests already the elusiveness of any authoritative position. The essential precariousness of all that is being so meticulously registered is implied in the high incidence of the verbal form «schien,» as well as by such interpolated phrases as «wie sie meinte» (p. 108), «meinte sie» (p. 114), «wie er meinte» (p. 133). It is a realm of conjecture that is being represented in indirect discourse. These characters judge and are judged both by the image they present to the world and by the image («Vorstellung» is another recurrent key word) of each other that they cherish. Because the narrator records their voices and their perceptions, and because, moreover, he abstains from evaluative elucidation, the reader is left to face the text on his own. The more closely he scrutinizes that terse, compact text, the more compellingly does he become aware of its innate slipperiness. What confronts him is a narrative that not only uses irony but that also is intrinsically ironic in structure.

The reader's difficulty in achieving a reliable interpretation of the text reiterates the characters' problems in disengaging appearance and reality. Double-dealing subverts both these endeavours to arrive at a definitive clarity. «Reality» in *Die Marquise von O...* can at best be posited as a provisional, tentative state, subject always to additional modification; it remains therefore for ever beyond the reach of certainty. As a result, such fundamental concepts as *Sein* and *Schein* cannot be retrieved from the instability in which they float. The outcome of these equivocations is a mobility that extends from the literary into the metaphysical sphere.

---

7 Wolfgang Kayser, «Kleist als Erzähler,» *GLL*, 8 (1954/55), 19–29; reprinted in *Die Vortragsreise. Studien zur Literatur* (Bern: Francke, 1958), p. 169–83; and in Walter Müller-Seidel, ed., *Heinrich von Kleist. Aufsätze und Essays* (Darmstadt: Wissenschaftliche Buchgesellschaft, 1967), p. 130–43. All references are to this most recent reprint; p. 233.
8 Kayser, p. 233.
9 Kayser, p. 236.

In centering its axis on the dichotomy between appearance and reality *Die Marquise von O...* is following the archetypal plot of irony. A disagreeable surface masks an admirable personality, and vice versa. The comic, social ramifications of this scenario are transacted in Jane Austen's *Pride and Prejudice* (1813). Darcy is eventually recognized, despite his flaws, as a generous man of honour, while Wickham is exposed as the unscrupulous cad that he is. The initial misjudgements are corrected, and painful though that process is to those involved, all's well that ends well. *Die Marquise von O...* also ends rather well in a conventional way with the marriage of the Marquise and the Count and «eine ganze Reihe von jungen Russen» (p. 143). However, this outward reconciliation is not partnered by a genuine resolution of the problem. Unlike Darcy, the Count is never fully rehabilitated: he seems *and* is angel *and* devil. Appearance and reality, instead of being finally disjoined, as is traditional in irony, are in *Die Marquise von O...* inextricably conjoined. Their contours, far from possessing distinct, circumscribed limits, are so blurred as to be fused. In other words, there are no absolute categories here, nor, by implication, any objective reality.

Because the lines of demarcation are so fluid, the notion of the role is of primary importance in *Die Marquise von O. ...* As an intermediary performative stage, the role erodes distinctions by hovering at times closer to appearance, at others closer to reality. Since the characters must assess each other (and we them) from the evidence of manifest conduct, the foregrounding of the role compounds the confusion surrounding both the pursuit of specific certainties and the larger issues of *Sein* and *Schein*. For instance, the Count is first seen in circumstances encumbered with doubt: «Der russische Offizier, der, nach *der Rolle zu urteilen, die er spielte,* einer der Anführer des Sturms zu sein *schien»* (p. 106; my italics). His entreaties for her hand in marriage are regarded, successively and separately, by the Marquise and by her father as an «Aufführung» (p. 110 and 111). Leopardo has a role foisted onto him – or perhaps it is an appearance that betrays a reality[10] in the same way as the Count's apparent «performance» belies a reality. The impossibility of accurately distinguishing between appearance and reality is evinced again in the erroneous report of the Count's death, which is never explained. The evidence of the senses and of the mind may be wholly misleading. The criteria by which men and women judge each other, like the categories in which they think, are shown to be brittle constructs that do not stand the tests of experience. Nor is the reader granted the privilege of exercising a discrimination superior to that of the protagonists. As readers we too are playing a role: the role of readers of irony. And we are as liable as the protagonists to become victims of our own

---

10 Some students argue that the scenario outlined by the Marquise's mother is quite convincing, and that Leopardo could indeed be the father of the Marquise's child. Others suggest that it might be her father, judging by his behaviour.

misreadings, or rather, the objects of an intensely sceptical irony that precludes any totally assured reading.

So the attempt to grapple with the ironies in *Die Marquise von O...* leads back to its central problem of knowledge. Not just the protagonists' scant and fallacious knowledge, nor even the narrator's, but ours as readers too. For we come to realize that, like the characters, we are in a quandary not readily amenable to resolution. Once we are in possession of the knowledge that the Count, who seems an angel, is a devil, we believe ourselves capable of grasping the irony implicit in *Die Marquise von O....* We learn ultimately that this is not so, that there is far more than meets even the clever eye. So we are made aware of the fragility of our initial sense of reasonable assurance vis-à-vis the text we are interpreting. Our confident superiority to the protagonists is impaired as we find ourselves confronting perplexities *with* them. Their predicaments are projected onto us as we begin to discover that we have been dealt not a manageable set of dualisms, but double-dealt, as it were, a refractory knot of philosophical enigmas. The irony of *Die Marquise von O...* is therefore an irony of duplicity, itself double and duplicitous. Its neat, almost schematic surface of dualities acts as a mask for the epistemological and ontological crises which it explores. Kleist has assumed the guise and the devices traditional to irony, but for his own ulterior purposes, for the covert exposition of problems far beyond the overt matter of his story. The ironic game being played with the reader is a complex and hazardous one.

So the reader is denied the ease of formulating issues in terms of the stark contrasts favoured by the protagonists: «Ein reines Bewußtsein und eine Hebamme!» (p. 122); «Vortreffliche» / «Nichtswürdige» (p. 135); pistolshot / «lange, heiße und lechzende Küsse» (p. 139). The narrative refutes the confident assertion of the Marquise's mother: «Und gleichwohl muß es doch notwendig eins oder das andere gewesen sein» (p. 121). The riposte to that affirmation comes in the Marquise's evasive: «Er gefällt und mißfällt mir» (p. 117). The ironic dualities in *Die Marquise von O...* do not cancel each other out; they co-exist. The Count seems/is angel/devil, i.e., things cannot be reduced to a univalent meaning. Not a single persona, including the narrator, is in a position to command a «sicheren Standpunkt, von dem aus eine endgültige Sinngebung und Wertung möglich wäre.»[11] The impasse in the search for knowledge that is reached within the fiction applies also to the interpretation of the fiction. The reader is caught in the same epistemological dilemma as the protagonists and the narrator: that of coping with the disconcerting information he has acquired.[12] Unwilling though he is to assume the stance «Ich *will*

---

11 Kayser, p. 234.
12 John M. Ellis has put forward a similar argument about *Das Erdbeben in Chili* in *Narration in the German Novelle* (London: Cambridge University Press, 1974), especially p. 49 and 69-71. But he seems to believe that the critic can escape the error made by the narrator and the characters by acknowledging all the conflicting interpretations as provisional.

nichts wissen» (p. 129), he has nevertheless to come to terms with the limits of his knowledge and of his powers of interpretation.

The unattainability of knowledge in *Die Marquise von O...* is in the last resort a reflection of the nature of its universe. It appears at the outset to be a well ordered world in which each individual has a clearly defined place in a close-knit social fabric. Even after the storming of the citadel, the persistence of certain conventions of polite bearing and of ceremonious speech between conqueror and conquered suggests that there has been no deep breach in the established order. «Alles kehrte nun in die alte Ordnung der Dinge zurück» (p. 109), for who could suspect that an officer who approaches a lady «unter einer verbindlichen französischen Anrede» (p. 105) could behave in so ungentlemanly a way? As Müller-Seidel has pointed out: «Die Konvention, das „Verbindliche" dieser Menschen verschärfen den Konflikt.»[13] That conflict shifts from the physical and social plane onto the metaphysical and ontological in the doctor's sarcastic rejoinder «daß er ihr die letzten Gründe der Dinge nicht werde zu erklären brauchen» (p. 120). The Kantian echoes of «Dinge» in this as in the earlier «Ordnung der Dinge» (p. 109) are an obvious allusion to Kleist's own struggle for a valid order. What happens in *Die Marquise von O...* may be seen as an allegory «von der Umwälzung der Weltordnung» (p. 122). It is significant that the word «Ordnung» of the first half of the story yields in the second half to the more non-commital «Einrichtung.» And «Einrichtung» is qualified initially as «groß,» «heilig,» and «unerklärlich» (p. 126), but at the close by the simple and telling «gebrechlich» (p. 143).

The world of *Die Marquise von O...* is made «gebrechlich» through the obtrusion of paradox. That the Count is an angel *and* a devil capable simultaneously of French courtesies and of rape shatters the foundations not only of the ethical framework within which this society operates, but also of the ontological beliefs on which it rests. In this sense *Die Marquise von O...* dramatizes Kleist's Kant crisis. Its irony is not «die handfeste Ironie der Bloßstellung, die einen eigenen und gesicherten Standort voraussetzte,»[14] but an irony of duplicitous double-dealing that distrusts and subverts every position. Instead of being «notwendig eins oder das andere» (p. 121) it is suspended in a state of indeterminacy and contradiction. The dualities of irony are potentiated into the dissonances of paradox.

---

13 Walter Müller-Seidel, «Die Struktur des Widerspruchs in Kleists *Marquise von O...*,» *DVjs*, 28 (1954), 497–515; reprinted in Müller-Seidel, ed., *Heinrich von Kleist. Aufsätze und Essays*, p. 255. Moehring, *Witz und Ironie*, p. 238ff. interprets the language of *Die Marquise von O...* as an ironical satirization of the speech of the aristocracy. That contention seems to me ill-founded.
14 Wolfgang Binder, «Ironischer Idealismus. Kleists unwillige Zeitgenossenschaft,» in *Aufschlüsse. Studien zur deutschen Literatur* (Zürich: Artemis, 1976), p. 311.

So in effect «Ironie ist die Form des Paradoxen»[15] in *Die Marquise von O...*, though not in the implicitly positive sense in which Schlegel conceived it. For Schlegel immediately qualified his aphorism with the rider: «Paradox ist alles, was zugleich gut und groß ist.» This assessment of the role of paradox (and of irony) seems to adumbrate the Hegelian movement from thesis through antithesis to synthesis. Paradox and irony are alike for Schlegel vital instruments of Romantic idealism. It is a measure of Kleist's dissent and departure from the Romantic credo that his irony, far from being the agency of transcendence envisaged by Schlegel, is rather the means for a *mise en abîme* or at least a radical questioning of the conventionally accepted «Ordnung der Dinge» (p. 109). But, curiously, despite this inversion of Schlegel's intended meaning, his phrase nevertheless forfeits none of its cogency: irony *is* the narrational form that paradox assumes in this *Novelle*. Its importance in *Die Marquise von O...* resides not so much in its function as a dramatic tool of deflation and exposure as in its position as, and at the very fulcrum of, the ontological and epistemological disorder that is the mainspring of the narration. This irony could be characterized as a progressive irony[16] insofar as it queries and queers its own ploys and cumulatively diminishes the confidence which the reader may invest in the narrator and in the narrative process, and, by metaphorical extension, in the world itself. The *entente* between the narrator and the reader that animates the reader's ready recognition of the ironic insinuations of the discourse yields to the suspicion that this ironist is himself the butt of the cruellest irony. For though he is able to perceive and to represent the paradoxicality of the human and the cosmic system, he remains as unable as the Marquise herself or, for that matter, the reader to decipher, to interpret, let alone to fathom it. So a progressive irony, because it remains always cognisant of the «gebrechliche Einrichtung der Welt» (p. 143), is the only appropriate mode in which to record this particular vision of the universe. Irony thus asserts its supremacy as the explicit locus of the paramount rift in Kleist's narrative and in his *Weltanschauung*.

---

15 Friedrich Schlegel, *Lyceumsfragment* No. 48, *Kritische Ausgabe,* II, ed. Hans Eichner (Paderborn: Schöningh, 1967), 153.
16 Insofar as Kleist's irony may be characterized as «progressive,» it is related to what is commonly known as «Romantic irony»; cf. Lilian R. Furst, *Fictions or Romantic Irony* (London: Macmillan & Cambridge, Mass.: Harvard University Press, 1984), especially p. 23-48 and 225-39.

«Guillotinenromantik»:
Zu Verständnis und Wirkung der Romantik bei Georg Büchner

HEINZ WETZEL, *University of Toronto*

Büchners Verhältnis zur Romantik war mehrdeutig. Sein Werk ist so sehr von romantischen Zügen geprägt, daß Friedrich Gundolf ihn unter die Romantiker zählte,[1] und noch Hans Mayer, der diese Einordnung mit Recht und viel Nachdruck zurückgewiesen hat, hielt wenigstens *Leonce und Lena* für ein «romantisch-ironisches Zwischenspiel.»[2] Daß auch dies gefehlt ist, weil die Komödie unter anderem eine gegen die Romantik gerichtete Literatursatire sei, ist eine noch neue Einsicht, die sich so schnell und unwidersprochen verbreitet hat,[3] daß es geraten scheint, nach den möglichen Grenzen ihrer Gültigkeit zu fragen.[4]

Zugleich aber finden sich immer neue Belege für Büchners Verwurzelung in der deutschen Romantik.[5] Immer mehr zeigt sich, daß das Romantische, das an der Oberfläche in den Volkslied- und Märchenzitaten in Büchners Werk schon immer sichtbar war, tief in dessen Substanz hineinreicht.

Wenn Büchner aber von der Romantik oder vom Romantischen sprach, hatte er meistens das Triviale ihrer Rand- und Späterscheinungen im Sinn, und er setzte sich dagegen ab. In einem Brief an Minna Jaeglé vom März 1834, also aus der Zeit seiner psychosomatischen Krise, kündigt er ihr seinen Besuch an, beklagt aber zugleich seinen Zustand, in den ihn die Gießener Verhältnisse ver-

---

[1] Friedrich Gundolf, *Romantiker* (Berlin: Heinrich Keller, 1930), abgedruckt in: Wolfgang Martens, Hrsg., *Georg Büchner,* Wege der Forschung, 53 (Darmstadt: Wissenschaftliche Buchgesellschaft, 1965), S. 82-97.
[2] Hans Mayer, *Georg Büchner und seine Zeit* (Frankfurt: Suhrkamp, 1972), S. 307-30.
[3] Vgl. u.a. Hajo Kurzenberger, «Komödie als Pathographie einer abgelebten Gesellschaft. Zur gegenwärtigen Beschäftigung mit *Leonce und Lena* in der Literaturwissenschaft und auf dem Theater,» *Georg Büchner III,* hrsg. Heinz Ludwig Arnold (München: edition text + kritik, 1981), S. 150-68; Henri Poschmann, «Büchners *Leonce und Lena.* Komödie des status quo,» *GBJb*, 1 (1981), 112-59; Jost Hermand, «Der Streit um *Leonce und Lena,*» *GBJb*, 3 (1983), 98-117.
[4] Vgl. Vf., «Das Ruinieren von Systemen in Büchners *Leonce und Lena,*» *GBJb*, 4 (1986), im Druck.
[5] S. die Arbeiten von Bernhard Böschenstein, «Umrisse zu drei Kapiteln einer Wirkungsgeschichte Jean Pauls: Büchner - George - Celan,» in: Böschenstein, *Leuchttürme* (Frankfurt: Insel, 1977), S. 147-59, und von Walter Hinderer, «„Dieses Schwanzstück der Schöpfung": Büchners *Dantons Tod* und die *Nachtwachen des Bonaventura,*» *GBJb*, 2 (1982), 316-42.

setzt haben. Er erliege fast unter dem Bewußtsein, «wie ich hier zusammenschrumpfe.»[6] Auf die ängstliche Frage, was wohl Minna «zu dem Invaliden» sagen werde, folgt das Besuchsprogramm: »Nous ferons un peu de romantique, pour nous tenir à la hauteur du siècle...» (II, 428).

Der Übergang vom «Invaliden» zum gemeinsamen «faire un peu de romantique» impliziert so deutlich wie ironisch, daß aus der Not mangelnder Vitalität immerhin die Tugend zeitgemäßen Schwärmens zu machen sei. Der plötzliche Übergang in die französische Sprache in dem sonst deutsch geschriebenen Brief gibt der ironischen Distanzierung von dem zur Modeerscheinung degenerierten Romantischen eine Richtung, die eher auf soziale als auf nationale Besonderheiten zielen dürfte. Er unterstreicht den Kontrast zwischen der unverbindlichen Konvention und dem wahren Gefühl, der in der Formel «faire un peu [!] de romantique» enthalten ist.

Als er Ende 1835 einen Gedichtband der Brüder Stöber an Gutzkow schickte, setzte Büchner sich wieder von einer bestimmten Richtung der Romantik ab:

> Sie erhalten hierbei ein Bändchen Gedichte von meinen Freunden Stöber. Die Sagen sind schön, aber ich bin kein Verehrer der Manier à la Schwab und Uhland und der Parthei, die immer rückwärts ins Mittelalter greift, weil sie in der Gegenwart keinen Platz ausfüllen kann. Doch ist mir das Büchlein lieb; sollten Sie nichts Günstiges darüber zu sagen wissen, so bitte ich Sie, lieber zu schweigen. Ich habe mich ganz in das Land hineingelebt; die Vogesen sind ein Gebirg, das ich liebe, wie eine Mutter, ich kenne jede Bergspitze und jedes Thal und die alten Sagen sind so originell und heimlich und die beiden Stöber sind alte Freunde, mit denen ich zum Erstenmal das Gebirg durchstrich. (II, 449f.)

Das Bekenntnis zur Landschaft und zu den Sagen des Elsaß wie auch zu der Freundschaft mit den beiden jungen Dichtern, die Erinnerung an die gemeinsamen Wanderungen, all das sind – in Büchners Formulierungen – Bekenntnisse zu romantischen Werten, die der Ablehnung der «Manier» auf dem Fuß folgen. Der Gegensatz zwischen modischer Prätention und echtem Gefühl wird hier ebenso deutlich wie in der Selbstironie durch die konventionelle Formel in dem Brief an Minna Jaeglé.

Auch in den Dichtungen finden sich vereinzelt direkte Anspielungen auf die Romantik oder auf Romantisches, vor allem in *Leonce und Lena*. Der angetrunkene Valerio will «romantische Empfindungen beziehen,» indem er seine Nase wie eine Rose aus dem Gras blühen läßt, während Bienen und Schmetterlinge sich darauf wiegen (I, 106). Schon das Programmatische des Vorhabens steht dem Wesen der «romantischen Empfindung» entgegen, ganz abgesehen von der absurden Profanierung. Aber auch diese Stelle bleibt zweideutig, denn sie stellt Valerios Auffassung der romantischen Naturempfindung mindestens ebenso sehr in Frage wie diese selbst.

---

[6] Soweit nicht anderes vermerkt ist, wird Büchner zitiert nach: *Sämtliche Werke und Briefe*, hrsg. Werner R. Lehmann, Bd. 1 und 2 (München: Hanser, 1979 und 1971). Belegstellen im Text mit römischen Band- und arabischen Seitenzahlen.

Und dann gibt es die Komposita. Als Leonce und Valerio die Einsicht in die Sinnlosigkeit ihrer Existenz durch Aktivität verdrängen wollen und Valerio unter anderem vorschlägt: «So wollen wir Helden werden,» relativiert Leonce das Heldenideal durch den Hinweis auf so unangenehme Begleiterscheinungen wie das Lazarettfieber, den Fusel, Leutnants und Rekruten, um zu dem Schluß zu kommen: »Pack dich mit deiner Alexanders- und Napoleonsromantik!» (I, 116). Wieder steht die Romantik für einen falschen Zauber, durch den hier Alexander und Napoleon zu idealen Heldengestalten werden. Der unangebrachten Glorifizierung des Einzelnen, Mächtigen, hatte Büchner allerdings schon in seinem «Fatalismus-Brief» an Minna Jaeglé vom März 1834 abgesagt, wo ihm «der einzelne nur Schaum auf der Welle, die Größe ein bloßer Zufall» war und wo er das Fazit gezogen hatte: «Es fällt mir nicht mehr ein, vor den Paradegäulen und Eckstehern der Geschichte mich zu bücken» (II, 426).

Als Leonce nachts im Garten Lena gefunden und sie geküßt hat und von dem Gefühl der Seligkeit überwältigt ist, will er sich nach einem ekstatischen Monolog, der auf der Grenze zur literarischen Parodie angesiedelt ist, in den Fluß stürzen. Doch Valerio stellt sich ihm in den Weg und ruft – mit einem deutlichen Anklang an Heine[7] – «Halt Serenissime!» Dann verweist er ihm «die Lieutenantsromantik» über die Leonce hinaus sein müsse (I, 125). Dadurch, daß der Ausbruch des überschäumenden Gefühls als Symptom für eine niedrigere Entwicklungsstufe erscheint, wird auch hier nicht nur Leonce charakterisiert, sondern zugleich auch die pragmatische Weltsicht des Valerio. Mit dem Kompositum «Lieutenantsromantik» bezieht er Leonces eben noch ganz einmalig und intensiv erscheinende Empfindungen auf eine sozial nur allzu fest umrissene, in ihrer Mentalität nur allzu genormte Kategorie von Menschen. Aber der Monolog Leonces ist nicht eindeutig ironisch zu lesen, und deshalb deutet sich in dem Urteil auch die Beschränktheit von Valerios Verständnismöglichkeiten an.

Als in der ersten Szene des ersten Akts von *Dantons Tod* Camille Desmoulins und Philippeau zu der Gesellschaft stoßen, in der sich Danton befindet, kommt es zu folgendem Dialog:

HERAULT. Philippeau, welch trübe Augen! Hast du dir ein Loch in die rothe Mütze gerissen, hat der heilige Jakob ein böses Gesicht gemacht, hat es während des Guillotinirens geregnet oder hast du einen schlechten Platz bekommen und nichts sehen können?

CAMILLE. Du parodirst den Socrates. Weißt du auch, was der Göttliche den Alcibiades fragte, als er ihn eines Tages finster und niedergeschlagen fand? «Hast du deinen Schild auf dem Schlachtfeld verloren, bist du im Wettlauf oder im Schwertkampf besiegt worden? Hat ein Andrer besser gesungen oder besser die Cither

---

7 S. «Seegespenst» aus dem *Buch der Lieder*, «Die Nordsee, Erster Zyklus,» Nr. 10 (Heinrich Heine, *Historisch-kritische Gesamtausgabe der Werke*, Band I, 1, *Buch der Lieder*, bearb. Pierre Grappin [Hamburg: Hoffmann und Campe, 1975], S. 387–89).

geschlagen?» Welche klassischen Republicaner! Nimm einmal unsere Guillotinenromantik dagegen!⁸

Büchner hat die Replik Camilles fast wörtlich aus Thiers übernommen, der sie seinerseits aus Camille Desmoulins' *Le vieux cordelier* zitiert. Die Druckanordnung in der Ausgabe des Dramas von T.M. Mayer zeigt auf den ersten Blick, daß Büchner nur am Anfang und am Ende eingegriffen hat, am Anfang, um diese Replik als Antwort auf die Zynismen Héraults anfügen zu können; am Schluß aber hat er das Adjektiv «klassischen» im vorletzten Satz eingefügt und den ganzen letzten Satz angeschlossen. Der Ausruf, mit dem Desmoulins im *Vieux cordelier* das Fazit gezogen hatte, lautet: «Quels républicains aimables!»⁹ Der Vergleich mit dem Terror Robespierres und Saint-Justs war darin nur impliziert. Indem Büchner ihn auf das Gegensatzpaar klassisch – romantisch bezieht, das er hier einführt, macht er ihn explizit und gibt ihm zugleich eine Qualität, den er bei Desmoulins nicht hatte. Hatte dort die Freundlichkeit der attischen Demokratie der Brutalität der französischen Revolution gegenübergestanden, so hat Büchner den Hinweis auf Athen mit dem Bildungsideal der deutschen Klassik verbunden: Maß und Harmonie bestimmen den sportlichen und künstlerischen Wettbewerb, in dem Alkibiades verloren haben könnte; selbst wenn er seinen Schild auf dem Schlachtfeld verloren hätte, so hätte Sokrates nichts Schlimmeres erwartet, als daß es ihm die Stimmung verdorben hätte. In dem Kompositum «Guillotinenromantik» liegt dagegen die Maßlosigkeit in ihrer letzten, destruktiven Konsequenz.

Die Vermutung Héraults, Camilles Genuß an diesem «Schauspiel» könnte durch schlechtes Wetter oder einen schlechten Platz beeinträchtigt gewesen sein, stellt der brutalen Grausamkeit des Guillotinierens die Empfindlichkeit und Irritierbarkeit des Zuschauers an die Seite, der die Größe des Ereignisses goutieren wollte. Die Ausschweifung, die dem «erhabne[n] Drama der Revolution» (I, 18) seine Einmaligkeit und Größe verleiht, erscheint in dem Kompositum als romantischer Zug, der, auf die Politik über- und in die Realität eingreifend, im Gegensatz nicht nur zum Maßvollen der attischen Demokratie steht, sondern auch zu deren Humanismus. Dies begründet die in Camilles Formulierung implizierte Abwertung der «Guillotinenromantik.»

Gleichzeitig verbindet Büchner hier den Begriff des Romantischen mit dem das ganze Drama beherrschenden Motiv des Schauspiels. Das Theatralische und der Mangel an Wirklichkeit in der Welt der Revolutionäre wird immer wieder an der Übernahme der Institutionen, vor allem aber der politischen Terminologie und Rhetorik aus der Römischen Republik exemplifiziert; dem wird dann immer wieder die Natürlichkeit der Griechen gegenübergestellt.

---

8 Zitiert nach der Ausgabe von Thomas Michael Mayer, in: *Georg Büchner, Dantons Tod. Die Trauerarbeit im Schönen,* hrsg. Peter von Becker (Frankfurt: Syndikat, 1980), S. 15.
9 M.A. Thiers, *Histoire de la Révolution Française,* 15. Aufl., Bd. 2 (Paris: Furne, 1853), S. 453. Leider war mir die Ausgabe Paris 1823-27, die Büchner benutzt hat, nicht zugänglich.

Danton ist zu der Auffassung gekommen, daß nicht nur die politische Aktion, sondern das ganze Leben Theater ist; um in dieser Welt leben zu können, müssen wir eine Rolle übernehmen, eine Maske aufsetzen, uns nach dem Drehbuch verhalten. In der letzten Konsequenz dieses Gedankens setzt er, wie auch Büchner dies in seinen Briefen wiederholt tat, die Menschen mit Marionetten gleich (I, 41). Erst im Sterben erreichen wir die Wirklichkeit: «Wir stehen das ganze Leben auf dem Theater, wenn wir auch zuletzt im Ernst erstochen werden.»[10] Dantons eigene Entwicklung im Drama bestätigt dies: Immer wenn der Tod ihm so nahe kommt, daß er ihn erschreckt und seinen instinktiven Lebenswillen wiedererweckt, übernimmt er wieder seine alte Rolle als Revolutionär; er fängt dann wieder an zu agieren, in beiden Bedeutungen des Wortes. Besonders sinnfällig ist dies in seinem theatralischen Auftritt vor dem Revolutionstribunal, wo er das Publikum mit seiner pathetischen Rhetorik dermaßen aufwiegelt, daß der Wohlfahrtsausschuß wieder Angst vor ihm bekommt (I, 52-54, 56f.).

Aber an eben diesem Punkt, an dem die akute Gefahr, die allein ihn noch zum Handeln reizen kann, gebannt erscheint, verliert er das Interesse. Die Einsicht, daß das Leben Theaterspiel ist, läßt ihn in seine Lethargie zurücksinken, wodurch er sogleich dem Tode wieder näher kommt. Dieses Oszillieren ereignet sich mehrmals, auf besonders engem Raum in der Flucht-Szene (I, 39), und jedesmal streift Danton seine Rolle etwas mehr ab, nähert er sich dem Tod etwas mehr. Die Sehnsucht nach der Ruhe im Tode, von der er mehrmals spricht, entspringt dem Abscheu vor dem Scheinhaften und der Lüge, die dem Theaterspielen inhärent sind und die am sichtbarsten in dem grandiosen historischen Schauspiel der Revolution in Erscheinung treten.

Danton ist so davon durchdrungen, daß man erst im Tode zur Ruhe und zu sich selbst findet, daß es ihm beinahe gelingt, seinen Gegner Robespierre zu der Einsicht zu bekehren, daß man, um überleben zu können, sich selbst betrügen, daß man edle Motivationen für egoistische Handlungen erfinden muß. Von Danton dazu verführt, in diesen Abgrund zu blicken, erkennt Robespierre plötzlich seine Gefahr, aus der er sich rettet, indem er sich in die politische Aktion, die Vernichtung Dantons, stürzt. Seine Skrupel überwindet er durch Selbstbetrug: «Ist's denn so nothwendig? Ja, ja! die Republik! Er muß weg» I, 28). Die Guillotine tritt in Aktion. Das «erhabne Schauspiel» der Hinrichtung Dantons und seiner Freunde wird stattfinden, und in der Tat wird das Schafott zur Bühne, die Akteure suchen nach einem originellen Abgang, und das Publikum spendet Beifall oder äußert Mißfallen (I, 73f.). Aber nichts an dieser

---

10 Vgl. dazu Heines Gedicht «Nun ist es Zeit...» *(Buch der Lieder,* «Die Heimkehr,» Nr. 44), wo dieses Motiv noch eine weitere Dimension erhält. Die Affinität der Romantik-Auffassung in *Dantons Tod* zu derjenigen in Heines Gedicht ist beträchtlich; abgesehen von der Beziehung zwischen Tod und Wirklichkeit, liegt sie vor allem in der Verknüpfung des Theatralischen, Scheinhaften, mit dem Romantischen (Heine, S. 257-59).

Szene ist erhaben; im Gegenteil: das Sterben dieser Menschen ist so armselig wie die Umstehenden mit ihren Kommentaren. Die Vorstellung vom großen historischen Ereignis erweist sich als Illusion, während die Wirklichkeit der nihilistischen Weltsicht der Verurteilten entspricht. Auf der Grundlage ihrer Erfahrung, der sinnlosen Leiden, die sie verursacht und erduldet haben, ist ihnen auch der Glaube an Gott unmöglich geworden. So haben sie am Vorabend ihres Todes keinen Trost, sondern nur die traurige Perspektive: «Morgen bist du eine zerbrochene Fiedel, die Melodie darauf ist ausgespielt. Morgen bist du eine leere Bouteille, der Wein ist ausgetrunken, aber ich habe keinen Rausch davon und gehe nüchtern zu Bett» (I, 66). Selbst dieser Nihilismus trägt in den Werten, die er verneint, noch romantische Züge.

Es bleibt aber nicht bei dieser Weltsicht. Dantons müde Gleichgültigkeit hat ihre Grenze in dem Gedanken an die Einsamkeit, in der er sterben könnte. Er sieht sich darin einer Marter ausgesetzt, die erst endet, als er die Gewißheit erhält, daß der Mensch, der ihm am nächsten ist, mit ihm geht: Darüber kommt es zwischen seiner Frau Julie und ihm zu einem Einverständnis, das unausgesprochen bleibt und auch von der physischen Gegenwart des anderen unabhängig ist. Die Unmöglichkeit der verbalen Kommunikation rational verstehbarer Inhalte zwischen Julie und Danton war schon gleich in der allerersten Szene des Dramas zum Thema geworden; die Unabhängigkeit ihres Verhältnisses von der konventionellen ehelichen und auch von der sexuellen Bindung war dann indirekt durch die Marion-Szene etabliert worden.

Durch diese negativen Bestimmungen erweist sich die emotionale Bindung, die sich in ihren Dialogen und in den auf ihr Verhältnis bezogenen Monologen manifestiert, als einzige Grundlage ihrer Beziehung. In dieser Absolutheit, in dieser ausdrücklich über alle gesellschaftlichen und physischen Bindungen, auch über jede rationale Begreifbarkeit erhabenen Beziehung liegt ein durchaus romantisches Element, das in den einerseits ins Universale ausgreifenden, andererseits Shakespeares Ophelia verpflichteten Bildern in Julies Todesmonolog sehr konkret hervortritt.

Aber nicht nur hier wird der negativen, in den Nihilismus mündenden Vorstellung vom Romantischen als dem theatralisch Scheinhaften, dem Maßlosen und Destruktiven ein Wert entgegengesetzt, der ebenfalls wesentlich romantisch ist. Noch einmal geschieht das in der Selbstdarstellung Marions. Marion ist so natürlich und naiv, daß sie außerstande ist, moralische Prinzipien zu begreifen. Sie erscheint wie die Allegorie einer idealen Natürlichkeit, die sich in der Realität kaum behaupten könnte. Ihre Schönheit, von der Danton vergeblich wünscht, daß er sie in sich aufnehmen könnte, beruht auf dieser reinen Amoralität, auf dieser allgemeinen Unfähigkeit zur Einteilung, Kategorisierung und Ordnung. Auch darin liegt etwas Absolutes, das schon äußerlich dadurch evident ist, daß Marion in keiner Weise in die Handlung des Dramas einbezogen ist. Sie tritt nur hier, in der fünften Szene des ersten Akts, auf und wird anderswo nicht einmal erwähnt.

«Guillotineromantik»

Vor allem aber sind die Bilder in ihrem Monolog mystischen Vorstellungen verpflichtet, wie sie, teils über den Pietismus, auf die Romantik gewirkt haben. Die Vorstellung der alles umgreifenden Einheit wird in den Bildern des Wassers, des Meeres, des Stroms, des Versinkens und Schmelzens vermittelt, die der Intensität durch die Glut und Abendröte, die jeweils, wie es der mystischen Tradition entspricht, mit Fließendem in Verbindung gebracht werden: «ich versank in die Wellen der Abendröthe...»; «Ich bin immer nur Eins. Ein ununterbrochenes Sehnen und Fassen, eine Gluth, ein Strom» (I, 22).

Auf dieselbe Tradition weist die Einheit von Erotik und Frömmigkeit, die Marion für sich beansprucht (I, 22). Marion, eine Gestalt aus dem Geist der Romantik, ist der anderen, der Guillotinenromantik gegenübergestellt. Sie verkörpert die Einheit; für sie verschmelzen «alle Männer... in einen Leib» (I, 21f.). Die großen Aktionen der Robespierres und Dantons dagegen zielen immer auf Trennung, derjenigen in Freund und Feind, und in der letzten Konsequenz enden sie in derjenigen des Kopfes vom Rumpf.

Am deutlichsten aber zeigt sich der Gegensatz zwischen Büchners Auffassung von der Romantik, wie sie sich in seinen gelegentlichen Äußerungen spiegelt, und den romantischen Einflüssen auf sein Werk in der dritten bedeutsamen Frauengestalt in *Dantons Tod*, besonders in der letzten Szene des Dramas (I, 75). Sie könnte mit dem Kompositum überschrieben sein, das Camille in der ersten Szene ironisch gebraucht hatte, doch handelt es sich hier um eine ganz andere Art der Guillotinenromantik.

Hier steht die Guillotine auf der Bühne als das zentrale Requisit; es ist der Abend nach der Hinrichtung Dantons und seiner Freunde. Zwei Henker sind «an der Guillotine beschäftigt» und singen ein krudes volkstümliches Lied, in dem vom Mond und vom Heimweg die Rede ist. Die Gefühllosigkeit in ihrer Routine wird durch den Kontrast verstärkt, als die wahnsinnige Lucile auftritt, sich auf die Stufen der Guillotine setzt und singt: «Es ist ein Schnitter, der heißt Tod...» Sie hatte den Tod ihres Camille ursprünglich nicht begreifen können. Indem sie das religiöse Volkslied aus *Des Knaben Wunderhorn* singt, nimmt sie den Gedanken in sich auf. In ihrem Wahnsinn, der auch sie, zusammen mit ihrem Gesang, zu einer literarischen Verwandten Ophelias macht, ist sie vor der Einsicht in die Wirklichkeit des Todes, wie sie Camille zuteil geworden war, geschützt. Sie redet die Guillotine an: «Du liebe Wiege, die du meinen Camille in Schlaf gelullt, ihn unter deinen Rosen erstickt hast. Du Todtenglocke, die du ihn mit deiner süßen Zunge zu Grabe sangst» (I, 75).

Instinktiv findet sie, nachdem sie die Trennung von Camille begriffen hat, eine Möglichkeit, sich wieder mit ihm zu vereinen, denn ganz spontan liefert sie der auftretenden Wache den Vorwand zu ihrer Verhaftung und Guillotinierung. Mit diesem romantischen Motiv endet Büchners Drama.

Die kritischen und ironischen Äußerungen über die Romantik, die er formuliert hat, und die Satire auf die Romantik, die gewiß Teil von *Leonce und Lena* ist, führen zu dem Schluß, daß er nicht erkannt hat, was er ihr, zumal in seinem ersten Drama, verdankt.

Novalis and Musil

CHARLES N. GENNO, *University of Toronto*

Much has been written in recent years on the subject of Novalis's influence on writers and thinkers as diverse as Schopenhauer, Carlyle, Hauptmann, and the French Symbolists. It is, therefore, surprising that the importance of his contribution to Robert Musil's literary development has been largely overlooked.[1] One possible explanation for this oversight might be found in the tendency among critics to treat Musil as a peculiarly Austrian writer. A blatant example of this is found in a recent article by Jean Gyory, in which Musil is described as «mit allen Fasern seines Seins ... wahrhaftig der HOMO AUSTRIACUS».[2] While it is easy to understand why the author of *Der Mann ohne Eigenschaften* would be given such an epithet, Musil, especially during the last decade of his life, resented being labelled an «Austrian» writer. He believed, quite correctly, that the scope of his works extended far beyond the geographical boundaries of his homeland. Only a few weeks after her husband's death in 1942 Martha Musil felt compelled to object on his behalf to an obituary in a Zurich newspaper. In a letter to a friend she wrote: »Robert wäre ... nicht recht gewesen, daß man ihn immer den „österreichischen" Dichter nennt.»[3]

With the exception of Ernst Mach, the major contributors to Musil's intellectual and literary evolution came from outside the Austro-Hungarian Empire. He discovered Novalis very early in his career. When he was eighteen, he began jotting down clinical accounts of his life and plans for his fictional writing in notebooks. The first reference to Novalis is found in one of these notebooks, in a sketch with the rubric «Vorarbeit zum Roman.»[4] This sketch, which introduces themes which will become major ones in his later works, is largely autobiographical and helps to explain his attraction to Novalis. His protagonist is a mining engineer who develops a passion for philosophy and literature. He has an all-consuming love affair which makes him conscious of his

---

1 Novalis's influence on Musil is mentioned briefly in Karl Corino's *Robert Musils «Vereinigungen»* (München: Fink, 1974).
2 Jean Gyory, «Musil, Homo Austriacus,» *Musil-Forum,* 7: 1–2 (1981), 19.
3 See Adolf Frisé, «Der Zeitgenosse Robert Musil,» *Musil-Forum* 7: 1–2 (1981), 23.
4 Robert Musil, *Tagebücher,* 2 vols., ed. Adolf Frisé (Hamburg: Rowohlt, 1976), vol. 1, 139. Further references to these volumes appear in the text preceded by *T*.

soul, but discovers that he cannot sustain the intensity demanded of the relationship. He describes the experience as a dream from which he is awakened. Standing at the bedside of his dying grandmother soon after, he thinks of his childhood and Novalis.

There are a number of interesting similarities between the two writers' biographies. Both received educations intended to prepare them for a science-related career but which led instead, via philosophy, to literature. Novalis's formal studies encompassed physics, philosophy, and law. He had a thorough grounding in mathematics and mining engineering, but was also well-versed in philosophy, particularly in the works of Plato, Plotinus, Kant, Fichte, Hemsterhuis, Baader, and Böhme.

Musil passed the state examinations in mechanical engineering at the Technical University in Brünn, where his father was a professor in the Faculty of Engineering, in 1901. After having held a junior post at the Technical University in Stuttgart for a year, he managed to persuade his father, on whom he remained financially dependent until 1911, to allow him to abandon his budding career as a scientist in order to study philosophy and psychology in Berlin. He received his doctorate from the Friedrich Wilhelm University in 1908 for a dissertation on the teachings of Ernst Mach. As his perception of the limitations of the sciences as channels to successful living grew, Musil began to share Novalis's enthusiasm for Plato and mystic philosophy. In a diary entry, dated 6 May 1905, he noted why he felt the sudden compulsion to immerse himself in mysticism at this juncture in his life: «Die Bilanz zwischen Bewußtem und Unbewußtem in korrektem Sinne muß notwendigerweise einmal gezogen werden ... Vorher muß man aber die beredeten Data gesichert haben. Da ich augenblicklich nicht reich an solchen Erkenntnissen bin, so ist es meine Aufgabe bei der Romantik u. Mystik in die Lehre zu gehen» (*T*, I, 139).

There are a number of compelling reasons why Musil felt a strong spiritual kinship with Novalis throughout his adult life. The numerous references to him in his diaries and essays provide some of the answers. But often one has to look deeper to find direct borrowings from him in Musil's writings. Karl Corino's claim that the titles *Vereinigungen* and *Der Mann ohne Eigenschaften* are a tribute to Novalis, who makes use of both terms, is very persuasive;[5] however, one can extend the argument much further to embrace the major themes not only of these works, but of most of his other prose fiction. This paper will attempt to shed light on five of these themes: the role of the scientist in society, the relationship between the sciences and ethics, the search for Utopia for society at large and for the individual, and functions of literature and of love in this search.

Both Novalis and Musil considered scientific training to be an essential requisite of successful living. Novalis professed this belief various times in his

---

5 Corino (n. 1), p. 406, 408.

works and in his correspondence. In a letter to Reinhold, a Jena professor, in October 1791, he explained that his recent decision to switch to the university in Leipzig to study mathematics, law, and philosophy was motivated by a strong desire to bring more discipline into his thinking: «Ich muß mehr Festigkeit, mehr Bestimmtheit, mehr Plan, mehr Zweck mir zu erringen suchen und dies kann ich am leichtesten durch ein strenges Studium dieser 3 Wissenschaften erlangen. Seelenfasten in Absicht der schönen Wissenschaften und gewissenhafte Enthaltsamkeit von allem zweckwidrigen hab ich mir zum strengsten Gesez gemacht.»[6] Six years later, in a letter to his dying brother Erasmus, he reiterated his faith in the power of the sciences to guide him through life: «Die Wissenschaften haben wunderbare Heilkräfte – wenigstens stillen Sie [sic], wie Opiate, die Schmerzen und erheben uns in Sfären, die ein ewiger Sonnenschein umgiebt. Sie sind die schönste Freystätte, die uns gegönnt ward. Ohne diesen Trost wollt ich und könnt ich nicht leben ... Es mag mir begegnen, was will; die Wissenschaften bleiben mir – mit Ihnen [sic] hoff ich alles Ungemach des Lebens zu bestehn» (IV, 202).

Like Novalis, Musil regarded the study of the sciences as a necessary and effective method for imposing self-discipline. In a diary entry, dated 14 October 1911, he attributed his passion for the sciences to an early personal need for exactitude (*T*, I, 244). He also recognized, of course, their broader social function. In his essay *Der mathematische Mensch,* published two years later, he extolled mathematics as a *sine qua non* for technological progress. But he was also conscious of its limitations. He believed that the primary value of a scientific education rested in its application to the field of ethics. Nearly all Musil's male protagonists are scientists who, sensing that contemporary European society is on the brink of spiritual collapse, struggle to imbue their own lives with deeper moral awareness. Musil's search for solutions to the crisis encompasses both society at large and the individual. In an early sketch of *Der Mann ohne Eigenschaften* he describes how Anders (= Ulrich) turns to mathematics to bring meaning to his life: «Es schien ihm folgerichtig, daß er sein Leben noch einmal ändere und er beschloß, um an die Quellen zu gehn, Mathematiker zu werden. Denn er kannte/glaubte zu ../ daß diese scheinbar lebloseste Wissenschaft das Geheimnis des Lebens selbst umschließe.»[7] In the final version Ulrich, schooled in mathematics and engineering, sets out into the world, only to discover that reality is at least one hundred years behind the time. Like Anders, he reaches the conclusion that a solution might be found in the application of mathematical methodology to life: «Wenn man statt wissenschaftlicher An-

---

6 Novalis, *Schriften,* 4 vols., ed. P. Kluckhohn and Richard Samuel, 2nd ed. (Stuttgart: Kohlhammer, 1960–75) IV, 97. Further references to these volumes will be made in the text by volume and page number.

7 Robert Musil, *Gesammelte Werke,* 9 vols., ed. Adolf Frisé (Hamburg: Rowohlt, 1978) V, 1979. Further references to these volumes appear in the text preceded by *GW*.

schauungen Lebensanschauung setzen würde, statt Hypothese Versuch und statt Wahrheit Tat, so gäbe es kein Lebenswerk eines ansehnlichen Naturforschers oder Mathematikers, das an Mut und Umsturzkraft nicht die größten Taten der Geschichte weit übertreffen würde» (*GW*, I, 40). The object of his application of scientific methods to problems of the emotions and conscience is to find a healthy balance between reality and phantasy, between *ratio* and the soul, both for society and for himself. The culmination of Ulrich's ruminations is his tongue-in-cheek proposal to Graf Leinsdorf that a General Secretariat for Exactitude and the Spirit be established to commemorate Franz Josef's jubilee.

The bleak depiction of the moral and spiritual state of the world in Musil's essays and fiction has its counterpart in Novalis's writings. He uses essentially the same polarities when he attempts to diagnose the ailments afflicting his world. In *Logologische Fragmente* (1798) he states, «Unser Denken war bisher entweder blos mechanisch – discursiv – atomistisch – oder blos intuitiv – dynamisch,» and wonders, «Ist jezt etwa die Zeit der Vereinigung gekommen?» (II, 524). Novalis shares Musil's conviction that mathematics can play an important part in the realization of this union because of its link with both reality and the transcendental. It is a point that he makes frequently in his writings.[8] In *Das Allgemeine Brouillon* he argues that early civilizations found in the science of numbers a deeply hidden treasure of wisdom, a key to all the closed doors of nature (III, 423); because of its hybrid nature, mathematics is a useful tool for uniting the seemingly incompatible poles of reality and the abstract world: «Alles aus *Nichts* erschaffene *Reale,* wie z.B. die Zahlen und die abstracten Ausdrücke – hat eine wunderbare Verwandtschaft mit Dingen einer andern Welt – mit unendlichen Reihen sonderbarer Combinationen und Verhältnissen – gleichsam mit einer mathem[atischen] und abstracten Welt an sich – mit einer *poëtischen mathem[atischen]* und abstracten Welt» (III, 440–41). The oxymoron here reinforces the argument; Novalis uses this literary device elsewhere, in phrases such as «musikalische Mathematik» and «poetische Physiologie,» for the same effect.

Besides reinforcing the argument, the final phrase in the above quotation introduces another, more effective way of combatting the spiritual degeneration of modern man: through poetry. Novalis regards the poet as a divine agent. In *Blüthenstaub* he likens him to the ancient poet-priest and envisions the day when his dual function will once again be generally recognized (II, 446). Novalis's poet views man and life as metaphors and considers his own task to be the revelation of the transcendent through the immanent. Novalis calls this «magischen Idealism,» a term he first used in the *Teplitzer Fragmente* of 1798 (II, 605). Since life is metaphorical, the poet should use metaphors to depict it.

---

8 For a detailed study of the influence of mathematics on Novalis see Martin Dyck's *Novalis and Mathematics* (Chapel Hill, NC: University of North Carolina Press, 1960).

In his «apotheosis of poetry,» *Heinrich von Ofterdingen,* Novalis attempted to put his theories into practice. In the various episodes the setting and the characters may change, but the message remains the same: the ability of poetry in concert with the natural sciences to bring man back to the state of harmony with nature, that he had once enjoyed in the Golden Age, and to guide him to knowledge of the transcendental. Heinrich is taught this lesson early in the novel on his journey to Augsburg by the merchants who relate fables about poets who have united opposing forces and tamed nature. The tale about Atlantis in chapter three is an allegory in which poetry, as personified in the beautiful princess, and the natural sciences, as embodied in the youth whom she meets in the forest, are united. At the end we are told that no one knows what has happened to their country. According to legend it was swallowed up in a great flood. The moral of the tale is clear: it must be rediscovered.

The best known, and most difficult tale in *Heinrich von Ofterdingen,* Klingsohr's *Märchen,* is a variation of the same theme. Again in allegorical form, it describes how the powers of poetry and love can solve the mysteries of life and help man to attain the transcendental. The father and mother in the fairy-tale personify Intellect and Feeling. The product of their marriage is Eros or Love. Eros's nursemaid and the father's mistress is Ginnistan or Phantasy, and her child, sired by the father, is Fabel or Poetry. Simply stated, intellect and phantasy together produce poetry, intellect and heart produce love. Thus love and poetry are siblings. The greatest threat to the harmony of the family is the father's scribe, the personification of Arch-Rationalism, who is so devoid of humour that he has to tickle himself in order to laugh. As long as Eros and Fabel are at home, he carries out their father's instructions and passes them on to the veiled figure Sophie or Wisdom, the spiritual guide of the family and Fabel's godmother. When Eros sets out with Ginnistan to find Freya, or Peace, who is asleep in the North, the arch-rationalist becomes mutinous and enchains the father and mother, Intellect and Feeling. As in all fairy-tales, everything turns out well in the end. Love and Peace are united, and Poetry has the task of securing victory and preparing the way for the advent of the Golden Age.

The central image in Novalis's writings is that of a new Golden Age. Inspired primarily by the Biblical triadic pattern of Paradise, Fall, and Redemption and by Winckelmann's idealized concept of the ancient Greeks, a number of German intellectuals in the second half of the eighteenth century speculated seriously about the possibility of ever realizing the millenium. In *Die Erziehung des Menschengeschlechts* (1780) Lessing expressed his faith in the advent of a Golden Age in which people would all do what was morally right, without the incentive of a reward or the fear of punishment affecting their behaviour. Schiller in his *Über die ästhetische Erziehung des Menschen* (1795) found paradise, like Winckelmann, in Greek antiquity, where, he believed, phantasy and reason had lived in harmony with each other. In his search for a lost

Golden Age Novalis did not go to Lessing's Old Testament world or to Schiller's Greek antiquity, but to the Middle Ages when Europe was united under Christianity. His «sermon» *Die Christenheit oder Europa* (1799) opens with a paean to this era of peace, harmony, and unity, and ends with a profession of faith in the birth of a New Jerusalem.

Novalis's chiliastic vision does not presume a recreation of the past, however. He never advocated the restoration of Catholicism as it existed in the Middle Ages, nor did he sympathize with those who were so preoccupied with ancient history that they lost touch with the realities of the present and the possibilities of the future. In a passage in *Blüthenstaub* he writes: «Nichts ist poetischer, als Erinnerung und Ahndung oder Vorstellung der Zukunft. Die Vorstellungen der Vorzeit ziehn uns zum Sterben, zum Verfliegen an. Die Vorstellungen der Zukunft treiben uns zum Beleben, zum Verkürzen, zur assimilirenden Wirksamkeit. Daher ist alle Erinnerung wehmüthig, alle Ahndung freudig» (II, 461).

In his *Rede zur Rilke-Feier* (1927) Musil claimed that Rilke was in a certain sense the most religious poet since Novalis, but went on to say «ich bin nicht sicher, ob er überhaupt Religion hatte. Er sah anders. In einer neuen, inneren Weise. Und wird einst, auf dem Weg, der von dem religiösen Weltgefühl des Mittelalters über das humanistische Kulturideal weg zu einem kommenden Weltbild führt, nicht nur ein großer Dichter, sondern auch ein großer Führer gewesen sein» (*GW*, VIII, 1240). Ironically, what he wrote about Rilke could equally well have been applied to his own situation. After reading the works of Nietzsche and Novalis as a young man, he came to think of himself also as a kind of poet-priest. When one reads his comments on the function of the writer in his early essays, one gets the feeling that nothing has really changed since Novalis's time. In *Der mathematische Mensch* he too argues that it is the poet's task to unite intellect and feeling, and in *Geist und Erfahrung* he emphasizes the need for a new evaluation of poetry and science, in light of the current battle being waged between scientific thinking and the demands of the soul. Like Novalis, Musil regards life as emblematic and believes that literature should reflect this. The task of literature, as a mediator between reality and phantasy through its metaphorical nature, is to teach man to recognize and accomplish his potentialities. In *Der Mann ohne Eigenschaften* Ulrich proposes that one should live one's life like a character in a book, stripping away all inessentials and living intensely in order to realize all the possibilities of existence (*GW*, II, 573).

Musil equates Utopia with possibilities – «Utopien bedeuten ungefähr so viel wie Möglichkeiten» (*GW*, I, 246) – and believes, like Novalis, that it must have a basis in reality. Ulrich is the character in Musil's works who experiments most with utopian possibilities. His first attempt, to escape the narrow prescriptions of society by living hypothetically, is soon dismissed as naive and supplanted by a Utopia of exactitude, in which he tries to combat the dangerous rift between exactitude in the sciences and inexactitude in other areas of life by a more universal application of scientific methods. His next attempt, the Utopia of essayism, places greater importance on man's emotional life and is directed at bringing it in harmony with his rational nature. All three are linked by their emphasis on man's ability to reason, and correspond in varying degrees to theories expressed earlier by Novalis. But it is Ulrich's fourth attempt, his Utopia of «the other state,» that best reveals his great debt to the Romantic poet.

Musil first uses the term «der andere Zustand» in his essay *Ansätze zu neuer Ästhetik* (1925) to describe a mental state in which the individual, shedding the conventional fetters of morality, enters into a direct mystical relationship with creation: «Man hat ihn den Zustand der Liebe genannt, der Güte, der Weltabgekehrtheit, der Kontemplation, des Schauens, der Annäherung an Gott ... und vieler andrer Seiten eines Grunderlebnisses, das in Religion, Mystik und Ethik aller historischen Völker ... wiederkehrt» (*GW*, VIII, 1144). Ulrich, in *Der Mann ohne Eigenschaften,* reflects a great deal about «the other state» and begins to read autobiographies and treatises by mystics, in the hope of finding the key for experiencing a *unio mystica*. His incestuous attraction to Agathe is an attempt to enter into «the other state» through love for another human being. It represents the last of a long series of such attempts in Musil's works.

For Novalis and Musil love in its highest form is a religious experience. Heinrich von Ofterdingen voices his author's faith in the religion of love in his famous rhetorical question: «Was ist die Liebe als ein unendliches Einverständnis, eine ewige Vereinigung liebender Herzen?» (I, 288). In a jotting, written in 1797, two years after the death of his young fiancée Sophie von Kühn, Novalis acknowledged that he had consciously mythologized her: «Ich habe zu Söfchen Religion – nicht Liebe. Absolute Liebe, vom Herzen unabhängige, auf Glauben gegründete, ist Religion» (II, 395).

Similar reflections on the nexus between love and religion are strewn throughout Musil's works. One of the earliest is found in a diary entry, dated 20 February 1902, in which he irreverently compares himself in a state of love to Christ and Buddha (*T*, I, 12). Elsewhere he states categorically: «Man kann überhaupt nur lieben, wenn man religiös ist» (*T*, I, 306).

Novalis's belief in love between man and woman as the most complete symbol of the driving passion for oneness in the individual can be traced to the influence of the naturalist philosopher Franz von Baader (1765-1841), whose theories stem mainly from Plato and Jakob Böhme. According to Baader, the first man Adam, as God created him in His own image, was both man and woman, a «whole» person. Because of his lust for the feminine part of his being, he sank from his higher nature into the corruption of the flesh. After this split woman was created from him and the image of God was destroyed. Baader believed that the goal of man should be the re-creation of the original divine image. When a man-soul and a woman-soul feel that they can produce the lost image of God, love arises.

Baader taught that love in its purest state was impossible without the sacrifice of masculinity and femininity. True lovers are hermaphroditic. Love between man and woman becomes a great metaphor of the physical and transcendental, of human and divine relationships. Man's salvation lies in the secret of love. Until now, with the exception of Adam, only one person has appeared on earth in whom both the masculine and feminine within him were united. This was Christ, who stands on the portals of the New Testament proclaiming the religion of love and the return to the lost paradise.[9]

The influence of these ideas on Novalis is evident everywhere in his works, but perhaps nowhere as clearly as in *Hymnen an die Nacht* and *Geistliche Lieder,* both composed in 1799 at the height of his religious zeal. In the six hymns the poet's love for Sophie becomes closely associated with his reverence for Christ. He uses the same erotic language to express his longing for mystical union with her and with Christ, as he moves from the personal to the universal. Just as Sophie initiates him into the secrets of night in the first hymn, so Christ, whose hermaphroditic nature is alluded to in the final stanza of the last hymn, initiates all mankind into the secrets of death. In the seventh of his *Geistliche Lieder* he again equates sexual love and love of Christ as manifestations of one cosmic force.

In the chapter «Romantische Liebe» in *Die Blütezeit der Romantik* (1899) Ricarda Huch discusses the influence of Baader's philosophy on Novalis. Musil read the book in April 1905, and recorded the impact that it made on him in his diary: «Ich lese Ricarda Huch, *Die Blütezeit der Romantik* ... Ein Satz von *Novalis* fällt mir auf: „*Was kann ich also für meine Seele tun, die wie ein unaufgelöstes Rätsel in mir wohnt? Die dem sichtbaren Menschen die größte Willkür läßt, weil sie ihn auf keine Weise beherrschen kann?"* Die darin liegende Auffassung der Seele ist eigenartig ... Bemerkenswert eigenartig ferner die aus Kant gezogenen Konsequenzen. Ich werde mir Baader auf seine Rolle als Mittestehender hin ansehen» (*T*, I, 137). The result of his study of Baader is evident everywhere in the prose works written after this time. The search for perfect love as a means of total communion with the metaphysical world becomes the central theme in his writings. Perhaps the best description of this ideal love, as both he, Novalis, and Baader envision it, is found in Musil's novella *Die Vollendung der Liebe* in his account of Claudine's relationship with her husband: «Es war ein dunkles Gefühl der Welt um sie, das sie aneinanderschmiegte, es war ein traumhaftes Gefühl der Kälte von allen Seiten

---

9 A systematic exposition of Baader's ideas is found in vol. 16 of Franz von Baader, *Sämmtliche Werke,* 16 vols., ed. Franz Hoffmann et al. (Leipzig: Bethmann, 1851-60). Other valuable sources are Julius Hamberger's *Die Cardinalpunkte der Franz Baader'schen Philosophie* (Stuttgart: Steinkopf, 1855) and David Baumgardt's *Franz von Baader und die philosophische Romantik* (Halle: Niemeyer, 1927).

bis auf eine, wo sie aneinanderlehnten, sich entlasteten, deckten, wie zwei wunderbar aneinandergepaßte Hälften, die, zusammengefügt, ihre Grenzen nach außen verringern, während ihr Inneres größer ineinanderflutet» (*GW*, VI, 159).

The major problem that Novalis and Musil encounter in their utopian concepts of love is reality: the fact that the individual, by necessity, is alone and isolated in the world. The attempt to escape from one's isolation and establish total communion with another soul is doomed to failure, because the intensity demanded in such an absolute relationship proves impossible to sustain. The only possible solution is some form of physical separation. Sophie von Kühn's death enabled Novalis to build his cult of love around her. His friend Ludwig Tieck suggests as much in his comment about his rather hasty engagement to Julie von Charpentier soon after the funeral: «Als eine Abgeschiedene verehrte er sie fast mehr, als da sie ihm noch sichtbar nahe war.»[10]

Musil, like Novalis, was interested in death as a key to understanding life. In his novella *Tonka* the protagonist – a young scientist who enjoys reading Novalis's *Tagebuchfragmente!* – recognizes the value of his naive, working-class mistress only after her death, when he suddenly relegates her to the realms of poetry and religion: «Tonka war in die Nähe tiefer Märchen gerückt. Das war die Welt des Gesalbten, der Jungfrau und Pontius Pilatus» (*GW*, VI, 289). In *Die Versuchung der stillen Veronika* the heroine, when she discovers that her yearning to dissolve and become wholly one with Johannes, her lover, will not withstand the pressures of reality, proposes that he commit suicide in order to keep their dream of love alive.

The theme is given an interesting twist in the novella *Grigia,* where it is the hero who dies, not the love partner. When Homo finds his love for his wife threatened by the intrusion of a third person, his own child, he flees from reality to the fairy-tale world of the Val Fersena where, through an affair with a peasant woman, he experiences a more complete union with his absent mate than he has ever known before. In order to perpetuate this *unio mystica* he chooses to die: «Er war kein dem Glauben zugeneigter Mensch, aber in diesem Augenblick war sein Inneres erhellt . . . es war nur ein herrliches, von Jugend umflossenes Wort: Wiedervereinigung da. Er nahm sie in alle Ewigkeit immer mit sich» (*GW*, VI, 241).

Of all Musil's tales, *Grigia* is the one that most often invites the reader to think of Novalis, particularly of *Heinrich von Ofterdingen*. Homo's journey to the south is in some ways reminiscent of Heinrich's trip from the rational world of his father to Klingsohr's land of poetry. The descriptions of the mountains, the mines, and the great lumps of rock-crystal and amethyst, «diese unheimlich schönen Märchengebilde» (*GW*, VI, 235), call to mind similar passages in Novalis's novel. Musil even introduces a symbolic flower that

---

10 Novalis, *Dichtungen,* ed. C. Grützmacher (Hamburg: Rowohlt, 1966), p. 223.

binds Homo to his beloved one, but here it is scarlet rather than blue (*GW,* VI, 240).

From our comparison of the two authors' views on the sciences, ethics, literature, and love, the reasons why neither Novalis nor Musil managed to complete his major utopian project should be clear. It seems fruitless to speculate on if or how Novalis would have completed *Heinrich von Ofterdingen.* Friedrich Schlegel's claim that he had told him on the last day of his life that he had completely altered his scheme for the conclusion (I, 187) tends to invalidate Tieck's theory on the proposed ending. Similar controversy surrounds Musil's ultimate design for *Der Mann ohne Eigenschaften.* The fact is that both men, in trying to find solutions for enormously complex issues in their works, faced the same formidable, perhaps insurmountable problem: how to reconcile their grand vision of a new Golden Age with the reality of their time. The result of their attempt in their creative works is proof that their efforts were not in vain. Perhaps Musil had an inkling of this when he wrote: «Eine Utopie ist aber kein Ziel, sondern eine Richtung.»[11]

---

11 Robert Musil, *Der Mann ohne Eigenschaften. Gesammelte Werke in Einzelausgaben,* ed. Adolf Frisé, 5th ed. (Hamburg: Rowohlt 1960), p. 1594.

Hermann Hesse and Novalis:
A Portrait of the Artist as a Young Dilettante

THEODORE ZIOLKOWSKI, *Princeton University*

In a revealing passage of *Demian* Emil Sinclair describes a drawing that he made at a crucial point in his youth. In the curiously androgynous portrait, which displayed a resemblance both to a young woman with whom he was infatuated and his friend Demian, Sinclair eventually came to recognize a symbolic representation of his own inner self – «mein Schicksal oder mein Dämon.»[1] During those same weeks, he continues, he had begun reading a work that he experienced more intensely than anything that he had previously read:

> Es war ein Band Novalis, mit Briefen und Sentenzen, von denen ich viele nicht verstand und die mich doch alle unsäglich anzogen und umspannen. Einer von den Sprüchen fiel mir nun ein. Ich schrieb ihn mit der Feder unter das Bildnis: «Schicksal und Gemüt sind Namen eines Begriffes.» Das hatte ich nun verstanden.

Some thirty years ago I used that passage as the point of departure for a dissertation on «Hermann Hesse and Novalis» (Yale, 1957). On the basis of empirical evidence it was easy to demonstrate Hesse's lifelong fascination with Novalis – first in the years around 1900 and later in the period from 1917 to 1935. Hesse's literary life begins, so to speak, with Novalis. The epigraph that heads his first published work, the slim volume of *Romantische Lieder* (1899), is a quotation from Novalis's poem «Der Fremdling»:

> Seht – der Fremdling ist hier – der aus demselben Land
> Sich verbannt fühlt, wie Ihr; traurige Stunden sind
> Ihm geworden – es neigte
> Früh der fröhliche Tag sich ihm.

The epigraph for Hesse's first prose collection, *Eine Stunde hinter Mitternacht* (1899), is likewise taken from the same asclepiadean poem:

> Streute ewiger Lenz dort nicht auf stiller Flur
> Buntes Leben umher? Spann nicht der Frieden dort
> Feste Weben? Und blühte
> Dort nicht ewig, was einmal wuchs?

---

1 Hermann Hesse, *Gesammelte Dichtungen* (Berlin: Suhrkamp, 1952), III, 178.

Finally, one of Hesse's earliest stories, «Der Novalis. Aus den Papieren eines Altmodischen» (1900), derives its narrative sequence from the peregrinations of an edition of Novalis's works.

Although Hesse's next book, *Hermann Lauscher* (1901), contains a few passing references to Novalis, its ironies and fantastic episodes stand essentially under the aegis of E.T.A. Hoffmann, whom Hesse had come to regard as the leading Romantic narrator. Between *Lauscher* (1901) and *Demian* (written 1917), however, Hesse falls conspicuously silent with regard to Novalis. There are random references, to be sure, as to the «stille goldene Tiefe des Novalis» in the introduction to *Der Zauberbrunnen,* an anthology of Romantic poems that Hesse edited in 1913. But the Romantic poet no longer dominates Hesse's imagination in a period when such poetic realists as Gottfried Keller provided new models for his fiction.

Then suddenly from 1917 to 1935 the name Novalis again figures conspicuously in Hesse's writing. The well known quotation from *Heinrich von Ofterdingen,* cited above in the passage from *Demian,* shows up significantly in the essay «Eigensinn» (1919) and again in the autobiographical narrative *Der Kurgast* (1924). In 1925, in collaboration with his nephew Karl Isenberg, Hesse edited a small selection of letters and biographical documents by and about Novalis with an appreciative afterword that suggests the considerable extent of his knowledge of the Romantic poet.[2] Novalis is one of the favourite writers cited by Harry Haller in *Der Steppenwolf* (1927). The four-volume edition of Novalis by Paul Kluckhohn is singled out by Hesse in his recommendations for *Eine Bibliothek der Weltliteratur* (1929). The narrator of *Die Morgenlandfahrt* (1932) not only meditates on words by Novalis; in the imaginative realm of the fantasy he also encounters the title-figure of *Heinrich von Ofterdingen.* In the introduction to *Das Glasperlenspiel* (written 1934) Novalis is cited as one of the spiritual forerunners of the symbolic game.

Against this background of empirical evidence, then, I sought to determine the significance of Novalis for Hesse's thought and writing. It was only in the earliest works that anything resembling «literary influence» was apparent to me. In the works following 1917, in contrast, we can speak more precisely of a certain spiritual or temperamental affinity between the two writers, as Hesse gratefully turns to Novalis for quotations that support his own intuitions. In the works written around 1920 - *Demian* (1917), *Klein und Wagner* (1919), and *Siddhartha* (1922) - Novalis's notion of «the inward way» («Nach Innen geht der geheimnisvolle Weg») turned out to be particularly productive: Hesse gave that title *(Weg nach Innen)* to a volume in which he collected the last two narrative works along with two others in 1931. «Magisches Denken» is the term that Hesse used to characterize his complex attitude towards the apparent duality

---

2 *Novalis. Dokumente seines Lebens und Sterbens* (Berlin: S. Fischer, 1925); reissued by Volker Michels as Insel-Taschenbuch, 178 (Frankfurt: Insel, 1976).

of the world, an attitude that Novalis knew as «magischer Idealismus» and a concern evident in Hesse's works from the essays of *Blick ins Chaos* (1920) down to *Der Steppenwolf* (1927) and *Narziß und Goldmund* (1930). The «inward way,» finally, brings both Hesse and Novalis by way of «magical thinking» to the recognition of an eternal spiritual tradition that they call «the Third Kingdom» and that is illustrated in *Der Steppenwolf, Die Morgenlandfahrt,* and especially *Das Glasperlenspiel.*

Now, thirty years later, I see no reason to revise my principal thesis. It is precisely that spiritual affinity that distinguishes Hesse's attitude toward Novalis specifically and Romanticism generally from that of Thomas Mann, in whose works – despite the plethora of references, allusions, and quotations – Hans Eichner has persuasively demonstrated the absence of that essential sense of life that characterized Romanticism.[3] Moreover, I found that the three categories provided a sound basis for my discussion of Hesse's later works in *The Novels of Hermann Hesse* (Princeton, N.J.: Princeton University Press, 1965). However, the wealth of new material that has appeared subsequently – notably the two volumes of letters and documents published under the title *Kindheit und Jugend vor Neunzehnhundert,*[4] the new edition of *Gesammelte Briefe,*[5] and the *Werkausgabe* of Hesse's *Gesammelte Werke*[6] – now enable us to see more clearly and to understand more precisely the emergence of Hesse's early interest in Novalis and the nature of its influence on his first works. I would like to take this opportunity to look again at those early years in an effort to illuminate through a specific case the survival or revival of Romanticism in the *fin de siècle.* To that end I propose to focus on the following questions. When and why did Hesse begin to read Novalis? Why did his initial interest cease so abruptly after 1900? What is the extent of Novalis's «influence» on Hesse's early works?

It is by no means as self-evident as I once assumed (along with most other students of Hesse's life and works), that Hesse should have been an enthusiastic reader of Novalis at the end of the nineteenth century. The second period of his enthusiasm – the years from 1917 to 1935 – paralleled extensively the scholarly and critical revival of interest in Romanticism generally and Novalis in particular, which had grown in intensity since the turn of the century. In 1926, for instance, Julius Petersen remarked that «die heutige Literaturgeschichte

---

3 Hans Eichner, «Thomas Mann und die deutsche Romantik,» *Das Nachleben der Romantik in der modernen deutschen Literatur.* Die Vorträge des Zweiten Kolloquiums in Amherst/Massachusetts, ed. Wolfgang Paulsen (Heidelberg: Lothar Stiehm, 1969), p. 152-73.
4 *Hermann Hesse in Briefen und Lebenszeugnissen,* vol. I (1877-1895), ed. Ninon Hesse (Frankfurt: Suhrkamp, 1966); vol. II (1895-1900), ed. Ninon Hesse and Gerhard Kirchhoff (Frankfurt: Suhrkamp, 1978).
5 Esp. vol. I (1895-1921), ed. Ursula and Volker Michels (Frankfurt: Suhrkamp, 1973).
6 Esp. vols. 11 and 12 (*Schriften zur Literatur,* I-II), ed. Volker Michels (Frankfurt: Suhrkamp, 1970), which contain many hitherto uncollected reviews and essays from the early years.

beinahe mit Romantikforschung gleichgesetzt werden kann»[7] and cited a number of now classic studies from the period – by H.A. Korff, Rudolf Unger, Paul Kluckhohn, Josef Nadler, Karl Joël, Oskar Walzel, Viktor Klemperer, Fritz Strich, Franz Schultz, and others – to prove his point. Similarly, while there had been no new edition of Novalis's work during the second half of the nineteenth century following the two-volume Schlegel-Tieck edition of 1802 (5th edition 1837; 3rd volume 1846), the twentieth century saw a succession of editions, both popular and scholarly, beginning with Carl Meissner's three-volume *Sämtliche Werke* of 1898 and leading by way of editions by Ernst Heilborn (1901), Josef Minor (1907), Hermann Friedemann (1913), and Ernst Kamnitzer (1924) to Paul Kluckhohn's standard four-volume edition of 1929. In 1923 Hesse could write that, while fifteen years earlier the readers of Hölderlin and Novalis had been a small and scattered group of eccentrics, «heute begegnen uns die Gestalten dieser Dichter jeden Tag, eine neue Jugend kennt, liebt, verehrt sie.»[8]

At the time when Hesse first became acquainted with Novalis, however, the situation was quite different. Hesse went to school and came to intellectual maturity during the period of which Rudolf Haym, in the first major study of German Romanticism (1870), wrote: «Im Bewußtsein der Gegenwart erfreut sich das, was man „romantisch" nennt, keinerlei Gunst.»[9] To be sure, Haym goes on, the days were past when the majority of Germans cared strongly enough to attack Romanticism «mit Leidenschaft und Haß.» Yet when people speak of Romanticism, «da meint man alles Unwirkliche und Wesenlose, Alles, was zu leben nicht fähig ist und zu leben nicht verdient.» Hesse clearly shared that prejudice of the day. On 29 May 1895, in one of the pompous literary evaluations that the seventeen-year-old wrote to his friend Theodor Rümelin, Hesse turns from Heine to the Romantics: «Im Prinzip sind mir die Romantiker zuwider.»[10] Even Eichendorff is too romantic for the taste of this discriminating young aesthete – not to mention Tieck and Brentano, whose works he puts aside after only a few pages. «Ihre schwüle Dämmerwelt hatte nicht festen Boden genug, deshalb wird außer Uhland kein Romantiker in seiner Eigenart lange fortleben.» The Romantics have influenced our literature, Hesse concedes, but they will endure only in a few folksongs. As far as the present is concerned, they are utterly irrelevant.»Unsere heutige Zeit vor allem ist nicht geeignet, ihrem Andenken Hochachtung zu zollen und zu bewahren.»

---

7 *Die Wesensbestimmung der deutschen Romantik: Eine Einführung in die moderne Literaturwissenschaft* (Leipzig, 1926; repr. Heidelberg: Quelle & Meyer, 1968), p. 2.
8 Review in *Vivos Voco*, 3 (1923), 290; cited in Annette Kym, *Hermann Hesses Rolle als Kritiker: Eine Analyse seiner Buchbesprechungen in „März", „Vivos Voco" und „Bonniers Litterära Magasin"* (Bern: Peter Lang, 1984), p. 144.
9 *Die romantische Schule: Ein Beitrag zur Geschichte des deutschen Geistes* (Berlin, 1870; repr. Darmstadt: Wissenschaftliche Buchgesellschaft, 1961), p. 3-4.
10 *Kindheit und Jugend*, I (n. 4), p. 472-73; subsequent references in the text are indicated by *KJ* and volume number.

Hesse's remarks conclude with a statement that alerts us to the source of his evaluation. «Wo die Romantik krank wird, und das ist sie mehrmals geworden, da wird sie allzu unerquicklich.» This refrain, in which we correctly sense the influence of Goethe's critique of Romanticism, continues to resound. A year later, in one of the book reports that Hesse sent home periodically from Tübingen to impress his parents, he pontificates: «Wo diese Anschauung krank wird, wo sie die Selbstherrlichkeit des Poeten auf alles, auf Denken und Leben, anwendet, nenne ich sie Romantik. Wenn die Goethesche Anschauung krank wird, was sie bei Goethe selbst nicht tut, wird sie zur romantischen, und Goethe allein steht fest wie auf festem Boden auf diesem schlüpfrigen höchsten Gipfel, zwischen Real und Ideal, zwischen Griechisch und Deutsch, zwischen Antike und Romantik.»[11] As late as February of 1897 Hesse protests to his friend Eberhard Goes: «Mir ekelt vor einigen betrunkenen Romantikern, die aus Wald und Mond und Marmorbildern Kapital schlagen, ohne je einer persönlichen Stimmung fähig zu sein» (*KJ*, II, 67). It should be stressed that Hesse, at this point, means by «Romanticism» essentially the writing of the later Romantics in the twenties and thirties, for he displays as yet little, if any, acquaintance with early Romanticism. But his condemnation covers everything that parades under the general label.

By what process, we must ask, did the young autodidact – who in early 1897 still spoke only with contempt of Romanticism and who up to that time had apparently never heard of Novalis – develop within only three years to the point at which he could publish an article culminating in the statement that Novalis «war der genialste Mitbegründer der ersten „romantischen Schule"»?[12]

When the eighteen-year-old Hesse arrived in Tübingen in October, 1895, to take up his position as an apprentice in the Heckenhauersche Buchhandlung, he set out consciously to train himself for his new job, recognizing that he required a systematic familiarity with German literature of the nineteenth century. Within weeks he writes home to his parents about his reading schedule, happy that his «private study» of aesthetics and literature is now consistent with the requirements of his profession. «Ich treibe noch immer Geschichte der deutschen Literatur von 1790 bis 1890 und hoffe, verhältnismäßig bald dies Stück Geistesgeschichte wirklich innezuhaben» (*KJ*, II, 53). Already at this time he has discovered the writer who was to become his principal touchstone for the next years: «Merkwürdig hat sich mir Lernen und Urteil erleichtert, seit ich mich zu Goethe schlug und damit einen bestimmten Standpunkt für die Beurteilung gewann. Es ist eigen, wie von Goethe aus sich auch die neusten Regungen verstehen lassen.» In the coming weeks and months Hesse reads and re-reads Goethe constantly. He protests that he would be con-

---
11 *Kindheit und Jugend*, II, 82.
12 *Gesammelte Werke*, XII, 229.

tent with a library that contained nothing but Goethe's works. He regales his parents with epistolary lectures on Goethe: «Was Goethe zum Einzigen, Größten macht, ist eben das, daß in ihm allein das Rätsel der Neuzeit sich gelöst hat» (*KJ*, II, 63).

Of course Hesse does not restrict his reading to one author. He studies the classics of world literature – but «alles als Vorarbeit zu Goethe» (*KJ*, II, 75). «In der Hauptsache ist mein Plan, die antike Dichtung, in die mich jetzt Vergil einleitet, in großen Hauptzügen (Homer, Sophokles, Euripides – Vergil, Ovid) zu erfassen, dann Ossian und andre, die Goethe'n direkt beeinflußten, etwas vollständiger kennen zu lernen und mit der Ästhetik Lessings die Vorarbeiten zu schließen» (p. 80). The young rebel, who only three years earlier had run away from school at Maulbronn in rejection of the disciplined curriculum, is led back to the classics, some of which he still reads in Latin and Greek, by his newly discovered passion for Goethe. «Ich hätte nie gedacht, daß ich mit solcher Wärme zu den Alten zurückkehren würde, daß ich, was mir früher lächerlich schien, ein Goldsucher würde, der mit Wonne in den Büchern der antiken Welt den lachenden Goldadern nachläuft. Wäre nicht Goethe mein Ziel, so würde mich wohl nichts so bald aus der trojanischen Ebene ... hinweglocken» (*KJ*, II, 85). More than a year later, in June of 1897, Hesse writes to his half-brother Karl Isenberg that, apart from the belletristic works that he consumes by the dozen to train himself for his job, he has read nothing except Goethe and a little Nietzsche (*KJ*, II, 191).

At the same time the young book-dealer seeks to educate himself by studying publishers' catalogues, newspaper feuilletons, and literary history, beginning in 1896 with Rudolf Gottschall's popular *Die deutsche Nationalliteratur [in der ersten Hälfte] des neunzehnten Jahrhunderts* ([1855] ³1872, frequently reprinted). The references to Gottschall (*KJ*, II, 64, 66, 93) are illuminating, for no work could have been better calculated to reinforce Hesse's anti-Romantic prejudices: «Die *Classiker* schufen uns die künstlerische Form nach antikem Vorbild und mit humanem Geiste,» Gottschall pontificates in the preface to the first edition. «Die *Romantiker* zerstörten diese Form wieder, um die Phantasie von gegebenen Traditionen zu emancipiren und die Dichtung *volksthümlich* zu machen, verfielen aber dabei in eine chaotische Urpoesie und in die Abhängigkeit von nur scheinbar volksthümlichen, mittelalterlichen Überlieferungen.»[13] Thanks to the labours of Hettner, Heine, Gervinus, and Rosenkranz, he continues, our understanding of Romanticism is so complete that it remains only to clarify a few details in the interpretation of individual works. This is hardly worth the trouble, however: «Die romantische Schule hat keinen Dichtergenius von nationaler oder universeller Bedeutung: sie hat Genialitäten im vagen Sinne des Worts, unausgegohrene Talente, deren Unfertigkeit der Urwüchsigkeit des Genies ähnlich sieht.» In Hesse's stern opinion

---

13 4th ed. (Berlin: Eduard Trewendt, 1875), I, xi.

Gottschall's condemnation does not go nearly far enough. «Gelesen habe ich hauptsächlich Gottschall's Nationalliteratur, die mir aber wenig neue Lichter aufgesteckt hat... Wenn es mir einmal einfiele, in Literaturgeschichte zu pfuschen, so ginge ich wenigstens etwas kecker und gewagter zu Werk und würde etwa die Rückenmarkstarre unserer Literatur direkt und allein vom romantischen Element, von Tieck und Brentano, ableiten: das gäbe doch einen winkelrechten Rahmen, wenn auch viel Späne abfielen» (*KJ*, II, 66).

Suddenly, in the summer of 1898 and without apparent motivation, the tone changes. In a letter of 23 June 1898 to Helene Voigt-Diederichs Hesse mentions Novalis for the first time. «Neben allerlei Lektüre treibe ich gelegentlich meine besondere Liebhaberei und weile Abende und Nächte bei den deutschen Romantikern, vor allem bei Tieck und Novalis. Für ruhige, hohe Stunden sind mir nächst Goethe die Meister Keller, Meyer und Storm befreundet» (*KJ*, II, 268). There is of course a certain amount of posturing in Hesse's letters to the beautiful young poetess who, six months earlier, had initiated their correspondence with a fan letter to him. For instance, concealing the fact that he was a book-dealer's apprentice, Hesse sought to give the impression that he was a *littérateur* of more or less independent means; and his preoccupation with such off-beat subjects as the Romantics certainly suited that image. At the same time, there is no reason to doubt the validity of the basic facts. A few weeks later, for instance, he is delighted to learn from his correspondent that her publisher-husband is preparing the first new Novalis edition in half a century (edited by Carl Meissner). «Ich bin in meiner Freizeit ganz mit ernstlichen Romantikerstudien beschäftigt,» he reiterates, «und Novalis ist mir besonders wichtig» (*KJ*, II, 273). Around the same time he reports to his parents that «meine Kenntnis der romantischen Schule geht vorwärts» (*KJ*, II, 274). Novalis along with Wackenroder is his favourite poet, but to our astonishment we register a totally new attitude toward previously despised writers: «Diese und Tieck kenne ich ziemlich, Eichendorff und andre kommen bald an die Reihe. Bei Brentano fand ich wenige, aber schöne, volksliedartige Gedichte. Er ist am meisten „Romantiker", und hat ein ungebändigtes, fahrendes Leben geführt und war voll von Künstlergedanken, die zumeist untergegangen oder verkümmert sind» (*KJ*, II, 274-75).

By the end of the summer it is clear that Hesse's reading in Romanticism has gone much further than casual perusal. And he is now concerned, in a mood of new discovery, with the writers of early Romanticism rather than with the poets and novelists of the 1820s and 1830s who had previously conditioned his understanding of the period. He begins one letter to Helene Voigt-Diederichs by explaining that he is stealing a few moments from Mundt's history of literature, Schlegel's critiques, and Novalis's *Hymns* in order to write to her. His obsession with Romanticism continues. «Diese Romantik!» he exclaims (*KJ*, II, 278). «Alles Heimliche und Jünglinghafte des deutschen Herzens ist in ihr, alle die Überkraft neben aller Krankheit, und vor allem eine Sehnsucht nach geistiger Höhe, eine jugendlich geniale Spekulation, welche unserer Zeit durchaus fehlt.» A telling phrase reveals the reasons for the young aesthete's enthusiasm. «Die Religion der Kunst – das ist für mich das Wesentliche, sie ist das Ziel der Romantik in ihren naivsten wie in ihren raffiniertesten Produkten» (*KJ*, II, 278). He finds ridiculous the mindless adoration of Nietzsche. How much richer was the age of the Schlegels, Hardenberg, Steffens, Schelling, Schleiermacher. «Wenn Novalis die sonst so wenig seltene Gabe der Schreibkunst, des Büchermachens gehabt hätte, so wäre er mehr als alle Literaten neben und nach ihm geworden» (*KJ*, II, 278).

The reference to Theodor Mundt's *Allgemeine Literaturgeschichte* (1846) is revealing, for in Mundt Hesse found an approach to German Romanticism that was quite different from that of Gottschall. Gottschall's history of nineteenth-century German literature devoted a few rather desultory chapters to Romanticism and then hastened on to devote three more volumes to the «modern» (= mid-century) literature that he approved (and to which as a prolific writer he himself belonged). For Mundt, in contrast, «die Literatur der Revolutionsperiode» represented the culmination of the world literature that he had surveyed in the first two volumes of his encyclopedic yet readable work. «Die Revolution ist der Mythus der neuen Zeit,» begins volume three, and here we find a wholly new attitude that sees in Romanticism the natural outgrowth of the phenomenon named Goethe. «Die *romantische Schule* begann und entwickelte sich, ihrem ästhetischen Glaubensbekenntniß nach, allerdings aus der *Goethe*'schen Poesie, an deren Verherrlichung sie zum Theil ihre Kritik ausbildete.»[14] Mundt goes on to elaborate with considerable subtlety the ambivalent relationship of admiration and opposition that characterized the Romantic view of Goethe, as exemplified especially in Novalis. Whereas Gottschall had devoted to Novalis only a few pages at the beginning of a long chapter on Tieck, Mundt places Novalis at the pinnacle of romantic achievement: «Der *Ofterdingen* von *Novalis* hätte ein eben so umfassendes Epos der romantischen Weltansicht werden können, wie *Dante's* Göttliche Komödie das Epos der katholischen Weltansicht war, und der Gedanke mag auch dem Dichter lockend genug vorgeschwebt haben.»[15] Novalis was prevented – both by his early death and by what Mundt characterizes as the excessively centripetal aspect of his nature, which was all centre and no periphery – from achieving his great goal. But the comparison to Dante must have been quite appealing to Hesse, in whose works – from *Eine Stunde hinter Mitternacht* down to *Demian* – the same coupling of names repeatedly occurs.

It would seem, then, that Hesse arrived at his new appreciation of Romanticism generally and Novalis in particular as a consequence of the obsession

---

14 *Allgemeine Literaturgeschichte,* zweite, verbesserte und vermehrte Ausgabe (Berlin: Simion, 1848), III, 91.
15 *Ibid.,* III, 150.

with Goethe that dominated his early Tübingen years. Just as the first year's reading revolved around the writers – from Homer and Vergil to Lessing and Ossian – who lead up to Goethe and then to an appreciation of such contemporaries as Schiller, the course of study by 1898 had led, with the assistance of Mundt, to an appreciation of Goethe's younger contemporaries who, in constant struggle with the great mentor, worked out their own form of emulation. In particular, the acquaintance with Novalis and the writers of early Romanticism served to offset the distaste for the writers of late Romanticism who had previously determined Hesse's response to the entire era.

At the same time, Hesse's course of reading had from the start involved not just Goethe but also the modern literature for which he was responsible in the bookstore and to which he saw himself, as an aspiring young writer, belonging. His letters from these years teem with references to contemporary literature: Keller, Meyer, Fontane, Bahr, Dehmel, Sudermann, Nietzsche. He is astonished to discover that Gerhart Hauptmann, whom he had not admired as the author of *Die Weber* and other naturalistic dramas, was capable of writing a play as poetic as *Die versunkene Glocke* (p. 157). And not just German literature: Ibsen, Tolstoy, Turgeniev, Zola, Jens Peter Jacobsen, D'Annunzio – the various masters of late-nineteenth-century European literature figure in his letters. Of these, however, none meant more to Hesse than Maurice Maeterlinck, of whom he expected more – as he confided to Helene Voigt-Diederichs – than from any other foreign writer (p. 280). One of the first reviewers of *Eine Stunde hinter Mitternacht* noted in those prose poems the influence of Maeterlinck, a debt that Hesse himself, in the preface to a 1941 edition of the work, readily acknowledged.[16] Maeterlinck, in turn, as Hesse observes in an essay of 1900, «hat sich nicht umsonst sein halbes Leben lang mit Novalis beschäftigt.»[17] Hesse is alluding here to the fact that Maeterlinck had recently (1895) published a French translation of works by Novalis; and the name Novalis occurs frequently in the essays of his widely acclaimed book *Le Trésor des humbles* (1896). In his discussion of that collection of philosophical essays Hesse writes: «Neben dieser scheuen, stammelnden Weisheit mutet Novalis wie ein Schulphilosoph an, und doch ist die Verwandtschaft der Maeterlinckschen Mystik mit seinen „Fragmenten" augenscheinlich.» More broadly and without specific reference to Maeterlinck, Hesse pointed out in November of 1899 that Neo-Romanticism in general had attached itself to Novalis. «Sie hat ihn erkannt, den lang verkannten, sie hat ihn neu entdeckt und hat an ihm ein verehrtes Haupt, das allen modernen Streitigkeiten und Kunsthändeln entrückt ist» (*KJ*, II, 401).

It seems likely, in short, that Hesse's sudden appreciation of Novalis came about as the result of a coincidence. His systematic course of reading around

---

16 *Gesammelte Werke*, XI, 19.
17 *Gesammelte Werke*, XII, 392.

Goethe, guided by such appreciative works as Mundt's *Allgemeine Literaturgeschichte,* brought Hesse to Novalis for literary-historical reasons almost precisely at the moment when, in his perusal of contemporary literature, he had discovered and become attracted to Maeterlinck, whose frequent citations of Novalis caused Hesse to regard the German Romantic poet with new understanding. From the late spring of 1898 until 1900, in any case, Hesse's letters are filled with references to Novalis, who is cited during this period with greater frequency than even Goethe or Nietzsche. In September, 1898, he reports that his «Privatstudium» of the Romantics has now led him to the fascinating correspondences of the Schlegels, Schleiermacher, Hardenberg, Tieck, Dorothea, Karoline. «Bis jetzt steht immer noch Novalis mehr im Mittelpunkt meines Interesses als Tieck» (*KJ*, II, 283). In November he is still reading Tieck, Friedrich Schlegel, and Schleiermacher. Above all, however: «Ich möchte fast ein Leben Novalis' schreiben» (*KJ*, II, 295). Later that month he writes a long letter of reassurance to his parents, who are alarmed by what they regard as their son's dangerous obsession with a writer whom they mistakenly take to be Catholic. Informing them that Novalis was not only Protestant but even the son of a Pietist, Hesse proceeds to provide a capsule sketch of this «liebenswürdigste tragische Gestalt jener Zeit» (*KJ*, II, 301) and his works, concluding: «Ich halte ihn für den edelsten Dichter der ganzen neueren deutschen Poesie darin, daß er nie ein Wort geschrieben hat, das bloß Wort und Zierat, Phrase, war» (*KJ*, II, 302). In December he urges Helene Voigt-Diederichs to read «den wunderlichen, lieben Novalis» (p. 311). If he ever succeeds in writing straight from the heart, without a touch of rhetoric, he continues, he would be indebted for that gift to Novalis, this «Lehrer der Wahrhaftigkeit,» «diesem Gewissenhaften der Rede» (*KJ*, II, 311). In February, 1899, he reports that, to calm himself in the evening, he must switch to books that are intellectually less agitating than the fragments of Novalis (*KJ*, II, 321). And in November of that same year he writes to his publisher: «Daß Novalis, der einzige innerlich Feste und seine Zeit Überragende unter dieser Gemeinde, – daß Novalis als Jüngling gestorben ist, das ist das Tragische der ersten romantischen Schule. Mit seinem Tode war ihre größte Hoffnung vernichtet, nach ihm erloschen die andern rasch und ruhmlos» (*KJ*, II, 401). Then, with the new century, the references to Novalis suddenly stop. The occasional mentions smack of recapitulation rather than of continuing study and discovery. In September, 1900, he writes to a friend that his studies in Romanticism have advanced so far «daß ich sie besser als irgendwer zu kennen und zu verstehen glaube, wobei ich als edelste Blüte des jungen Baumes den Ofterdingen, als süßeste Frucht der Spätzeit die Brambilla Hoffmanns empfinde» (*KJ*, II, 495) – a sentiment echoed in the «Tagebuch 1900» that concludes *Hermann Lauscher.* In October he reports to Diederichs: «ich bin wieder tief in die Romantica geraten, besonders Novalis ist mir teuer und unerschöpflich» (*KJ*, II, 500). Inexhaustible perhaps. But for the next twelve years the letters contain no mention of the poet who for two years had dominated his mind and imagination.

In sum, Hesse's period of intense concern with Novalis, when that romantic poet meant more to him than any other writer in world literature, can be dated with fair precision to the last year and a half in Tübingen – from the spring of 1898 to the fall of 1899 – and the first few months in Basel. The seemingly unmotivated turn to Novalis, following a period of outspoken contempt for all things Romantic, can be explained as the result of signals from Goethe and Maeterlinck. It remains to ask two questions. What did Hesse intend to do with his knowledge of Novalis? And why did his interest cease with such puzzling abruptness in 1900?

The evidence does not suggest that Novalis exerted any significant literary influence on Hesse's own writings at this time. Despite its motto, *Romantische Lieder* contains poems that were essentially all written in 1897 and 1898 before Hesse's acquaintance with Novalis. To be sure, the attentive reader easily picks up, in this collection of rather derivative poems, reminiscences of many writers.[18] For instance, despite Hesse's professed early aversion to Tieck, the «mondbeglänztes Heimwehreich» (in «Königskind») is an unmistakeable allusion to the «mondbeglänzte Zaubernacht» of Tieck's «Wunder der Liebe»; the titanic pathos of «Ich bin ein Stern» is distinctly reminiscent of Nietzsche's dithyrambs; «Der müde Sommer senkt das Haupt» (in «Jugendflucht») echoes Mörike's «Um Mitternacht»; and other poems contain allusions to Dehmel, Uhland, and other favourites of the young author. The title that Hesse chose for his collection suggests the new appreciation of Romanticism that he had gained by the summer of 1898 – not the contempt that he expressed during the period when he was actually writing the poems. Similarly, the motto betokens the new enthusiasm for Novalis by which he has just been overwhelmed – and not the guiding spirit of the poems themselves. By a curious coincidence, Hesse announces to Helene Voigt-Diederichs his intention to collect his poems of 1896–98 «auf das Drängen eines Freundes» in the very same letter of 23 June 1898, in which he first mentions his new obsession with Novalis.

Very much the same applies to the prose pieces of *Eine Stunde hinter Mitternacht,* which were written during the second half of 1898. Here again the alert reader can make out in the nine sketches curiously distorted echoes of Hesse's eclectic reading. The first piece («Der Inseltraum») is based on the story of Odysseus and Nausicaa and closely parallels Homer's account of Odysseus's sojourn among the Phaeacians. Yet the story is related in a poetic prose that owes more to Maeterlinck than to Homer. Another episode («Incipit vita nova») is sparked by Dante's *Vita nuova;* at the same time, the episode contains

18 The poems are reprinted at the beginning of the collected poems in *Gesammelte Dichtungen,* v, 375-414; also in the expanded two-volume edition of *Die Gedichte,* ed. Volker Michels (Frankfurt: Suhrkamp, 1977), I, 9-63.
19 In this connection see my discussion of «Die Erzählungen,» in Theodore Ziolkowski, *Der Schriftsteller Hermann Hesse* (Frankfurt: Suhrkamp, 1979), 11-26.

clear allusions to the third of Novalis's *Hymnen an die Nacht* when Hesse's «Schiffbrüchiger des Geistes» speaks of his recovery from the great sense of meaninglessness in life: «Eine stille, traurige Nacht wölbte sich tröstend und schläfernd über mir. Schlummer und Traum kamen zu mir wie Freunde zu einem Heimkehrenden und lösten eine tödliche Last wie ein Reisebündel von meinen Schultern.»[20] (We have already noted the coupling of Dante and Novalis that Hesse appropriated from Mundt.) Still another echo of the third hymn, uncomplicated by hints of Dante, is evident in the sketch «An Frau Gertrud,» which is also prompted by an experience at the beloved's grave:

> Ich stand in dichter Finsternis und wußte nicht, wo ich war, ohne Nähe und Ferne, wie von erloschenen Lichtern umgeben. Ich stand unbewegt und fühlte auf allen Seiten Abgründe neben mir offen, spürte nur meine ineinander gelegten Hände hart und kalt, und glaubte an kein Morgen mehr. Da stand der Tröster neben mir, umschlang mich mit festen Armen und bog mein Haupt zurück. Da sah ich im Zenith eines unsichtbaren Himmels inmitten der vollkommenen Finsternis einzig einen hellen, milden, strahlenlosen Stern von seliger Schönheit stehen.[21]

It would be a misrepresentation to suggest that this work is any more deeply indebted to Novalis than to Homer, Dante, or several other conspicuous influences. Yet it is appropriate that a motto from Novalis stands at the head of the collection. The association between these works and Novalis is established by the author himself. In the letter of 4 September 1898, in which he tells Helene Voigt-Diederichs that he is writing these prose poems, he also refers specifically to his intensive study of the *Hymnen an die Nacht:* «Der Gedanke der „freien Rhythmen" für Novalis' Hymnen ist ja nicht neu. Ich habe mich tief und lange in dieses Werk versenkt, ich kenne es genau und habe den Gedanken dieser Rhythmenform oft und ernstlich erwogen – und verworfen» (*KJ*, II, 280). Yet Hesse's epigraph betrays a curious misunderstanding of Novalis's poem. In «Der Fremdling» Novalis is referring to what he describes as:

> Jenes himmlische Land – keiner der Sterblichen
> Weiß den Pfad, den auf immer
> Unzugängliches Meer verhüllt.

Following this brief description of the submerged kingdom the poet turns and faces life as it lies before him. He greets the few «Heimatsgenossen» who were also saved from the deluge and «die eben, im Stillen / Heut ein häusliches Fest begehn.» It is a poem in praise of Frau Bergrätin von Charpentier, the mother of his second fiancée, and Novalis declares himself prepared to live contentedly in the intimate circle of new friends in Freiberg until death – «dem großen Geburtstag hin.» The poem expresses manly resignation and the positive acceptance of life following the death of Sophie von Kühn. Hesse, in contrast,

---

20 *Gesammelte Dichtungen*, I, 34.
21 *Ibid.*, I, 58–59.

turns away from life: the nine prose sketches of his book represent an attempt to create a land and life that have disappeared – «das Reich, in dem ich lebte,» as he put it years later in the preface to the 1941 edition, «das Traumland meiner dichterischen Stunden und Tage,... das geheimnisvoll irgendwo zwischen Zeit und Raum lag.»[22]

A third work from this period, to which allusion was made at the beginning of this essay, – «Der Novalis» (written in 1900; first published in 1907) – confirms the pattern that we have established. While the story revolves around an old Novalis edition – «eine „vierte, vermehrte" vom Jahre 1837, ein Stuttgarter Nachdruck auf Löschpapier in zwei Bänden»[23] – the style of the work owes more to Gottfried Keller and C.F. Meyer than to Novalis or any other romantic narrator. The tale belongs to the category known in the eighteenth century as «spy novels» – works, that is, in which a series of otherwise unrelated episodes is attached to an object (a gold coin, a pet animal, and so forth) that passes from owner to owner. In this case we learn the stories of various owners – Cand. phil. Rettig, his friend Hauslehrer Brachvogel, their mutual acquaintance Theologe Rosius, Brachvogel's son – from the year of the edition's first purchase in 1838 down to the time when it came into the narrator's possession. The plot has nothing whatsoever to do with Novalis: it could just as well have been an edition of Homer or Goethe or Dante. But several passages incidentally afford insight into Hesse's attitude toward Novalis around 1900.

The emotions that overcome Theophil Brachvogel when he peruses his new acquisition reflect Hesse's precisely:

> Ihn hatte seit einigen Tagen die sanfte Gewalt dieses tiefsten und süßesten Romantikers erfaßt, dessen dunkeltönige von Duft und Ahnung gesättigte Sprache sein williges Herz in ihre weichen Rhythmen zwang. Das klang so mystisch wohllaut wie ein ferner Strom in tiefer Nacht, von Wolkenflucht und blauem Sternlicht überwölbt, voll scheuen Wissens um alle Geheimnisse des Lebens und alle zarten Heimlichkeiten des Gedankens.[24]

This passage refers to the second paragraph of the first of the *Hymnen an die Nacht,* which Hesse quotes in part. Then it goes on: «Die schwermütige Schönheit der Nachthymnen zog durch die Brust des jungen Schwärmers wie ein Wetterleuchten durch eine dunkle, fruchtbare Frühsommernacht.» From that point on Novalis accompanies Brachvogel for weeks. Flowers and leaves used as bookmarks leave their imprint on the pages; pensive notes are jotted with a light pencil in the margin of the *Fragmente;* and the dates of happy days in the forest are noted on the blank page at the back of the volume. As the exposition progresses Hesse himself, in his capacity as narrator, enters the story. At various times he reads «die feinen tiefen Gedichte des alten Novalis»

---

22 *Gesammelte Werke,* XII, 18–19.
23 *Gesammelte Dichtungen,* I, 69. (This story is not included in the 1970 *Gesammelte Werke.*)
24 *Ibid.,* I, 74.

aloud[25] as well as *Die Lehrlinge zu Sais*. He is grieved when one of the company speaks facetiously about his favourite poet. The story reaches its high point when one character reads the famous fifteenth *Geistliches Lied* in order to praise the heroine of the tale, who is also named Maria. Yet in plot or style this story owes no more to Novalis than does C.F. Meyer's *Plautus im Nonnenkloster* to the Roman comedian.

The last major work of this period, *Hermann Lauscher,* represents a conscious turn to E.T.A. Hoffmann: indeed, the third episode (»Lulu«) is dedicated to Hoffmann's memory. Only in the final section («Tagebuch 1900»), which is essentially autobiographical, do we hear reminiscences of Hesse's devotion to Novalis. «Vor dem Schlafengehen,» we read at one point, «lasen wir den dritten der Hymnen an die Nacht.»[26] And elsewhere we sense a weakening of his admiration for early Romanticism: «Hoffmann tritt mir als romantischer Erzähler immer mehr an die erste Stelle, Tieck versagt doch öfters, auch in den Märchen, Novalis ist noch nicht fertig geworden, und Brentano ist doch zu bewußt formlos.»[27] At the same time – and this is Hesse's last published statement on Novalis from these years – Hesse/Lauscher concedes that *Heinrich von Ofterdingen* transcends mere literature and rises into the realm of pure poetry.

It seems clear, then, that Hesse's intense preoccupation with Novalis did not result in any slavish imitation – not even to the extent that he took E.T.A. Hoffmann and Maeterlinck as models for his prose of that period. To be sure, Novalis's «inward way» very much suited the mood of the young recluse of Tübingen, who spent his days selling books that he might spend his nights reading and writing them. Novalis was the perfect model for the ambitious young writer who, not yet having established himself, retreated nightly into aesthetic kingdoms «eine Stunde hinter Mitternacht.» But if Hesse did not attempt to compose his own literary works after the fashion of Novalis, he still hoped to make use of Novalis for literary purposes.

We have already seen that Hesse had toyed with the idea of writing a life of Novalis; indeed, that notion did not let him go for a quarter century until, in 1925, he collaborated with his nephew Karl Isenberg in a documentary biography of the poet. In 1898, however, his ambitions rapidly became larger. The letters to his parents, while grandiose in tone, always contain a nugget of truth. In October, for instance, he reports that, while his colleagues from the bookstore escape in the evenings to beer and cards in the taverns, he retreats from the exteriors of books to their insides «und betreibe planmäßig größere literarhistorische und überhaupt geistesgeschichtliche Studien, die, wie ich hoffe, sich später werden verwerten lassen» (*KJ*, II, 286). This systematic course of read-

---

25 *Ibid.*, I, 88.
26 *Ibid.*, I, 193.
27 *Ibid.*, I, 200.

ing was gradually leading him – according, incidentally, to the plan of Mundt's history – to «die glänzende Reihe von Fichte bis Schleiermacher.» The young autodidact sorely regrets his ignorance of Kant but is concerned at the moment with Schleiermacher's life (by which, as subsequent comments make clear, he means Dilthey's *Das Leben Schleiermachers)* as well as his *Reden über die Religion* and *Monologe.* A month later he confides that he is resting from his labours with «den überfeinen, verwirrenden états d'âme der Romantiker» (*KJ,* II, 298). At the same time, he is fascinated by the details of biography and says that, while he could never be more than a dilettante in art history, he feels a genuine urge to master literary history. He even postpones the study of French in order to pursue his readings in Romanticism. When we finally learn of his plan, in April of 1899, he is already pessimistic about its feasibility. «Ich weiß jetzt, daß ich meine „Deutsche Romantik" nicht oder erst als alter Mann schreiben werde» (*KJ,* II, 345). He has been working for weeks on a chapter about Novalis, but his health necessitated an interruption of the studies that he had been pursuing so intensively. He longs to get back to work, «vor allem an meine unterbrochenen Novalisstudien,» but realizes that he can do little more that summer (*KJ,* II, 355).

At this point we should remind ourselves that the literary histories with which Hesse was acquainted were written mainly not by literary scholars but by *littérateurs.* Gottschall and Mundt were after all professional writers who also produced popular literary histories as an aspect of their general literary oeuvre. When Hesse thought of literary history, therefore, he did not have in mind a scholarly work but rather a well-informed popular work that would provide for his generation more or less what Mundt had done fifty years earlier. In one sense his enterprise can be understood as the dilettante's revenge on the university community in Tübingen, where the young bookseller's apprentice was destined to remain an outsider or – after the title of Novalis's poem that he twice ransacked for mottoes – «der Fremdling.» Hesse's sense of timing was accurate. The recent popularity of Neo-Romantic writers had awakened an interest in older German Romanticism, whose centennial could now appropriately be celebrated in almost any year (p. 400). Hesse recognized the need for a good new book. He had read the older works; but apart from Dilthey in *Das Leben Schleiermachers* and Haym in *Die romantische Schule,* both works already thirty years old, «hat kein Literarhistoriker die Fülle und den eigenartigen Reiz dieser Zeit recht begriffen. Jahrzehntelang wurde unter der Etikette „romantisch" kritiklos ein ganzer Wust von Literatur zusammengefaßt und abgetan» (*KJ,* II, 230). This is the task that Hesse now set for himself – the goal of the intensive studies of the past two years, the fruit of the extensive detail-work in literary history and biography that he had undertaken to the point at which it had affected his health and his vision. This, he had come to believe, was *his* terrain – the realm that he had discovered and mastered better than any of the literary scholars of the period.

Then on 9 January 1900, the sobering notice to Helene Voigt-Diederichs: «Über Ricarda Huchs Buch war und bin auch ich sehr erfreut» (*KJ*, II, 434). To be sure, on the basis of two years' careful study of the same material he has penciled several critical notations in the margin of his copy. «Aber trotzdem – das Buch ist meisterhaft, und einige Hauptschwierigkeiten (vor allem Fr. Schlegel) sind glänzend gelungen.» It requires little imagination to appreciate the ambivalence with which the aspiring young critic greeted the masterly work, which had come virtually unheralded out of nowhere and whose first volume (*Blütezeit*, 1899) accomplished almost precisely the task that Hesse had set out two years earlier to do. Without transition and without even a break in the paragraph Hesse moves on – no doubt to mask his intense disappointment – to talk about the new interests, chiefly in art history, that have begun to occupy him in Basel. «Die frühere reichliche kunsthistorische Lektüre wird nun erst wirksam und zeigt sich nicht als unnütz. Vor allem aber ist Böcklin da, unvergleichlich berückend, und der geniale Holbein, der mich äußerst anzieht und beglückt.»

The references to Novalis do not stop absolutely following the publication of Ricarda Huch's *Die Romantik*. On 21 January 1900, Hesse published a brief piece on Novalis in the *Allgemeine Schweizer Zeitung* – the first of the hundreds of literary reviews that he was to publish in coming decades.[28] The piece begins with a sentiment that might have come straight out of Maeterlinck. «Es gibt gewisse stille Kinder mit großen, vergeistigten Augen, deren Blick schwer zu ertragen ist. Man prophezeit ihnen kein langes Leben und betrachtet sie wie vornehme Fremdlinge mit ebensoviel Ehrfurcht als Mitleid.» Hesse observes that the general public knows only Novalis's name and perhaps two or three songs. Few realize that he was the most brilliant among the founders of the early Romantic school, whose achievements were soon eclipsed by the trivial works of later writers who co-opted the label «Romantic.» One brief paragraph, which locates Novalis among his contemporaries and cites appreciatively the works of Dilthey and Haym, reveals the extent of Hesse's knowledge of the period that he calls one of the most fascinating in German literature. Novalis is more difficult to read than any other writer of the period, and we know his works almost exclusively in fragmentary form. Yet a single line of Novalis offers more enchantment than entire works by Tieck and others. Young Hesse's appreciation anticipates the ironic amusement of Harry Haller: «In den einzelnen Stücken seiner Arbeit, auch in seinen Liedern, ist ein ganz unbeschreiblicher Duft von Zartheit, von Seele; es gibt Worte von ihm, die uns berühren wie eine Liebkosung und solche, bei denen man den Atem anhalten möchte, um sich ganz dieser reinen, fast überirdischen Schönheit hinzugeben.» Following a paragraph on Novalis's personality and death, Hesse notes that his works appear to fall into two distinct categories – philosophy

---

28 *Gesammelte Werke*, XII, 229-34.

and poetry. But even his more philosophical works speak to us essentially as poetry. «Vielleicht hat überhaupt kein anderer Deutscher eine so überquellend poetische Seele besessen, und dieser eine fiel dem verzehrenden Geist seiner Zeit zum Opfer.» But this delicate blossom of Romanticism was despoiled by the fashionable writers of the twenties and thirties, who displaced Novalis and ruined the reputation of «Romanticism,» making it appear reactionary and outmoded. Among the best contemporary writers, however, one senses according to Hesse certain moods and efforts that are conspicuously close to those around 1800. Hesse closes his review with an expression of hope that the new edition of Novalis's works will serve as a touchstone by which the Neo-Romantics may measure their own achievements.

Although this piece constitutes Hesse's most elaborate statement on Novalis from these early years, it should not be read as a development beyond the earlier studies. It is after all the review of an edition that had appeared over a year earlier during the period of Hesse's most intense concern with Novalis and that he had studied at the time (December, 1898) with appreciation – even if the tone of the editor's introduction struck him as «schrecklich kühl» (*KJ*, II, 311). Read carefully, moreover, it is not a review at all but an essay justified as a review. In fact, we are most likely dealing here with an extract from the chapter on Novalis that gave Hesse so much grief during the spring of 1899. As such, it offers a sample of the kind of literary history that Hesse had in mind to write when his plans and ambitions were frustrated by the publication of Ricarda Huch's magisterial monograph.

Essentially the same is true of another piece that Hesse published in those early Basel months – «Romantik. Eine Plauderei.»[29] The article begins with a discussion of the term «romantisch» as it was used by writers and thinkers around 1800. Hesse moves on to cite again the confusion in the public mind of the genuine early Romanticism with the superficial products of later writers. «Novalis ward rasch vergessen, während der Romanschmierer Fouqué Erfolg um Erfolg erzielte.» Despite his acknowledgement of such late efflorescences as Eichendorff and Hoffmann, «Die echte Romantik dürfen wir allein bei Novalis suchen, denn die Schlegel waren beide, trotz tiefer Einsichten und sublimen Verständnisses, dichterisch impotent.» The article continues with a brief appreciation of Novalis – «Der „Ofterdingen" ist zeitlos, er spielt heute, hie und immer, er ist die Geschichte nicht einer Seele, sondern der Seele überhaupt» – and concludes with the hope that a new generation will be able to make productive use of his example. Again we are obviously dealing with paragraphs written originally for Hesse's own now superfluous monograph on Romanticism.

Otherwise Novalis hardly figures in Hesse's letters and other writings after 1900. Exactly how are we to understand this abrupt loss of interest in the poet

---

29 *Allgemeine Schweizer Zeitung* (17 June 1900); repr. *Gesammelte Werke,* XI, 105-09.

who for two years was virtually the spokesman of Hesse's mind and soul? With the benefit of hindsight we know that Novalis was later to re-emerge strikingly in Hesse's thought and imagination. So it would be an oversimplification to assume that his impact amounted to no more than the superficial fad of a fickle young man. The emphasis needs to be placed differently.

Despite the borrowed epigraphs and the plot-device of «Der Novalis» the romantic poet was never important to Hesse as a model for his writing. The *Romantische Lieder* were composed before the acquaintance with Novalis and *Hermann Lauscher* is already clearly dedicated to Hoffmann. Only in the prose pieces of *Eine Stunde hinter Mitternacht* does Novalis – notably the *Hymnen an die Nacht* – constitute a secondary influence after Maeterlinck and Dante. Although his admiration was profound and genuine, Hesse realized that Novalis could not serve as a literary archetype. He chose instead to communicate that admiration – and, incidentally, to establish his own reputation as a man of letters – with a major literary history of romanticism. When Ricarda Huch anticipated his project, he simply shifted his goals as critic and dilettante to the new interests that opened up before him in Basel. Under the pressure of ambition and more appropriate literary models Novalis was displaced.

It was seventeen years before Hesse, in *Demian,* turned back again to the favourite poet of his youth. Emil Sinclair recalls the volume of Novalis, with the aphorisms that attracted him mysteriously though he did not understand them. Now the encounter with Demian has changed his perception of these statements. «Das hatte ich nun verstanden.» Similarly Hesse himself came to a new appreciation of Novalis, whose works he had studied with a sometimes uncomprehending intensity during his Tübingen years. Now his own experiences of the war years – notably divorce, death, psychoanalysis, and war itself – had given him a new maturity and a new insight into Novalis. Hesse never wrote his history of German Romanticism: Ricarda Huch and the scholarly studies that soon followed her example had made that effort unnecessary. But in the thought and works of the mature Hesse Novalis played a fruitful role that he had never held in the works of the lonely young dilettante of the *fin de siècle.*

Thomas Mann and Novalis. On Thomas Mann's attitude to Romantic Political Thought during the Weimar Republic

HANS REISS, *University of Bristol*

«Thomas Mann and Novalis» is a story that tells us much about a crucial stage in Thomas Mann's intellectual development. What Mann took from Novalis and how he used it brings out vividly how he turned away from his German nationalism of World War I and began to champion both the Weimar Republic and cosmopolitan ideals. Moreover, Thomas Mann and German Romanticism is an important subject, and, not surprisingly, it is one on which Hans Eichner has written. Appropriately, too, it brings together two of the main areas of German literature and thought in which he has made his mark as a scholar. In his important article «Thomas Mann und die deutsche Romantik» he demonstrated[1] not only that Thomas Mann's interpretation of Novalis's political thought is implausible, but that it is a mistaken re-interpretation. Novalis was not, as Mann maintained, a republican. Hans Eichner reminds us[2] that the only purely political piece of writing that Novalis published (*Glauben und Liebe oder Der König und die Königin,* 1798) was written in praise of the Prussian monarchy, to mark the accession to the throne of Frederick William III and his consort Louise in 1797. His strictures are severe but just, when he writes: «es ist schwer zu rechtfertigen, daß Thomas Mann in seiner Rede „Von Deutscher Republik" die Weimarer Demokratie und das von Novalis verherrlichte Preußen, die sich unterscheiden wie Tag und Nacht, in denselben Topf warf. Es handelt sich um eine seltsame Form der Selbsttäuschung.»[3]

But it would be wrong to leave it at that. Rather we should pursue Hans Eichner's stimulating remarks a little further. Great writers are often as interesting when they get things wrong, as when they get them right. It would certainly be foolish to treat Mann's mistaken interpretation of Novalis as if he

---

1 Hans Eichner, «Thomas Mann und die deutsche Romantik,» *Das Nachleben der Romantik in der modernen deutschen Literatur,* ed. Wolfgang Paulsen, Poesie und Wissenschaft, 14 (Heidelberg: Lothar Stiehm, 1969), p. 152-73. Eichner writes: «Als Redner und Essayist bezog sich Thomas Mann vor allem deshalb so oft auf Novalis, um der deutschen Jugend der zwanziger Jahre den Gedanken der Demokratie näherzubringen – und dazu bedurfte es einer gewaltsamen Umdeutung dessen, wofür Novalis auf dem Gebiet des Politischen stand» (p. 155).
2 *Ibid.,* p. 155.
3 *Ibid.,* p. 155.

were a student who had committed a howler. There is no case for looking at his misleading interpretation in a condescending manner. Not that Hans Eichner encouraged us to do so.

Indeed, Eichner's concern in his essay was to show how the Romantics' approach to the world differed fundamentally from that of Thomas Mann: most Romantics were believing Christians, Mann was a sceptic.[4] Our aim here is, however, more limited and more specific. It turns on the question as to how and why Mann appropriated Novalis for his own purposes in the important address «Von Deutscher Republik» of 15 October 1922, given to mark Gerhart Hauptmann's sixtieth birthday, and in other writings.

For Mann to turn Novalis into a champion of democratic republicanism, as he did, is indeed an astonishing *tour de force*. But he did not rush into this position heedlessly. He knew Novalis well and had studied him carefully. From Novalis's work he selected, as was his wont, what suited him, and he ignored or rejected what did not. He thought that as an imaginative writer he had a right to do that.

What manner of political thinker was Novalis?[5] He never fully developed his political thought, for he died too young at the age of 28. But even if he had lived longer, it is doubtful whether he would have ever systematized his ideas. For he was not a systematic thinker, but rather threw out hints, leaving behind, as it were, a quarry of ideas which other Romantics mined to build their edifices. In fact, he wrote relatively little on politics. Much of his work, even *Glauben und Liebe,* is a collection of aphoristic sayings. And the only longer piece of writing that can be called political, *Die Christenheit oder Europa* (1799) remained a fragment. Yet his thought is interesting, pregnant with ideas and the suggestive power of a poet's imagination; for he possessed an intuitive understanding of political problems, even if some of his pronouncements may appear naive. That was certainly the view of the King of Prussia, Frederick William III, to whom *Glauben und Liebe* was dedicated; for he thought that its author expected more from a monarch than a human being was capable of achieving.[6]

Novalis, like other Romantics, rejected Kantian epistemology. He turned to Fichte, a far less important philosopher, for inspiration. But he was not an out-and-out Fichtean, though he may well have picked up from him the organic theory of the state which Fichte adumbrated in *Grundlage des Naturrechts*

---

4 Cf. *ibid.*, p. 155f. and also p. 172ff.
5 The following account is based on my book *Politisches Denken in der deutschen Romantik* (Bern: Francke, 1966), particularly p. 29–39 (with bibliography); see also the earlier English edition of this book, *The Political Thought of the German Romantics 1793-1815* (Oxford: Blackwell, 1955), p. 24–27. Cf. also Hans Wolfgang Kuhn, *Der Apokalyptiker und die Politik. Studien zur Staatsphilosophie des Novalis* (Freiburg: Rombach, 1963), reviewed by me in *PolVj,* 4 (1963), 438–41.
6 Cf. Max Preitz, *Friedrich Schlegel und Novalis* (Darmstadt: Gentner, 1957), p. 122.

(1796).[7] Above all, Novalis rejected the rational approach to politics as prosaic. What lay behind that (as Hans Eichner, in a brilliant article on «The Rise of Modern Science and the Genesis of Romanticism,» has recently shown[8]) was hostility to the rise of science. The scientific approach, if applied to social life, appeared to Romantics like Novalis mistaken in principle. This may appear surprising; for Novalis was, by training, a mining engineer, and by all accounts a successful one. But he believed that intuitive thought, or thinking by way of analogy, was more fruitful than scientific analysis. The poetic method alone could do justice to the diversity of life. It was imperative to focus attention on individual events and personalities: thus more could be learned about society than by seeking to establish general laws. Only then could individuality be preserved; but individuality would have to be submerged into an organic whole which would engender a true community, united by emotional bonds. He objected both to the French Revolution and enlightened absolutism because they were based on rationalist constructions. Therefore, they were inherently unstable and would not last.

A genuine monarchy had to be created; but to create it entailed a revolution in thought. For that new monarchy should inspire the people with an ideal which would counteract the forces unleashed by the French Revolution. For men need models to emulate – and that is why they need a monarchy. Novalis placed high hopes in the new Prussian King Frederick William III and his consort Queen Louise. He also believed that a royal couple could inspire men and women to rally round them and thus give the Prussian state a coherence which had hitherto been lacking. The machine-like manner by which Frederick the Great (1740-86) had administered Prussia was not good enough.[9] Indeed, it was destructive. Novalis had perceived the weakness of Prussia which in due course fell like a house of cards when confronted by the might of Napoleon's armies. (However, perhaps it was not all that difficult to perceive Prussian weakness after the defeat during the campaign in France of Autumn 1792!) Novalis felt that a state needed strength and stability to survive and recognized that rational arguments were not enough to bind men together. Emotional ties were needed to appeal to man's irrational nature. But Novalis's own conclusion drawn from this insight is by no means acceptable either. Admittedly, citizens ought to be committed to the state in which they live, if it is to survive. Novalis went further, however. He demanded that the whole personality be passionately engaged.[10] Cool, detached thought is inadequate. The principles

---

7 For Fichte see my account in *Politisches Denken in der deutschen Romantik*, p. 18-26 and in *The Political Thought of the German Romantics* p. 11-22 as well as my article «Fichte als politischer Denker,» *Archiv für Rechts- und Sozialgeschichte*, 47 (1959), 159-78.
8 *PMLA*, 97 (1982), 8-30.
9 Cf. Novalis, *Schriften. Die Werke Friedrich von Hardenbergs*, ed. Paul Kluckhohn and Richard Samuel, 2nd ed. (Stuttgart: Kohlhammer, 1960-75), II, 494. All further references in the text and in the notes are to this edition (abbreviated as *Schr.*).
10 *Schr.*, III, 313.

of the *Aufklärung* are mistaken and do harm. The unity of Europe can be achieved only if men turn away from intellectualism. The emotional and sensuous, the intuitive and imaginative have to be harnessed to the full. Only then will citizens be prepared to give full allegiance to the state.

Novalis's thought is incontrovertibly irrationalist, indeed often even obscurantist. To realize that men's motives are not purely rational and that irrational forces draw them together in society or in a state does not mean that we need to abandon rational discourse. Thomas Mann was convinced that, while we should be fully aware of, and indeed welcome, life's irrational side, we should nonetheless use our reason to cope with our irrational urges. Novalis, however, drew dangerous conclusions; by implication, he suggests that a war against reason ought to be waged. As a result, for instance, some necessary distinctions are glossed over. He claims – and Thomas Mann here sided with him – that a monarchy can be republican, and a republican can be monarchical,[11] deliberately obscuring the differences between the two forms of government and without depicting the institutional safeguards, such as separation of powers, needed to prevent abuse of power. On these Kant for one insisted, who also believed that a (constitutional) monarch could preside over a «republican» constitution. But Novalis was not interested in analysing institutions. His concern was with the spiritual life of a nation.

It is surprising indeed that Thomas Mann turned to Novalis as his principal witness when defending the Weimar Republic, bracketing him with Walt Whitman, that scion of American democracy, when for the first time he appeared in public to abjure his nationalist views which he had expounded at such formidable (and tedious) length in *Betrachtungen eines Unpolitischen* (1918). For in «Von deutscher Republik» he came out in favour of German republicanism, much to the astonishment and even indignation of those who had believed him to be an intellectual champion of German conservativism and nationalism and thus a supporter of the Hohenzollern monarchy.

Why did Mann speak in favour of the Weimar Republic? And why did he appeal to Novalis when he did so? Surely he could have found other German classics to support his new-found Republicanism – the works of Wieland, Schiller, or Kant could have been used more easily for that purpose, not to speak of later writers, such as Heine. But, of course, Heine would never have done. He was a Jew and would have carried no weight at all with the overwhelming majority of German youth whom Mann wished to «convert.» Wieland would likewise have been dismissed as a superficial rococo writer, suspect on account of his Enlightenment attitudes and of his style reminiscent of French culture.

---

11 Cf. *Schr.*, II, 490. Cf. also Thomas Mann, *Gesammelte Werke in dreizehn Bänden* (Frankfurt: Fischer, 1960), XI, 812. All further references in the text and in the notes are to this edition (abbreviated as *GW*). Mann writes: «Meine Heimat war ein republikanischer Bundesstaat des Reiches, wie diejenigen, aus denen es heute noch besteht.» (*GW*, XI, 818).

Kant was too abstract a philosopher to attract Mann. On the other hand, Schiller would have been a powerful witness. But despite his being elected an honorary citizen of France by the French National Assembly, he did not, in his prose writings, advocate a republic. And from the republican par excellence, Verrina in *Die Verschwörung des Fiesko zu Genua,* Thomas Mann explicitly distances himself since, with Schiller, he considers him to be too rigid an exponent of republican virtue. Still, Schiller's *Wilhelm Tell* might have served Mann's purposes, for instance, but he chose not to cite this drama. And perhaps with good reason; for he obviously felt that Novalis's writings were the *right* choice. Why was that so?

The actual facts are beyond contention. During the 1914-18 war Thomas Mann had temporarily abandoned work on his novel, *Der Zauberberg,* and unburdened himself of the ideas on culture and politics which he had been pondering for some years. He wrote essays, «Gedanken im Kriege» (1914), «Friedrich und die große Koalition» (1915), and finally the major treatise *Betrachtungen eines Unpolitischen.* Mann's own personal relations with his elder brother Heinrich clearly coloured his approach. Heinrich had opted for Western ideas: he defended the intellectual heritage of Enlightenment thought; he was a liberal, a radical, even a socialist; and above all, his fiction was politically committed. Thomas rejected all Heinrich's ideas and actions outright. Unlike Heinrich, Thomas believed that it was his duty to defend German culture against the Western allies and their propaganda. He preached the «unpolitical» nature of the Germans. For him that was the main feature of German culture, its specific individuality. He defended German national aspirations by claiming that «Kultur» made it superior to Western «Zivilisation» which, by comparison, lacked depth and strength. There is no need here to analyse the complex, tortuous, and unconvincing arguments of this infelicitous book. When Germany was defeated, Thomas Mann did not change his opinion immediately. For some time he still felt convinced of the superiority of German culture and of the inferiority of Western ideas. But he did not hark back for long to the world of Imperial Germany. After a few years he began to realize that the attack on the new Republic from the right was dangerous in the extreme. Barbarians, enemies of culture, were at work. The murder of Walther Rathenau, then Foreign Minister of the Republic, on 24 June 1922 (as T.J. Reed has pointed out) opened his eyes fully to the true nature of the situation.[12] From that moment onward there was no turning back for Mann. He felt that as a man of letters it was his duty to defend the Republic, for it was in real danger of being overcome by the forces of evil. The banner which Mann raised in the cause of the new state was that of *Humanität.* Goethe and Nietzsche were his mentors. For Goethe had opposed nationalist reaction and irrationalism after the Napoleonic wars, Nietzsche had protested against German chauvinism

---

12 Cf. T.J. Reed, *Thomas Mann: The Uses of Tradition* (Oxford: Clarendon, 1974), p. 289.

after the Prussian victory in the 1870-71 war against France in telling phrases; for him a victory of arms was not a victory of culture, but spelt a great danger: «ein großer Sieg ist eine große Gefahr...»[13]

There is no need here to chart the development of Mann's political attitudes in those years in any detail, for T.J. Reed, in his masterly study *Thomas Mann: The Uses of Tradition,* has done so succinctly and convincingly. Suffice it to say, there is no truth in Kurt Hiller's charge that Mann backed the Republic because his temperamental conservatism made him allegedly incapable of rebelling against anything. He was not, as Hiller claimed, a «Schöngeist» who had «eine leidenschaftliche Affinität zum jeweils Gegebenen ... während Liebknechts Zuchthauszeit war er ganz Preußische Prägung, unter Eberts Reichs-Chefschaft ist er ganz Demokratie»;[14] rather Mann was a responsible intelligence, as Reed believes,[15] moved by social concern.

But even when Mann's eyes were opened by Ernst Troeltsch, the great historian of ideas, to the true nature of German Romantic thought and its impact on German culture, he stuck to his guns. He did not throw Novalis overboard as later remarks (above all in his lecture of 1929 on «Die Stellung Freuds in der modernen Geistesgeschichte») reveal, although, by that time, he had undoubtedly distanced himself from some aspects of Romanticism. He reviewed a lecture by Troeltsch, delivered in 1922 shortly before the latter's death, at the Berlin *Hochschule für Politik* on «Naturrecht und Humanität in der Weltpolitik,» a striking piece of writing which, more than any other work, succinctly, but powerfully uncovers the distinction between the climate of thought of nineteenth-century and early twentieth-century Germany, on the one hand, and the Western world, on the other.[16] Thomas Mann, to judge by his short but important review published on 25 December 1923 (*GW,* XII, 627-29), was greatly impressed by Troeltsch's lecture. As Reed has argued,[17] this review is more of a watershed in Thomas Mann's political development than the much more famous lecture «Von Deutscher Republik» of 1922. Although Troeltsch's lecture was given in the autumn of 1922 it was not published until 1923. There is no evidence that Thomas Mann had seen it when he wrote «Von Deutscher Republik.» Troeltsch's argument is highly subtle and telling. He showed that German thought had moved away under the influence of the Romantic movement from the principal Western tradition based on Natural Law and on the

---

13 Nietzsche, *Werke in drei Bänden,* ed. Karl Schlechta (München: Hanser, 1966), I, 137.
14 Kurt Hiller, in a 1925 addition to his book, *Taugenichts - Tätiger Geist - Thomas Mann* (Berlin: Basch, 1917), repr. by Klaus Schröter (ed.) in *Thomas Mann im Urteil seiner Zeit. Dokumente 1891-1955* (Hamburg: Wegner, 1969), p. 73; cf. Reed, *Thomas Mann,* p. 309.
15 Reed. p. 309f.
16 Cf. Ernst Troeltsch, «Naturrecht und Humanität in der Weltpolitik.» *Deutscher Geist und Westeuropa,* ed. Hans Baron, (Tübingen: Mohr, 1925; repr. Aalen: Scientia, 1966), p. 3-27, (originally published in *Tätigkeitsbericht der deutschen Hochschule für Politik* (Berlin, 1923), p. 627-29.
17 Cf. Reed, *Thomas Mann,* p. 294-97.

Enlightenment, and that it had abjured cosmopolitanism and universalism with their roots in early Christianity and Classical Antiquity. Instead it had developed a genetic-historical approach which set up «principles of historical uniqueness» and advocated free individuality untrammeled by moral prescript. Germans considered the principles of Natural Law and the ideas of the Enlightenment, Troeltsch argued, to be arid and shallow while, from the vantage point of the Western tradition, German ideas appeared not profound, but obscure and confused, a blend of mysticism and brutality.[18] Troeltsch who, as his brilliant *Spektator-Briefe* (1918-22),[19] written under the impact of the German defeat and its aftermath, reveal, had sought to come to terms with the new realities of German politics, had grasped the threat to the Republic and civilized life coming from the right, and had felt that a realignment of German thought was necessary if Germany were to flourish and rejoin the community of nations. He therefore urged German thinkers to return once again to European culture and share the ideals of Natural Law.

To accept Troeltsch's view and yet at the same time to espouse Novalis, that quintessential Romantic royalist, as a champion of Republican political thought entails a basic contradiction. Admittedly, Mann's arguments in later years became more circumspect. After 1933 – and even in earlier years – he did, on occasion, issue warnings against Romantic attitudes, but Novalis remained one of the German writers to whom he admitted his indebtedness and of whom he spoke with pride (cf. *GW*, x, 935).

Why did Thomas Mann never jettison Novalis? Why did he not even do so when he fought against National Socialism, which had pillaged Romantic thought for its own nefarious purposes? The answer is complex.

Thomas Mann did not just blunder into the realm of Romantic thought, picking out at random those passages useful for his purpose. Nor did he blindly and sentimentally follow tradition. He was also a strategist who knew what he was about. He knew that in order to win over German youth to his side – that is, the side of the Republic – he had to make it feel that the Republic was a *German* Republic. Thus, the adjective in the title of Mann's lecture is significant, for he wanted to make his fellow Germans, and particularly young Germans, accept that the Republic was a *German* phenomenon and he said so explicitly in the lecture itself. And what would suit his campaign better than to call upon the most archetypal German movement, the Romantic movement, to support his arguments? The opponents of the Weimar Republic maintained that it was un-German to be a republican. Mann set out to take the wind out of their sails (*GW*, xi, 826) by discrediting their views. To be a Republican, he argued, was not disreputable for a German; on the contrary, it was honourable. Hostility to the Republic, not republicanism, was treason. What better witness

---

18 Troeltsch, «Naturrecht und Humanität,» p. 7.
19 Ed. Hans Baron (Tübingen: Mohr, 1924).

for this view could there be than Novalis? Even without having been enlightened by Troeltsch, Mann recognized the particular *German* flavour of German Romanticism and he knew of the attachment of youth to it. Indeed, he does not beat about the bush in the lecture itself, where he speaks of his intention of winning over the hearts of Germans for the Republic: «Mein Vorsatz ist, ich sage es offen heraus . . . euch für die Republik zu gewinnen und für das, was Demokratie genannt wird» (*GW*, xi, 819). And he made it quite plain at the beginning of his lecture that he was addressing not so much Gerhart Hauptmann, whose sixtieth birthday he had been invited to celebrate, but German youth. The choice of his words is a significant pointer to his strategy; for he says that he is expecting not merely German youth to be there and to listen, but he wishes to speak directly to young Germans, using their language and speaking in terms of their ideas: «Soll deutsche Jugend da sein und ihre Ohren spitzen, denn auch zu ihr will ich, über [Hauptmanns] Person hinweg, heute wieder reden, auch *mit ihr,* wie die Wendung lautet...» (*GW*, xi, 811). And what better way of winning the hearts and minds of German youth brought up in the intellectual climate of Romanticism than to invoke the words of one of its star thinkers? As Thomas Mann wrote to Ernst Bertram on 23 August 1922, at the time when he was composing «Von Deutscher Republik»: «O, o. Sie schwelgen da in Feudalismus, während ich der Jugend die Republik mundgerecht zu machen suche, indem ich sie zur deutschen Romantik in Beziehung setze.»[20]

Many of the listeners to the address in the *Beethovensaal* in Berlin on 15 October 1922 were indeed taken aback as their repeated sounds of discontent demonstrate (recorded in the printed lecture as «Scharren im Hintergrund» [*GW*, xi, 812]; «Verbreitete Unruhe» [*GW*, xi, 814]). But the plan was bold. For Mann was not dishonest when praising Romanticism. A traditionalist to the core, in «Von Deutscher Republik» he spoke as a conservative. Indeed, again and again he emphasizes that the author of *Betrachtungen eines Unpolitischen* and «Von Deutscher Republik» was one and the same person. He had changed his opinions, but not his basic attitudes of mind. As he wrote to Ida Boy-Ed on 5 December 1922: «Ich verleugne nichts. Dieser Aufsatz ist die gerade Fortsetzung der wesentlichen Linie der „Betrachtungen", glauben Sie mir.»[21]

Thomas Mann valued tradition. German literature was flesh of his flesh and bone of his bone; German culture was the air which he breathed; German Romanticism was an integral part of the European literary tradition. As a German writer who felt himself to be a representative (later on even *the* representa-

---

20 *Thomas Mann an Ernst Bertram. Briefe aus den Jahren 1910-1955,* ed. Inge Jens (Pfullingen: Neske, 1960), p. 113.
21 Thomas Mann: *Briefe an Otto Grautoff (1894-1901) und Ida Boy-ed (1903-1928),* ed. Peter de Mendelssohn (Frankfurt: Fischer, 1975), p. 22; cf. also *GW*, xi, 810.

tive of German culture) he had to stand for the whole German literary canon. However different the message of «Von deutscher Republik» was from *Betrachtungen eines Unpolitischen,* an undercurrent connects both works. Mann wanted to preserve and foster German culture in face of the danger that beset it. In World War I he felt, impelled by his personal conflict with his own brother, that the real enemy was the rhetoric of Western intellectualism. Therefore, he created the negative figure of the *Zivilisationsliterat,* modelled on his brother Heinrich. By 1922, far more justifiably, he had sensed the danger of rising fascism. He had become aware of the barbarism and mindless brutality of German chauvinism. But he still wished to defend what was deeply steeped in German literary traditions, including, of course, German Romanticism. Novalis was, as the Danish critic Georg Brandes, whose work Mann thoroughly studied, had shown,[22] a key figure of that movement. The more reason for Mann to defend Novalis – and even better – to turn the tables and use him to mount an attack on the barbarians and to entice German youth away from the worship of chauvinism and brutality of mind that gave rise to fascism. Thus, since tradition required Novalis's inclusion in the pantheon of German poets, it was good tactics to use the quintessential German Romantic poet, to appeal to German youth. And Novalis lent himself particularly for that purpose since his writings contain phrases that could be construed differently from the general tenor of his thought. After all, he did claim that a monarchy could be a republic, and a republic a monarchy (*Schr.,* II, 490), and that these distinctions were not what the theorists of Natural Law, the French revolutionaries and their followers, had thought. Mann eagerly seized the opportunities which Novalis's lack of precision opened up for him, believing he had found in Novalis sufficient intimations that Romanticism could help to establish a climate of thought favourable to the Republic. Thus, he wrote:

> ... daß meine natürliche Aufgabe in dieser Welt allerdings nicht revolutionärer Art, sondern erhaltender Art ist – in dem Sinne, den Novalis in einem Aphorismus mit zartester Kraft bezeichnet. «So nötig es vielleicht ist ... daß in gewissen Perioden alles in Fluß gebracht werde, so unentbehrlich ist es jedoch ebenfalls, die Krisis zu mildern und die totale Zerfließung zu behindern, damit ein Stock übrig bleibe, ein Kern, an dem die neue Masse anschließe und in neuen schönen Formen sich um ihn her bilde.» (*GW,* XI, 829; cf. *Schr.,* II, 490).

22 Georg Brandes devoted three chapters to Novalis in his *Den Romantiske Skole i Tyskland* (The Romantic School in Germany), the second volume of *Hovedstrømninger i det nittende aarhundredes litteratur* (Main currents in nineteenth century literature); my references are to an English edition (London: Heinemann, 1905), Chapter III, «Novalis,» p. 181-206; Chapter XIII, «Longing – The Blue Flower,» p. 207-29; Chapter XVI, «Romantic Literature and Politics,» p. 293-309. Thomas Mann, of course, used a German edition: *Die Romantische Schule in Deutschland,* 8th ed. (Charlottenburg: Barsdorf, 1900); cf. Hans-Joachim Sandberg, «Suggestibilität und Widerspruch: Thomas Manns Auseinandersetzung mit Brandes,» *Nerthus: Nordisch-deutsche Beiträge,* 3 (1972), 119-63, esp. 132-47. Steven Cerf, «Georg Brandes's View of Novalis,» *Colloquia Germanica,* 14 (1981), 114-29 also discusses Thomas Mann's attitude to Novalis.

Thus, Mann's tactics corresponded to an emotional need and a deeply-held conviction. And on receiving Käthe Hamburger's book *Thomas Mann und die deutsche Romantik* (Berlin: Junker & Dünnhaupt, 1932) he was delighted to discover that the author had demonstrated his close links with the German Romantic movement. He felt she had shown that he too belonged to the Romantic tradition. As he wrote to her on 12 October 1932: «Im Ganzen bin ich immer wieder überrascht, mir meine Zugehörigkeit zur deutsch-idealistisch-klassisch-romantischen Überlieferung so überzeugend nachgewiesen zu sehen wie bei Ihnen. Und sowas Treu-Echtbürtiges wird „international" gescholten!»[23]

Yet there are other reasons why Thomas Mann chose to quote Novalis. Although he rejected the Romantic yearning for death and opted for life he was unable to eradicate the fascination with disease and death from his range of experience. Just as in *Bruder Hitler* (1939) he claimed Hitler to be the evil brother of the artist, an outsider to society who was always on the verge of criminal conduct, so he always felt close to the appeal of death. He had learnt from Freud that «eros» and «thanatos» are closely linked. These undercurrents never cease to run in his work. He found it anything but easy to overcome sympathy with death. As an artist, he thought it quite inappropriate to speak unambiguously. As a political thinker, he had in the end no choice and condemned Nazism in absolute terms. But even by 1933 he had not relinquished Romantic thought. In his last public address in Germany, before he went into exile, «Leiden und Größe Richard Wagners,» delivered on 10 February 1933, he spoke with warmth of the composer's Romanticism, of his Romantic glorification of love and death, of the debt Wagner owed to Novalis, revealing an affinity and sympathy with his erotic philosophy. Aware of the dangers of Romanticism, he still assents to it since it allows «Wagners gesunde Art, krank zu sein, seine morbide Art, heroisch zu sein» and because it is «dermaßen komplex und schillernd» (*GW*, IX, 403).

The strategy demanded tactics which would accommodate Romanticism to the new-found political and intellectual principles. To do this it was necessary to have recourse to still deeper foundations than could be provided by a simple respect for tradtion. The limits of reason and the basic irrationality of man had to be appraised. Mann knew that men are not convinced by logical arguments alone. However plausible and admirable rational discourse may be, only rarely does it carry the day. That was one of the main, though by no means the only, reason for his criticism of the bourgeois rhetoric with which he identified his brother Heinrich. If a cause is to triumph, Mann felt, it must have deep roots. One of those roots in Germany was Romanticism. Novalis had criticized rationalism, but politics needs more than rational plans and principles, it

---

23 Thomas Mann, *Briefe 1889–1936*, ed. Erika Mann (Frankfurt: Fischer, 1961), p. 324. Cf. also his letter to Käthe Hamburger, 10 September 1932, p. 322f.

needs symbols. But had Germany not possessed a symbol in the Emperor who, after the defeat of 1918, had, so the men of the right maintained, been shamefully chased away? And was the Republic not bereft of that symbolic power that alone could radiate strength because it appealed to the irrational urges and impulses of its citizens? No, Mann argued, it was not so. The Emperor, in retrospect, appeared to have been a theatrical figure. And Mann, therefore, emphasizes that the new Head of State, the President of the *Reich*, Friedrich Ebert, is able to represent Germany, too:

> ... Der Vater Ebert zum Beispiel ist mir bekannt. Ein grundangenehmer Mann, bescheiden-würdig, nicht ohne Schalkheit, gelassen und menschlich fest. In seinem schwarzen Röcklein sah ich ihn ein paarmal, das begabte und unwahrscheinlich hoch verschlagene Glückskind, ein Bürger unter Bürgern, bei Festlichkeiten ruhig-freundlich sein hohes Amt darstellen; und da ich auch dem verwichenen Großherrn, einem dekorativen Talent ohne Zweifel, bei solchem Geschäft das ein oder andere Mal hatte zusehen können, so gewann ich die Einsicht, für die ich Teilnehmer werben möchte, daß Demokratie etwas Deutscheres sein kann als imperiale Galaoper. Kinder, Mitbürger, es ist jetzt besser – die Hand aufs Herz, uns ist im Grunde wohler, bei allem Elend, aller äußern Unwürde, als zu den Glanzzeiten, da jenes Talent Deutschland repräsentierte. Das war amüsant, aber es war eine Verlegenheit ... Dämmert uns heute nicht, in allem Jammer, die Möglichkeit der Harmonie? Ist Republik nur ein Name für das volkstümliche Glück der Einheit von Staat und Kultur? (*GW*, XI, 827).

Thus, Thomas Mann, like Novalis before him, had grasped the importance of symbols for a state. He therefore launches a counter-attack against the monarchists who deny that a republican citizen can do what a monarch alone is able to do – to represent the state in public. Indeed, Mann goes further: he suggests that Ebert does it better. The very words – «Vater Ebert» – make his conception quite plain. Ebert too, though shorn of pageantry and pomp, as *Reichspräsident* is a *Landesvater* like the monarchs of yore standing for a patriarchical conception of society; as a good *Landesvater* he represents the whole of the country. Novalis had felt that a monarch alone could fill that role, but Thomas Mann thought a monarch was no longer necessary.

Mann did accept Novalis's view that the state must be visually and emotionally felt and needs to exist by the strength of its outward appearance: «„Der Staat wird zu wenig bei uns verkündigt" ruft er [Novalis] aus. Es sollte Staatsverkündiger, Prediger des Patriotismus geben. Jetzt sind die meisten Staatsgenossen auf einem sehr gemeinen, dem feindlichen sehr nahe kommenden Fuße mit ihm» (*GW*, XI, 833; *Schr.*, III, 576). Mann here identifies himself with Novalis; for since the French Revolution, as he suggests (*GW*, XI, 833) inspired these views in the Romantic poet, so the revolution of 1918 and the Weimar Republic make him defend the existing state against its opponents. He equates the Prussia of Frederick William III with the Weimar Republic, a bold and questionable undertaking. He looks for help wherever he can get it. If «Vater Ebert» was one representative, Gerhart Hauptmann is another. He is a king even when there is no king, a king of the people, «ein Volkskönig, ein König der

Republik» (*GW*, XI, 812). In this context Novalis can once again be quoted in support, who, a royalist of a special kind, said: «man werde bald allgemein überzeugt sein, daß kein König ohne Republik und keine Republik ohne König bestehen könne» (*GW*, XI, 812; *Schr.*, II, 490). For Hauptmann – and by association he implies that it could be true of Ebert – possesses genuine popularity. It means that he is truly German; for he agrees with Novalis that genuine popularity, «echte Popularität» (*GW*, XI, 813), is the ideal of that which is truly German («das Ideal der Deutschheit» – *GW*, XI, 813). Novalis, too, had then fully appreciated the need of emotional attachment to the state. Indeed, Mann explicitly quotes, with approval, Novalis's extravagant demand made in a posthumous fragment – not in *Glauben und Liebe* (a sign of Thomas Mann's wide-ranging reading of the Romantic poet's work) – in which Novalis urged that we have to live in the state as if it were a beloved: «Nur wer nicht im Staate lebt in dem Sinne, wie man in seiner Geliebten lebt . . . wird sich über Abgaben beschweren, denn sie sind der höchste Vorteil» (*GW*, XI, 833; *Schr.*, III, 313). This demand, as of course Mann knew, is an extravagant one. Yet he appears to approve in principle of this social eroticism and links Novalis to Walt Whitman, whom he singles out as his other witness for the Republic. However extraordinary some of Novalis's observations may be, he is, in Mann's view, so important a witness that he must be defended, if at all possible. One of the charges that might have been made against him was that he is merely a romanticizing emotionalist. Not so, Thomas Mann maintains, Novalis's work is highly intellectual and therefore respectable. Did he not say: «„Der Sitz der eigentlichen Kunst . . . *ist im Verstande*. Dieser konstruiert nach einem eigentümlichen Begriffe. Phantasie, Witz und Urteilskraft werden nur von ihm requieriert. So ist Wilhelm Meister ganz ein Kunstprodukt – ein Werk des Verstandes"» (*GW*, XI, 839. *Schr.*, II, 641). By emphasizing this aspect of Novalis's thought, he does not merely wish to make Novalis intellectually respectable, but he also wishes to pull the rug out from under the feet of the «völkische Professoren» who are anti-intellectual. But more still, hostility to democracy is refuted by an appeal to Novalis. Mann succeeds in the remarkable feat of turning the organic theory of the state, implicit in Novalis's political writings, into a democratic force (*GW*, XI, 843). His conception of love as the binding force exerted on the state is for Mann both Romantic and democratic (*GW*, XI, 844).

However, to show awareness of the emotional basis of politics and to pay heed to the emotional forces that alone could give stability to a state was not enough. More positive action was needed. If the wretched body politic that was the Weimar Republic were to survive, it would have to enthuse its citizens. Therefore, Mann was anxious to show it in a favourable light. What could be more positive than to proclaim that to be a Republican meant being on the right road? In fact – and here is yet another reason for Mann's use of Novalis – the Republic, so Mann maintained, showed the way to the future just as

Romantic thought had done a century or so earlier. This claim is surprising. Indeed, Mann goes to some lengths to explain that his is a radical reinterpretation of the conventional view according to which Romanticism was not a backward-looking movement, but basically one which looked forward to the future. Indeed, the truly revolutionary principle, as Novalis said, is the will to look to the future. For Novalis the future mattered more than the past: «Was ist eigentlich Alt? Was Jung? ... Jung, wo die Zukunft vorwaltet. Alt, wo die Vergangenheit die Übermacht hat» (*GW*, xi, 820; *Schr.*, iii, 258). He also agrees with the dictum of Friedrich Schlegel, the main theorist of Romanticism and a close friend of Novalis's, who claimed that true German qualities were not to be found in the past: «An dem Urbilde der Deutschheit, welches einige große vaterländische Erfinder aufgestellt haben, läßt sich nichts tadeln als die falsche Stellung. Die Deutschheit liegt nicht hinter uns, sondern *vor uns*.»[24]

Thomas Mann goes to great lengths to argue that Romanticism is a radical movement looking to the future precisely because it is so radical. In doing so he follows an unscholarly course of action; for he does precisely what scholars ought not to do: he selects only the evidence that supports his argument and ignores what might refute it: «Die deutsche Romantik nun aber ist, so sonderbar es herkömmlichem Vorurteil klingen mag, wesentlich nicht historisch gestimmt, sondern zukünftig, und dies so sehr, daß man sie als die revolutionärste und radikalste Bewegung des deutschen Geistes bezeichnen kann» (*GW*, x, 266).

How does Thomas Mann manage that remarkable feat of turning Romanticism into a forward looking movement, when Romantics almost invariably yearned for a world that was dead and gone? He leaves no stone unturned to find support. In his address of 1929 «Die Stellung Freuds in der modernen Geistesgeschichte,» Mann even claimed that Georg Brandes, his mentor in matters of literary history, had spoken of «spiritual kinship between Romanticism and the French Revolution.» He adopted from Brandes the suggestion that both the followers of the Revolution and the Romantics were linked by the impact which the French Revolution had on both of them. The impact was profound in either case, but they drew different conclusions: the French revolutionaries' minds were deeply affected, whereas the Romantics' soul (the German translation which Thomas Mann read gives «Gemüt») was roused. (It is of course a misinterpretation of Brandes's views as Hans Eichner has pointed out.[25]) In fact, Brandes had maintained that Novalis, unlike Shelley, was not prepared to stand up and fight for the oppressed.[26] Mann, however,

---

24 *GW*, x, 658. Friedrich Schlegel, *Kritische Friedrich Schlegel Ausgabe*, II, ed. Hans Eichner (Paderborn: Schöningh, 1967), 151. Schlegel writes: «Diese ...» and does not italicize «vor uns.»
25 Cf. Eichner, «Thomas Mann und die deutsche Romantik,» p. 155f.
26 Brandes, *The Romantic School in Germany* (p. 187f.), writes: «Although Novalis is deaf to all the social and political cries of the period, and blind to all its progressive movements, and

dissented; for him Novalis boldly struck out on new paths and was a revolutionary, too. Mann thus wrote on the margin of his copy of the German translation of Georg Brandes's *Die Romantische Schule in Deutschland:* «auf seine Art auch. Auch er war kühn, und darauf kommt es an.»[27] A telling comment, indeed; for Novalis served Mann as a model for his own approach.

However, Mann was not alone in objecting to Brandes's interpretation. Another non-German student of Novalis, Henri Lichtenberger, professor at the Sorbonne and doyen of French Germanists, had, in 1912, published a study of Novalis in which he held that the latter was a republican, even with vaguely socialist sentiments. He wrote: «il [Novalis] était „républicain" et vaguement socialiste par son patriotisme civique qui absorbait l'individu dans le citoyen.»[28] There is no evidence that Thomas Mann had read Lichtenberger's book by 1922, though he had read it by 1926 (*GW*, XI, 67). He nowhere cites Lichtenberger in support of his case. It would in any case have been poor tactics at that time to call upon a French scholar for support when he wished to convert German youth. He might, of course, have quoted him in his Freud lecture of 1929 when speaking about Novalis, but did not choose to do so; he merely cited Brandes who was far better known in Germany than Lichtenberger.

In «Von Deutscher Republik» itself Mann is, as always, skilful. He seeks to rescue what he considers to be intrinsically Romantic – a regard for individual phenomena and individual experience or personality. For him, individuality is justified by being part of the wider world, of the cosmic or universal whole. He quotes Novalis:

> Alles Nationale, alles Temporelle, Lokale, Individuelle läßt sich universalisieren und so kanonisieren und allgemein machen. Christus ist ein so veredelter Landsmann ... Dieses individuelle Kolorit des Universellen ist *sein romantisches Element*. So ist jeder national und selbst der persönliche Gott ein romantisiertes Universum. Die Persönlichkeit ist das romantische Element des Ich. (*GW*, XI, 815; *Schr.*, II, 616)

> although he ends in the most grim and repulsive reaction, he is nevertheless, not merely influenced, but all unconsciously, completely penetrated by the spirit of the age. Between him – the quiet, introspective, loyal Saxon assessor – and the poor *sansculottes* who rushed from Paris to the frontiers, singing the «Marseillaise» and waving the tricolour flag; there is this fundamental resemblance, that they both desire the destruction of the whole outward and the construction of an inward world. Only, their inward world is reason, with its demands and formulae – liberty, equality, and fraternity; for him, the soul, with its strange nocturnal gloom, in which he melts down everything, to find, at the bottom of the crucible, as the gold of the soul – night, disease, mysticism, and voluptuousness.
>
> Thus, in spite of his violent animosity to his age, Novalis belongs to it; the direct opponent of all its enlightened and beautiful ideas, he is, despite himself, possessed by its spirit.»

27 The entry is on p. 222 of the edition of Brandes's study which Thomas Mann used.
28 Henri Lichtenberger, *Novalis* (Paris: Bloud, 1912), p. 252. Mann also referred to his having read Lichtenberger's study with pleasure in an as yet unpublished letter to Elisabeth Förster-Nietzsche of 6 June 1927.

There is also no problem in reconciling love of the past with a commitment to the future. Again he quotes Novalis:

> Beide Teile haben große notwendige Ansprüche und müssen sie machen, getrieben vom Geiste der Welt und der Menschheit. Beide sind unvertilgbare Mächte der Welt und der Menschenbrust: hier die Andacht zum Altertum, die Anhänglichkeit an die geschichtliche Verfassung, die Liebe zu den Denkmalen der Altväter und der glorreichen Staatsfamilie und Freude des Gehorsams; dort das entzückende Gefühl der Freiheit, die unbedingte Erwartung mächtiger Wirkungskreise, die Lust am Neuen und Jungen, die zwanglose Berührung mit allen Staatsgenossen, der Stolz auf menschliche Allgemeingültigkeit, die Freude am persönlichen Recht und am Eigentum des Ganzen und das kraftvolle Bürgergefühl. Keine hoffe die andere zu vernichten, alle Eroberungen wollen hier nichts sagen, denn die innerste Hauptstadt jedes Reichs liegt nicht hinter Erdwällen und läßt sich nicht erstürmen. (*GW*, XI, 830; *Schr.*, III, 522f.)

Novalis believed that in order to achieve a synthesis between these two elements it was necessary to invoke a higher force. This had to be the Church. In Mann's view this concept of a «katholisierender Romantiker» is no longer appropriate for the twentieth century, and he calls instead for another, a «third force» to mediate between the secular and the transcendental spheres. He then rather boldly maintains that this force is: «sozial und innerlich, menschlich und aristokratisch zugleich ... [daß sie] zwischen Romantizismus und Aufklärung, zwischen Mystik und Ratio eine schöne und würdige – man darf es sagen: eine deutsche Mitte hält» (*GW*, XI, 830f.). For him it is «das Element der Humanität» which can achieve that synthesis and it is in keeping with the German character. In a republic, *Humanität* can prosper more successfully; for there the individual is better capable of participating in political life. Here again Mann quotes Novalis:

> Dies ist freilich besser in Republiken, wo der Staat die Hauptangelegenheit jeder Person ist und jeder sein Dasein und seine Bedürfnisse, seine Tätigkeiten und seine Einsichten mit denen einer weitverbreiteten Gesellschaft verbunden, sein Leben an ein gewaltiges Leben geknüpft fühlt, so mit großen Gegenständen seine Phantasie und seinen Verstand ausweitet und übt und beinah unwillkürlich sein enges Selbst über das ungeheure Ganze vergessen muß. (*GW*, XI, 838)

But all this is rather vague. Mann does not map out what kind of institutions the Weimar Republic – or, for that matter, any republic – would need. All he offers is his tribute to the symbolic figure of the President of the Republic. Mann, despite his support for the Republic, does not actually advocate the modern parliamentary system: for he approvingly quotes Novalis's view that it can be dispensed with in a republic:

> Diejenigen ... die in unsern Tagen gegen Fürsten als solche deklamieren und nirgends Heil statuieren als in der neuen, französischen Manier, auch die Republik nur unter der repräsentativen Form erkennen und apodiktisch behaupten, daß nur das Republik sei, wo es Primär- und Wahlversammlungen, Direktorium und Räte, Munizipalitäten und Freiheitsbäume gäbe, die sind armselige Philister, leer an Geist und arm am Herzen, Buchstäb-

ler, die ihre Seichtigkeit und innerliche Blöße hinter den bunten Fahnen der triumphierenden Mode unter der imposanten Maske des Kosmopolitismus zu verstecken suchen, und *die Gegner, wie die Obskuranten, verdienen,* damit der Frosch- und Mäusekrieg vollkommen versinnbildlicht werde. (*GW*, XI, 818; *Schr.*, II, 490f.)

However, although cosmopolitanism fares badly in this quotation from Novalis, Thomas Mann finds other ammunition elsewhere in the poet's work to defend his views on the internationalism of the Republic. The modern spirit of commerce, the very feature of Western life so often denounced by nationalist Germans, receives praise from both Novalis and Mann. Novalis had said: «Der Handelsgeist ist der Geist der Welt. Er ist der großartige Geist schlechthin. Er setzt alles in Bewegung und verbindet alles. Er weckt Länder und Städte, Nationen und Kunstwerke. Er ist der Geist der Kultur, der Vervollkommnung des Menschengeschlechts» (*GW*, XI, 840; *Schr.*, II 490f.). Basing his arguments on this passage, Mann is able to assert that Novalis, although a Romantic poet, was deeply imbued with the spirit of the Enlightenment.

Thus, Novalis, as Mann writes in his speech on the occasion of the 60th birthday of Ricarda Huch, was not a reactionary. Goethe misunderstood him and was mistaken in not wishing to have *Die Christenheit oder Europa* published in the *Athenäum*. For Novalis opted for the future, where a better world might be found. He adopted a moral stance (cf. *GW*, X, 435). Romanticism, as he argued in his 1929 lecture on Freud, was fundamentally a radical movement, «die revolutionärste und radikalste Bewegung des deutschen Geistes» (*GW*, X, 266), because it enlarged human consciousness, anticipating Freud. Novalis was a pioneering spirit – he broke new ground by his spiritual journeys into the nocturnal caverns of our soul.

To attribute radicalism to the Romantic movement may indeed appear paradoxical. But that was deliberate. It was not a conjuring trick of «der Zauberer.» For Mann followed, as he explicitly stated (*GW*, X, 259), a line of argument mapped out by Nietzsche in *Menschliches, Allzumenschliches* (No. 26 «Die Reaktion als Fortschritt»),[29] where he described how reaction could amount to progress. Thus, in the wake of Nietzsche, Mann maintains that, despite its reactionary garb, Romanticism can in fact foster enlightened attitudes of mind and inspire men to follow the banner of the Enlightenment on which the names of «Petrarch, Erasmus, Voltaire»[30] are inscribed. This is at best a hazardous argument. In order to make his political stance respectable, Mann latches on to affinities and ignores differences. It allows him to paint a picture of Romanticism which is peculiarly his own – and, as would be expected, interesting and suggestive, even if it cannot withstand critical analysis. But then, as he wrote himself (in a letter to Ernst Bertram, 25 December 1922), he had not been all that accurate: «Mit dem Geistigen nehme ich es darin nicht

---

29 Nietzsche, *Werke*, I, 466f.
30 *Ibid.*, p. 467.

sonderlich genau,» and by implication justifying his lecture by calling it a «pädagogische Aktion.»[31]

Thomas Mann pleads the writer's right to use ideas as a dialectical means, to play with ideas as it befits a writer who wishes to use them for a purpose necessary for life:

> Kennt der Künstler den «Gedanken» nicht überhaupt nur als dialektisches Mittel? Kann er sich nicht spielend leicht so denken lassen, wie es dem lebensnotwendigen Zwecke dienlich ist? Man hat von Sophistik gesprochen, aber Sophistik hat nicht mit Lebensdienst zu tun. Ich bin im Grunde Pragmatist, Mann der praktischen Vernunft.[32]

The method is then anything but scholarly, yet the aim was praiseworthy. For Mann wanted to rescue as much as he could of German tradition in the cause of *Humanität*. For *Humanität* without tradition would, in his view, be insecurely based. It was the writer's task to preach a new humanism in an age where the onslaught of barbarism was stronger than ever. Again and again in letters, lectures, and essays he defends his stance as an attempt to make a humane attitude to life prevail, and that is for him the foremost need of the day. Undoubtedly he came to believe more and more that this new humanism should be seen in the context of Troeltsch's views, and that it should bring about the return of German thought to its origins in the Western tradition. This, however, did not mean that one should cut oneself off from the body of German Romantic thought. That would entail betraying the German past. Moreover, it would have meant for Mann an abandonment of his own intellectual heritage. He was not a man for radical gestures of that kind. He needed to enjoy a sense of continuity. It took him a long time – and his abhorrence at Hitler's rise to power – to repudiate the *Betrachtungen eines Unpolitischen*. For reasons of strategy and because of his attachment to his own intellectual experience, he found it difficult to recant. The more he could rescue from the German intellectual tradition the better. Thus, Novalis is appropriated in large measure, and with him much of Romanticism. Of course, after reading Troeltsch some Romantic ideas could not be retained and Mann had to distance himself from some Romantics. Romantic obscurantism was declared to be a misuse of Romanticism by ideologues, by blinkered men who ought to have known better, whether they were Romantic writers or German scholars. Thus in *Pariser Rechenschaft* (1926) he dissents from Alfred Bäumler who had praised the nocturnal side of Romanticism and rejected Novalis and Friedrich Schlegel since they still belonged to the eighteenth century. In contrast, Thomas Mann rejects: «Diese Nachtschwärmerei, diesen ganzen Joseph-Görres-Komplex von Erde, Volk, Natur, Vergangenheit und Tod, einen revolutionären Obskurantismus, derb charakterisiert» (*GW*, XI, 48). For to put these

---

31 Letter to Ernst Bertram, 25 December 1922 (see n. 20), p. 116.
32 *Ibid.*, p. 116.

obscurantist ideas forward is no longer right. It is not «an der Tagesordnung» (*GW*, xi, 48). It smacks of professorial ideology and the Romanticism of *Germanisten* (some of whom, given their record in Nazi Germany and their ultranationalist creed, are rightly chastised). Thus, in his essay, «Deutsche Ansprache» (1930), he writes:

> Dazu gehört eine gewisse Philologen-Ideologie, Germanisten-Romantik und Nordgläubigkeit aus akademisch-professoraler Sphäre, die in einem Idiom von mystischem Biedersinn und verstiegener Abgeschiedenheit mit Vokabeln wie rassisch, völkisch, bündisch, heldisch auf die Deutschen von 1930 einredet und der Bewegung ein Ingrediens von verschwärmter Bildungsbarbarei hinzufügt, gefährlicher und weltentfremdender, die Gehirne noch ärger verschwemmend und verklebend als die Weltfremdheit und politische Romantik, die uns in den Krieg geführt haben. (*GW*, xi, 878)

Humanität, on the other hand, was a positive concept. The new humanism embodied an affirmative attitude to life. It rejected the surrender to death, but this did not mean that death and disease should be ignored. In «Tischrede in Amsterdam» (1924), in the year of the publication of *Der Zauberberg,* he expressed his creed:

> Wir dürfen die Vorstellung menschlicher Vornehmheit nicht auf den Todesgedanken festlegen. Im *Herzen* dem Tode, der Vergangenheit fromm verbunden, sollen wir den Tod nicht Herr sein lassen über unsern *Kopf,* unsere *Gedanken.* Dem Pathos der *Frömmigkeit* muß dasselbe der *Freiheit* gegenüberstehen, dem aristokratischen Todesprinzip das demokratische Prinzip des Lebens und der Zukunft die Waage halten, damit das allein und endgültig Vornehme, damit Humanität entstehe. (*GW*, xi, 354)

In this context, too, Novalis is invoked. Death indeed is a fascinating phenomenon, but it is one's duty to turn to life. And this, so Mann argues, means replacing sympathy with death by sympathy with life. Novalis, so he rather surprisingly claims, thought so too: «Und ist es nicht dies, was den hektischen Träumer von ewiger Brautnacht zu seinen Ideen von Staat und schöner Menschengemeinschaft geführt hat» (*GW*, xi, 851). Whether Novalis was really moved by these intentions may well be doubted.

«Von Deutscher Republik» was written when Mann was still working on *Der Zauberberg* (1924) which is a novel of death and disease and tells of its hero's learning to cope with them. Novalis is of course pre-eminent among poets who celebrated disease and death. No wonder, therefore, that in those years Mann studied Novalis so closely. For he found in Novalis's diaries and fragments «große geistige Kostbarkeiten»[33] and in *Die Christenheit oder Europa* «unsterbliche Worte.»[34] On reading Brandes's *The Romantic School in Germany* he was surprised to find ideas in Novalis's work which belonged to the realm of *Der Zauberberg.* He noted in his diary on 5 July 1920: «verblüfft, bei Novalis

---

33 Thomas Mann, *Tagebücher 1918–1921,* ed. Peter de Mendelssohn (Frankfurt: Fischer, 1979), p. 515.
34 *Ibid.,* p. 515.

Gedanken zu finden, die sich bei der Durchdringung der Zbg. Welt einstellten, ohne daß ich mir ihrer etwaigen früheren Reception bewußt gewesen wäre.»[35] To judge by his pencil markings on the margin of the edition of Novalis which he most probably used at that time,[36] it was not only the Romantic poet's political views but also his attitude to disease and death that fascinated Mann. For Novalis disease and death were central experiences, just as they were for the hero of *Der Zauberberg,* Hans Castorp, and his creator. To chart the path which Castorp took through the valley of these shadows would go beyond the confines of this essay. Suffice it to say that Thomas Mann looked in Novalis for views which would confirm his own. But he did not merely find the spell which disease and death cast over a sensitive mind, but also believed he ascertained the positive response that would allow him to overcome it. Whether he read Novalis aright is another matter.

In *Der Zauberberg* the issues are also political. The main exponent of Romantic intellectual lore is Naphta, the Jesuit dialectician. But it would be wrong to label Naphta simply as a spokesman for Romantic political ideas. He is not; he is far too complex a figure. In fact, only in the last of Naphta's many debates with Settembrini, the liberal arch-rationalist and secular humanist, a debate that turns into a bitter quarrel and finally into a duel, does Naphta explicitly refer to the political ideas of German Romanticism, but he does not quote Novalis. Naphta puts forward a conception of freedom, such as was envisaged by Fichte (in his *Reden an die deutsche Nation,* 1807/8) and by Görres and Arndt (*GW,* II, 964ff.). Indeed, when speaking about Görres and Arndt Naphta uses words similar to those with which Thomas Mann had castigated what was for him a misuse of Romanticism. Naptha's praise of Romantic obscurantism rouses Settembrini to protest and to accuse him of indecencies («Schlüpfrigkeiten» [*GW,* III, 966]). For that is what these remarks constitute from Settembrini's point of view. For a liberal to define freedom in terms of the individual's subordination to the organic state, to the collective whole is indeed *la trahison des clercs,* a perversion of all that is most sacred to the Enlightenment – the right of the individual to freedom and equality. But Naphta's political thought is by no means only Romantic. There are other roots as well.[37] Some of them are Marxist, but they need not concern us in this context. Much of the right-wing ideological sectors of his thought belong to the arsenal of Romantic thought. But it is difficult, if not impossible, to be precise here, for many of them are medieval in origin, though of course medieval

---

35 *Ibid.,* p. 450.
36 Novalis, *Sämmtliche Werke,* ed. Bruno Wille, III, Leipzig, 1898; Ergänzungsband, Leipzig, 1901.
37 I am indebted to an as yet unpublished paper on Naphta read by my Bristol colleague A.J.B. Grenville on «Linke Leute von Rechts – Rechte Leute von Links» at the Conference of University Teachers of German in Great Britain and Ireland at the University of Bristol on 9 April 1984, published in *DVjs,* 59 (1985), 651-75.

doctrines were appropriated by the Romantics. The very concept of a theocratic «Gottesstaat» agrees for instance with a hierarchical concept of the state. Other arguments of Naphta appear to recall *Die Christenheit oder Europa* (*GW*, III, 560; III, 620), though Novalis's name is never mentioned. Likewise when Naphta demands that the individual should subordinate himself to the state, when he holds that German «Volksgenie» is freedom (*GW*, III, 561) and severely criticizes utilitarianism (*GW*, III, 561), his argument runs along Romantic lines.

To discover an influence in a novel does not amount to much; what matters is the part which these ideas (and the character who puts them forward) play in the novel. Naphta has, of course, anything but an attractive personality. By implication Mann warns us against his views. Yet Castorp is impressed by Naphta's brilliance and even finds some of his arguments convincing, but his manner far less so. He is understandably put off by his personality and his intellectual ruthlessness and harshness. But he does not side unambiguously with Settembrini, a far more attractive, even if also complex personality. Although Settembrini speaks with the voice of liberal humanitarianism he also appears as «Satana,» utters Mephistopheles's words in the *Walpurgisnacht* scene in Goethe's *Faust*, and in the end turns nationalist when the war breaks out. Moreover, his work on the encyclopaedia of suffering and his membership of the Freemason's league are dubious. The debates between Settembrini and Naphta leave Castorp confused. They seem mere words, rush past him like torrents, and appear in the presence of Peeperkorn, admittedly another ambiguous figure, to be lacking in real power; for Peeperkorn dwarfs both pedagogues by the force of his personality, though not by the trenchancy of his speech, which is in fact almost incoherent – incidentally a Romantic trait. Till the end of the novel, Hans Castrop is still groping to understand the world – and himself.

Novalis is not mentioned in the novel, though the fascination of death and the nocturnal realms of our inner life, so vividly conjured up in the novel, were deeply felt by him.[38] This is not Settembrini's attitude. Mann had, in the main, moved into Settembrini's political camp by the time he was finishing the novel, without sharing all of Settembrini's views on other subjects, yet neither Settembrini nor Castorp is Thomas Mann's mouthpiece. Mann has not fully abandoned his mistrust of rhetoric, which pained him in his brother Heinrich who shares one Christian name (Luis) with Settembrini (Lodovico). The novel is far too complex a work for that. Yet the allegorical message of the snow chapter is clear: we should not grant death dominion over our thoughts,

---

38 Cf. Bernard Guillemin, «Gespräch mit Thomas Mann über den Zauberberg,» *Berliner Börsen-Courier* (Berlin), Jg. 58, No. 509, (30.10.1925), p. 3, repr. by Hans Wysling and Marianne Fischer (eds.), *Dichter über ihre Dichtungen: Thomas Mann,* Bd. I (München: Heimeran, 1975), p. 506.

though we must be aware of its power. But the novel does not end with this chapter, though the knowledge gained through that vision may indeed subconsciously still affect the hero. Later on, Mann regretted that he had not been able to end the novel with this message, which was so dear to him,[39] but the story did not let him do so. It is of course a better work of literature for not being straightforwardly allegorical. Castorp, like Mann himself, found it difficult to cut his links with Romanticism. Thus, Schubert's song «Am Brunnen vor dem Tore» with its *Lindenbaum* symbol, for Mann the epitome of the misuse of Romanticism, casts its spell over Castorp. We last see him in the war, with this song on his lips, probably on his way to death. It determines his fate:

> Wir wissen, was wir sagen, wenn wir - vielleicht etwas dunklerweise - hinzufügen, daß sein Schicksal sich anders gestaltet hätte, wenn sein Gemüt den Reizen der Gefühlssphäre, der allgemeinen geistigen Haltung, die das Lied auf so innig-geheimnisvolle Weise zusammenfaßte, nicht im höchsten Grade zugänglich gewesen wäre. (*GW*, III, 905)[40]

Castorp's fate is a German, a very German, fate. It also tells us where sympathy with death may lead to: to death in war. That is how things were. How they ought to have been and ought to be – the snow chapter tells us. Through all the ambiguities we learn what Europe – and Germany in particular – was like, and what it could have been or could become. Political Romanticism, a dangerous, at best ambiguous body of ideas, was part of that story – and Novalis is a key figure. For, despite his newly found enlightened views to which Mann had not come easily, the deep undercurrents arising from the Romantic realm never ceased to affect him. He depicted its impact and his struggle against it. His work is the more fascinating for it.

Yet poets, as Mann perceived, need freedom to assimilate tradition and change it as their own creative power needs. They are by nature attracted to ambiguity. Novalis was, and Thomas Mann even more so. In that sense Mann felt he was able to preach Romantic ideas and *Humanität,* in that sense he could claim that national and universal elements were blended in German Romanticism which would always have a home in German hearts. But his attachment to Romanticism did not prevent his speaking out against Hitler when it would have been more convenient to temporize and try to climb onto the band-wagon that appeared to offer so many tangible rewards and a far larger German reading public. However strong his attachment to Romanticism, he became increasingly aware of its dangers – *Doktor Faustus* tells that story. Moreover,

---

39 *Ibid.*, p. 506.
40 Cf. Reed, *Thomas Mann,* p. 269, who perceptively points out the significance of this passage and of the «Lindenbaum» symbol (p. 305). Cf. also Thomas Mann's letter to Julius Bab, 23 April 1925 (*Briefe 1889-1936,* p. 239) in which Mann writes «Die Kandidatur Hindenburgs ist „Lindenbaum".» Cf. also *Zitat zum Verfassungstag* where he writes: «aus *„deutscher Seele",* die etwas anderes ist als unsere Romantiker glauben, – nicht Heimwehkrankheit nämlich nach dem „Lindenbaum", sondern Wille zum Opfer, zum Untergang, zur Neugeburt und zum ewigen Werden» (*GW*, XII, 634).

when he met my late friend and colleague William Rose after one of his lectures in London after World War II and the conversation had turned to Novalis he said: «die deutsche Romantik, das ist der Dorn in der Rose, das ist die Liebe zum Tode.» But he also knew that there are no roses without thorns, and thus, appropriately, the works of Novalis retained their place with other classics on the shelves of his library.[41]

41 I am indebted to A.J.B. Grenville, J. Hibberd and M.C. Morgan for their constructive criticism, to Professor Hans Wysling, the Curator of the Thomas Mann Archive, Zürich, for providing most helpful information, to the Thomas Mann Archive, Zürich itself for permission to consult books from Thomas Mann's library, in particular Georg Brandes, *Die Romantische Schule in Deutschland* (n. 22) and Novalis, *Sämmtliche Werke* (n. 36) as well as to the Universitätsbibliothek Düsseldorf, and to Professor Golo Mann for permission to consult one of Thomas Mann's as yet unpublished letters.

Music on Mann's *Magic Mountain:*
«Fülle des Wohllauts»
and Hans Castorp's «Selbstüberwindung»

RODNEY SYMINGTON, *University of Victoria*

«The novel is the highest example of subtle
interrelatedness that man has discovered.»
D.H. Lawrence

«Die Musik hat von jeher stark stilbildend in meine Arbeit hineingewirkt ...
Der Roman war mir immer eine Symphonie, ein Werk der Kontrapunktik, ein
Themengewebe, worin die Ideen die Rolle musikalischer Motive spielen.»[1] The
musical structure to which Thomas Mann was referring here is further enhanced in the case of *Der Zauberberg* by the use of music itself and of musical
motifs as a part of the contrapuntal textual web of the novel. Music does not
simply provide him with a technical literary device, it becomes itself a constituent element of the narrative, one of the ideas to which he referred above. The
very first word of the novel («Vorsatz») hints at the important role that music
is to play, and it is then given two whole sub-chapters to itself: «Politisch verdächtig» (p. 156–62), and «Fülle des Wohllauts» (p. 883–907).[2] Since the latter
sub-chapter (23 pages long) occurs almost at the end of the novel, and since it
contains one of the central experiences of Hans Castorp's sojourn at the Berghof – his analysis of Schubert's «Der Lindenbaum» – it is a reasonable assumption that its author intended to accord it some considerable significance.

In a speech given at his fiftieth birthday celebration in Munich, Thomas
Mann stated that he hoped the future would say of his work, «daß es lebensfreundlich ist, obwohl es vom Tode weiß (*GW*, XI, 368). Since *Der Zauberberg*
had appeared less than a year earlier, he could well have had that work principally in mind, when he explained himself further: «Es gibt zweierlei Lebensfreundlichkeit: eine, die vom Tode nichts weiß; die ist recht einfältig und
robust, und eine andere, die von ihm weiß, und nur diese, meine ich, hat vollen
geistigen Wert. Sie ist die Lebensfreundlichkeit der Künstler, Dichter und

---

1 Thomas Mann, *Gesammelte Werke in dreizehn Bänden* (Frankfurt: Fischer, 1974), Bd. XI, 611.
   All references to Mann's works will be cited in the text as *GW*. References to *Der Zauberberg*
   are from *GW*, III and will be given by page number in parentheses.
2 Cf. Henry Hatfield, *From the «Magic Mountain»: Mann's Later Masterpieces* (Ithaca and
   London: Cornell University Press, 1979), p. 56.

Schriftsteller.» He might also well have added: and of my novel's hero, Hans Castorp. For one of the few generally accepted conclusions one can draw from Mann's *Der Zauberberg* is that the hero in the course of the novel gains knowledge of life and death and learns to overcome his innate «Sympathie mit dem Tode.» The process of his «Bildung» teaches him to be «lebensfreundlich.»

However, it has troubled not a few critics that Castorp is not a hero in the mould of the conventional «Bildungsroman» and that he is not shown finally applying his lessons in any kind of social activity. It has even been suggested that «there would seem to be considerable evidence for a conclusion that Hans Castorp does not develop.»[3] The author of that statement also raised a troubling and justified question: «Do the last three chapters or so of the novel show us a hero who is manifestly in possession of certain values which he did not have at the beginning?»[4] The textual limit he mentions is flexible enough to include the sub-chapter «Fülle des Wohllauts,» and thus we feel justified in looking at this segment of the novel in order to try and see if we can establish whether or not Castorp, in fact, achieves any development and reaches any conclusions. Since by this stage of the novel all the verbal references have been well and truly established, it would be reasonable to expect that the verbal echoes might point not merely to the recapitulation of the novel's themes, but also towards some conclusions.

In the sub-chapter «Fülle des Wohllauts» we observe Castorp left to his own devices. Peeperkorn is dead, Chauchat has left the Berghof, and, while both Settembrini and Naphta are still in Davos, neither intrudes on the scenes we are about to witness.[5] This does not mean that they are not still present in spirit, but now Castorp can reflect upon his experiences with the seven major figures who accompanied him through the novel without their intruding in person on his thoughts. We should not be misled by the fact that the gramophone that is purchased by the administration of the Berghof is intended primarily to relieve the boredom and depression that has befallen the patients, including Castorp. What begins as a means of entertainment and diversion, becomes for him a major element in his pedagogical progress. He is saved from his card-playing craze by the arrival of the new device, but it quickly develops into a secret passion that dominates his life for an undefined period of time.

---

3 Martin Swales, *The German Bildungsroman from Wieland to Hesse,* (Princeton, NJ: Princeton University Press, 1978), p. 117. For a survey of critics who see a negative conclusion to the novel see: Jill Anne Kowalik, «„Sympathy with Death": Hans Castorp's Nietzschean Resentment,» *GR*, 58 (1983), 44–5. Apart from ample evidence that Castorp does indeed develop personaily and philosophically, as the present article is attempting to show, Hans-Martin Gauger demonstrates convincingly Castorp's growing linguistic awareness as a feature of his development of self-awareness; cf. «*Der Zauberberg* – ein linguistischer Roman,» *NR*, 86 (1975), 217–45, especially p. 228.
4 Swales (note 3), p. 107.
5 Cf. Charles E. Passage, «Hans Castorp's Musical Incantation,» *GR*, 38 (1963), 239.

It is ironically appropriate that the new gramophone, which resembles a coffin, should be brought in by Hofrat Behrens, whom Settembrini had nicknamed Rhadamanthus, one of the judges of the Underworld. The first records played by Hofrat Behrens on the record player are intended to introduce the guests at the Berghof to the pleasures of the new device. But, in addition to this function, these initial recordings – and not just the five that are discussed in detail as Castorp's favourites – also play a thematic role in the novel. Castorp's five favourite recordings, the effect of which on him is described in some detail by the narrator, have been the subject of considerable comment and analysis.[6] But the first ten pages of this section (which comprise 40% of the whole) have for the most part been passed over, as if they fulfilled no further function than that of filling out the text, or at the most of serving to lead us in a leisurely manner into the major part of this section. But these ten pages and the seemingly insignificant initial selections of recordings they describe serve both to recapitulate the themes of the novel and to hint at Hans Castorp's main preoccupations not only in this particular sub-chapter but also during the entire work. For example, it is particularly striking that of the first six selections that are mentioned specifically, five touch thematically on Castorp's relationship to Chauchat and on the complex of themes surounding her. Furthermore, when he returns to the salon by himself early the next morning to play some more records, both the recordings specifically named relate to Chauchat, and of his five favourite records that are discussed in some detail, four relate to her. Clearly, the departure of Chauchat from the sanatorium has neither exorcised his feelings for her nor reduced his interest in the corpus of themes that she embodies. That the author also intended this section in its entirety to be understood as important, is demonstrated by the fact that he structures the section around his favourite magical number: while Hans Castorp is in the presence of other patients the narrator describes seven selections (counting «dance tunes» as one),[7] and when he is alone, he likewise listens to seven recordings. In addition the repeated use of the word «Zauber» (both by itself and in compounds) throughout this segment of the novel indicates his intention to give it a «magical» significance: the magical nature of music and its mysterious effect on the human soul are to produce not only profound feelings within Hans Castorp, but also insights whose essence can only partially be framed in words. What Herman Weigand said about the rest of the novel is particularly applicable to

---

6 Cf. Passage (note 5), who reduces Castorp's five favourite records to expressions of his love for Joachim. A more cogent and convincing discussion is offered by Helmut Gutmann, «Das Musikkapitel in Thomas Mann's *Zauberberg*,» *GQ*, 47 (1947), 415–31. See also Swales (note 3), p. 115–17, and T.J. Reed, *Thomas Mann, The Uses of Tradition* (Oxford: Clarendon Press, 1974), p. 268ff.

7 They are treated in the text as one item (p. 887), only the «exotic» tango being specifically mentioned. Of the 14 musical selections in this sub-chapter all except the Figaro-aria have to do with love and/or death.

this sub-chapter about music: «the tissue of themes in the *Magic Mountain* is to a unique degree a tissue of „magic words with indefinitely ramified associations".[8]

In all but three of the cases where actual recordings are mentioned Mann plays a little game with the reader: he gives mere hints about the provenance of the music rather than precise details. We should not, however, overestimate the difficulty of this game: it is fairly easy to discover the titles of most of the pieces of music mentioned. They would all have been familiar to the average, cultured concert and opera-goer of Mann's own day (say, someone like himself), and thus the author is deliberately inviting us to make associations between the musical pieces he chooses to mention and his own work. As Hans-Martin Gauger so aptly commented: «Dieser Autor schreibt für seinesgleichen; und der Reiz des *Zauberbergs,* gerade für den „Gebildeten," beruht gewiß auch darauf, daß er diesem das behagliche Gefühl vermittelt, dazu zu gehören.»[9] Mann has selected, in fact, from the world's music those references that fit in with the novel's themes. It is also significant that of these musical pieces all but four include words.[10] When Castorp is left alone, all but one of the seven recordings he plays have an accompanying text. Thus it is not just the music itself that causes echoes to resound within Hans Castorp's being (and thereby in the mind of the reader also), but in each case the text allied with the musical selection also plays a considerable role in moulding his thoughts and feelings.

At the very beginning of this sub-chapter the gramophone itself is described in elaborate and ironical prose that hints at the nature of the music to come. But the cunningly laboured style hides veiled allusions to the main preoccupation both of this sub-chapter and of the whole novel: death. There is an immediate evocation of death in the description of the gramophone as «der mattschwarz gebeizte Schrein» (p. 884), while the machine's connection with Chauchat is hinted at in the description of the playing arm and its device for holding the needle (p. 884).[11] The effect that this new acquisition will have on the patients, and especially on Castorp, is indicated by Behrens' use of the word «Zauber» (p. 885) to depict the gramophone's possibilities.

The first piece chosen by the Hofrat is an overture by Offenbach. The use of the deceptively simple indefinite article is the narrator's clearly not too serious attempt to disguise the fact that this piece of music is the overture to «Orpheus in the Underworld» – a piece which bears a direct thematic relationship to the

---

8 Hermann Weigand, *Thomas Mann's Novel «Der Zauberberg»* (New York: Appleton-Century, 1933), p. vii–viii.
9 Gauger (note 3), p. 229.
10 When Behrens indicates the record albums, he declares ambiguously: «Da haben Sie die Literatur!» (p. 885).
11 Cf. Lotti Sandt, «*Mythos und Symbolik im „Zauberberg" von Thomas Mann*» (Bern und Stuttgart: Paul Haupt, 1979), p. 161.

Berghof in general, and to Castorp and Chauchat in particular. We note the multiple irony with which the author permits Hofrat Behrens – in his three roles as Director of the Berghof, «judge of the Underworld» (i.e., Rhadamanthus), and in Castorp's eyes his rival for Chauchat's affections – to be the one who selects this piece as the very first to be played. The Hofrat sets the scene, as it were, with a musical selection that comments ironically on his own institution and its inmates. The Berghof as the Underworld, and Castorp as Orpheus in forlorn pursuit of his Eurydice – the point does not need to be belaboured. But the narrator adds extra poignancy to the parallel by citing specifically the words of the aria «Ach, ich habe sie verloren,» which in the overture is, of course, a purely instrumental theme, and which by the mention of the words here is clearly meant to suggest Castorp's loss of Chauchat.[12] Even the description of the final section of the piece, «die Ausgelassenheit selbst ... ein unverschämter Cancan,» contains echoes of both the tenor of life at the Berghof in general and of Hans Castorp's Walpurgis Night experiences with Chauchat in particular. Hans did not ask her to cancan, but he did ask her to dance (p. 466). In the operetta this cancan is performed by a chorus line of gods and goddesses as part of a revel in Hades. Whether it is the ironic playfulness of Behrens or the narrator, it is only appropriate that this evocation of the Underworld should be not in serious mode, but rather as a comic opera, which serves as a comment both on the inhabitants of the Berghof and on Castorp.[13]

The next selection, Figaro's entrance aria from Rossini's *Barber of Seville,* is performed by an Italian tenor in Italian. This suggests an association with Settembrini, the more so since Rossini based his opera on Beaumarchais' *Le Barbier de Séville,* which in its day was regarded as a somewhat revolutionary plea for social equality.[14] But the reference in this instance is primarily an ironic one, since the comic aspects of the singer's bravura aria are especially stressed by the narrator and appreciated by the audience of patients. For is there not a hint of ironic criticism of Settembrini's polemical virtuosity in the narrator's description of the singer's performance? «Die Zuhörer wollten sterben vor Lachen über sein falsettierendes parlando, über den Kontrast dieser Bärenstimme und dieser zungenbrecherischen Sprechfertigkeit. Erfahrene mochten die Künste seiner Phrasierung, seiner Atemtechnik verfolgen und bewundern. Meister des Unwiderstehlichen, Virtuose des welschen Da capo-Geschmacks...» (p. 886). Settembrini's «Sprechfertigkeit,» Settembrini as «Meister des Unwiderstehlichen,» as «Virtuose des welschen Da capo-Ge-

---

12 If it is true that Offenbach's «Ach, ich habe sie verloren» is indeed a parody of «Che faro senza Euridice» from Gluck's *Orfeo ed Euridice,* then readers may have been expected to conjure up Gluck's French version («J'ai perdu mon Euridice») or the standard German text («Ohne Dich, du Heißgeliebte ...»).
13 Space limitations prevent the delineation of many further parallels between Offenbach's work and *Der Zauberberg.*
14 Cf. Georges Lemaitre, *Beaumarchais* (New York: Alfred Knopf, 1949), p. 82.

schmacks» (i.e., repetition of the previously stated), the singer's final triumphant gesture that mirrors Settembrini's own often repeated gesticulation,[15] – all this, plus the fact that he is generally associated with Figaro the factotum, represents a mild and playfully ironic criticism of Settembrini by the narrator through the medium of Hofrat Behrens, who once again chooses the record to put on.

There follows a paragraph that mentions any number of records that were played for the pleasure of the guests at this first demonstration. Even this list of titles and brief, suggestive descriptions contains important allusions to the novel's themes. «Ein Waldhorn vollführte mit schöner Vorsicht Variationen über ein Volkslied,» reads the sparse description of the next selection. It might be assumed that this vague reference is merely intended to evoke a somewhat «Romantic» mood and to prepare us (and Castorp) through the mention of the folksong for more weighty musical matters to come later in relation to «Der Lindenbaum,» but there are at least two thematic associations that this apparently innocent musical mention suggests.[16] Firstly, horns have already appeared in the novel as an important leitmotif. During his «Snow»-experience Castorp remembers the lifeguard blowing his horn on the beach at Sylt to warn those who dared to brave the dangerous surf (p. 658). The warning horn is transferred in his mind to Settembrini, whose cupped hands and cry of warning remind him of his childhood experience (p. 659) and who henceforth in this section is repeatedly identified with the warning voice of reason (cf. «Vernunfthörnchen» – p. 685). Thus the Waldhorn referred to here reminds us of the associations of the «Schnee» segment, particularly since we are told that it performs its piece «mit schöner Vorsicht» (p. 887), a phrase that recurs, moreover, in the discussion of the Lindenbaumlied (p. 906) in connection with Hans Castorp's memory of Settembrini's warning about regressing into «Romanticism.» But it suggests other allusions too: by specifically referring to the Waldhorn, the narrator is evoking the «French» horns of *Carmen*. Indeed, there is a direct verbal connection to the later discussion of that opera where the bugles that sound retreat are first called «Trompeten, Clairons» and then suddenly become «Hörner» (p. 899) and indeed «diese französischen Clairons – oder spanischen Hörner» (p. 900); thus the opera that has already been mentioned three times in the novel (p. 231, 330, 848), each time with gathering significance, is alluded to here, also. In this manner the French horn, performing «mit schöner Vorsicht,» hints at the basic thematic conflict of the novel: the corpus of themes that surround Chauchat and Naphta versus those that are represented by Joachim and Settembrini. We can see, therefore, that there is a

---

15 The narrator imagines the tenor with «offenbar die Hand in der Luft,» which is reminiscent of Settembrini's gesture either at the end of a successful speech (p. 225) or when particularly emphasizing a point (p. 462-3).
16 It is probably impossible to identify this piece of music.

complex interrelation between the numerous musical selections mentioned, be their description – as in this case – ever so brief.

Following this, the patients hear an aria from *La Traviata,* which the soprano «schmetterte, stakkierte und trillerte.»[17] This characterization of the performance together with the context in which it is mentioned indicates the famous coloratura aria «Ah, fors è lui...» from Act One of the opera, and in particular the well known and often performed third part of this aria, «Sempre libera.»[18] In the first part of the aria («E strano...») the consumptive Violetta asks herself if she could be truly in love, for if so, it would be the first time a man had set her heart on fire. In the following section she wonders whether Alfredo might be the man she has always dreamed about: «He, who in quiet vigil stood before my door and infected me with a new fever...» («e nuova febbre accese»). However, her lyrical mood is interrupted by renewed doubts about herself. She asks herself: «What can I hope for? What can I do?» She answers: «Find pleasure, perish in the vortex of the senses!» («Gioire, di voluttà nei vortici perir!») – at which point the music reaches a climax of lyrical and dramatic intensity. The final aria («Sempre libera») is an assertion that freedom and pleasure are the twin poles of her existence.

The relation of this aria to Chauchat is obvious – at least insofar as such a connection would be made in Castorp's mind. The verbal parallels between the Italian text of the aria and that of the novel are striking.[19] This merely hinted allusion by Thomas Mann points to future thematic references when Hans Castorp is alone and chooses his own records – to *La Bohème,* where the heroine also dies of something akin to consumption, and to the selection from *Carmen,* where freedom is a major theme. It is not clear whether it is again the Hofrat who chooses to play this aria from *La Traviata,* for at the end of the paragraph we are told: «Behrens hatte sich zurückgezogen» (p. 887), which leaves open the exact moment of his retreat. But he may well have made this selection also, since it comes comparatively early on in the session, and, if so, it is yet another example of the narrator's playful irony at Castorp's expense.

Even the briefest of references to «eine Romanze von Rubinstein» is not without thematic significance. Anton Rubinstein (1829–1894) was a Russian composer, the majority of whose works bear French titles.[20] He only wrote one

---

17 Sandt, (p. 162) suggests this might be the dying Violetta's aria «Lebt wohl jetzt, ihr Geschmeide, die ich einst getragen,» which hints at Castorp's visits to the dying and especially to Natalie von Malinckrodt, who was always changing her jewelry. But the dying Violetta's aria is scarcely one that one «schmetterte, stakkierte und trillerte.»
18 It is impossible to say what language is used on the Berghof's recording.
19 Note, in particular, the verbal parallel between Violetta's evocation of death and Chauchat's daring statement: «Il nous semble qu'il est plus morale de se perdre et même de se laisser dépérir que de se conserver» (p. 473) – an idea that Castorp absorbs and unconsciously reproduces, once in French to Joachim (p. 535), without knowing why the phrase came into his head, and once in German to Chauchat (p. 772) who does not recognize it!
20 For example, one «Romance» occurs in Opus 44 as the first of six pieces (for piano) entitled «Soirées à St. Pétersbourg.»

Romance specifically for the violin (Opus 86, «Romance et Caprice pour violon avec orchestre»), but the piece mentioned here could well be a transcription.[21] The association with the figures of Chauchat and by extension of Hippe, however, is obvious, the more so since we are told that the piece sounded as if it were being played «wie hinter Schleiern.» We are reminded of Castorp's fascination with Chauchat's arm behind its sleeve of gauze (p. 182, 288, 453), but even more of the repeated references to the voices of both Hippe and Chauchat as being «verschleiert» (p. 171, 173, 463, 771, 823). Hippe's eyes also sometimes darken themselves «ins Schleierig-Nächtige» (p. 171). It is also significant that Thomas Mann once described the French of *Der Zauberberg* (the language of the erotic in the novel) as a «Schleiergewand» (*GW*, xi, 602).

After the Hofrat's departure Castorp imperiously takes possession of the operation of the record player[22] and is initially content to play the requests of the other patients for dance-music.[23] Even this apparently minor detail is not without thematic resonance. For the cataclysm with which the novel ends – the First World War – is ironically described by the narrator as «das arge Tanzvergnügen» (p. 994), thus placing the stupidity of the war and its participants on the same level as the superficiality of the dancing in «Fülle des Wohllauts,» which is a precursor of the dance of death to come. And even the requests of Castorp's fellow inmates, whose superficial musical tastes and thoughtless behaviour Hans Castorp so disdains, do not leave him totally untouched, for they finally ask him to play the «Barcarolle» from Offenbach's *The Tales of Hoffmann,* a piece which, the narrator reports, «lieblich genug ins Ohr ging» (p. 888). The roguish narrator knows very well that this recording was «lieblich genug» to Hans Castorp's ears, for once again this is a piece which connotes striking associations with Castorp's own situation. In the opera Hoffmann (a bachelor) has a companion Niklausse, whose attitude of care and solicitation towards the poet becomes somewhat ambiguous as the plot unfolds. In the «Barcarolle» he joins in a duet with Giuliana, a courtesan who is out to destroy Hoffmann:

---

21 Catherine Drinker Bower, *Free Artist: The story of Anton and Nicholas Rubinstein* (New York: Random House, 1939), p. 378, 382. Joseph Szigeti (*With Strings Attached: Reminiscences and Reflections* [New York: Alfred A. Knopf, 1967], p. 155) thinks that he may be the performer on this recording.
22 Castorp believes the other patients would be too careless and not keep the records in the right place. In the next sub-chapter his own untidiness («schlampig» is used in both instances) causes the recording of Valentin's Prayer to be found in the room where the séance is being held.
23 We are told of only one specific dance-tune that is played, the tango, whose brief description («berufen, aus dem Wiener Walzer einen Großvatertanz zu machen» – p. 887) suggests, however, unbecoming behaviour, especially since earlier in the novel (p. 59) Castorp had heard waltz music while the Russian couple was making love in the next room.

> Le temps fuit et sans retour emporte nos tendresses.
> Zéphirs embrasés, versez-nous vos caresses,
> Zéphirs embrasés, donnez-nous vos baisers
> Belle nuit, ô nuit d'amour, souris à nos ivresses,
> Nuit plus douce que le jour, o belle nuit d'amour!

Whoever requested that particular record was perhaps well aware of Hans Castorp's amorous adventure in the Berghof! Furthermore, the ambiguity of the sexual roles in the opera (the figure of Hoffmann's male companion Niklausse being played by a mezzo-soprano) suggests Castorp's own fascination with sexual ambiguity – for example, his identification of Chauchat with Hippe, his attraction to his own «Blaue Blume,» the ranunculus («zwittrig übrigens,» as he comments to Joachim on page 505), his musings on the ambiguity of «son crayon» (p. 676), and his discussions of «res bina» (p. 705, 827) and «prima materia» (p. 705). His relationship to Joachim – which may well be latently homoerotic (see below) – is also perhaps suggested by this musical reference.

Thus the apparent innocuousness of these first musical selections can be shown to be quite the opposite: they are laden with evocative implications that relate to the major themes of the novel. While clearly intended primarily to be harbingers of the more significant pieces to come, they still in themselves contribute to the thematic web of the novel. The Berghof itself is first conjured up *(Orpheus in the Underworld)*, then Settembrini (Figaro), followed by a hint of Romanticism blended with intimations of rationalist warnings («Waldhorn,» «Volkslied») and Hippe/Chauchat (*La Traviata,* Rubinstein), and ending with Hippe/Chauchat again *(The Tales of Hoffmann):* in essence, this is a close recapitulation in musical themes of the structure of the first part of the novel.

When Castorp hastens to return to the salon early the following morning in order to continue his listening undisturbed, we are told of two pieces that particularly impress him. These are the first two of seven selections that he listens to alone. Firstly, he hears «Blick' ich umher in diesem edlen Kreise –» from Wagner's *Tannhäuser,* which constitutes Wolfram's entry in the «Sängerkrieg.» In this aria Wolfram sings of «der Liebe reinstes Wesen» which he imagines as «ein Wunderbronnen, in den mein Geist voll hohen Staunens blickt.» For Wolfram, pure love remains platonic, the source must never be sullied («Und nimmer möcht ich diesen Brunnen trüben»), and the lover is ever prepared to sacrifice himself for his love: «in Anbetung möcht ich mich opfernd üben,/ vergießen froh mein letztes Herzensblut!»

But as noble and pure as these ideals are – and as much as Castorp identifies himself with them – do they represent in any way that which he has experienced in relation to Chauchat? Even when his love for her was unrequited, it was scarcely «minne» in the medieval sense, even though he might have liked to see it that way. Here we have the first intimation in this section that he will interpret the recordings he hears in accordance with his own emotional needs. Thus it seems that Castorp regards Wolfram's aria from *Tannhäuser* as an accurate reflection of his own attitude to love; if so, it is a distortion of the true circumstances, a subjective identification of text and music with his own private concerns. In fact, his own experience of love is much closer to that of Wolfram's competitor Tannhäuser, who in his response in the opera declares: «Im Genuß nur kenn ich Liebe!»

The second piece that Castorp listens to alone is a «Zwiegesang aus einer modernen italienischen Oper.» Since we are given one of the lines sung by the tenor («Da mi il braccio, mi piccina»), we can deduce that the narrator is referring to Puccini's *La Bohéme,* and specifically to the duet between Rodolfo and Mimi at the end of the first act. That this duet also makes a profound impression on Castorp is clear from the qualification: «Zärtlicheres gab es auf Erden nicht» (p. 890-91). Furthermore, there is also nothing more tender on earth, we are told, than the tenor's line «Give me your arm, my little one» (with its suggestion of Castorp's fascination with Chauchat's arm) and «die simple, süße, gedrängt melodische kleine Phrase, die sie ihm zur Antwort gab» (p. 891). This simple, little phrase is «I obey, sir!» («Obbedisco, signor!»), whereafter he asks her to tell him she loves him («Che m'ami, di»), and she sings («with abandon,» according to the stage direction) «Io t'amo!,» and the two leave the stage arm in arm. The last lines of the act are heard off stage:

RODOLFO:	«Say that you love me!»
MIMI:	«I love you.»
RODOLFO and MIMI:	«Love! Love! Love!»

However, the actual starting point of the record must lie somewhat earlier than the quoted line («Da mi il braccio . . .»), since from there to the end the scene lasts less than a minute. In fact, the Berghof's recording of this famous scene could begin either with either of the famous arias, Rodolfo's «Che gelida manina» or Mimi's «Mi chiamano Mimi,» but it most likely begins with «O soave fanciulla . . .» («O lovely child . . . in you I behold the dream I would always dream!»), which quickly becomes a soaring duet and eventually leads into «Da mi il braccio . . .» Wherever the Berghof recording actually begins, it clearly reflects in Castorp's mind his love for Chauchat: he is Rodolfo, she is Mimi, and when left alone, they fall in love and exit arm in arm. What the narrator calls the «bescheidene und innige Gefühlsannäherung» (p. 891) between the two voices, is no less than Castorp's own wishful thinking. The tragic outcome of the opera is not mentioned, and we have no way of knowing if it, too, plays a role in Castorp's thoughts.

The author's artful irony is once more at work in this section: immediately after Mimi has sung «I obey, sir,» Mann allows Behrens to enter the salon. Just as when Settembrini entered Castorp's darkened room and embarrassed him in the middle of a phantasy about Chauchat (p. 270), so now his enjoyment of this reverie is impaired by the unwanted interruption of the Hofrat: «Hans

Castorp zuckte zusammen, da hinter ihm die Tür ging» (p. 891). His apparently guilty reaction reveals the sensitivity of the operatic allusions in his mind. When he hears the door being opened, he reacts without knowing who is entering. The fact that it is of all people the Hofrat makes the interruption ironically appropriate. However, the Hofrat leaves immediately after a perfunctory nod of the head, and Castorp can return to the opera. And yet he has probably missed Rodolfo's «Che m'ami di» and Mimi's response «Io t'amo,» two lines that surely would have made his own heart soar. The description here of the two singers («unsichtbar-wohllautend» - p. 891) indicates not only that they are «inside» the record-player, but that in the opera they are by now also invisible, being offstage, where they sing the last line together: «Amor! Amor! Amor!» In this case, too, there is no question but that Castorp identifies with the music and the situation, particularly since the text does not present any excessive linguistic demands on him.

If we turn our attention now to the five records that represent Castorp's favourites, we immediately encounter the problem of narratorial ambivalence that occurs so frequently in *Der Zauberberg*.[24] That is, are the descriptions and interpretations of the recordings in this sub-chapter those of Castorp or the narrator? In this case there is little doubt that we are invited to share in the interpretations of these pieces of music with Castorp, even though from time to time the narrator makes comments on his hero's thoughts and feelings. Castorp's interpretations, however, are highly subjective and represent in some instances a wilful distortion of both music and text. These distortions are, however, narratorially necessary, firstly in order that the music fit the circumstances, and secondly in order that we may understand more clearly Castorp's mood and, more importantly, become privy to his conclusions.

He listens to his favourite records in the same posture as he has always listened to music: «den Kopf auf der Schulter, den Mund geöffnet» (p. 892; cf. p. 58, 306), but now there is a change in his attitude towards the act of listening. At the beginning of the third chapter we are told that he loved music dearly and that its effect on him was «tief beruhigend, betäubend, zum Dösen überredend» (p. 58). In «Fülle des Wohllauts» music has quite a different effect on him: it is perhaps to some extent still intoxicating, but his development is revealed in the insights he now gains from the music he listens to. Whereas earlier music made him sleepy, now it spurs him to reflection and analysis. What was previously a soporific, is now an instrument of personal development.[25]

---

24 Cf. Francis Bulhof, *Transpersonalismus und Synchronizität* (Groningen: Van Denderen, 1966), p. 159ff. Gauger (p. 222), speaks of «eine ... Negation oder Zurückdrängung des Sprechens» in this sub-chapter. However, Castorp's thoughts and the description of his feelings are surely eloquent enough.
25 Kowalik (note 3) believes that Castorp «becomes, by the end of the novel, „vernarrt" (905), transfixed by his „Musiksarg" (907), and plagued by „Gewissenszweifel" (905).» But all these words have been taken out of context.

The first of Castorp's favourite recordings to be discussed – and perhaps for that reason of especial significance – comprises a group of records that bring the final scenes of Verdi's *Aida*. Here also the narrator forbears to give us the name of the composer and his opera, but decides instead to provide us with every possible clue so that the answer is obvious. But in this case he is not simply playing his customary little game with the reader and providing him merely with the chance to experience the pleasure of guessing the music correctly. The records, we are told, bring «die Schlußszenen des pompösen, von melodiösem Genie überquellenden Opernwerks, das ein großer Landsmann des Herrn Settembrini, der Altmeister der dramatischen Musik des Südens, in der zweiten Hälfte des vorigen Jahrhunderts aus solennem Anlaß, bei Gelegenheit der Übergabe eines Werkes der völkerverbindenden Technik an die Menschheit, im Auftrag eines orientalischen Fürsten geschaffen hatte» (p. 893). In plain prose: Verdi's *Aida* was commissioned by the Khedive of Egypt to commemorate the opening of the Suez Canal. Mann's playfully ironic description of the circumstances surrounding the composition of *Aida* allows him to adumbrate certain conclusions about the musical selection and even about Castorp's sojourn in the Berghof. The juxtaposition of Settembrini with Egypt (cleverly identified by the narrator with the «Orient,» so detested by the rationalist), and of the Suez Canal with the opera *Aida* offers a summary in motifs of some of the novel's central themes. Settembrini would no doubt approve of the description of the Suez Canal as a work of «völkerverbindende Technik,» since such a sign of technological progress must surely be grist to his rationalist mill, but this triumph of human cooperation is ironically qualified by the manner in which its completion is celebrated: the highly questionable (in Settembrini's words: «politically suspect») medium of music is employed, by one of his own countrymen under commission to an «oriental prince,» to portray a tale of reckless love and death – set in a country, moreover, that Settembrini would scarcely be likely to consider as belonging to the «civilised West.» And in fact, the effect of both music and story on Castorp has nothing to do with rational technology and everything to do with erotic love and death. Furthermore, whereas Castorp once considered himself to be an engineer, a profession that works, as he himself had said, «angeblich sogar in völkerverbindender Richtung» (p. 847), he has already admitted to Peeperkorn (where he speaks of his profession in the past tense, p. 847, a habit he had already acquired after only a few months in the sanatorium, cf. p. 408), that he was never especially attached to his profession and that he has given it up for the sake of Chauchat and all she represents: «Ihr zuliebe und Herrn Settembrini zum Trotz» (p. 848). In the case of the opera *Aida* then, Settembrini's defeat by Chauchat is complete. The «völkerverbindende Technik» of the Suez Canal means nothing to ex-engineer Castorp, the transfiguration of Aida and Radames on the other hand everything.

His reactions to the music of *Aida* are yet another example of his intuitive feeling for situations that conform to or compare with his own natural predilections. Thus, we are told that, although he does not understand precisely what is going on in these final scenes, he believes he is able to comprehend their essence «mit Hilfe seiner Kenntnis der Situationen und seiner Sympathie für diese Situationen, einer vertraulichen Anteilnahme, die wuchs, je öfter er die vier oder fünf Platten laufen ließ, und schon zur wirklichen Verliebtheit geworden war» (p. 893). His sympathy with the «situations» is no less than his subjective identification with the love triangle (Radames – Aida – Amneris) in the opera, with the question of honour and duty versus love, with the reuniting of the lovers at the end, and above all with their apparent heavenly apotheosis in eternity. This «sympathy with the situations» is, however, not simply his well known «Sympathie mit dem Tode» transferred to the opera and its characters, for Castorp's conclusions about the ending of the opera – as we shall see below – illustrate a new optimism and a developing transcendental vision that represent a victory over the darker side of life.[26]

Both the recounting of the plot of *Aida* and the actual quotation of lines (or parts of lines) are creatively selective so as to illustrate and underscore the themes that are being recapitulated. Thus, when reading of the events of the last few scenes of *Aida*, we are given only those parts of the libretto that are of particular significance to Castorp and his concerns.[27] For example, Castorp's view of these recordings is clearly determined by his own experiences: he sees the general Radames torn between love and honour, as he himself was, and is. The fact that Radames, having deserted his post and having planned to flee with Aida, can still maintain that «im Herzensgrunde [war] die Ehre unverletzt geblieben» (p. 894), then that is also Castorp speaking for himself. As long as he believes still in the «Intaktheit seines Innern» (p. 894), he can persist in his forlorn love for Chauchat: when urged to renounce, he must answer, with Radames: «Ich kann nicht!» and «Vergebens!» (p. 894) – both words twice over.

Castorp's fervent liking for this scene derives not so much from an exact parallel of the operatic situation with his own,[28] as from the inherent psychological truth that strikes him. From the very start of the novel he has been wrestling with the competing demands of the Flatland (work, honour, duty) and the innate tendencies of his character (irresponsibility, freedom, love). The thrice proclaimed exhortation: «Rechtfertige dich!» (p. 894–95) applies in Castorp's mind equally to himself, and just as Radames has no answer to this

---

26 Early in the novel Castorp unwittingly adumbrated his self-identification with Radames when he naively confused Settembrini's appellation for Behrens (Rhadamanthus) with the operatic hero – cf. p. 273.
27 The uncited libretto (Act IV, Scene i) evokes many associations with Castorp's situation.
28 Cf. Passage (p. 242–46), who argues that Joachim is Radames and Castorp is Aida.

imperative, neither does Hans. It is also significant that Radames' crime is not conveyed to us through the text of the libretto itself, but rather through a summary of it in a way that also underscores Castorp's own dilemma: «Der Oberpriester ... führte ihm in zugespitzter Form sein Verbrechen des Verrates vor Augen.» That the sentence of death is conveyed by the Chorus «der stimmgleich beieinander geblieben war» (p. 895), suggests the unanimous judgment of the society Castorp has left behind, while Radames' being buried alive is merely an operatic equivalent of Castorp's present condition: having spent now at least five or six years at the Berghof, he may well feel, «sein Los sei erfüllt, er sterbe den Tod der Verfluchten, unter dem Tempel der zürnenden Gottheit habe er lebend ins Grab einzugehen» (p. 895). As with all the musical interpretations we are given, Castorp views *Aida* not objectively, but as having particular relevance to his own situation and problems.

That this scene does indeed have a deep effect on him personally is demonstrated by the description of his behaviour when changing the records: «Castorp mußte die Platte wechseln, was er mit stillen und knappen Bewegungen, gleichsam mit niedergeschlagenen Augen, tat ...» (p. 895). The downcast eyes are those of a troubled, if not guilty man who has found no answer to the demand: «Rechtfertige dich!» Hence his relief that he can escape such an exhortation when listening to the following piece of music (p. 898).

As much as the scene just discussed has a profound effect on Castorp, it is surpassed by the attraction that the final scene has for him. Aida has hidden herself in the very tomb where Radames is to be buried alive, and Castorp's description of this scene leaves no doubt at all that he views it as an exact parallel to that wish-fulfilment for which he yearns: «Ja, sie hatte sich zu ihm gefunden, die Geliebte, um derentwillen er Ehre und Leben verwirkt ...» (p. 895).[29] Aida's return to the tomb, in order to share death with Radames: that is what Castorp wishes Chauchat would do for him. And that is why the final duets of the two lovers make such a deep impression on him, not merely because of the brilliance of the music but also because of the circumstances: «sie [i.e., the duets] waren es eigentlich, die es dem einsam-nächtlichen Zuhörer in tiefster Seele angetan hatten: in Hinsicht auf die Umstände sowohl wie auf ihren musikalischen Ausdruck» (p. 895). These duets lead Castorp to conclusions that are of profound significance both for himself and for the novel. For he describes them as «das Verklärteste, Bewunderungswürdigste, was ihm je untergekommen» (p. 896).[30] That we are not simply dealing here with the

---

29 Cf. Radames' first lines: «The fatal stone has closed over me ... This is my tomb. I shall never again see the light of day ... I shall never more see Aida.»
30 The word «Verklärung» recurs (p. 897) to describe the final effect of this music on Castorp. In essence, this interpretation of *Aida* offers us an example of «Liebestod,» as defined by Hans Eichner, «Thomas Mann und die deutsche Romantik,» *Das Nachleben der Romantik in der modernen deutschen Literatur,* hrsg. von Wolfgang Paulsen (Heidelberg: Lothar Stiehm, 1969), p. 166-67.

music or the performance is made clear by the following sentence: «Doch wäre er in das Lautliche weniger verliebt gewesen ohne die zugrunde liegende Situation, die sein Gemüt für die daraus erwachsende Süße erst recht empfänglich machte» (p. 896). Once again it is his identification with the *situation* that causes him to be so deeply affected by the music, and it is this operatic situation that in his mind parallels his own. With his limited Italian (it is, significantly, the only Italian line he quotes) he extracts from the libretto the one line that applies to his own yearning: «No, no! troppo sei bella,» a line, however, that he misconstrues completely. Whereas Radames is objecting that Aida is too beautiful to die, Castorp completely distorts the line's meaning to signify «das Entzücken endgültiger Vereinigung mit derjenigen . . . die er nie wiederzusehen gemeint hatte» (p. 896). Even when imagining this to be Radames' feeling when uttering the line, Castorp identifies totally with the operatic figure: «dieses Entzücken, diese Dankbarkeit ihm deutlich nachzufühlen, bedürfte es für Castorp keines Aufgebotes an Einbildungskraft» (p. 896). In other words, the operatic situation is his own, there is no need for him to imagine it, for he believes he is experiencing it at first hand.

The final result of this listening, reflection, and identification is the formulation of a conclusion that provides an illustration – by means of a musical example – of the philosophical message contained in the «Snow» experience. While listening to this final scene he is able, in a rather perverse manner, to imagine the sickening reality of being buried alive, the mine gas, the hunger pains, the decay and final death. But this recounting of the technical details of death and decay serves here quite a different purpose from the usually ironic employment of this device at other places in the novel:[31] here the recounting of the horrors of being buried alive provides Castorp with the opportunity to demonstrate his victory over that preoccupation with death that has dogged him all through the novel. For it is at this point in the discussion of the effect of *Aida* upon him, that we read one of the key sentences of the novel: «Was er aber letzlich empfand, verstand und genoß . . . das war die siegende Idealität der Musik, der Kunst, des menschlichen Gemüts, die hohe und unwiderlegliche Beschönigung, die sie der gemeinen Gräßlichkeit der wirklichen Dinge angedeihen ließ (p. 896). This Schopenhauerian conclusion represents the first evidence that Castorp is making progress in attempting to reconcile the influences to which he has been subjected. Moreover, the three key words of the above quotation («empfand, verstand und genoß») denote a synthesis of three levels of experience: feeling is now accompanied by understanding, and the new combination of those two elements can be enjoyed.[32] The significance of

---

31 For example, at Joachim's death, p. 744.
32 Cf. Herman Meyer, *Das Zitat in der Erzählkunst* (Stuttgart: Metzler, 1961), p. 227, who sees here a reference to Faust II and speaks of «Genuß mit Bewußtsein.» The connection of «regieren» and «genießen» may well also come from *Faust II* (2. 10,251), where the implication is, however, that the two together are incompatible – i.e., the reverse of what Hans Castorp achieves in this sub-chapter. See Reed (note 6), p. 271.

these three words for Castorp's «Bildung» cannot be overestimated, for we are witnessing here a «Steigerung» in Castorp's personality. The reality of death is triumphantly conquered and suppressed by the desire of the heart to believe in a future: «Für Radames' und Aida's Operngemüter gab es das sachlich Bevorstehende nicht» (p. 897). And we could add: nor for Castorp's soul either. The united victory of Radames and Aida over death, their belief in the grace of Heaven and the blessings of eternity – symbolized musically by their voices rising «unisono zum seligen Oktavenvorhalt» (p.897) – offers Castorp the opportunity, for the first time in the novel, to contemplate a concrete example of victory over death and to find in it a singular solace: «Die tröstliche Kraft dieser Beschönigung tat dem Zuhörer außerordentlich wohl» (p. 897).

Thus the description of the recording of *Aida* serves to recapitulate through musical analysis the seminal message of the «Snow» segment. It is, however, much more than merely a recapitulation, for it demonstrates not only that Castorp is fully aware of the technical aspects of death and decay, but also that he is able now to apply the lesson learned during his snow-experience which so quickly disappeared again from his conscious mind. In Castorp's reaction to *Aida* we see a clear illustration of Mann's message returning to his hero's consciousness. The final scenes from *Aida* contain for him not only the terrors of death but also the transfigurations that only a new attitude to life can bring.[33]

The second of Castorp's favourite records is Debussy's *Prélude à l'après-midi d'un faune,* a work he was wont to play after *Aida* in order to recover from the rigours the first piece occasioned within him. This orchestral work is infused with concentrated magic and has the «prudent» tendency to transport the listener into a dream. Castorp's dream is described in prose that conjures up an arcadian landscape in which the hero, transformed into a satyr and lying on his back with his head raised on a small mound of earth – that is, in a position very similar to that assumed during the «Liegekur»[34] – whiles away a hot summer's afternoon in blissful forgetfulness. Apart from the mention of his goat legs and the fact that the piece of music is of French origin, the scene as described contains scarcely a word that even hints at anything erotic, although usually the piece by itself is considered to be alluding to that suggestive realm.[35] In Castorp's mind, however, it portrays simply an escape from the moral burdens and social obligations of his earlier life: he does not have to justify himself, he does not have to be responsible, and no-one sits in judgment

---

33 The final duet of Radames and Aida is accompanied by a background refrain sung by Amneris: «Pace t'imploro» and thus suggests further connections to the novel, particularly to «Der Lindenbaum.»
34 This was also the posture assumed by Nijinski in his famous portrayal of the Faun in Paris in 1912. Cf. Richard Buckle, *Nijinksy* (London: Weidenfeld and Nicholson, 1971), p. 239.
35 Reed (p. 267), notes the erotic connection between *Aida, L'après-midi d'un faune* and *Carmen.*

upon him for having forgotten his honourable duty and gone missing.[36] The language of this passage makes it clear that the satyr in the meadow (i.e., Castorp himself) is relating directly to the finale of *Aida:* «Der junge Faun war sehr glücklich auf seiner Sommerwiese. Hier gab es kein «Rechtfertige dich!», keine Verantwortung, usw. . . .» (p. 898). The dream is one of total lethargy, of forgetfulness and timelessness: «Es war die Liederlichkeit mit bestem Gewissen, die wunschbildhafte Apotheose all und jeder Verneinung des abendländischen Aktivitätskommandos. . .» (p. 898).[37] The apotheosis of forbidden love which the final scene of *Aida* had depicted, is followed by an apotheosis of lethargy. Thus two of his most troubling problems are overcome by means of music. It is still wishful thinking, but for once Castorp feels no guilt, his conscience is appeased and he has now achieved a state of mind that would have been unthinkable in earlier days. Hence this recording also – as brief as the description of it is – is important to the portrayal of Castorp's development. To be sure, the achievement of the guilt-free enjoyment of lethargy is scarcely the traditional message of a «Bildungsroman,» but the text makes it quite clear that the call of the conventional «Bildungsroman» to social action («das westliche Aktivitätskommando») will no longer be blindly followed by this hero, nor will he feel guilty in not doing so. The rationalist would no doubt say that this was evidence of the corrupting effect of music, but it is a sign of Castorp's progress that he has overcome such restraints and that in this moment at least they are banished.

His third favourite piece of music is an extract from Bizet's *Carmen,* an opera that has played an important role in the novel already, having been mentioned on three previous occasions, each one more significant than the preceding. Since we are told belatedly in this sub-chapter that Castorp knew the opera well, because he had seen it often in the theatre (p. 898), the earlier references take on, in retrospect, added psychological significance. With each mention of the opera in the novel there is a growth in its significance for Castorp and his situation. But the breakthrough to mental clarity about Chauchat and Carmen does not come until he hears the records in the «Fülle des Wohllauts» section.

The Berghof's recording of *Carmen* begins with Act II, Scene iii, which takes place in the café owned by Millas Pastia. In this scene Carmen and Don José reveal the two opposing attitudes to life that Chauchat and Castorp demonstrated earlier in the novel: freedom versus duty.[38] It is important to

---

36 Considerable use is made in the novel of the leitmotif «abhanden,» event to the point of quoting the line of the verse from which it is taken: «Ich bin der Welt abhanden gekommen» (p. 823). The extra-textual musical reference (Mahler, «Rückert-Lieder») provides further striking parallels to Hans Castorp's circumstances: every word of the poem's twelve lines could apply to him.
37 Cf. Settembtrini's strictures against music in the sub-chapter «Politisch verdächtig.»
38 Hans Castorp had already expressed some uncommon thoughts about the conventional view of freedom – in French – on Walpurgis Night (p. 467).

note again two things about the plot description that follows: firstly, that it is highly selective, that is, it omits details that do not suit the forced parallel between Don José/Carmen and Castorp/Chauchat; and secondly, it contains alterations and additions to the original text that amplify the psychological relationship of the opera to Castorp's own situation.[39] While Carmen dances, Don José hears the bugles calling retreat: «Trompeten, Clairons» they are called, the use of the French word being significant. Don José's natural urge to return to barracks is couched in vocabulary that evokes the motif of «going home» – and thus is connected to the Lindenbaumlied, the sub-chapter «Snow» (p. 669–70) and even to «Valentin's Prayer.» These connections are, furthermore, strengthened by the important narratorial addition of «nach Haus» to the original text.

The argument that develops between Don José and Carmen over his conception of his duty and her total lack of concern for it, is framed in such a way as to mirror the same conflict between Castorp and Chauchat. The vocabulary used here in the narratorial analysis is not so much a paraphrase of the text as a reinterpretation of it in the light of Castorp's experience. The text of the libretto at this point reads as follows: «Tu ne m'as pas compris ... Carmen, c'est la retraite. Il faut que, moi, je rentre au quartier pour l'appel.» These simple sentences are paraphrased in the novel in the following manner: «Er war außer sich. Sein eigener Enttäuschungsschmerz trat ganz zurück hinter dem Bemühen, ihr klarzumachen, um was es sich handle und daß keine Verliebtheit der Welt gegen dieses Signal aufkomme. Wie war es denn möglich, daß sie so etwas Fundamentales und Unbedingtes nicht verstand!» (p. 899). Clearly, the commentary in the novel has read a good deal into Don José's three short and simple lines! In Castorp's mind we are dealing indeed with something fundamental: with the basic conflict between the call of duty and honour on the one side, and the natural inclination to love, irresponsibility, and freedom on the other.

Carmen's reaction – both angry and sarcastic – to Don José's pleading is likewise broadened by additions to the libretto in the novel's version of the action: it suits the novel's motifs, for example, to have Carmen say, when she is mocking Don José's anxious reaction to the retreat call by mimicking his apprehensions, that he «beim Schall der Hörner sein bißchen Verstand verloren habe» (p. 899), words that are not in the original. Carmen's taunting of Don José is an ironic echo of that which happened to Castorp: he lost his little bit of reason when he heard the horn (of Settembrini's warning cry) and embarked on his perilous snow-journey, just as he ignored the Italian's warning («Un po

---

39 Thomas Mann appears to have used the original German version of 1875 by D. Louis (pseud. for Julius Hopp), of which a more recent editor has said: «Die deutsche Übertragung von D. Louis (Julius Hopp) verfehlte und verfälschte ... ihren Charakter,» i.e., of the opera. Bizet, *Carmen,* hrsg. von Fritz Öser. Deutsche Übertragung der Originalfassung von Walter Felsenstein (Kassel: Alkor-Edition, 1964), p. iii.

di ragione, sa!» – p. 462) on Walpurgis Night. In this argument between Don José and Carmen we are invited not only to see the parallel to the similar situation of Castorp and Chauchat, but also to raise the operatic example to a universal paradigm. Carmen is elevated to a symbol of revolt against the very principle that is signified by the sound of the bugle-horns: that is, the call to duty and obedient service (p. 900).

Don José's aria «La fleur que tu m'avais jetée...» – in the novel the German version is used throughout – is one of Castorp's most cherished pieces of music amongst his list of favourites; we are told he plays it often by itself and that he listens to it «stets in achtsamster Sympathie» (p. 900). He is Don José, and like the latter Castorp is also «im schweren Arrest, worein er um ihretwillen geraten.» The rest of the analysis of the aria could just as well be a description of Castorp's feelings and sufferings vis-à-vis Chauchat. Like Don José he is imprisoned because of his love, and like the operatic hero he feels his life is forfeit because of his dilemma. Here again we have a narratorial addition to Bizet's libretto that underlines Castorp's problem more than Don José's. Whereas Don José sings (in the German version, but not in the French) «es war um mich getan,» he neither repeats it nor does he sing «auf immer also um ihn getan...» as the text of the novel would have us believe. The additions are there to emphasize Castorp's own emotions on listening to this aria.

After hearing this record to the end, Castorp is «schwergemut und dankbar» (p. 901). He does not listen to the remainder of this scene (which does not appear to be present on the recordings he has), in which Carmen exhorts Don José to go with her to the mountains: this part of the scene clearly would not have accorded with Castorp's situation, since Chauchat was never likely to ask him to go with her to the mountains or beyond them. Nor does he hear the beginning of Scene iv in which, just as Don José is about to leave, Zuñiga enters and an altercation ensues. Castorp's version resumes at the point where, we are told, the gypsies congratulate Don José on the fact that his encounter with the officer Zuñiga has made it impossible for him to return and he must now flee with them to the mountains. This is all very fine – except that it is not in Bizet's opera! It is clear that the language has been carefully chosen to connote once again Castorp's own circumstances. The novel's summary of the events states that «alle den jungen Don José beglückwünschen, daß ihm durch das Renkontre mit dem Offizier der Rückweg abgeschnitten war...» (p. 901). This is no less than a concise summary of Castorp's own story: his encounter with an officer (Joachim) cut off, so to speak, his return to the Flatland, and he has now deserted the colours (a repeated leitmotif of the novel) by staying in the mountains. In Bizet's opera, however, Don José still vacillates: during the Chorus's exhortation to flee to the mountains and freedom he is silent, managing no more than an anguished «Ah!» The decision to quote from the final lines of the Act likewise results from the attempt to draw parallels between Castorp's story and *Carmen*. «O folg uns in felsige Klüfte, / wilder, doch rein wehn dort die Lüfte –»: that is a deliberate reminder of the first pages of the novel, in which Castorp's perilous journey up into the mountains began (cf. p. 11–14). These two lines are again sung by the Chorus of Gypsies, and the fact that we are told «man konnte sie ganz gut verstehen,» denotes not just that their diction is impeccable, but that the symbolical significance of these lines is also clear to Castorp. The final four lines quoted from the opera have a similar function: they offer a concise summary of the lessons he has learned during the past five years or so:

> Offen die Welt – nicht Sorgen drücken;
> unbegrenzt dein Vaterland!
> Nur dein Wille gilt als höchste Macht,
> und voran: das seligste Entzücken,
> die Freiheit lacht! Die Freiheit lacht!» (p. 901)

The «Sorgenkind des Lebens» has learned to leave his cares behind him and to open his mind and heart to everything human. The child of Germany has broadened his horizons to encompass ideas and influences from the whole world (and even beyond), and thus freedom and joy have overcome duty and worry. Well might Castorp say when the record is finished: «Ja, ja!» Those words mean, in effect, that he believes he has just been listening to his own story.

The fourth piece of music among Castorp's favourites is Valentin's Prayer from Gounod's *Faust,* and on this occasion the narrator names the work for us. While he apologizes for the fact that it is once again a piece of French music, he nevertheless uses the German text, as he had done with *Carmen.* There is no secret about Castorp's reaction to this music: the character of Valentin is described as «jemand Erz-Sympathisches» (p. 902), but Hans identifies the voice on the recording with Joachim. Once again he transfers the operatic situation to his own circumstances by making the necessary imaginative leap in equating Valentin's posthumous protection of Margarethe with Joachim's looking down on him, so to speak, from Heaven. The pious nature of the aria («frommen Charakters») evokes one of the most frequently employed leitmotifs in the novel, one that repeatedly occurs in the relating of piety to the past and to death. The nature of Valentin's actions – not just brave and bellicose, but also audacious, reckless, and «French,» – remind us of Joachim's brave, but ill-considered departure from the Berghof to join his regiment and of his valiant and fervent battle against disease and death.

The vocabulary of this brief section is full of evocative epithets relating once again to the major themes of the novel. The tone of the middle part of Valentin's aria, for example, is described in part as «keck-chevaleresk,» the deliberate use of the French loan-word (instead of «ritterlich») initiating a string of French references that on the surface might seem paradoxical. What does the narrator mean, for example, by «das Französisch-Militärische»? If, indeed,

French is the language of the erotic in the novel,[40] what is the erotic doing combined with the military? This very antithesis portrays, of course, the essential thematic structure of the novel: love and death versus honour and duty. The soldier Valentin does his duty and seeks honour, but the achievement of the latter requires reckless abandon on the battlefield. The pious goal of the soldier can only be achieved through audacious means. Thus, the soldier on the battlefield embodies the thematic paradox: he who seeks honour must also seek death, from which there is no escape. Valentin is now described as «der Brave» (p. 902), the very adjective used both by Goethe (*Faust,* line 3775) to describe his Valentin, and by Thomas Mann (p. 688) and Castorp himself (p. 847) to refer to Joachim. In addition, much is made in this section of the fact that the singer is invisible («der Unsichtbare» occurs twice) and that he is inside the gramophone («der Kasten»; «dort drinnen»), which from the start was called «der mattschwarz gebeizte Schrein» (p. 884), the «Sarg aus Geigenholz» (p. 892), and later his (i.e., Castorp's) «Musiksarg» (p. 907), and which Castorp repeatedly gazes at (cf. p. 888: «den Schrein im Auge»). Thus the invisible presence of Joachim from the «coffin» makes itself deeply felt on him, and the four lines that the narrator chooses to quote from the libretto underscore the sense of loss and longing. Valentin laments his having to leave his homeland, as both Joachim and Hans have had to forsake their home on the Flatland.

The last two lines quoted from the libretto («O Herr des Himmels, hör mein Flehn, / in deinem Schutz laß Margarethe stehn!») would seem to have nothing at all to do with Castorp, except for the fact that we have been told that Valentin's use of «du» - although ostensibly referring to Margarethe - moved Castorp deeply. But Margarethe is not referred to by name. Rather, the narrator refers to her «Schwesterblut,» a circumlocution that permits Castorp to imagine it as meaning the family relationship of himself and Joachim. The nature of their association - so close, yet so reserved - merely hints at unplumbed depths, but Hans' reaction to his cousin's death (p. 743-44), his emotions when listening to this piece of music, and his response to the appearance of Joachim during the séance, all point to the extremely subtle portrayal of an emotional relationship that goes beyond that of mere blood and friendship. That the narrator uses Castorp's particular predilection for this piece as the very reason for talking so briefly about it may seem (and is) a paradox. But the laconicism of the narrator at this moment mirrors both the diffidence with which Hans and Joachim behave towards each other throughout the novel and the equally terse description of their relationship.[41]

---

40 Cf. Gauger, p. 237.
41 Thomas Mann's predilection for the homoerotic is by now well established; see Ignace Feuerlicht, «Thomas Mann and Homoeroticism,» *GR,* 57 (1982), 89-97. Charles Passage (note 5), has no doubt that Hans and Joachim have a homoerotic attraction to each other, while Alan

While the inclusion of the extract from Gounod's *Faust* in the list of Castorp's favourite records may seem to indicate simply his strong attachment to his dead cousin, we must not forget either the group of themes and motifs that are associated with Joachim. Castorp's admiration and affection for the latter signify also a pious respect for what he represents: honour, duty, devotion, etc. While he himself has been torn between the social demands of honour and duty on the one hand, and his innate inclination to laxity and irresponsibility on the other, his cousin's single-minded pursuit of health and service is an attitude he still respects, although he himself has by now progressed beyond it.

Of Castorp's five favourite records only the titles and composers of the two which have specifically German connections are given. The final record discussed, Schubert's «Der Lindenbaum,» is called «etwas sogar besonders und exemplarisch Deutsches» (p. 903), but why it should be considered exemplary only becomes clear at the end of the discussion. It is, in fact, the only thoroughly German piece among Castorp's five favourites. In this case, then, we are clearly dealing with a piece of music that is even more significant for Castorp than the other four. Even when he is still investigating the treasures hidden within the album covers, the special attraction for him of «Der Lindenbaum» is emphasized: amongst the «Lieder» he listens to when still familiarizing himself with the record collection is one, «eines zumal, das Castorp von Kindesbeinen an gekannt hatte, zu dem er aber jetzt eine geheimnisvollbeziehungsreiche Liebe faßte...» (p. 889). Just as his «Sympathie mit dem Tode» did not become conscious to him until it emerged in the hermetic atmosphere of the Berghof, so also the symbolical meaning of «Der Lindenbaum» only becomes apparent now, when he listens to the recording of it. The progress he has made is shown by the fact that what before he merely *felt*, now becomes an object for reflection, too.

Although musical analysis has been employed already elsewhere in this subchapter, it is significant that the discussion of «Der Lindenbaum» begins with a full page of technical analysis. A close reading of the long paragraph that describes the structure of the Lied and its performance reveals both some noteworthy as well as some puzzling aspects. For example, the analysis in the novel is based on the assumption that «Der Lindenbaum» consists of three eight-line stanzas, whereas countless editions of both Lied and poem alike have always presented it as consisting of six four-line stanzas. Moreover, in Schubert's Lied the final stanza is repeated (a fact which is also noted in the novel), which in a performance gives us seven (!) stanzas in all. The technical

---

Latta, («Symbolic Structure: Toward an Understanding of the Structure of Thomas Mann's *Zauberberg*,») *GR,* 50 (1975), 50, takes the view that their relationship is no closer than that of warm friendship. Thomas Mann made several references in his Diaries to the close connection between homosexuality and the military, e.g., *GW,* XII, 734.

analysis of the key changes (from major to minor and back to major) is accurate, but thereafter we enter a particularly problematical section of the analysis: «Die eigentlich bezwingende Wendung der Melodie erscheint dreimal, und zwar in ihrer modulierenden zweiten Hälfte, das drittemal also bei der Reprise der letzten Halbstrophe „Nun bin ich manche Stunde"» (903). The important «Wendung» (i.e., musical phrase) occurs three times over in the song: «Diese zauberhafte Wendung, der wir mit Worten nicht zu nahe zu treten mögen, liegt auf den Satzfragmenten „So manches liebe Wort," „Als riefen sie mir zu," „Entfernt von jenem Ort"...» (p. 903-04). The narrator finds something compelling and magical in the musical phrase to which each of those three lines is set, and yet he forbears to approach this magic too closely with words. The reader is expected simply to understand the mystery of this music that has such a profound effect on Castorp, «daß sie dem Zuhörer auf ungeahnte Weise ans Herz griff» (p. 904). Thus the secret, compelling and magical effect of music helps Castorp to attain his most important insight into himself, but the message of this music is one that is intuited rather than being derived through the power of reason.

The analysis of the significance of this recording for Castorp brings us to one of the most crucial passages of the entire novel. It is rendered all the more significant by the fact that the narrator issues a caveat to *himself* about the tone of the comments to follow and prefaces his revelations with a theoretical excursus on what a symbol is and why it is important. He takes great pains to inform us of two things. Firstly, he gives us (following Goethe[42]) his definition of a symbol: a symbol is significant in so far as it points beyond itself to something universal. Whoever loves the object that is the symbol reveals his relationship to the world that the symbol denotes. And the second, and even more important point: Castorp is conscious («bewußt,» and it is printed in italics) of the significance of the object of his devotion and of his love towards it. This is a key moment in the novel, for it is the first time that its hero has demonstrated any measure of intellectual clarity about the sum of his manifold experiences. Thus we have arrived at a point in the novel, where Castorp's years in Davos are finally to lead to valuable conclusions. The «Lindenbaumlied» denotes for Castorp that world of «forbidden» love and death to which he had always had a leaning. The Lied evokes both a sphere of feeling and an intellectual disposition to which Mann attaches the convenient label «Romantic» and which stand in opposition to those attitudes evoked by the name Settembrini.[43]

Castorp's innate personality had predetermined his predilection for the realm of death that lies behind the words of «Der Lindenbaum.» But the latter is a work of art, an aesthetic artefact combining music and literature; the living

---

42 Cf. Gutmann (note 6), p. 418.
43 Cf. Thomas Mann on the «Sympathie mit dem Tode»: «Formel und Grundbestimmung aller Romantik» (*GW*, XII, 432).

symbol («stellvertretendes Gleichnis» – p. 905) of the world to which he is attracted is Clawdia Chauchat, and for long he was infatuated with her, and hence with the world she represents. But it is the singular achievement of the Berghof atmosphere that this infatuation, this fascination with the «Romantic» side of life did not remain static. Here the narrator makes perfectly explicit the pedagogical process to which Castorp has been subjected. To be sure, it was his «fate» to be predisposed to the world of erotic love and death, but it is at this point that one of the novel's most helpful and productive comments appears: «Eben dieses Schicksal aber hatte Steigerungen, Abenteuer, Einblicke mit sich gebracht, Regierungsprobleme in ihm aufgeworfen, die ihn zu ahnungsvoller Kritik an dieser Welt, diesem ihrem allerdings bewunderungswürdigen Gleichnis, dieser seiner Liebe reif gemacht hatten und danach angetan waren, sie alle drei unter Gewissenszweifel zu stellen» (p. 905). Surely this sentence provides as clear an answer as one could wish to the question: What does Castorp learn on the Magic Mountain? He has matured to the point where he is able not only to achieve clarity about his own personality and its predilections, but also – and this is the most important pedagogical conclusion of the novel – to regard it critically and to subject it to sceptical questioning. Thus he is now able to look critically at Chauchat (although she is still «absolut bewunderungswürdig»), at the world she represents, and at his love for both her and that world. It is true that all along he has had a guilty conscience about both his inclinations and his behaviour, and those doubts were never more real and troubling than now when he contemplates the message of «Der Lindenbaum.» The lessons that Settembrini had attempted to inculcate into him may have been regarded critically (and even at times scornfully), but they have not been forgotten, nor have they been entirely rejected.[44] Settembrini's sermon on the dangers of slipping backwards into a world of Romantic yearning for love and death has left its mark on Castorp, of whom it is now said: «Er fand es ratsam, diese Unterweisung mit Vorsicht auf seinen Gegenstand zu beziehen» (p. 906).

That we are indeed talking here about «Romanticism» and all that that word connotes, is substantiated by Castorp's reflections about Settembrini's strictures: the latter had made it clear that a relapse would be a sign of sickness. A relapse into what? Not just into the view of life that favours disease and death, but also even into the intellectual epoch from which that view of life originates. There can be little doubt that by the use of the term «die Geistesepoche» (p. 906) in this context the era of Romanticism is meant. That era of Romanticism is past, to be sure, but its legacy can be found in a world view that encompasses a fascination with love and death. Here Castorp is reflecting critically on the two opposing attitudes to life: the «rational» humanistic approach personified by Settembrini, and the «irrational» Romantic

---

44 Cf. Gutmann (note 6), p. 421. Several of the points in the following discussion can also be found in Gutmann (passim).

tendencies that he himself possesses. It is important to note that he subjects both approaches to life to critical scrutiny. Thus his reflections occasioned by hearing «Der Lindenbaum» bring him along the path to pedagogical maturity. The knowledge of the two opposing worlds is combined into a new and fertile synthesis that expresses a message of progress and cautious optimism rising above the competing creeds and philosophies. The fascination with death is declared to be «das Gemütlich-Gesundeste auf der Welt» (p. 906), since life, like a fruit, consists of the antinomies of health and decay, beauty and death. Castorp's achievement is to overcome whatever negative aspects his previous view of life had contained and to reach a new level of optimistic awareness of life's paradoxes. Even Settembrini's reservations are included in this hopeful synthesis: this fruit of life, which at the same time contains the seeds of death, is perhaps the greatest miracle of the human soul, but at the same time it is «jedoch mit Mißtrauen betrachtet aus triftigen Gründen vom Auge verantwortlich regierender Lebensfreundschaft» (p. 906-07). Thus, Castorp has finally come to demonstrate what Mann himself characterized as the novel's basic theme: «Todesromantik plus Lebensja.»[45] And yet there is a small qualification here. Castorp's victory over his inborn inclinations is not necessarily valid for all people nor even for himself for ever: it is qualified by the phrase «nach letztgültigem Gewissensspruch» (p.907) – thus allowing for individual variations and possible changes of mind at a later date. The process of reflection about life is never over.[46]

Castorp therefore achieves his insight and consequently his «Selbstüberwindung» while listening to the «Lindenbaumlied,» and this ultimately is the message both of this sub-chapter and of the novel as a whole.[47] However, it is a message that he only intuits, but does not see clearly: his «Gedanken, oder ahndevolle Halbgedanken ... gingen höher, als sein Verstand reichte» (p. 907). The vague and visionary language of the final paragraph of «Fülle des Wohllauts» would leave us with various interpretative possibilities, were it not for the fact that Mann indicated his meaning for us by using both this paragraph and some of the preceding discussion as the basis for a speech he gave on the occasion of a musical celebration of Nietzsche's eightieth birthday on 15 October 1924, just two weeks after the publication of *Der Zauberberg*. His starting point was Nietzsche's love of music; but that love was full of doubts and criticism (and here Mann spoke of Nietzsche's «Regierungs- und Gewis-

---

45 Thomas Mann to Ernst Bertram, 21.9.1918, in *Dichter über ihre Dichtungen: Thomas Mann, Teil I: 1889–1917*, hrsg. von Hans Wysling (Passau: Heimeran/Fischer, 1975), p. 459.
46 This is the opposite conclusion from that of Michael Beddow in *The Fiction of Humanity* (Cambridge: Cambridge University Press, 1982), p. 279–80. Martin Swales (note 3) also believes that Hans Castorp's insight in regard to «Der Lindenbaum» is «a falsity.» Reed (p. 272-74), does see a positive, if not too concrete, message in the novel, as does Sandt, p. 160, 178.
47 Mann made several references to this. Cf. *GW*, XI, 20–21.

senszweifel» – *GW*, x, 182). The combination of music and romanticism Mann called «almost» typically German and it was both Nietzsche's fate and his mission to face this problem and to overcome it. The «problem» was for Mann the Romantic attraction of death, and for him the later nineteenth century produced two individuals, Wagner and Nietzsche, each of whom dealt with this problem in his own way. The former gave in to the attraction of death, the latter overcame it. Of Nietzsche Mann said:

> Dies ist er uns: ein Freund des Lebens, ein Seher höheren Menschentums, ein Führer in die Zukunft, ein Lehrer der Überwindung all dessen in uns, was dem Leben und der Zukunft entgegensteht, das heißt des Romantischen. Denn das Romantische ist das Lied des Heimwehs nach dem Vergangenen, das Zauberlied des Todes, und das Phänomen Richard Wagner, das Nietzsche so unendlich geliebt hat und das sein regierender Geist überwinden mußte, war kein anderes als das paradoxe und ewig interessante Phänomen welterobernder Todestrunkenheit» (*GW*, x, 182).

Thus the «Seelenzauber mit finsteren Konsequenzen» is Romanticism with its attendant dangers, and the «Seelenzauberkünstler» who conquered the world with his colossal works is Richard Wagner. Mann regarded the problem of Romanticism as a specifically German phenomenon which in the latter part of the nineteenth century and the beginning of the twentieth century produced the imperialistic posturings of Wilhelm II, who debased the true message of Romanticism until it became – in Mann's fanciful analogy – cheap electrical gramophone music. For Mann the way to overcome the dangers of Romanticism – and hence the way for Germany to overcome them, too – was to follow the example of Nietzsche, who consumed himself in his attempt to conquer the negative and dangerous aspects of Romanticism, but who died, «das neue Wort der Liebe und der Zukunft in seinem Herzen» (p. 907). Thus in demonstrating Castorp's «Selbstüberwindung,» and in pointing to the example of Nietzsche, Mann is also indicating, in the first instance, an optimistic solution for the future of Germany.

The five musical selections that comprise Castorp's favourites do not offer us a simple continuum, in which there is a progression from one to the other until a clear conclusion is reached. Just as the novel is built up on diachronic and synchronic principles, so in the segment «Fülle des Wohllauts» the musical references reflect both thematic synchronicity and chronological progress towards pedagogical enhancement. That is, the five major recordings recapitulate once again the main themes of the novel, they «talk around them,» so to speak, and amplify their resonances in Castorp's personality. But since these themes are ever present within him, since none is ever abandoned or left behind, the discussion and recapitulation of them is circular in nature. The novel's web of themes is constructed of a highly complex pattern of synchronic cross-reference and interrelatedness that allows, for example, Castorp to claim that he already loved Chauchat when he loved Hippe (p. 827). But at the same time a narrative is diachronic: the story has to be told with one event succeeding another. In «Fülle des Wohllauts» we witness the interaction of these two narratorial principles.[48] Although Castorp clearly listens to his favourite recordings many times over, the narrative gives the impression at times that he does listen to them in a certain order. For example, we are asked to believe that *L'après-midi d'un faune* follows *Aida,* and «Valentin's Prayer» follows *Carmen,* not just in the text of the novel, but also in Castorp's private sessions with the gramophone. While the musical descriptions cause thematic echoes to resound from many other parts of the novel, yet there is at the same time a chronological development: Castorp does attain greater clarity and insight into his situation during the course of his listening. As Mann hisself said of his hero: «Seine Geschichte ist die Geschichte einer Steigerung» (*GW*, XI, 612). In hearing *Carmen* Castorp is attracted finally to the exhortation of the gypsies to abandon duty and embrace freedom, while *L'après-midi d'un faune* enables him to welcome lethargy without guilt. In both *Aida* and «Valentin's Prayer» he sees the transfiguration of love and affection beyond the grave. But it is not until the discussion of «Der Lindenbaum» that all these thematic threads are drawn together and woven into a positive conclusion that represents his newly-won attitude to life. It is significant that all five musical analyses end on a positive note *for Castorp,* irrespective of the conclusion in the original. From having laughed at death in the first few pages of the novel (p. 19), he then became fascinated with and drawn towards it, and now he has achieved mastery over it. «Sein Ziel ist die Zukunft,» said Thomas Mann (*GW*, XI, 731), and he also wrote in like manner to Julius Bab: «Hans Castorp ist am Ende ein kleiner Vorkriegsdeutscher, der durch „Steigerung" zum Anticipieren gebracht wird . . . und während der Arbeit sagte ich immer: «Ich schreibe von einem jungen Deutschen, der vorm Krieg schon über den Krieg hinauskommt.»[49]

While reflection is able to take Castorp a considerable distance along the path to enlightenment, the end is never actually reached, it is only finally perceived through a combination of intuition and reflection: only the magic of the imagination could let him sense the ultimate goal. It is only fitting that the most Romantic of the arts, music, should be at the same time the culmination of Castorp's Romantic experience and his means of overcoming it. While there are two more narrative segments before the conclusion of the novel, they illustrate but do not alter materially the fundamental conclusions that have been gained and stated in «Fülle des Wohllauts.» The fact that the final page of the novel underscores the conclusions of «Fülle des Wohllauts» (even to the point of repeating its key vocabulary), demonstrates the significance of that musical segment. In his concluding remarks the narrator, addressing Castorp directly,

---

48 Cf. Beddow (note 46), p. 258, Swales (note 3), p. 123., and also Thomas Mann, «Einführung in den *Zauberberg*», *GW*, XI, 612.
49 Briefe (note 51), p. 239.

states: «Augenblicke kamen, wo dir aus Tod und Körperunzucht ahnungsvoll und regierungsweise ein Traum von Liebe erwuchs» (p. 994). The segment «Fülle des Wohllauts» had offered Castorp several such moments, culminating in the dream that went beyond reason in his contemplation of the «Lindenbaumlied.» The narrator continues: «Abenteuer im Fleisch und Geist, die deine Einfachheit steigerten, ließen dich im Geist überleben, was du im Fleisch kaum überleben sollst» (p. 994).

The musical selections of «Fülle des Wohllauts,» in particular the five that were dealt with in detail, offered Castorp concrete examples of the survival of the spirit. The messages that he had culled from his musical favourites were themselves expressions of the spirit and enabled him to envision the survival of his own spirit and that of mankind as a whole. Thus there is a direct link between the sub-chapters «Schnee,» «Fülle des Wohllauts,» and the final pages of the novel. The «Romantic» fascination with death has been overcome, and that means that Hans has overcome his own innate personality. He has achieved a fortunate synthesis of all the forces and influences that have acted upon him for seven years and has progressed beyond them to attain a level of growth and maturity that embodies the author's hope for humanity. He has had his fill of music and philosophy, and through music he has achieved, if not complete harmony, then at least a euphonious blending of the influences to which he has been subjected.[50] That he does not act on his new-found insights does not mean that the message he personifies is not valid or valuable. Why Mann did not show him engaged in useful social activity may have something to do with the view he expressed in a letter to Paul Amann in 1916: «Das eigentlich Deutsche, zugleich Protestantisch-Christliche und nach meinem Begriff Bürgerlich-Geistige ist die Weigerung, das Überindividuelle ins Soziale zu verlegen, die Scheidung von «Philosophie» und «Politik,» d.h. die Scheidung des metaphysischen vom sozialen Leben.»[51] And is it mere coincidence that Mann's supposedly unconventional «Bildungsroman» corresponds closely to the definition of the genre that had been formulated by Wilhelm Dilthey just a few years before Thomas Mann began working on the novel: «Eine gesetzmäßige Entwicklung wird im Leben des Individuums angeschaut, jede ihrer Stufen hat ihren Eigenwert und ist zugleich Grundlage einer höheren Stufe. Die Dissonanzen und Konflikte des Lebens erscheinen als die notwendigen Durchgangspunkte des Individuums auf seiner Bahn zur Reife und zur Harmonie.»[52]

50 Cf. Thomas Mann to Robert Faesi (21 November 1925): «Hans Castorp ist ein Opfer, ein kleiner, forcierter Vorläufer. Seine Sittlichkeit ist das Experiment. Er „widersteht nicht dem Bösen." Aber auf diesem Wege lernt er, bevor er in den Krieg gerissen wird, von zukünftiger Humanität etwas ahnen» (*Briefe,* note 51, p. 250.)
51 *Thomas Mann: Briefe an Paul Amann, 1915–52,* hrsg. von Herbert Wegener (Lübeck: Veröffentlichungen der Stadtbibliothek Lübeck, Neue Reihe, Bd. 3, 1959), p. 50.
52 Wilhelm Dilthey, *Das Erlebnis und die Dichtung* (Stuttgart: Teubner, 1957), p. 250. The book first appeared in 1905.

Narrative Accommodations:
The Legacy of the Romantic *Künstlernovelle*

MARTIN SWALES, *University College, London*

> Romanticism is, perhaps predominantly, a desperate rearguard action against the spirit and the implications of modern science – a rearguard action that ... liberated the arts from the constraints of a pseudoscientific aesthetics but that was bound to fail in the proper domain of science.[1]

So writes Hans Eichner in a splendid (and, as the response to it proved,[2] splendidly provocative) article entitled «The Rise of Modern Science and the Genesis of Romanticism.» He stresses the strength and the depth of Romantic aversion to the model of a mechanistic universe obeying the necessary laws of matter. In defining the counter-claims of the Romantic world view Eichner borrows a formulation of Isaiah Berlin's: «the Romantics ... sought not to discover truth but to invent it.»[3] The agency that made possible such inventiveness was, supremely, the imagination (rather than reason). In their impassioned advocacy of the creative imagination, the Romantics were concerned to dethrone notions of law-based generality and universality and to insist on the (psychological, socio-cultural, and historical) particularity of any quest for truth. Eichner summarizes their epistemological position as follows:

> Knowledge of God and the Infinite is obtained not through reason, which is the same in everyone, but through the imagination, which is different: individuals can only grasp and reveal that knowledge in the light of their own personalities, from their own individual and unique perspectives.[4]

Precisely because the individual personality is the source of such truth, the mode of expression by which truth is to be conveyed will necessarily be poetic (rather than prosaic, or discursive):

---

1 Hans Eichner, «The Rise of Modern Science and the Genesis of Romanticism,» *PMLA*, 97 (1982), 8–30 (p. 18).
2 See *PMLA*, 97 (1982), 408–12.
3 Eichner, p. 17.
4 Eichner, p. 19.

> The higher truths that are revealed through the irrational or suprarational powers of the imagination cannot, the Romantics held, be expressed directly: such revelations can only be communicated *symbolically,* and hence the higher poetry, which is concerned with these higher truths, must be symbolic.[5]

Eichner leaves us in no doubt as to his view of the status and value of the Romantic attempt to supplant Newtonian mechanics. Its importance, as far as science itself is concerned, is negligible – which must, he insists, call into question its claims as an epistemology. But, as a contribution to art and aesthetics, its impact has been immense. All of this implies, so Eichner concludes, that we nowadays live with a sense of two different kinds of truth impinging on our lives: one is that of science and technology whose impact has been enormous and whose functional effectiveness is beyond dispute – Eichner speaks of the «technology that really works ..., the technology that, for example, enables us to dial a ten-digit number and ten seconds later to talk to a friend on the other side of the Atlantic.»[6] And the other is the non-testable truth of poetry, of those experiences which answer our deepest imaginative needs. One question obviously has posed – and continues to pose – itself: what, if any, is the relationship between these two different kinds of truth? I have no wish to rake over the coals of (among others) the Leavis-Snow controversy. What I hope to do in this paper is simply to trace a literary genre which (for reasons that Eichner has helped us to see) emerged into prominence in the Age of Romanticism and which continued to engage some of the very finest literary talents of German-speaking culture for the subsequent one hundred years or so. The genre in question is the so-called «Künstlernovelle.» I wish to suggest that it is a potent legacy from Romanticism; and that much of its potency derives from the fact that it addresses, both thematically and structurally, precisely those issues to which Eichner has so eloquently drawn our attention. Where Romantic epistemology could stridently hypostatize the creative imagination, the Romantic «Künstlernovelle» thematizes – in other words, problematicizes – it.

I shall in the course of this paper make reference to the following stories (the dates are those of first publication): E.T.A. Hoffmann's *Ritter Gluck* (1809), *Don Juan* (1813), *Der goldne Topf* (1814); Georg Büchner's *Lenz* (1839); Franz Grillparzer's *Der arme Spielmann* (1848); Eduard Mörike's *Mozart auf der Reise nach Prag* (1855); Thomas Mann's *Tonio Kröger* (1903) and *Der Tod in Venedig* (1912); Franz Kafka's *Ein Hungerkünstler* (1922) and *Josefine die Sängerin oder das Volk der Mäuse* (1924). With this list I make no claims for exhaustiveness. I would simply argue that these works are significant narrative achievements that by common consent would be held to belong to – and constitute the tradition of – the «Künstlernovelle.» I do not thereby wish to advance any grandiose generic claims for the existence of the «Künstlernovelle»

---

5 Eichner, p. 19.
6 Eichner, p. 23.

as some kind of *Ding an sich*. I shall merely seek to highlight certain family resemblances between the stories, and to suggest that the recurring features of theme and mode contribute to an insistent debate about the place of imaginative endeavour in the quotidian world. The stories provide a matrix for the ever-renewed exploration of some of our profoundest cultural dilemmas.

A number of features common to all these texts can immediately be distinguished. All are concerned with a central character who is of imaginative and artistic temperament. Yet the artist figure is never the narrator. Rather, the tales are narrated from the perspective of an onlooker who registers both the creative endeavour of the artistic temperament and the everyday social world within which that temperament has to exist. Often (as we shall see) there is something uncompromising about the artist figure: and the narrative voice conveys both that unaccommodated selfhood and the familiar – compromising and perhaps also compromised – processes of practical existence outside it. Thereby the narrative voice acknowledges the everyday world in two important ways: first, there is the recognition of a world that (to borrow Eichner's phrase about telephone technology) «really works»; secondly, there is the perception that the vision of the creative individual could – or might – relate to the familiar social universe, or that, if it does not so relate, this disjunction needs to be registered. In this sense the «Künstlernovelle» partakes of the broader traditions of the Novelle genre which I explored in my study *The German Novelle:*[7] time after time the collision between the everyday and familiar on the one hand and the exceptional and unprecedented on the other provides for the characteristic effects of theme and mode. The «Künstlernovelle» concentrates on a particular definition of what is «einmalig»: it is the uniqueness of the creative individual to which the narrative voice bears witness – whether sceptical, grudging, sympathetic, or enthusiastic.

I shall begin by tracing the narrative logic of those «Künstlernovellen» where there is an immediately identifiable – because characterized – first-person narrator. In Hoffmann's *Ritter Gluck* the narrator introduces himself as an habitué of Berlin cafés – even mentioning one particular establishment by name: «bald sind alle Plätze bei Klaus und Weber besetzt.» In fact the name is that of the proprietors, not of the café itself: thereby the narrator presents his credentials as knowledgeable inhabitant of Berlin – he is initiated into the metropolitan shorthand, as it were.[8] Yet immediately we note that he is a solitary figure in the crowd of pleasure seekers: «Da setze ich mich hin, dem leichten Spiel meiner Phantasie mich überlassend, die mir befreundete Gestalten zuführt, mit denen ich über Wissenschaft, über Kunst, über alles, was dem Menschen am teuersten sein soll, spreche.» It is only with creatures of

---

7 *The German Novelle* (Princeton: Princeton University Press, 1977).
8 See Klaus Kanzog, «Berlin-Code, Kommunikation und Erzählstruktur» *ZfdPh,* 95 (1976), Sonderheft, 42–63.

his imagination that the narrator can converse about the truly important things of life. But alas, his reverie is soon put to flight by the abysmal sounds of the café orchestra – «das verwünschte Trio eines höchst niederträchtigen Walzers reißt mich aus der Traumwelt.» But precisely this aversion to debased music brings the narrator into contact with the mad musician who believes himself to be the composer Gluck. They are united in being outsiders for whom the transcendental mystery of music is being daily prostituted in Berlin. The narrator's affinity with the mad artist has to do with the reverence both of them feel for the realm of the imagination. And even the madness of the Gluck figure – whom the narrator at one point calls «meinen Sonderling» – is not allowed to obscure the fact that potentially he is a creative musician of the highest calibre. «Nun spielte er herrlich und meisterhaft,» we read; reference is made to the «viele neue geniale Wendungen»; his music is «die Glucksche Szene gleichsam in höherer Potenz.» The stance of the narrator cannot provide a reconciliation between the world of the Berlin cafés and that of the doomed composer: but what it can do is to make us, the readers, acknowledge the kinds of value and truth which can be ascribed to both worlds.

Something similar applies to the narrative in *Don Juan*. The narrator is, we are told, a «travelling enthusiast,» a composer who happens to stay one night in a hotel which adjoins an opera house. He attends a performance of *Don Giovanni* which proves a revelation to him. It is a revelation of the existential truth of this, the supreme opera; and its truthfulness is not only asserted by the narrator, it is lived out by the soprano who so identifies with the role of Donna Anna that she dies some hours after the end of the performance, consumed by the terrible spiritual crisis that Mozart's fictional character undergoes. The philistines are impervious to this grandiose drama. Indeed, they resent the fact that the performance, in its intensity, overstepped the bounds of socially acceptable entertainment. But they vouch for the fact that the death of the soprano occurred as an event in the world «that really works.» And thereby they provide confirmation (albeit unwittingly) of the «fabelhafte Begebenheit» which the narrator chronicles and interprets.

Where E.T.A. Hoffmann was uncompromising in his validation of the imaginative realm, subsequent writers prove more sceptical. Grillparzer's *Der arme Spielmann* has striking affinities to *Ritter Gluck* in terms of its narrative structure. The narrator meets the «Spielmann» of the title one day at a «Volksfest» in Vienna. He is struck by the strangeness of the old man's appearance and behaviour, and seeks him out to discover his life story. Some two years after their meeting he hears of the musician's death, witnesses his funeral, and, as a last contact with the old man, visits Barbara, the girl (now married) whom the musician loved. Throughout his account, the narrator is at pains to maintain a scrupulous distance from the «Spielmann.» Time and time again he asserts his overtly *scientific* detachment. There is no admission of sympathy, let alone affinity such as we find in *Ritter Gluck*. Grillparzer's narrator insistently

The Legacy of the *Künstlernovelle*

aligns himself with the world «that really works.» He is a writer, but one who asserts the value and dignity of the common world (whether it is the «Volksfest,» «in dem denn doch zuletzt das Göttliche liegt,» or whether it is the enthusiasm for a play evinced by a packed house). Similarly Barbara repudiates the incompetent, impractical «Spielmann» and enters the world «that really works» with her marriage to a butcher. Unlike Hoffmann's artist figures, Jakob, the poor musician, is a failure at everything – including the one thing that matters most to him, which is his work as a creative composer. And yet, behind the barrage of disparagement, the story implies an acknowledgment of Jakob that is as devastating as it is inadmissible. At the «Volksfest» both the narrator and the «Spielmann» are oddities, unaccommodated figures. Both of them stand apart from the crowd. The narrator's obsessive interest in the oddity suggests more than simply «anthropological» or «psychological» curiosity – particularly as the moment of their meeting deflects the narrator entirely from that mass spectacle which he has praised as «eine Wallfahrt, eine Andacht.» The narrator's assertions of the divinity of the common mass of humanity are challenged by that other divinity of which the «Spielmann» speaks: a divinity denied substantiation in the real world. His music is likened to a prayer, his attempts to compose are attempts to «den lieben Gott spielen.» At one level the story implies that the failure of that attempt may be to do with Jakob's incompetence. But it also intimates another possibility: that Jakob's failure may have to do with the sheer irreconcilability of the two worlds. At the end of the story the narrator visits Barbara and offers to buy the old man's violin from her. She reacts with gestures and words that accord the violin a spiritual status far in excess of its objective worth as a musical instrument. And the story leaves us with Barbara's acknowledgment, in her tears, of the old man.

The narrative stance of the worldly onlooker occurs again in two stories by Franz Kafka (who, it should be mentioned, once said of Grillparzer's tale that he was as ashamed of it as if he had writtten it himself). With Kafka, however, the doubts and bad conscience that beset Grillparzer's one attempt at the «Künstlernovelle» become further radicalized. The story *Ein Hungerkünstler* concerns a performance that cannot easily be described as art: for it is an art that consists purely and simply in abstaining from that activity that sustains life – eating. And the narrator figure, as Roy Pascal has shown,[9] is an impresario-cum-showman, somebody who is acutely aware of the «business» of the circus, the fairground, the sideshow. Gradually, public interest in such displays of fasting wanes. Finally the «Hungerkünstler» is replaced by a panther who does not lack for an audience. Our narrator is, as always, concerned with the public reaction to the show being presented. And in the closing lines he chronicles the panther's success: «die Freude am Leben kam mit derart star-

---

[9] Roy Pascal, *Kafka's Narrators* (Cambridge: Cambridge University Press, 1982), p. 105–35.

ker Glut aus seinem Rachen, daß es für die Zuschauer nicht leicht war, ihr standzuhalten. Aber sie überwanden sich, umdrängten den Käfig und wollten sich gar nicht fortrühren.» It is noteworthy that the people are overawed by the animal's abundant joy in life. If they have to «overcome themselves» in order to confront such a spectacle, perhaps we can begin to understand why and how the sight of a man denying all «Freude am Leben» could also, at certain times, claim public interest and enthusiasm. If art calls into question the bases of efficient living, this may be a message that people need to hear and experience.[10] The artist now is not just a «Sonderling» *(Ritter Gluck)*, an «Original» *(Der arme Spielmann):* he is a freak. But perhaps even freakishness can have a certain purchase on the intact and familiar world.

In *Josefine die Sängerin oder das Volk der Mäuse,* Kafka's last story, the narrator has become explicitly the spokesman for a whole community. He is an unremarkable member of the mouse nation, and he offers a quizzical account of the value of Josefine's art for its audience. Continually, his account seems to suggest that her performance is little better than a confidence trick. Certainly, the sounds she emits appear in no way distinct from the noises that all the members of the mouse community produce daily. Yet the confidence trick does «really work»: if for no other reason than that the audience colludes with the performer, invests the experience with the particular aura of aesthetic value. In the process the community comes to notice what it does daily – it notices because it does not take itself and its doings for granted. Kafka's story is both the epitaph to the tradition of the «Künstlernovelle» and its amazing reinstatement. It claims nothing for the art as such: yet it offers a weighty validation of the relevance of art to the world «that really works.» It claims both more and less than did E.T.A. Hoffmann.

So far I have been considering stories in which we have an identifiable first-person narrator, and I have suggested that that narrator figure functions as a kind of mediator between imagination and fact. A similar function can also be detected in those «Künstlernovellen» in which the narrator is not a particularized figure. The voice that recounts *Der goldne Topf* is one that both registers Anselmus's incompetence and clumsiness within the bourgeois world of Dresden, and at the same time urges us to make common cause with the protagonist in his process of gradual translation into the higher spirit world.[11] We are asked to acknowledge both Dresden and Atlantis. And just as the student Anselmus is initiated into the spirit world by copying the strange signs and symbols of Londhorst's books, so too the narrator, on his own account, pens his tale at night (when the quotidian world relaxes its hold on the mind), and owes his

---

10 See Sabina Kienlechner, *Negativität der Erkenntnis im Werk Franz Kafkas* (Tübingen: Niemeyer, 1981), p. 61–73.
11 See John Reddick, «.E.T.A. Hoffmann's *Der goldne Topf* and its „durchgehaltene Ironie",» *MLR,* 71 (1976), 577–94.

tale of Anselmus's life in the realm of poetry to a kind of automatic dictation from the spirit world. The narrator can vouch for the truth of the mythological world of salamanders and spirits precisely because he also recognizes the existence of Dresden, Heerbrand, and Paulmann.[12]

In Büchner's *Lenz* we have a strangely dispassionate – almost documentary – narrative tone which coexists with frequent moments of near-identification as the narrator reports, through such devices as *erlebte Rede,* the nightmarishly vivid metaphors and hallucinations of Lenz's tormented mind. In Mörike's *Mozart auf der Reise nach Prag* we have a narrator who sees – and cherishes – his protagonist as someone both happily, and creatively, part of society and also as a lonely, unaccommodated figure, doomed by the intensity of his imaginative life to know of the ever-present abyss. In Thomas Mann's *Der Tod in Venedig* we have a narrative performance that seems to embody the aesthetic principles of Aschenbach's own creativity – a chiselled perfection of form, a classicizing prose style. Yet Aschenbach himself confuses aesthetic and ethical values in that he allows form, in the sense of orderliness, to supplant all other values. He drifts into a degrading homosexual infatuation with a young boy, and his worship of form renders him impervious to all promptings of moral scruple. As his decline accelerates, the narrator stands back from his protagonist and judges him as «betört,» «starrsinnig.» But the judgment coexists with a complicity in precisely the cast of mind that makes Aschenbach so vulnerable. In its amazingly sophisticated, self-reflexive way, then, *Der Tod in Venedig* remains true to the tradition I have been tracing: the narrator may, on occasion, identify with the artist hero; but he never becomes identical with him.

One sub-theme emerges from the commerce between hero and narrator which I have been at pains to document: the sense of the oddity of the artist within the framework of socially accommodated living. We are constantly given details of his strange appearance, aberrant behaviour or utterance.[13] Anselmus is discovered embracing a tree, Lenz plunges into a freezing fountain, the «Spielmann» has sheet music with him but cannot even give a recognizable performance of simple tunes; Mozart, in a fit of artistic abstraction, picks an orange in a garden which he has no right to enter, Josefine throws «artistic» tantrums. The list could be extended almost indefinitely. But one particular point emerges very forcefully. As Herman Meyer pointed out in a famous book,[14] there has been no shortage in German literature of «Sonderlinge.» And, indeed, other European literatures have not been indifferent to the ap-

---

12 See Roland Heine, *Transzendentalpoesie: Studien zu Friedrich Schlegel, Novalis, und E.T.A. Hoffmann* (Bonn: Bouvier, 1974), p. 154–98.
13 See Jochen Schmidt (ed.), *Deutsche Künstlernovellen des 19. Jahrhunderts* (Frankfurt: Insel, 1982), «Nachwort,» p. 404.
14 Herman Meyer, *Der Sonderling in der deutschen Dichtung* (München: Hanser, ²1963).

peal of the «outsider.» But it must be stressed very firmly that the *Künstlernovelle* is not concerned with the outsider as a psychological or pathological phenomenon. The (actual or potential) creativity of the artist figure is central to the thematic argument of the stories: it is not simply a contingent version of «outsiderdom» which could be replaced by other aberrations (sexual, economic, or whatever). This accounts for a particular and insistent strand to the stories I am considering: a thematizing of the creative discourse of the artist in relation to the everyday concerns (and discourses) of society. The issue is nowhere more urgent – or more demonstrable – than where we are concerned with stories where the artist figure is a writer: that is to say, where the medium of the artist's creativity is the same as the medium of the narrator's account – language.

I have already commented on the theme of «automatic writing» in *Der goldne Topf,* which embraces both protagonist and narrator. Anselmus is employed by the Archivarius Lindhorst as a copying clerk: and, at the end of the tale, the narrator finds that he has penned the vision of Atlantis without knowing that he did so:

> Die Vision, in der ich nun den Anselmus leibhaftig auf seinem Rittergute in Atlantis gesehen, verdankte ich wohl den Künsten des Salamanders, und herrlich war, daß ich sie, als alles wie im Nebel verloschen, auf dem Papier, das auf dem violetten Tische lag, recht sauber und augenscheinlich vor mir selbst aufgeschrieben fand.

The central notion here is that the spiritual realm can only speak to an inhabitant of the modern bourgeois world if the accommodated (and self-censoring) consciousness is by-passed. Hence the chapters are called «Vigilien»: that is, they are written at night when the mundane preoccupations of the empirically perceivable world are in abeyance. Büchner's *Lenz* similarly brings the tormented perceptions (and discourse) of the threatened artist figure close to the operations of familiar discourse.[15] I have already drawn attention to the fact that the language which conveys Lenz's responses to us is highly charged and metaphorical: it is a language which we notice because it contrasts starkly with the register of sober reportage which characterizes some of the narrator's statements (as in the opening sentence of the story: «Den 20. Jänner ging Lenz durchs Gebirg»). The story closes with an account of Lenz's collapse into total apathy and indifference. The protagonist loses all contact with – and perception of – the natural world around him. The narrator writes: «die Erde war wie ein goldener Pokal, über den schäumend die Goldwellen des Mondes liefen.» The context makes it entirely clear that this formulation cannot be *erlebte Rede,* that it must derive from the narrator himself. The point of this «purple passage» is surely that the narrator thereby reminds us that metaphor is a property of all language – even of common-or-garden discourse – and is not

---

15 See Roy Pascal, «Büchner's *Lenz:* Style and Message,» *OGS,* 9 (1978), 68–83.

confined to poetic utterance. And it is primarily at this level of linguistic mediation that the text makes us share in Lenz's anguished visions. The narrative spectrum of Büchner's tale extends from dispassionate reportage to the eccentric, even aberrant responses of the unhinged poetic consciousness. And in that all-important final paragraph, the narrator, by his use of metaphor, asserts that the linguistic spectrum does not admit of hard divisions whereby «normal» discourse can be separated from «abnormal.» The spectrum is, in other words, a continuum in which we find common ground even with the radically unaccommodated consciousness of Lenz.

Tonio Kröger chronicles a painful growth process from adolescence to maturity. In this sense it has a psychological theme which clearly informs every chapter. Yet if we analyse the story in psychological terms, we soon find that it is a very slender piece, the sum total of whose wisdom would amount to something like «accept yourself as you are.» Yet what gives substance to an otherwise slender theme (and story) is the whole issue of creativity and language. Time and time again Tonio laments the curse of literature: that its maker has to stand aside from all substantial human concerns in order to be, precisely, a «maker,» a craftsman. Yet at the end he promises, in a letter written to a friend, that he will be able to «Besseres machen,» because he need no longer deny the substantial content that will give flesh to the artistic form. This credo is expressed in the words that end the story: «Schelten Sie diese Liebe nicht...; sie ist gut und fruchtbar. Sehnsucht ist darin und schwermütiger Neid und ein klein wenig Verachtung und eine ganz keusche Seligkeit.» These words echo the sentences which close the first section of the story: but there the words are spoken of Tonio by the narrator. At the end of the story he uses them himself. The process of psychological development, then, is underpinned by – and made possible through – a growth in artistic understanding. Tonio develops to the point of being narrator to his own experience: his discursively formulated commitment to future artistic creativity is reinforced by the existence of the text that we have been reading. Creative possibility becomes narrative actuality at the end of *Tonio Kröger.*

Der Tod in Venedig, too, makes the link between the discourse of the creative artist and the social world outside the realm of art: and it does so by thematizing the particular mode and character of the artist figure's creativity. In a moment of self-reflectivity the narrator comments on that ethos which informs both Aschenbach's life and art and the text itself (which is, as I have already suggested, closely implicated in Aschenbach's mind and discourse). Thereby the text thematizes its very own mode. The narrator writes:

> Damit ein bedeutendes Geistesprodukt auf der Stelle eine breite und tiefe Wirkung zu üben vermöge, muß eine geheime Verwandtschaft, ja Übereinstimmung zwischen dem persönlichen Schicksal seines Urhebers und dem allgemeinen des mitlebenden Geschlechtes bestehen. Die Menschen wissen nicht, warum sie einem Kunstwerke Ruhm bereiten..., aber der eigentliche Grund ihres Beifalls ist ein Unwägbares, ist Sympathie. Aschenbach

hatte es einmal an wenig sichtbarer Stelle unmittelbar ausgesprochen, daß beinahe alles Große, was dastehe, als ein Trotzdem dastehe.

Only a page later we are told that Aschenbach was the spokesman «all derer, die am Rande der Erschöpfung arbeiten, ... all dieser Moralisten der Leistung. ... Ihrer sind viele.» The ethos of form, of (to put it as a non-aesthetic category) orderliness and discipline is what provides the subterranean connection between Aschenbach's art and the climate of his time. That Thomas Mann's story both enshrines and criticizes the complex ethos that unites artistic and social discourses is not the least of its achievements.

Much of this mediation between artist and society derives, then, not only from the persona of the narrator but also from the style and mode of his account. The thematic correlative of this commerce is to be found in the notion of a secret possessed by the artist and revealed to the non-artistic (that is, uninitiated) world. *Der goldne Topf* has at its centre a myth of a paradise possessed, forfeited – and regained. At the end of the tale we are told that the harmony of which the myth speaks is cognate with the harmony of «das Leben in der Poesie, der sich der heilige Einklang aller Wesen als tiefstes Geheimnis der Natur offenbaret.» In *Ritter Gluck* the mad musician laments: «ich verriet Unheiligen das Heilige.» In *Don Juan* the mystery at the centre of Mozart's supreme opera is revealed to be a titanic drama in which man's spirituality is doomed by its material housing to search for experiences whose promise will never be redeemed. The narrator insists time and time again in such phrases as «nun erst,» «jetzt,» «jetzt erst» that the meeting with the soprano singing Donna Anna reveals to him what he had previously only dimly sensed about *Don Giovanni*. And the secret is confirmed in the price it exacts in the death of the singer who was so well initiated into its awful mystery. Equally catastrophic in its implications for the accommodations of everyday living is the secret which is at the heart of the life led by «der arme Spielmann.» When he speaks of his attempts to create his own music, he employs biblical language: «das Gebet gehört ins Kämmerlein.» The confession of the intense inner life is attended by «Beschämung über das verratene Geheimnis seines Innern.» That secret may appear only in distorted form (in the music that the old man actually plays): but so radical is the disjunction in his life between «Absicht» and «Werk» that the secret remains hidden to all but those who are attuned to its devastating disparagement of the material world. Mörike's *Mozart auf der Reise nach Prag* concentrates on a few unstrenuous and unproblematic hours from the life of the great composer. Many of the events chronicled are light-hearted, even seemingly trivial. Yet we must recall a phrase used by Madame Mozart of the wedding present she gives to the young couple – «daß es lediglich nur durch seine Geschichte einigermaßen interessieren kann.» The «story» which gives significance to the humble object is that it is «ein Stück gemeinen Hausrat, welches Mozart ausgewählt»: it is something that has been touched by Mozart's unique sensibility. Mörike's story persuades us of the imaginative intensity of the composer's life, one which he can neither control nor moderate. Even when he is relaxing in congenial company, Mozart embroiders, improvises on facts and circumstances. The amazingly prodigal inventiveness of his spirit is the story Mörike has to tell. It is the secret of Mozart's life and music: it is his glory and his doom – «genießend oder schaffend, kannte Mozart gleich wenig Maß und Ziel.» To that dark secret his greatest music bears witness. The piano on which he played is locked at the end of the story. It, too, will be cherished because of its «Geschichte.» And the import of that story is summarized in the incomparable poem with which Mörike's *Novelle* ends.

The final stages in this theme of the artist's secret are charted by Franz Kafka. Ultimately, the secret may be (as in *Ein Hungerkünstler*) rather like the punch line of a shaggy dog story. For the climactic disclosure of what sustains the hunger artist's amazing asceticism is: «weil ich nicht die Speise finden konnte, die mir schmeckt. Hätte ich sie gefunden, glaube mir, ich hätte kein Aufsehen gemacht und mich vollgegessen wie du und alle.» What the public has admiringly taken to be a superhuman exercise in self-denial proves to be a form of anorexia. As in so many of the stories we are considering, the artist figure is uncompromisingly divorced from common human experience; yet, in Kafka, he has no higher, no alternative values to offer. The secret is that there is no secret worth bothering about, no Atlantis, no mission such as that which sustained Grillparzer's poor musician to express «den lieben Gott» through art. Similarly, Josefine offers to her people an art that seems to be indistinguishable from the utterances that are produced daily by the mouse nation. There is, literally, nothing to it: it is «dieses Nichts an Stimme, dieses Nichts an Leistung.» The value of her art resides not in the art itself but in the expectations that her audience brings to bear on her performance. For, by attending to her performance, the hearers attend to what they themselves do daily without thinking about it. Kafka's last story is a wonderfully ironic legitimation of art: in place of proud claims for higher or transcendental insight, he suggests that art helps men and women to perceive what otherwise would go unremarked. It is a modest – but by no means unworthy – conclusion to the theme we have traced.

One final theme deserves mention, if only briefly. Almost inevitably the *Künstlernovelle* raises the issue of the success or failure of the artist figure. This may seem to be an obvious issue. But it brings into play various – and on occasion conflicting – value scales. One obvious possibility is that of the irreconcilable clash of worldly and spiritual criteria in respect of success and failure. Yet often, as we have seen, the stories do not operate with an undifferentiated distribution of plusses and minusses. If the Gluck figure and Lenz are failures, they are so even when judged by criteria of artistic creativity. Yet their failure is commended to us for our sympathy and even respect.

Mozart's amazing success is bought at a terrible price. «Der arme Spielmann» is arguably a failure in every realm, including even the one that matters most to him – but everything depends on whether, to borrow a phrase from the story, we judge «nach unseren Absichten» or «nach unseren Werken.» And Kafka's Josefine is both success and failure; the marvellously intricate dialectic of the mouse's account is the richest incarnation of the problematic that informs the tradition of the «Künstlernovelle.» For her art is, if the Heideggerian pun may be allowed, in-valuable: both worthless and amazingly precious.

We have come a long way from the Romantic love affair with the creative self.[16] And the journey is one charted by some of the finest creative talents in German literature. That they returned again and again to the problem of the artist, not as a psychological but as an epistemological theme, may, at one level, imply a penchant for voluptuous introspection, for writing about themselves and their craft. But there is more to it than this. Every story we have looked at has implied, through its narrative argument, a sense of the scale and urgency of the problem posed by the problematic commerce between the individual creative imagination and the corporate world that really works, that «wirkt.» The issue matters not only to creative writers. Behind the tradition of the «Künstlernovelle» there vibrates a cultural debate whose origins Hans Eichner has sketched for us with exemplary clarity. The richness of the legacy has to do with the fact that we are still part of that debate. And Kafka's *Josefine* story reminds us that it may take art to alert us to the full measure of the profound dilemmas that we enact every day of our lives.

---

16 See Lothar Pikulik, *Romantik als Ungenügen an der Normalität* (Frankfurt: Suhrkamp, 1979).

Nachdenken über Christa T. and the *Bildungsroman*

ROMAN S. STRUC, *University of Calgary*

«Politisch verdächtig» or
«Placet experiri.»?

Before turning to the issue at hand, i.e., the relationship of Christa Wolf's novel, *Nachdenken über Christa T.,* to the tradition of the *Bildungsroman,* I feel obliged to deal with two issues which have occupied most commentators discussing this novel. The first is the political controversy surrounding the book and the presence of political problems in the novel itself. It is clear not only how the novel became a political event, but also that it had to become one, considering the complexities of the relationship between the two Germanies. Within the GDR the novel was felt to be an audacious experiment in the art of the Novel. Thematically it appeared to be a challenge to the political and ideological establishment which, *a priori,* censures literature in which the relationship between the individual and the state is not presented with the clarity envisioned and demanded by the establishment. This clarity was absent. For even though Christa T. in the course of her short life initiates and undertakes efforts to bring about a better relationship between herself and the various forces identifiable with the monolithic ideology, either she or both sides fail to achieve an harmonious relationship which would validate the vision of the socialist state.[1]

It has been noted that the reception of the novel in other socialist countries has not been as harsh as it has been at home. In fact, the voices coming from Warsaw, Prague, and even Moscow accepted with much more readiness and greater understanding the peregrinations of Christa T. in her honest search for a place in the sun.[2] The reaction in the Federal Republic, on the other hand, was marked by cheers at the triumph of a free spirit and courage over a fossilized ideology.[3] A number of reasons account for these divergent attitudes in

---

1 The «affair» is thoroughly and competently treated by Alexander Stephan in *Christa Wolf: Autorenbücher* (München: Beck, 1976), p. 59-92.
2 Stephan, p. 91.
3 A representative sampling of critical comment is offered by Manfred Behn, ed., *Wirkungsgeschichte Christa Wolfs «Nachdenken über Christa T.»* (Königstein: Athenäum, 1978).

both Germanies. In the GDR, a socialist country with, however, a tarnished political past and therefore ever mindful of ideological purity and total allegiance to the cause, the reaction had to be what it was. Thus, as a result of the ideological watchfulness official reaction at the time of the novel's appearance verged on paranoia.

The reaction of the West German critical establishment predictably emphasized the political aspect of the novel, sensitive to the signs of overt and covert *Ideologiekritik,* at times to the point of excluding other facets of Wolf's novel. The forces impeding Christa T.'s progress «Zu-sich-Selber» were identified exclusively as those inherent in a socialist state. In other words, both sides, either in disapproval or benevolent approval, more or less explicitly, thoroughly politicized the novel. The reader in perusing critical commentaries on the novel will be somewhat taken aback, perhaps not unlike Hans Castorp on being told by Settembrini that music is «politically suspect.»

Thematically, the novel of the nineteenth century was concerned with the variety of relationships between the individual and the world at large. It also dealt with the degree of integration into society or lack of it, on the part of the individual. In the German literary tradition many of these novels range from the tragic case of *Werther,* to *Wilhelm Meister,* to other classical novels of formation, and the forces which impede those characters in their fulfillment are not all that different from those we observe in *Nachdenken.* Nor are they all that easily identifiable. Structurally, say, *Der grüne Heinrich* is not so different from *Nachdenken,* keeping in mind that in both cases society demands «Anpassung. Anpassung um jeden Preis» (p. 112).[4] Such conflicts and such imperative advice are likely to be encountered in the past as well as in the present, both in the East and in the West. Therefore, to say that Christa T. does die of leukemia, but is ill with GDR, is very clever indeed, but excessively reductive.[5] Individual and social structures have always been in a state of tension. This potentially tragic configuration is of an older vintage than A.D. 1968; it is at least as old as *Antigone.*

The second problem in *Nachdenken* criticism with which I do not quite sympathize but feel that I must comment on, is the relationship of Christa Wolf the author, with Christa T., the ostensible protagonist, and Christa T.'s surviving friend, the nameless narrator. The intention of the critics who pursue this «problem» seems to be the establishing of similarity, if not of identity, between the two figures in the novel, and, furthermore, the identification of the author with the two principal characters in ther novel. As «evidence» for

---

4 Page numbers in the text refer to Christa Wolf, *Nachdenken über Christa T.* (Darmstadt/Neuwied: Luchterhand, 1983).
5 Marcel Reich-Ranicki «Christa Wolfs unruhige Elegie,» *Die Zeit* (23 May 1969). Reprinted in Behn (see n. 3), p. 59-64. «Sagen wir klar: Christa T. stirbt an Leukämie, aber sie leidet an DDR» (p. 62).

this, critics note such similarities as those of «biography,» names, etc., etc.⁶ One prominent critic even remembers Christa T. from Leipzig.⁷

One is tempted to dismiss this non-problem with a shrug; yet, in view of its persistence, one is forced to speculate on the reasons for it. In my opinion, they are again political. If this novel, as many claim, represents political dissent, and if Christa Wolf is identical with Christa T., is she not a political dissident in the GDR?

Christa Wolf, unwittingly perhaps, has done her share to make such speculations possible though, I venture to say, more in the spirit of literary than political mystification. In the preamble to the novel, over the letters C.W., we read: «Christa T. ist eine literarische Figur.» Out of curiosity I consulted the English translation of Wolf's novel. There, this phrase reads, «Christa T. is a fictional character.» However, Christa Wolf would have said «erfunden» rather than «literarisch,» had she meant «fictional.» She uses this somewhat uncommon characterization because she wants to stress the heroine's «literariness,» her belonging to literary tradition. The phrase does mean, indeed, that Christa T. is a figure in a literary work but also, and perhaps foremost, that she is a figure made up of other literary figures. The authors from whom she borrows are as diverse as Goethe, Kleist, Dostoevsky, Flaubert, Thomas Mann, and others. At times Christa T. repeats the phrases of Goethe's Feline, just as in her musings she echoes the dark thoughts of Dostoevsky's Underground Man; in other words, Christa T. is a figure whose components are derived to an unusual extent from literature, but also from the author's imagination, as well as from the author's own life. There is nothing unusual about all this. Perhaps the most suitable epigraph to this discussion might be Magritte's inscription over his painting of a pipe: «Ceci n'est pas une pipe.»

Two important studies on the *Bildung* and the *Bildungsroman,* Bruford and Swales respectively, quote Thomas Mann on the subject. In the context of the present essay, the passage is also worth quoting as it contains an elegant and profound account of this problem. It is also significant because Thomas Mann's presence in Christa Wolf's *Nachdenken* is quite prominent:

> Die schönste Eigenschaft des deutschen Menschen, auch seine berühmteste, auch diejenige, mit der er sich selbst wohl am liebsten schmeichelt, ist seine Innerlichkeit. Nicht umsonst hat er der Welt die geistige und hochmenschliche Kunstgattung des Bildungs- und Entwicklungsromanes geschenkt, den er dem Romantypus westlicher Gesellschaftskritik als sein Eigenstes entgegenstellt und der immer zugleich auch Autobiographie, Bekenntnis ist. Die Innerlichkeit, die Bildung des deutschen Menschen, das ist: Versunkung; ein individualistisches Kulturgewissen; der auf Pflege, Formung, Vertiefung und Vollendung des eigenen Ich oder, religiös gesprochen, auf Rettung und Rechtfertigung des eigenen Lebens gerichtete Sinn ... Der tiefste Widerstand, so meine ich damit, dem der republikanische

---

6 As an example I mention Christa Thomassen, *Der lange Weg zu uns selbst* (Kronberg/Ts.: Scriptor, 1977), esp. p. 20-40.
7 Hans Mayer: «Christa Wolf, *Nachdenken über Christa T.,*» *NR,* 81 (1970), 184.

> Gedanke in Deutschland begegnet, beruht darauf, daß der deutsche Bürger und Mensch das politische Element niemals in seinen Bildungsbegriff aufgenommen hat, daß es tatsächlich bis jetzt darin fehlte...[8]

It is important to note that neither of the authors who quotes Mann nor he himself speak of a specific goal – such as an harmonious integration of the protagonist into the social or political fabric – which the protagonists might hope or expect to reach. In surveying the so-called classical *Bildungsroman,* it seems to be clear that «the goal attained» can just as easily be understood as either another station in the process of *Bildung,* or a conventional device for bringing the story to a close. Martin Swales in discussing this problem makes the following observation:

> Of course, the notion of a goal still has a place within human affairs. Yet, ultimately, the meaning of the growth process, of the *Werden,* is to be found in the process itself, not in any goal whose attainment it may make possible. The grasping for clarity and losing it, the alternation of certainty of purpose with a sense of overriding randomness of living, these are seen to be the very stuff of human experience and such meaning and distinction as men are able to attain. The Bildungsroman, then, is written for the sake of the journey, and not for the sake of the happy ending toward which that journey points.[9]

This concept of the process of life as being both becoming and the goal itself is powerfully expressed in *Nachdenken.* In an italicized passage, therefore presumably recorded by Christa T. herself, we read: «*Leben, erleben, freies großes Leben! O herrliches Lebensgefühl, daß du mich nie verläßt! Nichts weiter als ein Mensch sein...*» (p. 46); and somewhat further, the narrator discovers something which cannot be fully grasped, because its very nature is movement. She describes its emergence in this manner:

> Christa ging dann doch. Sie hat diesen Vorgang – wegzugehen – später noch öfter wiederholt, dahinter verbirgt sich ein Muster, schon ablesbar beim erstenmal: hinter sich lassen, was man zu gut kennt, was keine Herausforderung mehr darstellt. Neugierig bleiben auf die anderen Erfahrungen, letzten Endes auf sich selbst in den neuen Umständen. *Die Bewegung mehr lieben als das Ziel* [my emphasis] (p. 46).

I read these passages – other such utterances can easily be found in the novel – as signals to the reader of how the novel is to be read and Christa T. understood. Again Thomas Mann and his *Magic Mountain* come to mind (Christa T. reads *The Magic Mountain* in the hospital!) and specifically Settembrini's

---

8 W.H. Bruford, *The German Tradition of Self-Cultivation: «Bildung» from Humboldt to Thomas Mann* (Cambridge: Cambridge University Press, 1978) and Martin Swales, *The German Bildungsroman from Wieland to Hesse* (Princeton: Princeton University Press, 1978). To these two studies I am gratefully indebted. I was especially pleased to see Swales include Christa Wolf's *Der geteilte Himmel* and *Nachdenken* in his references to the contemporary variety of the *Bildungsroman* (p. 162). Thomas Mann, «Geist und Wesen der deutschen Republik: Dem Gedächtnis Walther Rathenaus,» *Gesammelte Werke in zwölf Bänden,* xi (Frankfurt: Fischer, 1960), 854–55.

9 Swales, p. 33–34.

recommendation *placet experiri* which Castorp embraces as an imperative and Claudia Chauchat criticises for being typically German. But then this is what «German» does mean in the context of *Bildung*, a dynamic process of *leben* but also *erleben*, a process which goes on beyond the book, as it were. The reader is challenged to continue the process of reflection begun in *Nachdenken über Christa T.* for his own sake. In the prologue to the novel, the narrator says: «Sie braucht uns nicht. Halten wir also fest, es ist unseretwegen, denn es scheint, wir brauchen sie» (p. 10). Swales claims that this is an important feature of the *Bildungsroman:* «it is the *reader* who is initiated into the wholeness and complexity of *Bildung;* the hero and the world through which he moves are only redeemable through the symbolic transformations made possible by an artistic labour of love.»[10]

Nachdenken über Christa T. finely delineates the reader's position in the novel's scheme. The process of *Bildung* consists of three perspectives. Christa T. is, of course, the subject and the agent through and by whom the events and episodes are activated. Her ability to make sense, to make patterns out of these episodes is necessarily limited. Of course, she cannot think of herself as some kind of symbol, although those around her sense that she is. In Christa T.'s life there is a powerful impulse to capture the dynamics of life: her poetic ventures appear to do just that in a fragmentary, «romantic» form. Everything we learn about Christa's literary experiments points to this somewhat vague, though persuasive dialectic between the desire to fix the experience, while simultaneously conveying it as a process. The very fragmentary nature of her experiments, it seems, is capable of doing both: she records reality as movement. Her fear of *Festlegung* is identified with death (p. 174); «Es [life] muß andauernd entstehen, das ist es. Man darf und darf es nicht dahin kommen lassen, daß es fertig wird» (p. 166). In part through her literary activity, her diaries, and notes, the reader can make out some patterns of movement. But it is actually through the narrator, Christa's friend, that the reader is offered more than intimations. One of the first episodes – Christa's blowing a tune on a rolled up newspaper – represents Christa's spontaneous action, performed without deliberate intention. The very essence of the episode is its spontaneity, its movement; but reflection necessarily interludes and for the narrator it is an action emblematic of something which she can express only vaguely: «Ich wollte an einem Leben festhalten, das solche Rufe hervorbrachte, hoohaahoo, und das ihr [Christa] bekannt sein mußte» (p. 18). In relating the incident the narrator ascribes to it a meaning which goes beyond the episode itself, but it is not spelled out for the reader.

The reader is challenged to complete the process by tracing and retracing Christa's life through reflection («Nachdenken»). Quite explicitly the narrator warns against cultivating memories of her: «Die Farbe der Erinnerung trügt»

10 Swales, p. 32.

(p. 9). The challenge to the reader is not unlike that of Brecht's to the viewer. What Brecht demands from his public is indeed *Nachdenken,* i.e., the completion of the writing process in life. The narrator explains to the reader the difference between sentimental memories and the process of reflection («Nachlässige Trauer und ungenaue Erinnerung und ungefähre Kenntnis haben sie zum Schwinden gebracht, das ist verständlich») (p. 10). «[Der] *Versuch, man selbst zu sein* (p. 9), must be completed through reflection and action: «Ein für allemal. Sie braucht uns nicht. Halten wir also fest, es ist unseretwegen, denn es scheint, wir brauchen sie» (p. 10).

This is of course the stuff of which *Bildungsromane* are made: experiences of the protagonist which the reader must convert into a *Bildung* for himself. What makes this novel deliberately more challenging is that the reader is offered two incomplete perspectives which must be dealt with. If one assumes that literary texts necessarily require concretization in Ingarden's sense, this novel makes it its task to force the reader into co-authorship. If this assumption is correct, then the somewhat unusual elliptic form and style of the novel, the confusing chronology, the uncertainty of the sources of the narrator's stories, and other such devices which increase the «indeterminacy» of the text are not only experimentation with form, but a component of the pedagogical intent of the novel. Therefore the form of *Nachdenken,* more than normally, is part of its predication. This very elliptic manner allows the novel to convey a wealth of more and less «raw» material. This depends on the narrator's proximity to the events or the availability of recorded material.

For the sake of convenience one can look at three spheres of experience which allow us to arrive at discernible patterns: first, childhood and adolescence; second, Christa in the social context, and, third, her private life. None of these spheres can be considered in isolation. One touches on the other, as for example in her marriage, in which a very private commitment is at the same time a social one. Thus, Christa T. appears before us as a loving woman, but also as «Tierarztfrau in mecklenburgischer Kleinstadt» (p. 36).

Unlike most novels of *Bildung,* this work does not make much of Christa T.'s childhood. One can go as far as to say that both childhood and adolescence are treated briefly and somewhat schematically. The reader hears «Frisch-Fromm-Froh-Frei» of the girls in brown skirts and white blouses; Christa is glad not to have to raise her arm in salute during the singing of the *Deutschlandlied* as she is holding a baby in her arms; a cat is cruelly smashed and killed against the wall; a boy dies in the severe winter of 1944; a schoolmate denounces his father to the authorities, and so on. There is little in those experiences or actions that is totally idiosyncratic. What remains of them in Christa T. is disgust, fear, abhorrence of violence, which in her adult life make her reactions toward similar occurrences distinctly pronounced.

The record of Christa T.'s life up to the point of the encounter in Leipzig is indeed paradigmatic. This record is prepared for those who had seen the flood of the refugees flowing from the eastern provinces, for those who had experienced the brutality and vicissitudes of that time, for those who frequently had identified themselves with the cause of Nazi Germany and in shame, disgust, and deep disappointment had had to renounce it. However, even at that time Christa T. begins to acquire a distinct individual profile. «ICH denkt das Kind, ICH bin anders» (p. 28). These are the first conscious reflections in the process of individuation. Such direct statements are, however, relatively rare. To a large extent such and similar fomulations are already the work of the narrator who, with the aid of sparse written evidence and her knowledge of Christa T., reconstructs and invents the figure of the departed friend, endowing it with patterns, rendering her life symbolic. All this is done, however, with qualifications. For the narrator gives the reader so much and no more. She herself partakes too directly of the evolving process of her friend's life to be able to cast Christa as an unequivocal symbol. If at all, the reader must do that. This is the reason for the eminently episodic character of the record, which is precisely what is intended: to convey Christa not as a fixed character, but as a phenomenon involved in process. Therefore the novel is largely composed of gestures, of incomplete sentences, often presented as puzzles for both the narrator and the reader. Thus, for example, Christa anonymously lays some flowers on the desk of a far from well-liked maths teacher. The gesture remains an enigma until the narrator, years later, discovers a notation in Christa's diary: this teacher was the only person, «die sie [Christa] nicht unfrei und unglücklich machte» (p. 18). The narrator does not grasp this remark in all of its significance. Even after Christa's death she is still slightly offended: «wie töricht dieser Stich nach all der Zeit» (p. 18). It is only in the course of her *Mutmaßungen* that her friend realizes Christa's desire to live «als habe sie auf sich genommen, überall zu Hause und überall fremd zu sein, zu Hause und fremd in der gleichen Sekunde» (p. 19-20). What kind of person is this? On the one hand she appears to be a utopian personality with total freedom to come and go, to be in the midst of life and at the same time apart. She seems to dwell passionately with others, but to be at liberty to absent herself. Yet it is a utopia not without its burdens. Hofmannsthal, in describing the modern poet, formulates the situation similarly and not without bitterness: «fremd und doch daheim.»[11] This concept which constitutes Christa's ideal contains its own hamartia, and this makes her life so problematic. It is no accident that the novel is punctuated by commitments and disengagements, unexpected arrivals and sudden departures. Her longing vacillates between the vision of the gypsies leaving the village in their green wagon («Da hat sich der grüne Wagen schon im Dunkel verloren, ... Sehnsucht, ein bißchen Angst und etwas was einer Geburt ähnelt» (p. 28) and another that of a house, «eine feste Burg,» on

---

11 Hugo von Hofmannsthal, «Der Dichter und seine Zeit,» *Ausgewählte Werke in zwei Bänden,* II (Frankfurt: Fischer), 451-52.

the lake, reflecting echoes of Hofmannsthal, of Thomas Mann's *Tonio Kröger,* of the poetic existence «zwischen zwei Welten.»

For Christa T. is a poet. «Auf dem Deckel steht in kindlicher Krakelschrift: *Ich möchte gerne dichten und liebe auch Geschichten*» (p. 22). And so, even in her childhood, emerges the old silhouette of the romantic artist «in dürftiger Zeit,» or perhaps even more generally, a human being between freedom and necessity. Christa's short life, from childhood on, when she formulates her independence: «Ich bin anders» (p. 61), finds its correlative in poetry. Poetry emerges for Christa as a means to negotiate between personal imperatives and the demands of necessity. There appear to be two primary functions of poetry. As a child, still quite vaguely, she muses: «Dichten, dicht machen, die Sprache hilft. Was denn dicht machen und wogegen?» (p. 23). Obliquely, the reader learns that Christa's poetic attempts are in response to the intimations of death. «Nun war sie wohl für immer in die andere Welt geraten, die dunkle, die ihr ja seit je nicht unbekannt war – woher sonst ihr Hang, zu dichten, dichtzumachen die schöne, helle, feste Welt die ihr Teil sein sollte? Die Hände, beide Hände auf die Risse pressen, durch die es doch immer wieder einströmt, kalt und dunkel . . . Da ist der Trost entdeckt: in den geschriebenen Zeilen» (p. 26). The solace of poetic utterance is but one aspect. Soon comes the realization that the world of objects can be held in check by the same means: «*Daß ich nur schreibend über die Dinge komme!*» (p. 39). Reverberations of Rilke's poetics are quite unmistakable.

If a conclusion were possible, it could be said that two things emerge from her childhood with its powerful though not untypical experiences of violence and brutality: the realization of her freedom endangered constantly by the demands of conformity; and the insight into the necessity of poetic utterance as the means of liberation from the tyranny of objects: «Dann haben sie [die Dinge] keinen Ausweg: nicht den der Ungenauigkeit, nicht den der Lüge» (p. 39).

One is little surprised that Christa T. experiences difficulties in the sphere of social relations. The social sphere in the context of this novel cannot be clearly separated from that of politics. The trauma of the Germany of her adolescence appears to be behind her at least superficially. But the new Germany, of which she sincerely approves as a genuine solution, makes demands on a personality which is mobile, restless, uncompromising and opposed to any conformity. There also emerges a gulf between the vision of the new world, derived from the brochures and works which she hungrily absorbs in the course of the post-War-re-education and the new reality. Christa is very willing indeed to do her share for the sake of the new world. She is envious of those who do not dwell on the distance between thought and deed: «Sie hat,» says the narrator, «nichts inniger herbeigewünscht als unsere Welt,» and yet «mir graut vor der neuen Welt der Phantasielosen. Der Tatsachenmenschen. Der Hopp-Hopp-Menschen, so hat sie sie genannt» (p. 55). She is trapped even when she is willing to make the necessary commitment: «Also gut, sagt sie, warum nicht Lehrerin» (p. 35). But the blueprint for «happiness» and her vision of life do not coincide: «In ihrer Kammer damals, aufsehend von den strengen, erleuchtenden Sätzen der Broschüren, tritt sie ans Fenster. Der Blick auf die siebzehn Pappeln» (p. 36). This «romantic» *Leitmotiv* expresses in all contexts Christa's vague but unmistakable longing for a life free of constraints of whatever nature. The dream of the fullness of life cannot be reconciled with the claims, interpersonal, social, or political, which are constantly made on her. The aspirations of her fellow students formulated as «Lehrerin, Aspirantin, Dozentin, Lektorin» (p. 40), hold little fascination for her. Her answer to them is a line from one of her poems: «*Sehnsucht, du Vogel mit dem leisesten Schlaf*» (p. 41). This is the point at which Christa emerges as a utopian personality. A former fellow student says of her, «Ich möchte sagen, sie war gefährdet.... Durch ihre Vorstellungskraft ... Sie hat es nicht fertiggebracht, die Grenzen anzuerkennen, die jedem nun einmal gesetzt sind» (p. 52). As much as Christa might be endangering her life through excess of imagination, by the same token her life form calls into question the lives of those who acknowledge those «natural» limits. Mockingly, the question is asked, what kind of paradise will it be that is promised in brochures and speeches: «Würde es mit Atomstrom geheizt sein, unser Paradies? Oder mit Gas?» (p. 56). The paradise, the Crystal Palace of the future, will it also be for those with imagination? «sich auslöschen, Schräubchen sein» (p. 60). Or: «Einmal im Leben zur rechten Zeit sollte man an Unmögliches geglaubt haben» (p. 56). What is that impossible dream? «Was fehlt der Welt zu ihrer Vollkommenheit? Zunächst und für eine ganze Weile dies: die vollkommene Liebe» (p. 64). And she is willing to risk the experiment of perfect love: «Wenn ich dich liebe, was geht's dich an. ... Wenn ich spiele, was kümmert's dich?» (p. 64-65). What emerges is «das Grundmuster,» as the narrator assures us: «Hingabe, was immer daraus folgt. Mangel an Vorsicht und Zurückhaltung. Das Erlebnis bis auf seinen letzten Rest. Wenn schon Spiel, dann mit hohem Einsatz» (p. 65). The reply from the world of necessity is brutal: «Bettinen, sagt er, und Anetten gibt es nicht mehr, solltest du das nicht wissen? Das heißt? fragt sie ihn. Daß du unzeitgemäß bist. Ja, sagt sie. Das mag sein. Dann werde ich nicht lange leben. Du aber, mein lieber Kostja, wirst sehr alt werden» (p. 65). So ends her bid for love. Kostja gets his blue-eyed Inge («beziehungsreicher Name» p. 61) and Christa T. «waffenlos, ausgeliefert, hält stand, lächelnd, spielend, verwundet von Liebe» (p. 65).

Young Tonio Kröger's melodrama is re-enacted some sixty years later. The dreaming poet and the dance of necessity, as in Christa's favourite writer, Storm, are with us again. The dream of the perfect love has no room in this reality, now or then.

The pattern, the conflict between the time of her own and the time in which she has to live, emerge from each episode in which she is involved. A discussion of *Kabale und Liebe* must show «Den Vorrang der gesellschaftlichen vor den persönlichen Motiven im Verhalten Ferdinands» (p. 70); and a student willingly and thoughtlessly confirms, «Unglückliche Liebe sei, in der neuen Gesellschaft, kein Grund mehr, sich umzubringen» (p. 70). The new society no longer allows for «unglückliche Liebe»; does it allow for love at all? Questions do not cease. «Wann soll man leben, wenn nicht in der Zeit, die einem gegeben ist?» (p. 74). These thoughts and questions lead to an intellectual and emotional crisis. Death appears to be a way out, a termination of unresolved paradox. «Kannst Du verstehen, was das heißt? Ich kenne alles, was falsch an mir ist, aber es bleibt doch mein Ich, ich reiß' es doch nicht aus mir heraus!» writes Christa in a letter. And she pleads: «Ich bin kein Einsiedler. ... Aber kein Zwang darf dabei sein, es muß mich zu ihnen drängen. Dann wieder muß ich allein sein können, sonst leide ich» (p. 74). She also pleads for her right to find her own sphere of activity: «Aber meine Wirkungsmöglichkeiten sind, soviel ich sehe, schriftlicher, mittelbarer Natur. Ich muß mich mit den Dingen in Stille, betrachtend, auseinandersetzen können. ... Das alles ändert nichts, unlösbarer Widerspruch, an meiner tiefen Übereinstimmung mit dieser Zeit» (p. 74). She must, if at all, come to terms with the world in her own way, presumably not unlike her literary hero Storm whose «Weltverhältnis „vorwiegend lyrisch" ist» (p. 97). But the world around her is not ready to make concessions. Her literary activity meets with incomprehension, even from her friends: «Er [Günter] glaubte zu fest daran, daß alles Bestehende nützlich zu sein habe, und es quälte ihn die Frage, wozu eine Erfindung von ihrer Art nötig gewesen war» (p. 88). In other contexts she hears the same. The psychotherapist, who is to help her out of her depressions, concludes: «Bei Ihrer Intelligenz ... Sie werden sich anpassen lernen» (p. 76). A former student, now a physician, announces his great discovery: «Der Kern der Gesundheit ist Anpassung ... Anpassung um jeden Preis» (p. 112). Even the patronizing fortune teller, a retired *Generaloberst,* advises: «die Extreme meiden: ein klein bißchen Lebenskunst, mein liebes Fräulein, auch Ihnen würde sie nottun» (p. 84). These demands and claims on her are made from all sides: «die Gesellschaft hat dich studieren lassen» says a fellow student, «Nun will sie eine Gegenleistung von dir sehen, das ist recht und billig, oder nicht? ... Recht ist es. Aber nicht billig, weißt du. Ich würde sogar sagen: teuer» (p. 89), is Christa's answer. The principal of the school where Christa teaches, reproaches her when she complains about the complacency and opportunism of her pupils: «Ihr wollt alles auf einmal haben ... Macht und Güte und ich weiß nicht, was noch. ... Plötzlich begreift sie ... Er hat sich erzogen, nur so viel zu wollen, wie er erreichen kann» (p. 106).»

These demands do not occur only in the social or political sphere. To that extent the novel can indeed be seen as an age old conflict between the demands of society and state, and the individual, especially one of such uncompromising a character as Christa. But she exhibits the same traits in the sphere of personal and intimate relations. The devoted friendship of the narrator can also be a burden. She, like Goethe's Feline, must have the freedom to love. «Sie lieben gern, sagt ihr General, oder wer ist es, der dies sagt? Sie lieben zärtlich und innig, aber ihre Liebe ähnelt der Freundschaft: daher haben sie gute Freunde, sind kameradschaftlich, mitfühlend. Bis diese Unzufriedenheit sie überkommt, sie wissen wohl, wovon ich rede» (p. 85). «Sie lieben gern,» that seems to be so, and the general might be right. But in intimate situations, she must be the one who makes decisions for both. A companion of her summer love knows this «... ich weiß. Was auch passiert, du gehst. Ich kann dich nicht halten. ... Du denkst Tag und Nacht, daß du um jeden Preis weggehen wirst und daß keiner dich halten kann. ... Bleibe doch, sagt sie da. Bleib. Bloß sie hat es sein müssen, die wählte, hier und immer. Versprechen, sagt sie, versprechen kann ich allerdings nichts» (p. 45–46). It is not frivolity which makes her speak and act so. Later, in a conversation with the narrator, she reflects almost ironically: «Sommerliebe ... der Sommer wird nicht lang und nicht kurz gewesen sein, die Liebe nicht zu schwer und nicht zu leicht. Das Nachbardorf ... nicht zu nah und nicht zu weit. Der Weg um das Dorf noch vertraut und schon fremd. Sie aber sich selbst bis zum Überdruß bekannt und schmerzhaft unbekannt. ... Sie soll erfahren haben, was sie wissen mußte, und gegangen sein» (p. 46). The reader might have doubts whether her exits have been as painless as she presents them. «Christa T. niemals hat auseinanderhalten können, was nicht zusammengehört,» says the narrator condescendingly, «den Menschen und die Sache, für die er eintritt, die nächtlichen Träume und die begrenzten Taten im Tageslicht, Gedanken und Gefühle» (p. 68). This makes her vulnerable in all spheres; this makes her suffer in her «affair» with Kostja. But even such disappointments she seems to accept as a price to be paid for starved desire to love and to know. The relationship with Justus, which culminates in marriage and three children, exhibits similar features. At times the reader feels as if Christa had arrived at the place where she will stay. The quality in Justus which makes her feel unthreatened is «die Gabe, im rechten Moment das Rechte zu tun.» But also: «Wie sie sich nach der Leidenschaft sehnt!» (p. 115). And when she makes the phone call to Justus to agree to their first intimate meeting «sagt sie sich, als sie aus der Telefonzelle tritt, versprechen kann ich natürlich nichts» (p. 116). «Wäre es nicht möglich, das Netz, das für sie geknüpft und ausgelegt wurde, erwiese sich am Ende als untauglich, sie zu fangen?» (p. 117). This the narrator writes not only with regard to Christa's marriage, but about her whole person: the ineffability of the self.

Her marriage does stem from a serious commitment, and «Christa konnte nicht sagen, daß sie ihre Rolle nicht selbst gewählt hätte, sie sagte es auch nicht. Im Gegenteil, sie benannte sich, ironisch natürlich ... Tierarztfrau in mecklenburgischer Kleinstadt» (p. 136). Obviously, in view of the personalities involved, the narrator cannot say whether or not passion was part of their marriage; that component which on one occasion Christa records as «*Sinne, liebe Sinne*» (p. 77). We do know that «ihr Gefühl sagte ihr, wie gefährlich Gefahrlosigkeit sein kann» (p. 139). As if acting on this self-admonition, «Sie sagte mir, sie habe sich in einen anderen Mann – verliebt, glaube ich, oder wie mag sie es sonst genannt haben?» (p. 153). A *literary* name is conjured up: Madame Bovary (p. 153). Responding to her friend's «Es geht nicht. Und warum nicht? fragte sie herausfordernd. Findet *ihr* [my emphasis], daß ich dazu bestimmt bin, treu zu sein?» (p. 153). The time of her marriage is subtly, atmospherically related to *The Magic Mountain*. During her confinement with her first child, «Sie las den Zauberberg und gab sich Mühe, selbst in eine ungegliederte Zauberberg-Zeit zu versinken, sonst kann man's gar nicht aushalten, sagt sie. Ich frage nicht, was sie nicht aushalten konnte. Die *sieben* [my emphasis] Jahre ihrer Ehe waren sie [Christa and her husband] selten getrennt» (p. 128). On the basis of the records and reports, it is difficult to reconstruct a full picture of those seven years. The routine of being a housewife is punctuated by the birth of her children, the fleeting «affair» («die Verführung, wenn überhaupt die Rede davon sein kann, ist von ihr ausgegangen» [p. 154]), now and then a guest. One of them is Günter, of her university days: «Es stellte sich heraus, daß Günter unverheiratet geblieben und daß die Verbindung zwischen ihm und Christa T. nie abgerissen war» (p. 162). These cryptic hints impart a certain ambivalence of her new role. In her diary Christa T. records: «*Viel mehr Gefühle morgens beim Aufwachen, als der Tag je verbrauchen kann. . . . Die unverbrauchten Gefühle fingen an, sie zu vergiften*» (p. 155). It is in this period of somewhat ambivalent serenity that the idea of the house is born: «Dieses ganze Haus war nichts weiter . . . als eine Art Instrument, das sie benutzen wollte, um sich inniger mit dem Leben zu verbinden, ein Ort, der ihr von Grund auf vertraut war, weil sie ihn selbst hervorgebracht hatte, und von dessen Boden aus sie sich allem Fremden stellen wollte. Sicherheit, ja, auch das» (p. 151–52). The house is obviously one of the last stations on her road of continuous self-realization. On the one hand it seems to represent a synthesis. Thought and feeling, idea and action seem to coalesce. Poplar trees would re-establish the link between now and then. The house, built with her own hands, erected by her imagination but in solid material, a structure which would shield her from the wind coming from the lake and from darkness. Christa now tries her hand at a material more resilient than paper; she attempts to accomplish in reality what she had previously attempted through writing. In this «concrete utopia» she means to dwell in a manner which suits her best: to be at home and a stranger in every second of her life. Yet there is no denying that there is something melancholy about her last concerted effort. It can be seen as a «Gehäuse», in Jaspers' terms, with the ensuing ambivalence. It might provide her with security but its nature is incomplete; for time and society, in whatever form, are banned from her utopia. The house stands «abseits» from the main road. Christa T., an empathic reader of Storm's, would know it. Thus, the house is not the final «Nach-Hause-Finden,» as some claim,[12] nor is it a «Rückzug ins private Glück im Winkel,»[13] but merely a station, with all its possibilites, another attempt at realization of her potential and at that one from which the world at large is excluded. Christa T. herself understands the questionable nature of her undertaking. When the narrator half asks, half asserts: «Und du wirst dich vergraben. Sie [Christa] lächelte und sagte: «Ich grab' mich aus» (p. 149). Therefore, indeed, the house is endowed with perhaps more striking symbolism than other gestures, events, and episodes. Yet the reader must be on guard against ascribing to any of them an absolute validity. For the goal of Christa's life is movement and not the arrival. Until the very final stages in her illness Christa T. tries to be on the move. Shortly before her irreversible collapse, her third child is born as if in defiance of death, as if to rejoin once again the process, the movement of life. She is now afraid of death. The fear of death equals «Angst vor Enge» (p. 176). For her death is that phenomenon which spells an ultimate fixation («er [der Tod] scheut die Festlegungen nicht» (p. 174), the cessation of all movement.

At all points of the narrative, attempts are made to make sense of a life which was both ordinary and extraordinary, dull and exciting; a life which seemed to exhibit disorder and arbitrariness, but also unusual tenacity in controlling those aspects which seemed essential to Christa T. Both the narrator and the protagonist even try their hand at summing up. The former writes: «Ihr Geheimnis ... war gar kein Geheimnis mehr. ... Ihr langes Zögern, ihre Versuche in verschiedenen Lebensformen, ihr Dilettieren auf manchem Gebiet deuteten in dieselbe Richtung. ... Daß sie ausprobierte, was möglich war, bis ihr nichts mehr übrigblieb.» And the protagonist, writing of herself in the third person, makes a similar claim: «SIE, mit der sie sich zusammentat, die sich hütete, beim Namen zu nennen, denn welchen Namen hätte sie IHR geben sollen: SIE, die weiß, daß sie immer wieder neu zu sein, neu zu sehen hat, und die kann, was sie wollen muß. SIE, die nur die Gegenwart kennt und sich nicht das Recht nehmen läßt, nach ihren eigenen Gesetzen zu leben» (p. 168). These laws are only infrequently spelled out completely. They are implied in Christa T.'s actions, thoughts, and literary formulations. At times they are clear, but more often, opaque. One such note reads: «*Man selbst, ganz stark man selbst werden.*» And yet this overriding direction of Christa T.'s life, the longing «*Ganz stark man selbst werden,*» is coupled with the insights «über die Schwierigkeit, „ich" zu sagen» (p. 167). The difficulty of self-realization comes from various quarters. It is the general socio-political environment

---

12 Horst Haase, «Nachdenken über ein Buch. Christa Wolf: *Nachdenken über Christa T.,*» *NDL* (1969:4), 174–85. Quoted by Thomassen, p. 133.
13 Günter Zehm, «Rückzug ins private Glück im Winkel,» *Die Welt der Literatur* (3 July 1969). Quoted by Thomassen, p. 133.

which is determined to bring about a new world at the price of reducing people to «Schräubchen . . . der absoluten Perfektion und Zweckmäßigkeit des Apparats» (p. 60). Sacrifices are expected and demanded which would encroach on her as an individual. The same is true of her personal relationships; there too she is weary of entering into commitments which would violate and reduce her individuality. She is also a woman facing a world of men, where she sees that which is denied her as a woman, the freedom of choice, of unencumbered commitment, the freedom of loving without being circumscribed. In Christa T.'s life, the realization of these postulates occurs only infrequently: in her writing at times, in an episode or gesture. What remains constant to the very end is the will to challenge necessity at every step and at all times. Wilhelm Dilthey, in describing the classical *Bildungsroman,* writes, «Eine gesetzmäßige Entwicklung wird im Leben des Individuums angeschaut, jede ihrer Stufen hat einen Eigenwert und ist zugleich Grundlage einer höheren Stufe. Die Dissonanzen und Konflikte des Lebens erscheinen als die notwendigen Durchgangspunkte auf seiner Bahn zur Reife und zur Harmonie.»[14] There are elements in this assessment which are applicable to Christa T. There are also significant deviations. «Reife» and «Harmonie,» the projection and striving for this ideal do not appear to figure large in Christa's life. Her longing is for life here and now; not as a slow, organic process implied in the classical concept of «Bildung,» but as an imperative: «Wann, wenn nicht jetzt?» (p. 183). Perhaps a better point of comparison would be Thomas Mann's *The Magic Mountain,* a novel in the tradition of the *Bildungsroman,* containing at the same time its critique. Hans Castorp's experiences – at first glance at least – appear to be arranged in a pattern of «Steigerung.» And yet, as has been noted, even the most momentous of those, such as the «Walpurgisnacht» or «Schnee,» are not the points of arrival but merely stations in the string of a process whose imperative remains, «placet experiri.» Therefore Mann can say that the story is told not for the sake of the «hero,» but for its own sake.

The narrator of *Nachdenken* in a preamble to one of the chapters toys with the idea of casting Christa T. as an *exemplum:* «Ach, hätte ich die schöne freie Wahl erfundener Eindeutigkeit. . . . Nie wäre ich, das möchte ich doch schwören, auf sie verfallen. Denn sie ist als Beispiel, nicht beispielhaft, als Gestalt kein Vor-Bild. . . . Einmal nur, dieses eine Mal, möchte ich erfahren und sagen dürfen, wie es wirklich gewesen ist, unbeispielhaft und ohne Anspruch auf Verwendbarkeit» (p. 48–49). Here the old problem of the purpose and use of this curious German genre surfaces. As firmly as the *Bildungsroman* is fixed in the literary tradition, it has always remained a problematic product. No longer can we, with the certainty of the past, claim for it a clear-cut *telos.* With justified scepticism we reread these novels of the past and often find the point of arrival, their *telos,* not as unequivocal as the readers of the past. Writers such as

---

14 *Das Erlebnis und die Dichtung,* 8th ed. (Leipzig/Berlin: Teubner, 1922), p. 395.

Thomas Mann, Robert Musil, and more recently Max Frisch in their major novels akin to the *Bildungsroman,* end their novels in equivocation. Friedrich Schlegel, in his appraisal of *Wilhelm Meister,* notes, rightly so, both the ironic *and* pedagogical tendency of Goethe's novel; the aforementioned modern writers bracket out of their novels pedagogy and a discernible *telos,* thereby shifting the onus for these from the author onto the reader. «Die Verwendbarkeit,» of which the narrator of *Nachdenken* speaks, is not in the book. *Bildung* must then be accomplished by the reader in the process of «Nachdenken»: «Nachdenken, ihr nach-denken. Dem *Versuch, man selbst zu sein*» (p. 9), is the opening line of the novel. The modern German novel of formation shares with the old tradition of *Bildungsroman* the exploration of life forms, the conscious experimentation with situations and masks, but the pedagogy, the «Verwendbarkeit» is left to the reader. The reader must be the reflecting and receptive component. The very structure, the episodic character, the disjointedness of chronology and experiences of the novel force us as readers to search for patterns, to re-form within ourselves that which eventually could become for us part of our *Bildung.*

*

A brief postscript is in order. My discussion of Wolf's novel assumes that both thematically, and to some extent artistically, it is related to the *Bildungsroman.* Less explicitly, however, another assumption was made, namely, that this novel is also related to that period in the history of German letters which, in part, gave rise to this sub-genre, specifically to Romanticism. This assumption cannot be substantiated throughout, but there are features in the novel which clearly have their antecedents in Romanticism.

First, and perhaps most important, is the so-called *Künstlerproblematik.* There is no doubt that the Romantics – though not only they – identified the problem of the artist with unusual intensity, and often endowed it with tragic implications. Hölderlin, Wackenroder, Novalis, and E.T.A. Hoffmann in their verse and prose created figures of artists whose salient existential characteristic is «das Leiden an der Alltagswelt,»[15] as Korff puts it. Their utopian, idealistic, and fantastic sensibilities stood in constant conflict with the world of the Philistine who confronted artistic sensibility and imagination with contempt or viewed such qualities as a threat. The artist, in turn, also felt threatened. Says Christa T., «mir graut vor der neuen Welt der Phantasielosen,» (p. 55), echoing, as it were, the anguish of her Romantic predecessors. If the free play of imagination characterizes the Romantics, Christa T. is that person for whom imagination and its deliberate exercise are indispensable for a life which must follow its own dictates. In words and gestures Christa T. rebels against the «Tatsachenmenschen,» though she is finally defeated and withdraws be-

---

15 H.A. Korff, *Geist der Goethezeit,* IV (Leipzig: Koehler & Amelang, 1956), 547.

yond their reach into death. Before this ultimate withdrawal, she retreats within herself, but not without paying a price. Her rich emotional and imaginative life, which finds no outlet in the world around her, turns on her. «Die unverbrauchten Gefühle fingen an, sie zu vergiften» (p. 155), claims her friend. In many respects, Christa T. stands close to the figures of Hoffmann's «Enthusiasten.» There is a difference, however. Insofar as Hoffmann's characters are capable of humour, irony, and often madness, and thus put a distance between themselves and the indifferent or hostile world, they survive after a fashion. In *Nachdenken* there is no humour, no irony, no relief. Christa T. suffocates from the superfluity of an inner life without vents. The poison accumulated kills her.

In the spirit of Romantic anthropology, Christa T. must be mobile. She is not a fixed character. Like Eliot's Prufrock, she refuses to be formulated and «pinned and wriggling on the wall,» she must float freely with an ability to move in whichever directions take her to new experiences. The form of this novel closely matches the to and fro of her experiments. If at times its structure is opaque or even chaotic, it serves as an approximation for her unpredictable character in the process of becoming.

In some respects Friedrich Schlegel's postulate concerning Romantic poetry (esp. «Athenäum» fragment 116) is applicable to Wolf's novel. The personality of the protagonist is illuminated in a variety of ways, from a multitude of perspectives, and through lyrical, dramatic, and epic forms, but permeated by the spirit «der poetischen Reflexion» (Schlegel), whose equivalent here is the notion of «Nachdenken.»

It would be an exaggeration to call Christa Wolf's *Nachdenken* a Romantic novel; it would be equally wrong not to be aware of and point to the affinities with the heritage of Romanticism.

Appropriating Romantic Consciousness: Narrative Mode in Christa Wolf's *Kein Ort. Nirgends*

LINDA DIETRICK, *University of Manitoba*

The definition and exploration of our cultural and especially literary heritage has always been a matter of self-definition and self-exploration. The space between then and now, between «them» in the past and «us» at this moment, is bridged by a relationship of similarity and difference which is both presupposed and continuously discovered. It sees in the historical progression of events and works a pattern of continuity and change that has as much to say about the past as it does about the present and its potential. This process of «appropriation» has, of course, political and ideological implications. The pronoun «we,» so far as it signals the collective character of social, historical, and cultural experience, includes the isolated individual in a common identity. Yet it can also signal presumption: there are always the others, past and present, who are imposed upon or excluded. The glib invocation of «our» cultural heritage, in the service of selling products or governments, evokes a familiar weary resentment. To be meaningful and productive, the «we» of cultural relatedness must evidently be discovered anew and critically reflected in the subjective experience of each individual.

This is well illustrated by the changed reception of Romanticism in the GDR during the last decade.[1] Still in the long shadow of Georg Lukács and the official norms of socialist realism, writers rediscovered such literary figures as Hölderlin, Kleist, and Karoline von Günderrode, whose works and lives, measured against Goethe's classicism, had been devalued or dismissed as solipsistic, reactionary, or decadent. The resulting series of sympathetic literary treatments,[2] portraying without apology the subjectivity of the suffering

---

1 For detailed discussions of this development, see Patricia Herminghouse, «Die Wiederentdeckung der Romantik: Zur Funktion der Dichterfiguren in der neueren DDR-Literatur,» *AbnG*, 11-12 (1981), 217-48; Monika Totten, «Zur Aktualität der Romantik in der DDR: Christa Wolf und ihre Vorläufer(innen),» *ZdPh*, 101 (1982), 244-62; and also Peter Beicken and Rolf J. Goebel, «Erzählerische Selbstverständigung: Christa Wolf zwischen Moderne und Tradition,» *Monatshefte*, 74 (1982), 59-71.
2 They include: Stephan Hermlin, *Scardanelli* (Berlin: Wagenbach, 1970); Gerhard Wolf, *Der arme Hölderlin* (Berlin: Union, 1972); Anna Seghers, «Die Reisebegegnung,» in *Sonderbare Begegnungen* (Berlin: Aufbau, 1973); Günter de Bruyn, *Das Leben des Jean Paul Friedrich Richter* (Halle/Saale: Mitteldeutscher Verlag, 1975); and Franz Fühmann, *Fräulein Veronika Paulmann aus der Pirnaer Vorstadt oder Etwas über das Schauerliche bei E.T.A. Hoffmann* (Rostock: Hinstorff, 1979).

writer during the Napoleonic Restoration, clearly reflected a personal experience of isolation and professional self-questioning on the part of writers who understood their social situation analogously.

It would be easy to reduce this trend, especially in light of the Biermann affair (1976), to a phenomenon of dissidence, were it not also an expression of political commitment, at least to the potential of socialist society and to a literature that contributes to that society. Years before (1938–39), in a famous exchange of letters with Lukács, Anna Seghers had advocated a more flexible concept of realism.[3] In her view, it should allow for the direct representation of the writer's inner experience, not for its own sake, but as conditioned by social and historical circumstance. Romantic and Modernist experiments with form could thus be seen as seismographic indices, and hence properly «realist» reflections, of the confrontation with historical crisis and change. For GDR writers in the 1970s, Seghers' long-neglected plea provided justification and impetus for their own personal and literary appropriation process. And the non-canonical Romantics, emotionally related to contemporary writers by their common (and at that time thwarted) goals and calling, but historically and culturally distant, offered a suitable subject matter. As might be expected, socialist critics were initially alienated, but most have meanwhile come to accept and indeed support these developments.[4]

In their forefront was Christa Wolf, both as a critical essayist and as a writer of fiction. After *Nachdenken über Christa T.* (1968) and *Kindheitsmuster* (1976), both complex explorations of the writer's and others' subjective experience, and set in contemporary or comparatively recent times, her own rediscovery of Romanticism culminated in an essay on Karoline von Günderrode, another on Bettina von Arnim, and the story *Kein Ort. Nirgends* (1979).[5] The latter narrates the «erwünschte Legende» (p. 6) of an encounter between Günderrode and Kleist in Winkel am Rhein in 1804, at a salon-like tea-party hosted by the merchant Joseph Merten; the guests include such prominent persons as Clemens and Bettina Brentano and Carl von Savigny. Something akin to a lyrical drama is played out, except that it is narrated, and the silent mono-

---

3 «Ein Briefwechsel zwischen Anna Seghers und Georg Lukács,» in G. Lukács, *Probleme des Realismus I: Essays über den Realismus,* vol. 4 of the *Werke* (Neuwied & Berlin: Luchterhand, 1971), p. 345–76.
4 Totten, p. 257–61 and Herminghouse, p. 231–34.
5 «Der Schatten eines Traumes,» foreword to Karoline von Günderrode, *Der Schatten eines Traumes: Gedichte, Prosa, Briefe, Zeugnisse von Zeitgenossen,* ed. Christa Wolf (Berlin: Der Morgen, 1979 and Darmstadt: Luchterhand, 1979); repr. in Chr. Wolf, *Lesen und Schreiben: Neue Sammlung: Essays, Aufsätze, Reden,* Sammlung Luchterhand, 295 (Darmstadt: Luchterhand, 1980), p. 22–83; «Nun ja! Das nächste Leben geht aber heute an. Ein Brief über die Bettine,» afterword to Bettina von Arnim, *Die Günderrode* (Leipzig: Insel, 1980); repr. in *Lesen und Schreiben: Neue Sammlung,* p. 284–318; *Kein Ort. Nirgends,* Sammlung Luchterhand, 325 (Darmstadt: Luchterhand, 1981). Page references to this edition will be given in the text.

logues of the isolated main characters flow almost imperceptibly into each other and into spoken dialogue. The tale is premised on the reader's awareness that both Günderrode and Kleist will choose suicide (in 1806 and 1811 respectively), and that both, as writers and as persons (inseparable categories for Wolf), will be denied recognition by their contemporaries and – expecially in the woman's case – by later generations, including the author's own.

Wolf forcefully articulates the programmatic nature of her undertaking in the Günderrode-essay:

> Die Literaturgeschichte der Deutschen ... hat sich leichtherzig und leichtsinnig der als «unvollendet» abgestempelten Figuren entledigt, bis in die jüngste Zeit, bis zu dem folgenreichen Verdikt, das Georg Lukács gegen Kleist, gegen die Romantiker aussprach. Der Dekadenz, zumindest der Schwäche, der Lebensuntüchtigkeit geziehen, sterben sie zum zweitenmal an der Unfähigkeit der deutschen Öffentlichkeit, ein Geschichtsbewußtsein zu entwickeln, sich dem Grundwiderspruch unserer Geschichte zu stellen; ein Widerspruch, den der junge Marx in den lapidaren Satz faßt, die Deutschen hätten die Restaurationen der modernen Völker geteilt, ohne allerdings auch ihre Revolutionen zu teilen.[6]

The strong rhetorical tone clearly identifies Wolf's preoccupation with the unrecognized Romantics as a personally significant rescue project like those of her writer-colleagues. Meticulously researched, *Kein Ort. Nirgends* recovers «jene unerwünschten Zeugen erwürgter Sehnsüchte und Ängste» (ibid.) from oblivion. This thematic concern and its relationship to GDR cultural politics have been widely discussed.[7] What I wish to examine, on the other hand, is the formal aspect of the text. For here, in a fictional enactment of the subjective process of appropriation, the rhetorical attitude gives way to something more complex.

Following Franz Stanzel's heuristic model of narrative types, one can place *Kein Ort. Nirgends* primarily in the category of the figural narrative situation (the «personale Erzählsituation»). It is distinguished from the other two situations – authorial and first-person – by three constituents.[8] The first and in this case main one is mode, the manner whereby the fictional world appears to be mediated to the reader. Narrative is always mediated by a story-teller, but in the figural situation, signals indicating that the story is being told by a narrator in

---

6 «Der Schatten eines Traumes,» p. 226.
7 See Herminghouse, p. 242-48; Beicken and Goebel, p. 69-70; Totten, who summarizes the initial critical reaction to the text in the GDR (p. 259-61); Karen Jankowsky, «Difficult Hoping: Tenuous Utopian Consciousness in Christa Wolf's *Kein Ort. Nirgends*,» NG, 2: 1-2 (1982), 31-38; and Sigrid Bock, «Christa Wolf: Kein Ort Nirgends,» WB, 26: 5 (1980), 145-57.
8 Franz Stanzel, *Theorie des Erzählens*, Uni-Taschenbücher, 904 (Göttingen: Vandenhoeck & Ruprecht, 1979), esp. Chapter 3, «Die Neukonstituierung der typischen Erzählsituationen,» p. 68-69, and p. 222-23. Readers familiar with Stanzel's earlier work should note that this volume represents a careful re-working of his theory, in the light of criticism, so as to account for the gray areas between the typical narrative situations, which of course rarely appear in «pure» form. His conceptualization of the situations is no longer three-branched, but circular, so as to allow for the transitions.

a recognizable communicative act are suppressed; instead, one has the impression that the fictional world is being reflected directly at the conscious level of the main characters – the «reflectors.» In *Kein Ort. Nirgends,* the absence of quotation marks, the sparing use of *inquit* formulae like «er sagt» or «sie denkt,» descriptions reduced to minimal stage directions or assimilated in tone to Kleist's and Günderrode's subjective attitudes, extensive use of interior monologues which even incorporate quotations from the actual historical persons – all these indicate the reflector-oriented mode. This is not to say that a narrator's mediation is never perceptible, for indeed it is, particularly in the many passages of *erlebte Rede,* which is a narrated form of monologue as opposed to a quoted one.[9] These and other hints of an authorial voice are significant, as we shall see.

The second constituent of narrative situation is person. Figural narration tends to employ the third person, with a narrator who does not belong to the spatio-temporal world of the text. In this story, the quoted interior monologues often function in effect as first-person narration from within the fictional world, but these passages are divided between the two main characters and are not autonomous; they depend on a surrounding third-person context. The third constituent is perspective, the angle from which the fictional world is viewed. Here again, one finds the characteristics of figural narration: the world of the text is generally presented from the internal point of view, from the spatially, temporally, and subjectively conditioned standpoints of the main characters. With respect to both person and perspective, however, there are also interesting ambiguities: traces of a narrating «wir» who seems almost physically present with the characters, or perhaps unites them; and elements of an aperspectivism that transcends their point of view.

The trend toward figural narration (or limited-perspective first-person narration), away from the clear hierarchical distinction between reliably omniscient narrators and the characters whose lives they plot, marks modern narrative practice. Narrators have tended either to fade into ghosts of their traditional all-knowing selves or to join the common ranks of flawed and limited humanity. This has enabled authors to represent complex areas of the psyche more immediately and intensively, to reflect the apparently disjointed particularity of a modern world, and at the same time, to hold up the challenge of understanding both. For many readers, of course, these technical developments have carried a moral price: the author has surrendered his or her podium.[10] The long insistence by Lukácsian theorists on the retention of

---

9 I adopt Dorrit Cohn's useful designations in *Transparent Minds: Narrative Modes for Presenting Consciousness in Fiction* (Princeton: Princeton Univ. Press, 1978), p. 12–14 and 99–107.
10 The best-known account of the moral complexities and confusions engendered by modern narrative techniques is Wayne C. Booth's *The Rhetoric of Fiction,* 2nd ed. (Chicago: Univ. of Chicago Press, 1983); see in particular Chapter 13, «The Morality of Impersonal Narration,» p. 377–98.

authorial narration can be understood in this light. For them, responsible literature could not let the reader enter unguided into a subjectively limited, opaque fictional world. The condescension and rigidity of this norm has drawn sharp criticism from Wolf. In her view, it reduces literary figures to fixed objects, mechanically manipulated by a self-certain narrator through a pre-determined plot. In effect, it duplicates formally the social relationship of domination; it cuts short the exchange between the reader and the world of the text, thus undermining its own social and moral effectiveness.[11] For similar reasons, however, Wolf also rejects the other extreme of Robbe-Grillet and the *nouveau roman:*

> Er, der mit einem «neuen Roman» die «Realität konstruieren» wollte, endet bei dem praktischen Versuch, die minutiöse Beschreibung einer Dingwelt zu geben, von der die Kenn-Nummer Mensch sich kaum noch als widerstehendes, aufbegehrendes, rebellierendes Individuum abhebt. Als sei das unkommentierte «Da-Sein» der «Dinge» im Roman möglich und erstrebenswert; als brauche die Kunst nicht die Vermittlung des Künstlers, der mit seinem Lebensschicksal und Lebenskonflikt zwischen der «Realität» und der leeren Seite steht und keine andere Wahl hat, ... als die Auseinandersetzung zwischen der Welt und sich selbst darauf zu projizieren. (*Lesen und Schreiben,* p. 202-03)

The middle course between the two extremes – a narrator who neither imposes commentary nor avoids it, a projection of self that still respects the unique subjectivity of the characters as «others,» a fictional world that is neither falsely transparent nor hopelessly opaque – poses great technical difficulties. In *Kein Ort. Nirgends* the ambiguities of mode, person, and perspective are crucial to the solution.

«Wer spricht?» (p. 6, 113). The question, near the beginning and end of the story, invites one not only to read the text as overlapping layers of discourse – that of the characters, that of the narrator – but also to distinguish between them.[12] The story is preceded by a pair of related, first-person quotations attributed explicitly to Kleist and Günderrode. The figures are thus introduced as two separate, inwardly divided and historically distant individuals whose lives and words the text will then try to connect – to each other, within their own introspections, and to the present experience of author and reader. This

---

11 Wolf's critique of socialist realism appears in the essay «Lesen und Schreiben,» in *Lesen und Schreiben: Aufsätze und Prosastücke,* Sammlung Luchterhand, 90 (Darmstadt: Luchterhand, 1972), p. 181-220; repr. in *Lesen und Schreiben: Neue Sammlung,* p. 27-30; and in «Die Dimension des Autors: Gespräch mit Hans Kaufmann,» *WB,* 20: 6 (1974); repr. in *Lesen und Schreiben: Neue Sammlung,* p. 73-75. For extensive treatments of Wolf's poetics, see Beicken and Goebel, and also Jürgen Nieraad, «Subjektivität als Thema und Methode realistischer Schreibweise: Zur gegenwärtigen DDR-Literaturdiskussion am Beispiel Christa Wolf,» *LJbGG,* 19 (1978), 289-316.
12 Cf. Horst Nalewski, «Monologisches Sprechen: Christa Wolf: *Kein Ort. Nirgends,*» in *Selbsterfahrung als Welterfahrung: DDR-Literatur in den 70er Jahren,* ed. H. Nalewski and Klaus Schumann (Berlin: Aufbau, 1981), p. 149-62, 252-54. He states with reference to «Wer spricht?»: «Es spricht einer, der Erzähler. Durch wessen Mund auch immer – will es Kunst sein ...» (p. 149).

endeavour, as a theme, but also as a formal, indeed grammatical, process, is presented in a lyrical prelude:

> Die arge Spur, in der die Zeit von uns wegläuft.
> Vorgänger ihr, Blut im Schuh. Blicke aus keinem Auge, Worte aus keinem Mund. Gestalten, körperlos. Niedergefahren gen Himmel, getrennt in entfernten Gräbern, wiederauferstanden von den Toten, immer noch vergebend unsern Schuldigern, traurige Engelsgeduld.
> Und wir, immer noch gierig auf den Aschegeschmack der Worte.
> Immer noch nicht, was uns anstünde, stumm.
> Sag bitte, danke.
> Bitte. Danke.
> Jahrhundertealtes Gelächter. Das Echo, ungeheuer, vielfach gebrochen. Und der Verdacht, nichts kommt mehr als dieser Widerhall. Aber nur Größe rechtfertigt die Verfehlung gegen das Gesetz und versöhnt den Schuldigen mit sich selbst. (P. 5)

The passage is permeated by a vocabulary of separation – historical, spatial, ontological, communicative, and moral. The lines «Sag bitte, danke. / Bitte. Danke.» even suggest prototypical social politics, politics of the word, with those who speak it on one side, those who parrot it on the other. Yet who is the «uns» of the first line? The Kleist and Günderrode of the preceding quotations, a voice from the present, or both? Does the «arge Spur» of time reach only as far as, or beyond the present of, Wolf's readers? What «wir» still desires the word and is not silent: the speakers or listeners of today, or the historical figures who are now permitted to speak? No finite verb forms indicate what might belong to a narrated past and what to the present until the last two sentences. And yet, are they the general observations of a narrator or the thoughts of the figures, articulated for them but also open to doubt? The indeterminacies of pronoun and time references hinder the attribution of this discourse to a clearly defined consciousness – to «them» in the past or to some inclusive «us» in the present.[13] The theme of separation is thus offset by the bridging element of formal ambiguity, which forces the reader to work out the relationship.

This introductory passage is exceptional in that the signals that suggest the presence of a mediating narrator are still relatively strong. Thereafter, figural narration becomes primary, and the reader is drawn into the subjective experience of the reflector-figures, who emerge as unique and complex individuals. Yet a number of techniques continue to suggest the voice of a narrating consciousness, speaking about the characters as well as through them. A central technique is the use of the present as the tense of narration throughout the text.[14] Consider the following passage:

13 Cf. Nalewski's interpretation of this passage, p. 15, 9–61, which tends to resolve the ambiguities.
14 Flashbacks into the figures' pasts, which in past-tense narration would be signalled by the pluperfect, are given in the imperfect tense in Wolf's story.

> Wer spricht?
> Weiße Handknöchel, Hände, die schmerzen, so sind es meine. So erkenne ich euch an und befehle euch, loszulassen, um was ihr euch klammert. Was ist es. Holz, schön geschwungen, Lehne eines Sessels. Der Sitzbezug schimmernd, in ungewisser Farbe, silberblau. Glänzendes Parkettmosaik, auf dem steh ich. Menschen zwanglos über den Raum verteilt, wie das Gestühl, in schöner Anordnung. Das verstehen sie, man muß es ihnen lassen. Anders als wir in Preußen. Üppiger, feiner. Geschmack, Geschmack. Sie nennens Kultur, ich Luxus. Höflich bleiben und schweigen, die kurze Zeit.
> Diesen Monat, das ist ausgemacht, denkt Kleist, will ich zurück. (P. 6)

Until one reaches the words «Preußen» and «denkt Kleist,» the pronoun reference («meine,» «ich») is unclear. It could just as well signal a first-person narrator whose body is here conjured into being. The question of corporality – whether it is the body of a narrator or a figure, whether located in the fictional world or not – will determine how the story is read: as first-person narration, as authorial narration with a narrator who reflects on present, personal experience within the text (a technique familiar to readers of *Kindheitsmuster*), or as figural narration with quoted monologues. The rhetorical direction of the text depends on this distinction. As it happens, this passage touches on aesthetic concerns: tasteful, luxurious order versus something different and preferable. Are these Kleist's sentiments alone? The disconcerting confusion of time and pronoun reference, though later clarified, suggests that they may also be the author's, especially since her geographical loyalties correspond to Kleist's.

In traditional narrative, the present has often signalled the *ex cathedra* pronouncements of an authorial narrator. Using this «gnomic» present tense, which is clearly distinguished from the surrounding imperfect-tense narrative, an authorial voice addresses for a moment the general human condition – the way things *are*.[15] Where this rhetoric is not contradicted by other textual elements – e.g., evidence of a limited point of view – one can assume it is endorsed by the author. In modern figural narration, on the other hand, the present tense, together with the first person, is a signal of quoted speech and interior monologue. Even when a character's discourse is not introduced by quotation marks or *inquit* formulae, the change in tense will set it off from the context. The imperfect tense is thus normally left to signal either the neutral discourse of the narrator or the mixed form of narrated monologue.

Where the tense of narration is the present, however, these distinctions are blurred, as in the example cited above. In order to locate the source of the discourse in the consciousness of a figure, the reader must rely on other indicators. These include the use of proper names, *inquit* formulae, and verbs of cognition (e.g., «denkt Kleist»), which signal the separate, mediating role of a narrator reporting about the characters. They also include word-choices and deictic referents that distinctly reflect the figures' own attitudes or their spatial and

---

15 See Cohn, p. 28, and Stanzel, p. 145–46.

temporal orientation (e.g., «Preußen»).[16] In the story, such signals, which reinforce each other, are usually supplied, though perhaps not right away. Within the predominantly figural narrative situation which is so established, the present tense creates a sense of vivid immediacy: the historical figures, lost in the past, are recovered for the present. The reader, however, must work to disengage their voices from an authorial voice that may or may not be speaking with them.

Often, the distinguishing features are withheld, as in the following example. It begins with Kleist's direct speech:

> Einmal in meinem Leben, Herr Hofrat, möcht ich dem Menschen begegnen, der mir ohne versteckten Vorwurf erlaubt zu sein, der ich bin.
> Wie soll zurechtkommen, wer sich in das Gegebene nicht zu schicken weiß.
> Manchen Menschen hat die Natur einen Schutz gegen jedes Unmaß mitgegeben. Übertriebene Taten und Gedanken stoßen sie ab. Nicht ohne eine gewisse Genugtuung denkt Kleist an den Augenblick, da der Doktor wie vor dem Gottseibeiuns vor ihm zurückfuhr. (P. 56-57)

The middle sentences, because of their aphoristic quality and the generality of their grammatical subjects, look much like the gnomic pronouncements of an authorial narrator. The paragraphing, which often marks a change of speaker, would seem to support this, as well as the fact that the narrative reporting of a cognitive event in Kleist's consciousness immediately follows. Yet the statements also fit into the flow of the figure's thoughts; the narrator does not necessarily stand behind them.

Here and throughout the text, Wolf relies on the fact that Kleist and Günderrode are writers: their conscious thoughts, their generalizations about the human condition, can easily appear in well crafted literary language. Indeed, it is their vocation to speak not only for themselves, but also for the «uns» of humanity. Descriptive passages, even though they may be sharply observed and literary in flavour, can also be incorporated into interior monologue without straining plausibility. But all of this, of course, compounds the problem of disentangling the figures' discourse and perspectives from the narrator's.

This is particularly true in the case of a technique that is ambiguous even in past-tense narration: narrated monologue *(erlebte Rede)*. Because it employs the third person and the same tense as the narrative (normally imperfect; here, present), only the context and the subjective, undistanced quality of the statements tell one that it represents the character's thoughts. It is a mixed form, partly authorial (third-person reference), partly figural (unsignalled representation of consciousness). Hence it can flow almost imperceptibly into or out of the discourse of the narrator *about* the character, which may in turn partially

---

16 Stanzel, p. 222-23. See also Lubomir Doležel, «Discriminative Features in Czech Represented Discourse,» in his *Narrative Modes in Czech Literature* (Toronto: Univ. of Toronto Press, 1973), p. 20-40.

adopt features of the character's discourse such as its deictic or attitudinal orientation. Alternatively, the narrated monologue may at times lack those subjectively determined features that clearly locate it in the consciousness of a character.[17]

One example will suffice to illustrate this point. It is preceded by Günderrode's recollection of a dream in which she, in the role of a deer, receives an arrow-wound from Savigny, whose hand later heals it.

> Wieso aber am Hals? So ist es nicht ausgemacht. Sie kennt die Stelle unter der Brust, wo sie den Dolch ansetzen muß, ein Chirurg, den sie scherzhaft fragte, hat sie ihr mit einem Druck seines Fingers bezeichnet. Seitdem, wenn sie sich sammelt, spürt sie den Druck und ist augenblicklich ruhig. Es wird leicht sein und sicher, sie muß nur achten, daß sie die Waffe immer bei sich hat. Was man lange und oft genug denkt, verliert allen Schrecken. Gedanken nutzen sich ab wie Münzen, die von Hand zu Hand gehn, oder wie Vorstellungen, die man sich immer wieder vors innere Auge ruft. An jedem Ort kann sie, ohne zu zucken, ihren Leichnam liegen sehn, auch da unten am Fluß, auf der Landzunge unter den Weiden, auf denen ihr Blick ruht. (P. 9)

The first two sentences, a deliberative self-questioning response to the recalled dream, are clearly to be read as Günderrode's monologue. What follows, however, is apparently straight narration. It would be difficult to transpose it into the first person and imagine her thinking: «Ich kenne die Stelle . . .» Still, the modal verb in the clause «wo sie den Dolch ansetzen muß» could be understood in terms of subjective, as opposed to «anatomical,» necessity. This narrative report, which in the context takes on the quality of a memory, slides in the direction of narrated monologue, a clear instance of which then follows: «Es wird leicht sein und sicher, sie muß nur achten, daß sie die Waffe immer bei sich hat.» Then come two aphoristic statements with the impersonal subject «man.» Although they are probably a continuation of Günderrode's monologue (considering the colloquialisms «gehn» and «vors»), the absence of a specific pronoun reference, as we have seen before, makes the statements grammatically equivalent to the gnomic pronouncements of a narrator. A narrating voice does in fact re-emerge in the last sentence quoted; Günderrode's fantasizing about her own corpse is reported, though in a way that adopts her speech-level («sehn») and spatial perspective («da unten am Fluß»). Throughout the passage, the two levels of discourse seem alternately to merge and to separate.[18] One is not sure how to judge these thoughts which, if objectively presented, would be exceedingly alienating. The text contains many such examples.

In their monologues as well as in their conversations with other members of the gathered society and with each other, Kleist's and Günderrode's constant

---

17 On narrated monologue in general, see Cohn, p. 99-140. The problem of demarcating internal and external reality, characters' discourse and narrator's discourse, is discussed on p. 132-34; see also Doležel, p. 50-55.
18 This is what Doležel (p. 51-53) calls the «diffused» type of narrated monologue.

theme is the thwarted search for integration, the integration of the unconditional, utopian desires that nourish their lives as writers with the practical requirements of their society, which cannot recognize or understand them. In a characteristic narrated monologue of Günderrode's, we read: «So hält sie sich zurück, an Zügeln, die ins Fleisch schneiden. Das geht ja, man lebt. Gefährlich wird es, wenn sie sich hinreißen ließe, die Zügel zu lockern, loszugehn, und wenn sie dann, im heftigsten Lauf, gegen jenen Widerstand stieße, den die andern Wirklichkeit nennen ...» (p. 10). Kleist's view of himself is similarly represented: «Er hat die Wahl – falls das eine Wahl zu nennen ist –, das verzehrende Ungenügen, sein bestes Teil, planvoll in sich abzutöten oder ihm freien Lauf zu lassen und am irdischen Elend zugrunde zu gehen» (p. 31). Once again, the third person reference lends these thoughts the force of narrative authority. The lines of conflict are sharply drawn when the figures, in conversation with more conventional, socially «adjusted» members of the party, come to defend their inability to compromise. Savigny, for instance, claims «daß es wohltätig eingerichtet ist, wenn das Reich der Gedanken von dem Reich der Taten fein säuberlich getrennt bleibt» (p. 50). This problem of integration also applies, of course, to Kleist's and Günderrode's outsider status with respect to the GDR literary canon, and it is acute for Wolf because of her own situation.

Yet through the reflection of the characters' dilemma from «within,» on their own terms, and in a form that lends it the validity of an authorial narrator's statements, the beginnings of a resolution are fictionally enacted. The voices of the figures, as writers, are made public without being pre-judged, labelled, and objectified. By virtue of the manifest honesty with which they view themselves, their critique of a society that dismisses their utopian vision carries an authority no conventional narrator could claim. Günderrode and Kleist are brought into an emotional and spiritual contact that belies their own expressed sense of isolation. The contact occurs not only at the level of the plot, but also through those formal techniques that blur the transitions between their voices and seem to combine them into that of a single gnomic observer.[19] Particularly towards the end, this is registered by the use of a «wir» that could be attributed to either figure:

> Sich selbst vernichten: Unnatur. Sie hat gegen ihr Gewissen anzuarbeiten. Der Widerstand wird stärker.
> Wenn wir Ruhe fänden!
> Unrühmlich ist es, denkt Kleist, sich von seiner Zeit zerbrechen zu lassen. Warum, warum nur soll ich nicht leben können mit diesen hier. (P. 77)

Later, in a kind of dual interior monologue, the «ich»-references of each figure coalesce into one sustained «wir»-reference: »Ich bin nicht ich. Du bist nicht

---

19 Cf. Beicken and Goebel, p. 69, Jankowsky, p. 36, and Herminghouse, p. 243.

du. Wer ist wir? Wir sind sehr einsam. Irrsinnige Pläne, die uns auf die exzentrische Bahn werfen ...» (p. 109).

At the same time, however, the narrator remains a separate voice, never fully absorbing or absorbed by the discourse of the characters. Even minimal narrative elements like «denkt Kleist,» «sagt Günderrode,» or merely «er» and «sie,» logically imply another, mediating consciousness that is not congruent with the characters and that is capable of orienting the reader from a broader point of view. The same holds true for those summaries of background information that cannot simply be read as figural monologues. In the examples quoted above, the bridging effect of the «wir» would not be possible if the separateness of the characters were not first established by narrative elements. Were it not for the clear instances of a distinct narrator, the aphoristic generalizations that run through the text could be attributed without second thought to the limited perspectives of the figures, and so perhaps dismissed. As it is, they *could* be seen as a narrator's rhetoric, but they need not be. The absence of features that would clearly mark such passages as figural monologue does not constitute an argument for the presence of a sympathetically commenting narrator.[20] The text thus creates a kind of rhetorical tension: the reader is neither led by the hand nor left completely unguided, and the decision whether to identify with the characters' vision is his or hers.

The use of two main characters, male and female, naturally allows for a rich thematic exploration of their differences as well as their kinship. On the one hand, there is Günderrode, closed in the narrow circle of domesticity, loving unconditionally, empathic, introspective, with the gift of lyric; on the other hand, Kleist, rejecting the realm of practical public activity that is open to him, incapable of intimacy, is a more acute observer of others than of himself, with the talent for drama and the novelle. By playing upon the contrasting values and personalities of the two, Wolf creates an internal dialectic that can substitute for the comments of an obtrusive narrator. But the dialectic still depends on the quiet stage directions and pronoun changes of an effaced narrator. The narrative technique itself thus sets the dramatic and lyrical principles in productive tension, with the objective showing of human relationships at one moment, the subjective working-through of those relationships at the next.

With respect to Kleist, the narrator occasionally emerges as a sharply distinct and distanced voice, as in the following:

> Jünglingin. Kurioser Einfall, weg damit.
> Kleist unterdrückt das Wort, das ihm zu passen scheint. Dem Widerwillen gegen Zwitterhaftes geht er nicht auf den Grund. (P. 21)
>
> Kleist beginnt die Gründe für seine Irrfahrt zu vergessen, die Einsicht in seine Handlungen, die er einmal besessen haben muß, schwindet ihm. (P. 55)

---

20 The tendency to read the gnomic statements unambiguously as those of an authorial narrator prevails among the GDR critics and reviewers; see for instance Bock, p. 154-55, and Nalewski, passim.

In both cases, the narrator reports the psychological event of repression; Kleist does not want to see his own androgyny reflected in Günderrode or to acknowledge his wish to join the army of his nemesis Napoleon. Elsewhere, he dismisses Günderrode as a woman who «doch immer noch ihren Liebhaber finden kann, ein bescheidnes Haus, in dem sie Kinder um sich versammeln und ihre Jugendgrillen vergessen mag» (p. 108). This contrasts ironically with the evidence of her greater insight into her own fate as well as into Kleist's. It is apparent that Wolf's stronger sympathies are with the woman,[21] who is a wholly forgotten poet and hence perhaps more in need of the public rediscovery the story enacts. Because the narrator's discourse diverges less sharply from Günderrode's, the figure's despair appears more absolute, not so much conditioned by her times or her individual circumstances. But the separate voice that mediates – as opposed to adopting – that despair still remains. As for Kleist, it is significant that the most pessimistic predictions in the text – using again a «wir» that might suggest authorial narration – are attributed to his less lucid consciousness: «Kleist hat die Vision eines Zeitalters, das sich auf Gerede gründet anstatt auf Taten ... Und da sitzen wir immer noch und handeln mit den Parolen des vergangenen Jahrhunderts, spitzfindig und gegen unsre stärkere Müdigkeit ankämpfend, und wissen: Das ist es nicht, wofür wir leben und worum wir sterben könnten. Unser Blut wird vergossen werden, und man wird uns nicht mitteilen, wofür» (p. 79).[22]

Wolf has clearly stated that *Kein Ort. Nirgends* was a rehearsal of the characters' problems for herself, a «Selbstverständigung.»[23] Does this imply that the text is merely a disguised presentation of her own situation in the GDR? Does it thus deny historical progress and argue instead for a view of the writer as forever locked into solipsism and incapable of productively influencing society? The story has been amply criticized by marxist critics for an imputed hopelessness and lack of historical and social objectivity.[24] As I have tried to show, however, the rhetorical tension generated by a narrator who seems alternately to merge with the characters and to stand aside from them prevents a facile identification – or an easy dismissal of what they represent. Kleist and

---

21 This is noted by Ursula Püschel, «Zutrauen kein Unding, Liebe kein Phantom,» *Neue deutsche Literatur* 27: 7 (1979), 135. On Günderrode's role and the theme of women's writing, see Herminghouse, p. 244–46, and Sara Lennox, «Trends in Literary Theory: The Female Aesthetic and German Women's Writing,» *GQ*, 54 (1981), 71–72.
22 Cf. Bock's comments on the passage: «Die „Sicherheit" solcher Sentenzen steht in einem eigenartigen Mißverhältnis zur Rolle des Erzählers als eines Fragenden. Zugleich stören diese direkt in die dargestellte Handlung eingreifenden Kommentare auch die Kollektivität der Rezeption» (p. 155).
23 Christa Wolf, «„Kultur ist, was gelebt wird",» (Interview with Frauke Meyer-Gosau), *Alternative,* 25: 143/144 (1982), 117–27; here, p. 117. The interview has been reprinted as «Culture is What You Experience – An Interview with Christa Wolf,» tr. Jeannette Clausen, *NGC,* 27 (1982), 89–100.
24 E.g., by Bock, p. 154–56; Nalewski, p. 153–56; and Jürgen Engler, «Herrschaft der Analogie,» *NdL,* 27: 7 (1979), 132–33.

Günderrode appear neither as autonomous reflectors of their own isolation, nor as prejudged products of socio-historical mechanisms. Romantic consciousness – the unconditionality of their desire for self-fulfillment, the utopian vision against which they measure their society – is «appropriated» without being fully embraced. Its productive relationship to historical change can thus still be affirmed. Indeed, it is re-activated in the reader's efforts to distinguish the characters' voices from the narrator's, the past from the present, «them» from «us».[25]

The «wir» of the final pages is still ambiguous. It can embrace the characters of the past in our present, but it need not:

> Was reden sie noch, oder denken sie?
> Wir wissen zuviel. Man wird uns für rasend halten. Unser unausrottbarer Glaube, der Mensch sei bestimmt, sich zu vervollkommnen, der dem Geist aller Zeiten strikt zuwiderläuft. Ein Wahn?
> ...
> Einfach weitergehn, denken sie.
> Wir wissen, was kommt. (P. 119)

Are the «wir»-statements to be read as the quoted dual monologue of the characters or as the generalizations of a narrator speaking both for them and us? The latter reading cannot be set aside, but to accept it without reservation would imply the imposition of a viewpoint that runs counter to the consistent delicacy of the text, its respect for the figures' unique, historically conditioned subjectivity. The story, as a representation of two persons bound for suicide, is a means of exploring not only the power of unconditional longing, but also its dangers.

---

25 On the dimension of the reader, see Herminghouse, p. 243, Totten, p. 261, and Nieraad, p. 301–02.

Von romantischer Kunstandacht zur nationalen Kunsterziehung: Die Politisierung eines ästhetischen Begriffs um die Jahrhundertwende

HILDEGARD NABBE, *Waterloo University*

Betrachtet man die Wirkungsgeschichte der als Kunstandacht bekannt gewordenen religiös-ästhetischen Auffassung Wilhelm Heinrich Wackenroders,[1] so sind es gewöhnlich zwei sich deutlich abzeichnende Entwicklungen, die sich ideenmäßig auf das Werk des Dichters zurückführen lassen. Zunächst sei hier auf die Nazarener verwiesen, eine Gruppe von Künstlern, deren Malweise direkt durch die verinnerlichte Kunstanschauung in den *Herzensergießungen eines kunstliebenden Klosterbruders*[2] beeinflußt worden ist. Dieses im Jahre 1796 (mit der Jahreszahl 1797) anonym in Berlin erschienene Büchlein, von Wackenroder und seinem Freund Ludwig Tieck verfaßt, gilt als das initiatorische Manifest der deutschen Frühromantik. Neben der Bildkunst der Nazarener läßt sich im Literarischen ein weiterer wirkungsgeschichtlich bedeutender Zug erkennen: Es ist die fragwürdige Beziehung des Künstlers zur modernen Gesellschaft, wie sie sich in der den *Herzensergießungen* beigefügten Erzählung «Das merkwürdige musikalische Leben des Tonkünstlers Joseph Berglinger» darbietet und eine Problematik aufzeigt, die durch die Interdependenz von ätherischem Enthusiasmus und dem niedrigsten Elend gekennzeichnet ist.[3] Es gibt jedoch einen weiteren das geistesgeschichtliche Erbe der Kunstschriften betreffenden Aspekt, der bisher von der Sekundärliteratur kaum tiefer erforscht worden ist, und dessen nähere Untersuchung einen aufschlußreichen Beitrag zum Verständnis des Weiterlebens der Ideen der Frühromantik liefern kann. Gemeint ist das Hervortreten von gewissen, jedoch teilweise abgewandelten Elementen der ursprünglichen Wackenroderschen Kunstandacht in den stark vom Emotionalen und Irrationalen bedingten ästhetischen Theo-

---

1 Wertvolle Hinweise und eine umfassende Bibliographie der Sekundärliteratur zu Wackenroders kunsttheoretischen Aussagen finden sich in Martin Bollacher, *Wackenroder und die Kunstauffassung der frühen Romantik. Erträge der Forschung* (Darmstadt: Wissenschaftliche Buchgesellschaft, 1983).
2 Zitiert im folgenden als *Werke* nach Wilhelm Heinrich Wackenroder, *Werke und Briefe*, Gesamtausgabe in einem Band (Heidelberg: Lambert Schneider, 1967).
3 Eine weitere wirkungsgeschichtlich interessante Erscheinung ist die im George-Kreis um 1900 wiederauflebende Raphaelsverehrung, welche gewisse Züge der Wackenroderschen Kunstandacht in sich birgt. Siehe dazu Martin Bollacher, «Wackenroders Kunstreligion. Überlegungen zur Genesis der frühromantischen Kunstanschauung,» *GRM*, 30 (1980), 386.

rien der sogenannten konservativen Kunstbewegung, die um die Jahrhundertwende einsetzte.[4] Die Vertreter dieser sich fast ausschließlich aus dem Bildungsbürgertum zusammensetzenden Gruppe, deren Ziel es war, ihren Anhängern durch eine ausgesprochen manipulierende Kulturpolitik den Geist eines chauvinistischen Nationalismus einzuprägen, haben einen wichtigen Teil ihrer Ideologie von den Ideen der frühromantischen Kunstanschauung abgeleitet. Obwohl im allgemeinen bekannt ist, daß die Einstellung dieser Leute von einem als «Kulturreligion»[5] zu bezeichnenden Idealismus beherrscht ist, so haben Kritiker und Historiker jedoch kaum die ästhetischen Elemente dieser konservativen Doktrin im Lichte gewisser Kerngedanken der Wackenroderschen Kunstandacht erforscht. Besondere Beachtung verdient hier die für die *Herzensergießungen* charakteristische Vorstellung von der Vereinigung der Seele des Betrachters mit dem Werk des Künstlers, wobei der stattfindende innere Prozeß in die Richtung des Sakralen weist und zu der göttlichen Gabe der Offenbarung in Beziehung gesetzt wird (*Werke*, S. 80). Dieses Konzept eines geistigen Vertiefens in den Bildinhalt gibt den Auftakt zu einer gefühlsbetonten Auffassung in der Ästhetik, die ihre Apotheose in dem exaltierten Kulturchauvinismus der konservativen Kunstbewegung findet. Während jedoch sowohl in der Frühromantik als auch bei den Nazarenern der grundlegenden Rolle des Emotionalen noch gewisse Grenzen gesetzt sind, haben die Vertreter der Kunstbewegung die Möglichkeiten von Gemüt und Gefühl in der Kunst bewußt ausgebeutet.

Wie bei so manchen richtungsweisenden Werken ist das starke Echo, das die *Herzensergießungen* bei ihren Zeitgenossen hervorgerufen haben, nicht so sehr auf die Originalität der Ideen, sondern eher auf die als neuartig empfundene, eindringliche Weise ihrer Darstellung zurückzuführen. Viele Vorstellungen in diesem schmalen Band, in dem das künstlerische Programm dieser Jahre zum ersten Mal in echt romantischer Form ausgesprochen wird, sind ideenmäßig der damaligen literarischen Welt vertraut gewesen.[6] Das für diese Zeit bezeichnend Aktuelle liegt in Wackenroders inspirierendem Unterfangen, die Sphäre des Sakralen und der Andacht mit der Ebene der Kunst zu verbinden. Bis dahin hatte man in der deutschen Kunstbetrachtung den Zusamnenhang von Kunst und Religion noch nie so bewußt vor Augen geführt.[7] Die Bedeutung dieses Bestrebens kann nur im Vergleich mit den zu diesem Zeitpunkt

---

4 Zum Begriff «Kunstbewegung» siehe Edgar Herrenbrück, *Literaturverständnis im Wilhelminischen Bürgertum. Eine Untersuchung konservativer Literaturzeitschriften zwischen 1900 und 1914* (Göttingen: Georg August Universität, 1970), S. 6f.

5 Zur Bedeutung von «Kulturreligion» in ihren ideologischen Auswirkungen siehe Fritz Stern, *The Politics of Cultural Despair. A Study of the Rise of Germanic Ideology* (Berkeley & Los Angeles: University of California Press, 1963), S. xxv.

6 Vgl. Helene Stöcker, «Zur Kunstanschauung des XVIII. Jahrhunderts: Von Winckelmann bis Wackenroder,» *Palaestra*, 26 (1904), 9-26.

7 Siehe Heinz Lippuner, *Wackenroder/Tieck und die bildende Kunst. Grundlegung der romantischen Ästhetik* (Zürich: Juris, 1965), S. 29.

noch stark vorherrschenden Tendenzen des Neoklassizismus ermessen werden; denn im Gegensatz zu dessen rational urteilender Haltung gegenüber dem Dargestellten läßt der «Klosterbruder» der *Herzensergießungen* die Auseinandersetzung mit einem Kunstwerk nur als ein von Grund auf bewegendes emotionales Erlebnis gelten, wobei von dem Einzelnen lediglich ein gänzliches Aufgehen in den Gegenstand seiner Betrachtung gefordert wird. Das entscheidende Moment in diesem Prozeß der Verinnerlichung ist eine getreue Übertragung des Andachtsmäßigen in die Sphäre der Kunst, ein Vorgang, bei dem auch die sinnliche Fülle der Antike vom Geistig-Religiösen nicht ausgeklammert wird.[8] Somit ist der fromme Kunstbetrachter alles andere als ein ausgeklügelter Kunstkenner, dessen Genuß von einer vorgeprägten Geschmacksrichtung bestimmt ist. Ähnlich wie der wahre Gläubige soll er sein Gemüt in Demut auf den Gegenstand seiner Verehrung vorbereiten. Erst dann erlangt er jene Ebene der inneren Hingabe, die ihn befähigt, sich dem Kunstwerk in diesem sakralen Sinne zu nähern. Gleich wie die aufeinanderfolgenden Phasen der Andacht, so sollen diese Stufen der verinnerlichten Kunstbetrachtung zu einer der göttlichen Offenbarung entsprechenden Erfahrung führen.

Eine zergliedernde und urteilende menschliche Sprache wird jedoch niemals in den Bereich des Göttlichen eindringen können, denn Worte gleichen einem vom Intuitiv-Emotionalen ablenkenden «mühsamen Umweg» (*Werke*, S. 25). Ein sicheres Geleit bietet der Klosterbruder in den «zwei wunderbaren Sprachen,» die über ein verstandesmäßiges Erfassen hinausgehen, weil sie uns befähigen, den geheimnisvollen Pfaden des Schöpferischen nachzuspüren. Es liegt eine zwingende Unmittelbarkeit in ihnen, denn «sie bewegen ... auf eine wunderbare Weise unser ganzes Wesen und drängen sich in jede Nerve und jeden Blutstropfen, der uns angehört» (*Werke*, S. 67). Die erste dieser Sprachen redet Gott durch die Natur; die zweite ist die Sprache der Kunst, die noch viel tiefgründiger wirkt, weil sie im Gegensatz zur Natur sich in Bildern mitteilt und somit eine Art von «Hieroglyphenschrift» darstellt, in deren Macht es liegt, «das Geistige und das Unsinnliche auf eine so rührende und bewundernswürdige Weise in die sichtbaren Gestalten» so hineinzuschmelzen, daß der Betrachter «von Grund auf bewegt und erschüttert wird» (*Werke*, S. 69). Diese Umformung grenzt an das Wundersame, und somit erscheint der Künstler als ein Auserwählter, als ein Vermittler, der durch seine Imaginationskräfte die Spuren des Göttlichen zu enthüllen vermag und neben Gott als eine Art zweiter Schöpfer zu einer ehrfurchtsgebietenden Gestalt erhoben wird.

8 «Da nun das übernatürliche, das von Gott eingegebene Ideal der Schönheit, ja geradezu die Idee der göttlichen Eingebung ist, widerspricht sie nicht der heidnischen Schönheit, sondern versöhnt sich bis zu einem gewissen Grade mit ihr.» Ladislao Mittner, «Galatea. Die Romantisierung der italienischen Renaissancekunst und -dichtung in der deutschen Frühromantik,» *DVjs*, 27 (1953), 559. Siehe auch Friedrich Strack, «Die „göttliche" Kunst und ihre Sprache. Zum Kunst- und Religionsbegriff bei Wackenroder, Tieck und Novalis,» *Romantik in Deutschland. Ein interdisziplinäres Symposium*, hrsg. Richard Brinkmann (Stuttgart: Metzler, 1978), S. 371.

Wenn Wackenroders Ideen zu seiner Zeit einen solchen Anklang gefunden haben, so liegt das zu einem nicht geringen Maße an der Tatsache, daß er keine lehrmäßige, dogmatisch bestimmte Religiosität vertritt. Im Mittelpunkt steht das einfache, kindliche Gefühl der Ehrfurcht gegenüber einer Gottheit, die sich der staunenden Menschenseele in den Erscheinungen der Natur widerspiegelt. Ebenso ehrfürchtig nähert sich der Mensch dem Kunstwerk. Die wunderbare Sprache der Kunst erreicht ihre wahrhaft vertiefte Ausstrahlung nur durch eine gänzlich verinnerlichte Hingabe, die sich kaum von der Inbrunst eines Gebetes unterscheidet. Verglichen mit dem demütigen Betrachter ist der Künstler in diesem sakralen Zusammenhang in einer höchst privilegierten Position, denn er kann in seinen Schöpfungen direkt auf die göttliche Inspirationsquelle zurückgreifen. Der Schauende muß zunächst mit dem Bilde eins werden, ehe ihm auch nur ein flüchtiger Blick in das Heiligtum gewährt wird. Es ist vornehmlich diese emotionale Identifikation mit dem verehrungswürdigen Bildgegenstand, die den Begriff der Kunstandacht von der rational bedingten Kontemplation des Neoklassizismus unterscheidet. Es ist daher nicht erstaunlich, daß für den von dem Gedanken der verinnerlichten Schau geleiteten Betrachter Kunstwerke sich nicht darum darbieten, «daß das Auge sie sehe, sondern daß man mit entgegenkommenden Herzen in sie hineingehe, und in ihnen lebe und atme» (*Werke,* S. 81). Wörtlich genommen könnte man diese Aussage als eine sich rein auf das Emotionale beschränkende Aufforderung interpretieren. Sicherlich ist die Vorstellung eines nahezu ekstatischen Sicheinfühlens in ein Kunstwerk eine der wesentlichsten Ideen in den *Herzensergießungen*. Es wäre allerdings irreführend, wenn man dieses Sichhineinversenken ausschließlich von dem religiös-gefühlsmäßigen Blickwinkel her betrachten würde, ohne sich Wackenroders besonderes Verhältnis zum Historischen zu vergegenwärtigen.

Mit der Einführung der beiden bevorzugt behandelten Künstlerfiguren, Raphael und Dürer,[9] wird eine historische Perspektive geschaffen, die entscheidend ist für die Entwicklung der romantischen Kunstästhetik. Daß es sich hier um eine Art Geschichtsverfälschung handelt[10] – die Hochrenaissance wird wie das Mittelalter beschrieben – ist offensichtlich; diese Verschiebung der Grenzen ist jedoch ganz im Sinne Wackenroders; sie hat den Zweck, seine Botschaft zu verkünden. Ohne die idealisierten Künstlergestalten, deren Tugenden einem früheren Zeitalter entliehen sind, wäre es schwierig, die tiefere Bedeutung der charakteristisch emotionalen Haltung zu würdigen, denn der Gedanke der Kunstandacht erhält erst durch die zeitliche Rückwendung seine eigentliche Prägung. Durch die Hinwendung zum Mittelalter mit dessen enger Verbin-

---

9 Vgl. den Abschnitt «Ehrengedächtnis unseres ehrwürdigen Ahnherrn Albrecht Dürers,» in dem der Nürnberger Meister gleichberechtigt neben Raphael gestellt wird (*Werke,* S. 57-66).
10 *Kritische Friedrich-Schlegel-Ausgabe,* Bd. IV, hrsg. Hans Eichner (Paderborn: Schöningh, 1959), xvi (künftig zitiert als: *KA*).

dung von Kunst und Religion werden Raphael und Dürer in verehrungswürdige, mythische Wesen verwandelt, die sich in erster Linie durch ihre christlich fromme Lebens- und Empfindungsweise auszeichnen. Raphael erscheint als der erhabenere «göttliche» Künstler, dessen Werke eine heiter gelassene Vollkommenheit ausstrahlen, wohingegen Dürer hauptsächlich als die Verkörperung des biederen mittelalterlichen Meisters gilt, der in seiner «unbefangenen Einfalt» (*Werke*, S. 61) treu und ehrlich seine Werke schafft. In dieser Charakterisierung einer sorgfältigen und bedächtigen Arbeitsweise liegt ein Hinweis auf deutsche Tugenden, die die «kalte, geleckte» Art (*Werke*, S. 63) und das glatte, technische Können der Neoklassizisten weit übertreffen. Wackenroders eigenwillige Darstellung eines im Grunde weltoffenen Renaissancekünstlers als den Inbegriff eines mittelalterlichen frommen Meisters ist richtungsweisend für das Entstehen eines Nationalbewußtseins in der deutschen Kunst, das zunächst seinen Ausdruck in Friedrich Schlegels Ideen und in der Bewegung der Nazarener gefunden hat.

*

Ein besonders aufschlußreicher Hinweis auf den Idealismus und das leidenschaftliche Engagement der Nazarener findet sich in den Memoiren des mit den beiden Malern Friedrich Overbeck und Peter Cornelius gleichermaßen eng befreundeten Dr. Johann Nepomuk von Ringseis, der sich 1818 als der Begleiter des Kronprinzen Ludwig von Bayern in Rom aufhält:

> Nur soviel von unseren deutschen Künstlern ... Alle sind überzeugt, und es ist nicht bloß ein gesagter, sondern ins Leben übertragener Ernst, daß man das sein müsse, was man im Bilde darstellen wolle; sie sind überzeugt, daß Gegenstände religiösen und geschichtlich vaterländischen Inhalts etc. der Darstellung am würdigsten sind, daß man aber innerlich christlich und innerlich deutsch sein, daß das Christenthum und die Deutschheit Fleisch und Blut müssen geworden sein, damit die Darstellungen von beiden wahrhaft seien.[11]

In dieser Aussage spiegelt sich nicht nur die eigentliche Überzeugung der Nazarener wider, sondern hier zeigt sich auch die methodische Weiterführung der Kernidee der Wackenroderschen Kunstandacht durch Friedrich Schlegel. Die *Herzensergießungen* sind nach ihrem Erscheinen zwar mit Begeisterung von einer Gruppe von Malern aufgenommen worden,[12] es ist jedoch zweifelhaft, ob ihre Botschaft ohne den katalytischen Einfluß von Schlegel so nachhaltend auf jene eingewirkt hätte. Wie überzeugend Wackenroder die Sterilität der akademischen Malerei auch bloßstellt, so bleibt er doch fast gänzlich im Ab-

---

11 Zitiert nach Christoph Heilmann, «Kronprinz Ludwig von Bayern und die Nazarener-Bewegung,» in *Die Nazarener in Rom. Ein deutscher Künstlerbund der Romantik,* Deutsche Ausgabe des Ausstellungskatalogs *Nazareni a Roma,* hrsg. Klaus Gallwitz (München: Prestel, 1981), S. 58f. (künftig zitiert als: *Die Nazarener in Rom*).

12 Siehe das Nachwort zu Friedrich Schlegel, *Gemälde alter Meister,* hrsg. Hans Eichner und Norma Lelless (Darmstadt: Wissenschaftliche Buchgesellschaft, 1984), S. 213.

strakten stecken, wenn es sich um die Beschreibung eines Gemäldes handelt.[13] Bei Schlegel jedoch, vor allem in seiner Zeitschrift *Europa,* bieten sich dem aufmerksamen Leser sprachlich glänzende Schilderungen, in denen es um das Charakteristische eines Kunstwerks geht. In diesen Gemäldebeschreibungen findet eine von ästhetischer Sensibilität und von einer außerordentlichen Fülle des Wissens getragene Bildkunstkritik ihren Ausdruck, die den Autor mitsamt seinen Forderungen an die zeitgenössischen Künstler zum «größten literarischen Anreger der religiösen Malerei seiner Zeit» (*KA*, IV, xxvi) macht. Obwohl Schlegel ähnlich wie Wackenroder die Malkunst «als eins der wirksamsten Mittel» erkennt, «sich mit dem Göttlichen zu verbinden, und sich der Gottheit zu nähern,»[14] so geht er jedoch durch seine betonte Hervorhebung der sogenannten Primitiven der frühmittelalterlichen italienischen Malerei über den historischen Horizont der *Herzensergießungen* hinaus. Hierdurch erhält Wackenroders Kunstfrömmigkeit eine greifbare kunsthistorische Dimension, denn nach Schlegel sind es gerade diese frühen Maler, in deren Werken man die Idee der christlichen Schönheit besonders einleuchtend dargestellt findet. Aber es bleibt nicht bei einer Beschränkung auf die Anfänge der Malerei jenseits der Alpen; auch die altdeutschen Kunstschätze spielen in diesem Wiederbelebungsprozeß eine wichtige Rolle, da gerade in der einheimischen Kunst die Tugenden einer maltechnischen Arbeitsweise und einer wahren Frömmigkeit ihren prägnantesten Ausdruck finden. Wenn Schlegel die ältere und weitgehend vernachlässigte Tradition wiederbelebt, so ist er gleichzeitig entschlossen, das christliche Ideal der inneren Beseelung im Gegensatz zum zeitgenössischen Dogma von der vollkommenen Form und sinnlichen Schönheit als exemplarisch hervorzuheben. Nicht die Antike soll der Künstler nachahmen, sondern sich in symbolisch-allegorische Vorstellungen vertiefen, wobei Begebenheiten aus dem Alten und Neuen Testament als echte Quellen für eine fromme Inspiration dienen sollten. Ebenso sollen «Gegenstände der vaterländischen Geschichte» (*KA*, IV, 231), Themen und Episoden aus der Zeit des deutschen Mittelalters, als Stoffe für eine betont patriotische Malerei gewählt werden. Ein sicherer Weg sei es, «den alten Mahlern zu folgen, besonders den ältesten und das Rechte und Naive so lange treulich nachzubilden, bis es dem Geiste zur anderen Natur geworden wäre.»[15] Durch seine eindringliche Empfehlung, sich ganz in die Malweise der frühen Tradition zu versenken, fordert Schlegel im Grunde eine Bekehrung zu jenen Idealen, die in der christlichen Kunst verkörpert sind, denn ein «bloß angenommener und wie erlernter oder nachgesprochener Begriff» (*KA*, IV, 260) vom Christentum würde höchstens von akademischem Interesse sein. Beim Entstehen eines echten Kunst-

---

13 Ladislao Mittner (S. 557f.) bemerkt dazu folgendes: «Wackenroder sieht ... nie ein Bild in seiner konkreten Wirklichkeit und ist nicht fähig, es zu beschreiben, sondern beschränkt sich darauf, von der tiefen religiösen Rührung zu sprechen, die die Bilder in seiner Seele auslösen.»
14 *Europa. Eine Zeitschrift* (1803); reprogr. Nachdruck 1983, Bd. II: 1, 109.
15 *Europa* (1805), II: 2, 144f.

werks seien somit weder glänzendes technisches Können noch fromme Gefühle allein ausreichend; hinzukommen müsse ein Schaffen im «göttlichen Lichte der inneren Beseelung» (*KA*, IV, 260).

In diesen Ausführungen des berühmten Kunstkritikers spürt man zwar Wackenroders Einfluß, doch zeigen sich darüber hinaus wichtige Momente, die auf ein lebendiges geschichtliches Bewußtsein hindeuten, das dem so stark zum Mythisieren neigenden Vorgänger allerdings fehlt. Wie entschlossen auch die Wiederbelebung der christlichen Kunst in der *Europa* und den späteren Schriften ins Auge gefaßt wird, so steht daneben doch die klare Erkenntnis, daß ein solches Bemühen nicht nur von gläubiger Frömmigkeit getragen werden kann. Unabhängig von seiner eignen religiösen Überzeugung ist sich Schlegel durchaus bewußt, daß ein Hineinversenken in die Gesinnung und die Ideen einer gegebenen Epoche nicht allein eine rein gefühlsmäßige Angelegenheit sein kann. Genauer gesagt: Schlegel erkennt selbst, daß die frühen Meister, deren Werke einer zukünftigen Generation von Malern als Inspiration dienen sollen, in ihrem Kunstschaffen im Begriff der «christlichen Schönheit» lebten und atmeten, obwohl dieser «noch unbewußt und unentwickelt [darin] schlummern mochte» (*KA*, IV, 259). Bei den Nachahmenden dagegen geht es zunächst vornehmlich um ein Wiederbesinnen auf die leitenden Ideen und Vorstellungen, die den Schaffensprozeß ihrer verehrten Meister beseelten, ein Bemühen, auf das nachdrücklich hingewiesen wird: «Wir müssen auch die Hervorbringungen und die Werke dieser alten christlichen Kunst, um sie ganz zu verstehen und richtig aufzufassen, in eben jenem Lichte der Seele betrachten, welches sie hervorgerufen hat und worin überhaupt die innersten Grundzüge der christlichen Denkart und Ansicht über alle Gegenstände enthalten sind» (*KA* IV, 261f.). Für eine Wiederbelebung der Gesinnung der frühmittelalterlichen Kunst ist das Verständnis der kulturellen Traditionen eine ernstliche Notwendigkeit, und in diesem Sinne verweist Schlegel auf das Vertrautsein mit der Kunstgeschichte als einen unerläßlichen Teil der künstlerischen Ausbildung, denn es ist vornehmlich diese Kenntnis, «welche die Gedanken selbst in ihm [dem Künstler] hervorruft, den wahren Kunstgeist weckt und rege erhält, und den Künstler das eigentliche Wesen der Kunst, wenn auch nicht theoretisch ergrübeln, doch richtig fühlen und beurteilen lehrt» (*KA*, IV, 230).

Erweisen sich die Überlegungen bezüglich der Geschichtlichkeit des künstlerischen Schaffens schon allein in theoretischer Hinsicht als von beträchtlichem Interesse, so sind sie umso aufschlußreicher, wenn man ihre Wirkung auf die Bewegung der Nazarener betrachtet. Indem Schlegel nämlich ihre Suche nach einer gefühls- und andachtsmäßig bedingten Ausdrucksform durch seine Ideen und Ansichten von der christlichen Kunst leitet und unterstützt, spielt er eine bedeutende Rolle in der künstlerischen Verwirklichung der ästhetisch suggestiven Lehre von der Kunstandacht. Die erhellenden Ausführungen hinsichtlich der Wichtigkeit mythisch-allegorischer Vorbilder für das Hervorbringen von gemeinschaftsbindenden Werken stimmen klar mit dem religiösen Ethos der Gruppe überein. Die Nazarener verstehen es, ihrer grundsätzlich naiven und gefühlsbetonten Sehweise in solchen Themen und Motiven Ausdruck zu verleihen, wie sie ihr gelehrter Mentor für empfehlenswert für die Wiederbelebung einer wahrhaft christlich-vaterländischen Kunst erachtet. Die Entschiedenheit dieser Gruppe, ihre Vorstellungen zu verwirklichen, läßt sich an ihrem Eifer ermessen, monumentale Werke zu schaffen, und zwar durch «die Wiedereinführung der Fresco-Malerei, so wie sie zu Zeiten des großen Giotto bis auf den göttlichen Raphael in Italien war,» wie es in dem berühmten Brief von Cornelius an Joseph Görres vom 3. November 1814 heißt.[16] Diese Gemeinschaftsarbeiten, wie z.b. die Freskenzyklen «Joseph und seine Brüder» in der Casa Bartholdy, Dantes «Divina Comedia» und Tassos Gedichte in dem Casino Massimo in Rom gehören zu den überzeugendsten künstlerischen Leistungen der Nazarener-Bewegung.[17] In seiner Besprechung der deutschen Kunstausstellung im Jahre 1819 in Rom ist Friedrich Schlegel auch recht zuversichtlich, daß die neue christliche Malerei nicht in eine leere Nachahmung ihrer ursprünglichen Quellen absinken könne, und somit kommt es zu einer entsprechenden Zukunftsvision: «Es wird unsre Zeit und die fortschreitende Sinnes-Entwicklung der christlichen Weltansicht, nach der jetzt herrlichen geistigen Stimmung, auch eine ihr eigentümliche Kunst und neue Epoche derselben mit sich führen und hervorbringen ...» (*KA*, IV, 261).

Schlegels optimistische Erwartungen erweisen sich jedoch als eine Illusion. Anstatt ihre Werke mit dem Geist der frühchristlichen Malerei zu beseelen, tendieren einige der wichtigsten Vertreter der Nazarener immer stärker zu einer ausgesprochen didaktischen Richtung, wobei der in den frühen römischen Freskozyklen durchscheinende märchenhafte Charme verlorengeht. Diese Neigung zu einem gelehrten und schwerfälligen Verfahren zeigt sich nirgends so deutlich wie in Friedrich Overbecks «Der Triumph der Religion in den Künsten» (1840, Städelsches Kunstinstitut, Frankfurt a.M.), ein monumentales Werk, für das der Künstler eine umfangreiche Druckschrift zur Erläuterung seines aufgestellten Programms beifügt.[18] Für den Kritiker und Philosophen Friedrich Theodor Vischer, der das Gemälde kurz nach seiner Vollendung gesehen hat, ist es «eine Rekapitulation der Kunstgeschichte, ein Kursus über ihre Vergangenheit, der zugleich eine Moral für ihre Zukunft enthält.»[19] Jeglicher Versuch, ein solch kompliziertes allegorisches Programm aufzustellen,

---

16 Zitiert nach Hans-Joachim Ziemke, «Die Anfänge in Wien und in Rom,» *Die Nazarener. Ausstellungskatalog,* hrsg. Klaus Gallwitz (Frankfurt: Städelsches Kunstinstitut, 1977), S. 48 (künftig zitiert als: *Städelkatalog*).
17 Siehe Frank Büttner, «Die römischen Freskenzyklen der Nazarener,» in dem Ausstellungskatalog *Die Nazarener in Rom,* S. 283–87.
18 Bezüglich Overbecks Druckschrift siehe Hans-Joachim Ziemke, «Zum Begriff der Nazarener,» *Städelkatalog,* S. 18f.
19 Friedrich Theodor Vischer, *Kritische Gänge,* Bd. 5, hrsg. Robert Vischer (München: Meyer & Jessen, 1922), S. 7.

um die Gültigkeit einer verlorenen Tradition hervorzuheben, ist für diesen hellsichtigen Zeitgenossen wie ein Werk von «Ideenmalern.» Niemals zuvor hätten Maler «mit dem Pinsel einen Vortrag über Geschichte der Kunst gehalten, um eine *fabula docet* daraus zu ziehen, um eine gewisse Ansicht über diese Geschichte als die einzig richtige aufzustellen.»[20] Vischers satirische Behandlung der monomanischen Bemühungen Overbecks läßt sich auch auf andere Nazarener übertragen, die ähnlich wie ihr geistiger Führer bestrebt sind, ihren Ideen in monumental angelegten Projekten den geeigneten Ausdruck zu verschaffen. Von Ludwig I., dem König von Bayern, werden diese Künstler beauftragt, Museen und öffentliche Gebäude im Sinne der ausgesprochen nationalen Auffassung des Herrschers zu dekorieren. Obzwar beide Seiten sich in ihrem Eifer für die christlich-vaterländische Kunst einig sind, fordert der König darüber hinaus, daß gerade die Geschichte in der Belehrung seiner Untertanen eine vornehmliche Rolle spielen sollte.[21] Indem die Künstler diesen im Grunde irrigen Vorstellungen folgen, verfallen sie dem Zwang, höchst komplexe und ikonographisch vielfältige Programme zu ersinnen, um eine Reihe von gegensätzlichen Traditionen sowohl ideenmäßig als auch künstlerisch unter einen Hut zu bringen. Trotz dieser Schwierigkeiten sind sie entschlossen, in dem ihre individuelle Aussagekraft beengenden allegorischen Schema ihr eigenes Weltbild zu behaupten, wie z.B. die grandiosen Pläne von Peter Cornelius zeigen.[22] Solch unlösbare und widersprüchliche Aufgaben bringen die Gefahr des Sichfestfahrens in akademischen Dogmen, von denen sich die Nazarener anfangs so zielbewußt hatten distanzieren wollen. Ironischerweise geraten sie im Rahmen ihrer Bemühungen in einen ausgesprochenen *circulus vitiosus,* da «über der angestrengten Durchdringung humanistisch-christlicher Gedankenketten und deren typisierter Darstellungsweise die lebendige künstlerische Individualität» vernachlässigt wird.[23]

Man würde den Nazareneren nicht ganz gerecht werden, wenn man ihre Mängel allein im Lichte ihrer ästhetischen und religiösen Überzeugung betrachtete. Denn wie stark sie auch an ihren Leitideen festhalten, so können sie doch nicht dem Sog des Historismus entgehn. Die nachfolgenden Schüler der Nazarener, besonders der zwischen Cornelius und der späteren theaterhaften Geschichtsmalerei stehende Wilhelm von Kaulbach (1804-74), entwickeln eine äußerst lehrbuchhafte Gestaltungsweise, über die sich die älteren Vertre-

---

20 Vischer, S. 8.
21 Siehe Keith Andrews, *The Nazarenes. A Brotherhood of German Painters in Rome* (Oxford: Clarendon Press, 1964), S. 53.
22 Für Querschiff und Chor der Ludwigskirche in München entwirft Cornelius in den dreißiger Jahren einen Trinitätszyklus, mit dem er ein christliches Epos der Malerei, eine «Comedia Divina» schaffen will. Siehe Ellen Spickernagel, «Zur Monumentalmalerei der Nazarener in Deutschland,» *Städelkatalog,* S. 267.
23 Christoph Heilmann, «Kronprinz Ludwig von Bayern und die Nazarener-Bewegung.» in *Die Nazarener in Rom,* S. 59.

ter der Bewegung empören.²⁴ Es ist nicht erstaunlich, daß die Museen dieser Epoche «die Heiligtümer des geschichtlichen Selbstbewußtseins» werden.²⁵ Friedrich Theodor Vischer, ein kritischer Gegner dieser belehrenden Tendenz in der zeitgenössischen Malerei, präsentiert einen bemerkenswerten Katalog der verschiedenartigsten Themen und Motive, von denen die Kunstszene beherrscht wird:

> Nun, was malen denn wir? Wir malen Alles und noch einiges Andere. Wir malen Götter und Madonnen, Heroen und Bauern, so wie wir griechisch, byzantinisch, maurisch, gotisch, florentinisch à la Renaissance, Rococo bauen und nur in keinem Stil, der unser wäre ... Wir sind der Herr Überall und Nirgends. Da ist keine Mitte, keine Hauptgattung, kein Hauptgericht zwischen all den Zuspeisen, Süßigkeiten, Zuckerbäckereien, unter denen die Tafel seufzt. Reflektierend und wählend steht jetzt der Künstler über allen Stoffen, die jemals vorhanden waren, und sieht den Wald vor Bäumen nicht. Dies ist das bedenkliche Prognostikon unserer modernen Kunst.²⁶

Die intensive Suche nach immer neuen Themen, verbunden mit einer musealen Gelehrsamkeit, zeigt die grundsätzliche Wurzellosigkeit dieser Künstler, denen in der Hauptsache das Aufblühen eines akademischen Historismus zuzuschreiben ist, der in der Gründerzeit, wie z.B. bei Hans Makart, ins ÜppigÜberschwengliche ausarten sollte.²⁷ Die gekünstelte und pompöse Malweise um die Mitte des 19. Jahrhunderts widerspricht gänzlich den von Friedrich Schlegel gesetzten kunsttheoretischen Richtlinien. Anstatt als belebendes Grundprinzip einer vorbildlichen Darstellungsweise die Kunstwelt zu beherrschen, ist der christliche Bildinhalt nur noch einer unter vielen in dem ständig anwachsenden Repertoire dieser Künstler. Die in den besten Leistungen der Nazarener durchscheinende überzeugende Symbolik ist aus den mehr und mehr im Akademischen wurzelnden Bildideen verschwunden, und kaum noch ist ein Anklang an jene religiöse Intensität wahrzunehmen, die überall in den Schöpfungen der romantischen Kunst als ihr tragender Grund spürbar wird.²⁸ Das immer größer werdende Interesse am geschichtlich Besonderen im Gegensatz zum menschlich Allgemeinen, wie es z.B. noch die Bilder Franz Pforrs von «Rudolf von Habsburg» (Städelsche Kunstinstitut, Frankfurt a.M.) ausstrahlen, ist eins der klarsten Zeichen eines Säkularisationsprozesses, in dessen Verlauf die Funktion der Kunst selbst in Frage gestellt wird. Aber obwohl die einst bei den Nazarenern tragende religiöse Gefühlswelt für die nachfolgende Malergeneration weitgehend irrelevant wird und die echte andachtmäßige Hal-

---

24 Gemeint sind hier besonders Kaulbachs riesige Fresken zur Kunstgeschichte außen an der Neuen Münchener Pinakothek. Vgl. Ludwig Justi, *Deutsche Malkunst im 19. und 20. Jahrhundert* (Berlin: Julius Bard, 1932), S. 149.
25 Werner Hofmann, *Das Irdische Paradies. Motive und Ideen des 19. Jahrhunderts* (München: Prestel, 1974, S. 72.
26 Vischer, S. 37.
27 Richard Hamann und Jost Hermand, *Gründerzeit* (Berlin: Akademie, 1965), S. 25ff.
28 Vgl. Herbert von Einem. *Deutsche Malerei des Klassizismus und der Romantik 1760–1840* (München: Beck, 1978), S. 170.

tung sich verflüchtigt, bleibt dennoch untergründig, als Erbe der frühromantischen Tradition, ein starkes Residuum einer ehrfurchtsvollen, ästhetisch erhöhten Empfindsamkeit gegenüber dem Kunstwerk, die um die Jahrhundertwende in der Auffassung und Ideologie einer einflußreichen konservativen Kulturbewegung eine wichtige Rolle spielt.

*

In einer im Jahre 1908 erschienenen Besprechung der Werke des Malers Fritz von Uhde (1814–1911) durch den Kunstkritiker Fritz von Ostini findet sich folgende Beschreibung:

> Aber aus der Kunst erwuchs ihm [von Uhde] wieder eine neue fromme Innigkeit, eine Ehrfurcht vor dieser Welt des Glaubens; sein Lichtproblem und dessen Träger wurden ihm nach und nach identisch, eines heilig wie das andere ... Wie der Künstler in seinem malerischen Problem so aufging, daß er die höchste Innerlichkeit der Wirkung erreichte, so durchdrang er auch seinen Stoff so tief wie irgendein Bibelgläubiger.[29]

Der feierliche Ton und die weihevolle Stimmung dieser Schilderung klingen wie ein fernes Echo jener Ergriffenheit, die dem Leser und Betrachter seit den *Herzensergießungen* so vertraut geworden ist. Zweifellos liest sich diese Passage, als ob sie von einer Dichternatur wie Wackenroder inspiriert worden wäre. Diese Kritik, die die besondere Gestaltungsweise eines zeitgenössischen Künstlers zu erfassen sucht, vermittelt den Eindruck einer ausgesprochen andachtmäßigen Haltung, in der Kunst und Religion ineinander aufgehen. Aus dieser Perspektive gesehen erscheinen die Bilder des Malers von Uhde als der Inbegriff einer ehrfurchtsvoll religiösen Hingabe, die an Wackenroders Kunstandacht erinnert. Sicherlich lassen sich hier von dieser Art der Kunstkritik – sowie von vielen ähnlich empfundenen Beiträgen während dieser Zeit – wichtige Momente auf die ursprüngliche Auffassung zurückführen. Es wäre jedoch verfehlt, wenn man das Wiederaufleben dieser charakteristisch emotionalen Haltung in der Kunst allein aus der Sicht der Frühromantik erklären wollte. Die Veränderung ist eng verbunden mit einer Ideologie, die den kulturellen Idealismus des mittleren Bürgertums im Wilhelminischen Deutschland widerspiegelt. Bei näherer Betrachtung läßt sich erkennen, daß die Kunstauffassung dieser Gruppe – im Gegensatz zu derjenigen der Frühromantik und der Nazarener – gänzlich einer bestimmten Weltanschauung verpflichtet ist. Die Ideen dieser Gesellschaftsschicht zeichnen sich wohl kaum durch Brillanz und ursprüngliche Frische aus. Wollte man diese mit religiösem Pathos vorgetragenen Ansichten jedoch ignorieren, so hätte man keinen Zugang zum Verständnis eines Umwandlungsprozesses, in dem wichtige Elemente einer ästhetischen Tradition von den Vertretern einer kulturell einflußreichen Gruppe gesinnungsmäßig umgebogen werden, um ihren erziehungspolitischen Zielen zu dienen.

---

29 Fritz von Ostini, «Fritz von Uhde,» *Die Kunst,* 17 (1908), 12.

Die um die Jahrhundertwende einsetzende sogenannte Kunstbewegung ist Teil einer weitläufigen konservativen Reformbewegung unter den Gebildeten, deren Hauptziel darin besteht, den liberalistischen und technologischen Tendenzen der Zeit mit einem betonten Kulturnationalismus entgegenzuwirken. Richtungsweisend für diese Gruppe sind die Ideen von August Julius Langbehn, die er in seinem notorischen Werk *Rembrandt als Erzieher* verkündigte.[30] Dieser Autor sieht in der Kunst die einzige Möglichkeit, Deutschland von einem seelenlosen Materialismus zu befreien, und um dies zu erreichen, stellt er die Forderung nach einem, jeglichem Tagesgeschehen übergeordneten, rein national-kunsterzieherischen Programm. Für Langbehn ist daher Politik allein als Kunstpolitik zu verstehen. Die Anhänger der Kunstbewegung, die sich von diesem kunstbesessenen Ideologen angesprochen fühlen, sind größtenteils Vertreter einer gebildeten Mittelklasse, die nun die Kunst als Hilfe und Maßstab für eine neue zukünftige Gesellschaftsordnung propagieren. Als ethische Idealisten[31] distanzieren sie sich von jener auf Erfolg hin orientierten Haltung, die sich seit dem ökonomischen Aufschwung der Gründerzeit mehr und mehr verbreitet. Dieser Idealismus kristallisiert sich in dem unerschütterlichen Glauben an die Notwendigkeit und Macht der Bildung, in der diese Kreise das Kennzeichen ihrer Gruppenidentität erkennen. Auf Grund dieses besonderen Standesbewußtseins sind sie als eine Gesinnungsgruppe zu bezeichnen; als solche verfolgen sie eine von ihrer bildungsbedingten Weltanschauung inspirierte Kulturpolitik. Da sie sich als die berufenen Kulturträger betrachten, ist es nicht erstaunlich, daß sie nach Mitteln und Wegen suchen, um aufnahmebereite Gemüter für ihre Vorstellungen zu gewinnen. Das Zustandekommen eines später erfolgreichen literarischen Organs zur Verbreitung ihrer volkserzieherischen Ideen ist zu einem entscheidenden Maße den publizistischen Fähigkeiten des Schriftstellers Ferdinand Avenarius zu verdanken. Als Gründer und Herausgeber der einflußreichen Zeitschrift *Der Kunstwart*[32] spielt er eine äußerst wichtige Rolle in der Förderung einer um die Jahrhundertwende sich manifestierenden kulturkonservativen Weltanschauung. Avenarius wendet sich «an eine zunehmende Gebildetenschicht, der die Familienblätter nicht mehr genügten, und die auf einer höheren, wenn zwar immer noch populären Stufe über die Fragen und die Vorgänge im gegenwärti-

---

30 Das zuerst 1890 anonym erschienene Werk *Rembrandt als Erzieher. Von einem Deutschen* wurde 1922 mit einer detaillierten Einleitung von Langbehns langjährigem Vertrauten, dem Maler Benedikt Momme Nissen, im Verlag C.L. Hirschfeld (Leipzig) neu herausgegeben.

31 Siehe Gerhardt Kratzsch, *Kunstwart und Dürerbund. Ein Beitrag zur Geschichte der Gebildeten im Zeitalter des Imperialismus* (Göttingen: Vandenhoeck & Ruprecht, 1969), S. 27.

32 Unter dem Herausgeber Ferdinand Avenarius (1855–1923) belief sich die Zahl der Abonnenten im Zeitraum von 1909–1913 auf durchschnittlich 23 000, und damit wurde *Der Kunstwart* zur weitverbreitetsten Revue seiner Zeit; siehe H. Fred Krause, «Der Kunstwart,» *Deutsche Zeitschriften des 17. und 20. Jahrhunderts,* hrsg. Heinz-Dietrich Fischer (Pullach bei München: Dokumentation, 1973), S. 219.

gen Kulturleben belehrt werden wollte.»³³ Um den in seiner Zeitschrift verfolgten Zielen mehr Nachdruck zu verleihen, gründet der geschickte Publizist um 1902 den «Dürerbund,»³⁴ der eine kulturpolitische Vereinigung zur ästhetischen Erziehung weiterer Volksschichten darstellt.

Wenn die Ideen von Avenarius und vielen ähnlich gesinnten zeitgenössischen Kritikern noch heute von beträchtlichem geistesgeschichtlichem Interesse sind, so hängt dies damit zusammen, daß sie eine Kunstauffassung dokumentieren, in der gewisse Momente der frühromantischen Kunstästhetik wiederbelebt werden, die dann allerdings sogleich eine ideologische Unterwanderung erfahren. Die Gestalt Albrecht Dürers als Schutzheiliger einer weitverzweigten Gesinnungsgruppe ist ein klares Anzeichen dieser Tendenz, denn der Meister von Nürnberg wird als der «Allerdeutscheste»³⁵ aller Maler bezeichnet, wobei auch die führenden Eigenschaften von Frömmigkeit und Innerlichkeit betont werden. Wie wichtig auch immer das vom Klosterbruder her bekannte vergeistigte Künstlerporträt sein mag, zeigt es doch nur einen Aspekt des idealisierten Dürerbildes der Kunstbewegung. Der Maler wird nun in erster Linie als der «Führer» betrachtet, als der kühne Ritter, der «in der großen Hunnenschlacht»³⁶ gegen die verhaßte Macht der ausländischen Einflüsse zu Felde zieht. Schwerlich ließe sich ein überzeugenderes Bild der Grundhaltung der konservativen Kulturbewegung zeichnen, denn hier erkennt man, wie sehr der Künstler schlechthin – denn Dürer ist nur ein Beispiel – zu einer charismatischen Gestalt geworden ist. Die Werke eines solchen Künstlers können nur durch unmittelbare Erfahrung erfaßt werden, und eine kritisch-analytische Betrachtungsweise wäre deshalb in den Augen der Kunstbewegung völlig unergiebig. Der Gegensatz von Künstler und Betrachter gilt als verderblich, denn er «zerreißt die innige seelische Verbindung zwischen dem Künstler und seinen Mitmenschen; er macht jenen unfruchtbar und diesen teilnahmslos.»³⁷ Man sollte nicht versäumen, dieser Aussage nähere Beachtung zu schenken, denn sie ist symptomatisch für ihre Zeit. Durch den Hinweis auf «innige seelische Beziehung» zwischen dem Künstler und seinem Publikum wird das zentrale

---

33 Kratzsch, S. 130.
34 Der Dürerbund war eine kartellartige Zusammenfassung zahlreicher Reformvereinigungen mit mehr als 300 000 Mitgliedern, die zur gebildeten Mittelschicht gehörten. Die Aufgabe dieser Organisation war die Hebung der deutschen Gesinnung und des Geschmacks. Vgl. Berthold Hinz in: *Dürers Gloria. Kunst, Kult, Konsum.* Ausstellungskatalog. Staatliche Museen Preußischer Kulturbesitz Berlin (Berlin: Gebrüder Mann, 1971), S. 43.
35 Ferdinand Avenarius, «Zum Dürer-Bunde. Ein Aufruf,» *Der Kunstwart,* 14: 24 (1901), 471 (zitiert im folgenden als *KW*).
36 *Dürer als Führer. Vom Rembrandtdeutschen und seinem Gehilfen (Julius Langbehn und Momme Nissen). Mit einem Brief von Hans Thoma und achtzig Bildern in Kupfertiefdruck nach Dürer* (München: Josef Müller, 1923), S. 15f. Zuerst erschienen in *Kunstwart,* 17: 15 (1904), 93-102. Der genaue Text hier, der typisch ist für viele andere Stellen, lautet: «Man folge den Bahnen Dürers ... In der großen Hunnenschlacht, für oder gegen das Seelische, welche innerhalb der heutigen Kunst gekämpft wird, streitet der Geist Dürers in den Wolken mit.»
37 Karl Steinacker, «Künstler und Laie,» *Der Türmer,* Jg. 1909/10, Bd. I, S. 607.

ästhetische Motiv der Kunstbewegung hervorgehoben. Für die kulturkonservativen Kreise ist diese Erfahrung ein unumgängliches Erfordernis. Somit wird die Kunst in erster Linie als ein Drang nach Kommunikation der Innerlichkeit empfunden, der als «Mitteilung des Fühlens und Schauens von Menschenseele zu Menschenseele»[38] charakterisiert wird. Diese zentrale Stellung der Verinnerlichung in der Kunstauffassung um 1900 erinnert zweifellos an die gefühlsbetonte seelische Unmittelbarkeit, die der ursprünglichen Kunstandacht der Frühromantik zugrunde liegt. Andererseits wird durch die dringliche Forderung nach einer «Mitteilung des Fühlens und Schauens» ein völlig neues Element eingeführt. Genau betrachtet, erfährt die Idee der «Innerlichkeit» gegen Ende des 19. Jahrhunderts einen Bedeutungswandel, in dessen Verlauf sie von einem der Lebensphilosophie entstammenden Erlebnisbegriff unterwandert wird. Erlebnis wird nun als das ausgesprochene Medium der Kommunikation erachtet, das den Künstler befähigt, seine Gefühle unmittelbar dem Betrachter mitzuteilen.

Die Tatsache, daß der Erlebnisbegriff sich von den Biographien der Dichter und Künstler im 19. Jahrhundert ableiten läßt,[39] ist aufschlußreich, wenn man die ästhetischen Ansichten der Kunstbewegung betrachtet. Erlebnis ist in diesen Schilderungen mehr als eine bloße Erfahrung, weil es auf das Leben des Einzelnen einen besonderen Nachdruck ausübt, der dem Moment bleibende Bedeutung verleiht. Das in dieser Weise gewonnene Erlebnis erreicht «einen neuen Seinsstand im Ausdruck der Kunst.» In seinem Buch *Das Erlebnis und die Dichtung* hat Wilhelm Dilthey als erster dem Wort eine begriffliche Funktion zugewiesen, sodaß es «bald zu einem beliebten Modewort und zur Bezeichnung eines so einleuchtenden Wertbegriffs aufsteigen sollte, daß viele europäische Sprachen es als Fremdwort übernommen haben.» Charakteristischerweise greift die Kunstbewegung diesen Erlebnisbegriff begierig auf, wobei sie ihn, um ihrer ideologischen Zielsetzung zu genügen, willkürlich abgewandelt hat. Anstatt das in Diltheys Methodologie dargelegte hermeneutische Verfahren zu beobachten, beschäftigen sie sich in ihrer Auseinandersetzung mit dem Werk jenes einflußreichen Philosophen ausschließlich mit den vitalistischen Aspekten, sodaß das Leben selbst, in seiner begrifflichen Unfaßbarkeit, ein wichtiges Element ihrer Kunstanschauung wird. Diese Tendenz wird von Adolf Bartels, einem der führenden Mitarbeiter des *Kunstwart,* klar dargelegt: «Das Leben ist das erste und hat an und für sich Wert, die Kunst (und auch die Wissenschaft) ist das zweite, das Abgeleitete oder, wenn man lieber will, eine feinere Form der Lebensbetätigung, die nur auf Grund vorhandenen Lebens möglich ist.»[40]

38 *KW* 13: 2 (1899), 45.
39 Hier und im folgenden siehe Hans-Georg Gadamer, *Wahrheit und Methode, Grundzüge einer philosophischen Hermeneutik* (Tübingen: J.C.B. Mohr [Paul Siebeck], 1960), S. 57f. Siehe auch Karol Sauerland, *Diltheys Erlebnisbegriff. Entstehung, Glanzzeit und Verkümmerung eines literarhistorischen Begriffs* (Berlin: de Gruyter, 1972).
40 Adolf Bartels, «Kunst und Wissenschaft als Völkermesser,» *KW* 13: 19 (1900), 244.

Bartels' Äußerung ist eine Bejahung der Tendenz, die Kunst als einen Teil einer unergründlichen Lebensmacht zu sehen; in ihrem Wirkungsbereich geht ein jegliches Vermitteln nur auf emotionalem Wege vor sich. In diesem Zusammenhang ist das Gefühlsleben der Künstler außerordentlich bedeutsam für die Kunstbewegung, denn es wird als die beseelende Kraft der Innerlichkeit erachtet. Aus diesem Grunde wird das Gefühl als das einzige Medium anerkannt, durch das die Kunst vermittelt werden kann. Um darzulegen, wie natürlich es ist, eine innere Gemeinsamkeit zwischen den Emotionen des Künstlers und denen seiner Mitmenschen zu finden, verwenden die Vertreter der Kunstbewegung eine höchst verzerrte Version des Begriffs «Nacherleben,» der eine Leitidee des Diltheyschen geisteswissenschaftlichen Verfahrens ist.[41] Avenarius und seine Gesinnungsgenossen fühlen sich von diesem im Grunde sehr komplizierten Vorgang deshalb angezogen, weil sie darunter ein einfaches einfühlendes Versenken verstehen,[42] eine Methode, die einen unmittelbaren Zugang zu den Emotionen des Künstlers ermöglicht. Durch ein Erfassen seines Gefühls- und Stimmungszustands glauben sie auch sein Werk begreifen zu können. In diesem Schnellverfahren wird dem Prinzip des «Verstehens», das einen so zentralen Bestandteil in Diltheys kritischem Vorgehen darstellt, keinerlei Beachtung geschenkt. Denn obwohl der Philosoph die grundlegende Bedeutung der Gefühlselemente anerkennt, behandelt er sie doch als Teil eines «Wirkungszusammenhanges,»[43] der sich nur als hermeneutisches Verfahren vorstellen läßt. Im Gegensatz zu den Ideologen der Kunstbewegung, die sich allein von der Wirkung der Affekte führen lassen, ist Dilthey mit Hilfe seiner «verstehenden» Methode im Grunde an der Wiederherstellung eines kulturellen und historischen Zusammenhanges interessiert. Solch ein konzentriertes intellektuelles Bemühen ist nicht im Sinne der Kulturkonservativen; bei Avenarius heißt es: «Das Leben hungert nicht nach Literaturwissenschaft und Kunstgeschichte, sondern es lechzt nach Leben, nach seinesgleichen, nach Einnahme dessen, was der Nächste gedacht und gefühlt hat, nach Ausgabe dessen, was er selber denkt und fühlt ... »[44] Solch ein unvermitteltes Erfassen erfordert eine direkte Anschaulichkeit, ein Bildbewußtsein, das jegliche verstandesmäßige Annäherung ausklammert. Nach den Theoretikern der Kunstbewegung ist der Kern eines jeden Kunstwerks ein inneres Bild, das von dem Kunstgenießenden unmittelbar erfaßt werden soll. Ein Gemälde mit prüfenden und urteilenden Augen zu betrachten, wird nicht zu einem echten ästhetischen Erlebnis führen. Ein bloßes «Sehen» muß durch ein «Schauen» ersetzt werden, denn nur durch das letztere wird dem Betrachter der «Seelenzustand» des Künstlers und «seine Stimmung beim Erfassen und Festhalten» seiner Ein-

---

41 Siehe Wilhelm Dilthey, *Gesammelte Schriften,* Bd. VII (Stuttgart: Teubner, 1961), 213ff.
42 Siehe Kratzsch, S. 170.
43 Dilthey, VII, 257ff.
44 Ferdinand Avenarius, *KW,* 14: 1 (1901), 4.

drücke offenbar werden.⁴⁵ Es ist bezeichnend für die Theoretiker der Kunstbewegung, daß das Hineinversetzen oder Einfühlen in das Kunstwerk zusammen mit dem unvermittelten bildhaften Erfassen die einzige Erkenntnismethode dieser Ästhetik bilden.⁴⁶

Die zielstrebigen Bemühungen der kulturkonservativen Intellektuellen um die Pflege und das Bewußtmachen des Begriffs der «Innerlichkeit» sind eng mit dem ideologischen Eifer der Reformbewegung der Gebildeten verknüpft. Die im Grunde verbohrte Kunstauffassung dieser Leute ist sowohl vom ideengeschichtlichen als auch vom soziokulturellen Standpunkt her gesehen bedeutsam, insofern hier die Ästhetik in ein ideologisches Schema gezwängt wird, um einer ausgesprochen nationalistischen Weltanschauung zu dienen, die besonders in der chauvinistischen Verherrlichung deutscher Kunst zutage tritt. In einem im Jahre 1900 veröffentlichten Artikel «Deutsch und französisch» von Avenarius heißt es: «Die Zeit des Nachahmens ... des Französelns ... sollte jetzt endlich vorüber sein, wo der germanische Geist der Kunst, wo die Kunst nicht als Formenspiel, sondern als Ausdruck in Dichtung und Musik und selbst in bildender Kunst erobernd durch die Welt vordringt. Wie wir sehen, wie wir empfinden, das muß das Letzte und Entscheidende ... sein.»⁴⁷ Wie augenfällig deshalb auch das Thema «ästhetische Kultur» im Schrifttum behandelt wird, es ist doch nur ein Aspekt einer viel breiter angelegten höchst idealisierten Vorstellung, nämlich jener von der «Ausdruckskultur,» die in dem Jargon des «Kunstwart» und Dürerbunds mit sittlicher oder «Willenskultur» gleichbedeutend ist: Ästhetische Kultur ist «auf das engste mit der sittlichen, mit der Willenskultur verschwistert. Ernsthafte ästhetische Kultur ist eine Form sittlicher Kultur.»⁴⁸ Mit anderen Worten, alle Bereiche des Lebens werden einer umfassenden ethischen Gesinnung untergeordnet, die den wahren germanischen Geist der Nation wiedererwecken soll. Im Sinne dieser programmatischen Auffassung ist das Kunsterlebnis des Einzelnen – seine höchst verinnerlichte Beziehung zur deutschen Kunst – letztlich nicht viel mehr als ein pädagogisches Mittel, um das nationalistische Selbstbewußtsein zu heben. Bezeichnenderweise wird die zielbewußte Kulturpolitik der Kunstbewegung als «eine soziale Hygiene des Geistes» charakterisiert.⁴⁹

---

45 Ferdinand Avenarius, «Sehen und Schauen», *KW*, 17:1 (1903/04), 566.
46 Die von der Kunstbewegung angewandte Methode des «Einfühlens» ist eine popularwissenschaftliche Verkürzung und Vergröberung von zeitgenössischen Studien, die sich mit den verschiedenen Ebenen des menschlichen Erkenntnisvermögens beschäftigen. Die Einfühlungstheorie, die quellenmäßig auf G.Th. Fechners Schrift *Zur experimentalen Ästhetik* (1871) zurückgeht, wird um 1900 von Konrad Lange, Johannes Volkelt und besonders von Theodor Lipps entwickelt. Lipps' *Grundlegung der Ästhetik* (1903) enthält die umfassendste Behandlung dieser Lehre; vgl. dazu Herrenbrück, S. 47ff.
47 Zitiert nach Kratzsch, S. 177.
48 Kratzsch, S. 177.
49 Ferdinand Avenarius, «Über Kunstpolitik,» *KW*, 22: 16 (1909), 181.

Obwohl «ästhetische Kultur» und «Ausdruckskultur» mit der aggressiven Weltanschauung der kulturkonservativen Vertreter eng verquickt sind, so lassen sich in diesem merkwürdigen Ideengefüge doch zwei klar erkennbare miteinander verflochtene Motive unterscheiden. Einerseits begegnet einem im Schrifttum dieser Kreise der ständig mit Pathos vorgetragene Aufruf und die Ermunterung zur Innerlichkeit, die durch ein gefühlsmäßiges Vertiefen in ein Kunstwerk erreicht werden soll. Andererseits wird der Leser beinahe überwältigt von den fast leidenschaftlich vorgebrachten Aufforderungen zur Entwicklung einer nationalistischen Gesinnung, die paradoxerweise jegliche individuelle Vergeistigung den kulturpolitischen Zielsetzungen unterordnet. Betrachtet man die ideologische Einstellung der führenden Köpfe der kulturkonservativen Bewegung, so fragt man sich, inwiefern ihr Begriff der Verinnerlichung dem der Kunstandacht in der Frühromantik und in der Malerei der Nazarener vergleichbar ist. Es gibt zumindest eine allgemeine Vorstellung, die beiden Gruppen gemeinsam ist: Um dem Betrachter eine gewisse Gesinnung nahe zu bringen, fordert man von ihm – als einzigen möglichen Zugang – ein gänzlich gefühlsmäßiges Vertiefen in das Kunstwerk. Ein wesentlicher Teil dieser Einstellung besteht aus der emotionalen Identifizierung des Betrachters mit dem Kunstwerk, wie sie zuerst in den *Herzensergießungen* so eindringlich nahegelegt worden war. Die Auffassung des Klosterbruders vom Einswerden des Schauenden mit dem Bildinhalt kann hier nicht genug betont werden, denn diese Idee ist der Leitfaden, der bis in die Ästhetik der Kunstbewegung führen sollte. Aber während die verinnerlichte Haltung der Frühromantik von echten religiösen Gefühlen getragen wird, ist den kulturkonservativen Kreisen diese Art von verwurzelter Gläubigkeit weitgehend fremd. Das Andachtsmäßige, das der früheren Tradition ihr unverkennbares Gepräge gibt, wird um die Jahrhundertwende durch eine ausgesprochen rhetorisch-emotionale Mentalität ersetzt, in der man der Gestalt des Künstlers eine quasi sakrale Bedeutung zumißt. Das ästhetische Erkenntnisvermögen des Betrachters wird zudem von einem allumfassenden Erlebnisbegriff unterwandert, der jede kritische und geschichtsbewußte Annäherung an das Kunstwerk verneint. Daher ist die Verinnerlichung im Sinne der Kunstbewegung lediglich ein rein emotionales Sichhineinversetzen in ein Kunstwerk, ohne jegliche Rücksicht auf dessen kulturellen Zusammenhang oder seine tiefere ästhetische Bedeutung. Letztlich aber ist die treibende Kraft, die sich in dieser Denkweise manifestiert, eine höchst nationalistische Ideologie, die in der turbulent-irrationalen kulturellen Atmosphäre der Wilhelminischen Epoche ihren charakteristischen Ausdruck findet.

«Wer hat Euch Wandervögeln die Wissenschaft geschenkt...?»
Zur Deutschromantik der Jugendbewegung

HANS SCHULTE, *McMaster University*

Die sogenannte Jugendbewegung, wie sie sich von 1896 bis 1933 – vom «Wandervogel» der Vorkriegszeit zur «bündischen» Jugend der Nachkriegsjahre – entwickelte, war das bedeutendste Ereignis in der kulturellen Wirkungsgeschichte der deutsch-romantischen Kulturtradition nach 1848. Der Energie, mit der sie dieses Erbe wahrnahm, entsprach das Maß ihrer Ausstrahlung, ja bewußtseinsbildenden Kraft im deutschen Bürgertum. Wenige der zwischen 1885 und 1915 geborenen geistigen bzw. politischen Führungskräfte in Deutschland wurden *nicht* von der Jugendbewegung berührt oder geprägt.[1] Die Literatur zur Geschichte oder zu Teilaspekten der Bewegung ist denn auch überwältigend.[2]

Die deutsche Literaturwissenschaft freilich, traditionell die Sachwalterin deutscher Romantik vor allen anderen Disziplinen, hat deren letzte produktive Phase nahezu ignoriert.[3] Bezeichnend ist Wolfgang Paulsens Sammelband über das Nachleben der Romantik, der der Jugendbewegung einen einzigen Satz widmet.[4] Und wenn Jost Hermand die Hammannsche Kulturgeschichte (der Moderne) bearbeitet, kommen dabei drei sehr beiläufige Seiten (von zirka 1800) für die Jugendbewegung heraus.[5]

Wie begreifen wir dieses Desinteresse? Zwei erklärende – nicht entschuldigende – Gründe spielen gewiß eine Rolle. Für eine Literaturgeschichte im traditionellen Sinne war eine Kulturepoche vergleichsweise unfruchtbar, die sich eher aus dem Kultus und der Lebensreform denn als «Kunstperiode» ver-

---

1 Vgl. die bisher fünfbändige Zusammenstellung der *Namen und Werke* ehemaliger Bundes- oder Gruppenführer von Hinrich Jantzen (Frankfurt: Dipa, 1972ff.).
2 Der 1960 erschienene Antiquariatskatalog eines ehemaligen Aktiven (A. Kistner, *Die deutsche Jugendbewegung*. Katalog Nr. 68, Buchh. Edelmann, Nürnberg, 1960) enthält Titellisten auf 183 engbedruckten Seiten, plus Nachtrag.
3 Allgemeine wissenschaftliche Darstellungen zum Thema deutsche Literatur und Jugendbewegung gibt es nicht. Zu bestimmten Einflüssen s. Fritjof Eberhard Korn, *Das Motiv der deutschen Jugendbewegung im Werk von Manfred Hausmann* (München: ohne Vlg., 1958), und Christiane Völpel, *Hermann Hesse und die deutsche Jugendbewegung* (Bonn: Bouvier, 1977).
4 *Das Nachleben der Romantik in der modernen deutschen Literatur* (Heidelberg: Stiehm, 1972), S. 104.
5 *Epochen deutscher Kultur* (Frankfurt: Fischer, 1977), v, 170–73.

stand.⁶ Und von dem interdisziplinären Betrachter verlangt diese Jugendkultur nicht weniger als eine souveräne Verbindung politisch-historischer, geistesgeschichtlicher, soziologischer, pädagogischer, musikologischer und literarhistorischer Perspektiven.

In jedem Fall scheint es an der Zeit, die Jugendbewegung mit ihrer Ausstrahlung in alle Bereiche der Kultur und Gesellschaft der deutschen Literaturwissenschaft erinnerlich und zugänglich zu machen, und die «Deutsche Bewegung» nicht 1830, sondern 1933 enden zu lassen, so wie das der Wandervogel Hermann Nohl schon früh gefordert hatte. Wir sollten insofern auch nicht von einem «Nachleben» der Romantik im engeren Sinne sprechen, sondern eher von einem Fortleben oder Fortzeugen. Die Jugendbewegung war echtbürtige, nicht epigonale Romantik. Die soziale und geistesgeschichtliche Krise um die Wende zum 19. Jahrhundert wiederholte sich an der Wende zum 20., und zwar in einer verschärften Form, die zu radikaleren Lösungen zwang. Die Problematik des cartesischen Ich und der Individuation führte in beiden Fällen zu universalistischen, religiösen und «völkischen» Lösungsversuchen, nur in der nach Hofmannsthals Wort «konservativen Revolution» der Jugend zu einer viel weitergehenden Bereitschaft der Unterordnung unter ein «Ganzes». Auch die krisenhafte Erfahrung der Entfremdung des Menschen in einem profanierten und mechanisierten Dasein – die sogenannten Romantiker machten die Aufklärung, die Jugend um 1900 das kapitalistische Bürgertum verantwortlich – schien angesichts der weit bedrohlicheren Entmenschung gleichsam hinauszudrängen über den Glaubensweg einer Erlösung durch die Kunst: zu einer aktiv organisierenden, auf ein Volksganzes zielenden Gemeinschaftskultur. Die Leitbilder und -ideen sind dabei fast durchweg die gleichen: das universalistische Mittelalter (mit einer blühenden Ritter- und Burgenromantik); die Volkskultur (Lied, Spiel, Tanz, Brauch, Mythos); das Ewig-Jugendliche; Freundschaft und Bund; das Wandern, die Spannung von Heimat und Fremde, das Prinzip Sehnsucht, die blaue Blume; die Natur als Heimat und Bewährung; die mystisch-religiöse Tendenz; die Hochachtung des Unbewußten und Irrationalen; der nationalpädagogische Idealismus; politische Überparteilichkeit. Dies wird im folgenden zu zeigen sein. Daß die zweite dieser so nah verwandten romantischen Bewegungen ihre Lehrmeister in der ersten fand (vor allem Fichte, Novalis, Eichendorff, Görres, auch Nietzsche als später Nachfahr), versteht sich. Auch solche Beziehungen sind an Beispielen zu verdeutlichen. Vor allem aber muß die Bewegung als Ganzes, ihre Grundlegung, Entfaltung und Produktivität, dem kulturhistorischen Interesse nahegebracht werden, soweit das möglich ist in diesem engen Rahmen. Daran anschließen soll eine Untersuchung der wichtigsten Grundbegriffe. Auch eine kommen-

---

6 Dem widerspricht nicht der auffällig bekennerische Publikationsdrang der bündischen Jugend, die über tausend eigene Zeitschriften zu ihrer Selbstaussprache benötigte.

tierte Kurzbibliographie soll der Einführung in dieses von der Germanistik kaum je betretene Gebiet dienen.

*

Die deutsche Jugendbewegung entstand gleichsam explosiv, ohne Anregung «von oben.» Ein kleiner gymnasialer Stenographenverein unter der Leitung des Studenten Hermann Hoffmann-Fölkersamb in Berlin-Steglitz geriet im Jahre 1896 ins Wandern.[7] Diese befreiende Aktivität mitsamt ihrer Führer- und Gefolgschaftsstruktur breitete sich nun wie ein Lauffeuer durch ganz Deutschland aus. *Spiritus rector* und Organisator dieser ersten «Wandervogel»-Bewegung[8] wurde Karl Fischer, ein Mitglied der ersten Steglitzer Gruppe. Nach seinem Beispiel entfaltete sich in Hunderten von Ortsgruppen ein allen Annehmlichkeiten moderner Zivilisation entsagendes Naturleben, auf Fahrten mit Blechtopf und Klampfe am Rucksack, in Freiheit und selbstauferlegter Disziplin, dessen Breitenwirkung und Inbrunst einzigartig scheint. Weder die Sozialphänomene der Naturschwärmerei in der Vergangenheit des 18. und 19. Jahrhunderts halten den Vergleich aus, noch die spätere Hippie-Bewegung.

Hier ist nun gleich nach dem Wesen dieser romantischen Revolution zu fragen, in der die deutsche Jugend sich rousseauistisch lossagte von der Wertewelt der Eltern, mit dem ausgesprochenen Ziel, ein «neues Reich» der Innerlichkeit zu begründen. Da ist zunächst das «Prinzip Jugend» selbst, dessen schöpferisch überlegene Humanität, ja soziale Erlösungsfunktion zwar seit der romantischen Ära[9] literarisches Gemeingut war, in der gesellschaftlich-pädagogischen Realität aber keinerlei Entsprechung fand. Erziehung war Drill, Jugend nur Vorstufe erwachsener «Reife.» Die Jugendlichen schlossen nun diese Lücke mit der Schaffung eines von den sozialen Zeitstrukturen abgesonderten, autonomen «Jugendreichs,» einer «Jugendkultur» (Wyneken), eines Systems der Selbsterziehung in der Gemeinschaft. Im romantischen Erbe lag für sie zunächst etwas Zweideutiges: der Weg zu einer Erneuerung der gesamten Lebenskultur aus einem Gemeinschafts«ursprung» *und* – bloße Literatur. Sie wollten *das Leben* in seiner geistsinnlichen Totalität; die Botschaft, die sich nicht in Tat und Lebenspraxis umsetzen ließ, bedeutete ihr nichts. Die ästhetische «Schwelle» Eichendorffs, wie sie Richard Alewyn beschrieben hat, die den einsamen Schauenden-Lauschenden etwa am offenen Fenster festhält – sie wird programmatisch überschritten, in Richtung auf die Sache selbst. Die

---

7 Friedrich Borinski und Werner Milch haben auf den romantischen Sinn dieses stenographischen Bundes aufmerksam gemacht. Stenographie war den Mitgliedern eine Erwachsenen unbekannte Hieroglyphik mit dem Ursprungsreiz zeichenhaft magischer Beschwörung (*Jugendbewegung*, S. 24f.).
8 Den Namen der neuen Bewegung fand die Steglitzer Gruppe auf einem Ausflug im ersten Vers einer Grabinschrift, – s. Obertitel dieser Studie.
9 Ich begreife hier und im folgenden die «romantische» Kunstperiode als die Kultur der «Innerlichkeit» von der Geniezeit zur Heidelberger Romantik.

Führungsrolle der alten Romantik beruhte allein auf ihren prophetischen Visionen. Die deutsche Jugend des Jahrhundertbeginns, und weit mehr noch der völkisch gesteigerten zwanziger Jahre, empfand ihre Zeit als die historische Stunde der Wahrheit und sich selbst als Organ ihrer Erfüllung.[10]

Dem widerspricht auch nur scheinbar die Tatsache, daß das Buch des «Rembrandtdeutschen» Julius Langbehn[11] einen so tiefen Eindruck auf diese Jugend machte. Denn Kunst war in diesem Buch kein ästhetisches Phänomen, sondern Parole: Künderin eines mystisch-religiösen Daseinsgrundes, eines ursprungshaften Ganzheitsideals in wissenschaftlich fragmentierter Zivilisation, und als solche nur in einem bäuerlich ländlichen *Volkstum,* wie bei Rembrandt, ganz zu Hause. Langbehn und sein älterer theologischer Mitstreiter, der gleichfalls vielgelesene Rückert-Schüler Paul de Lagarde, waren enterbte Romantiker, deren zivilisatorische, politische und kulturelle Verzweiflung sich ganz auf die Idee einer spirituellen Wiedergeburt der deutschen Nation aus dem natürlichen «Volk» warf, aus *einer* das Volk umfassenden und ausdrückenden Religion (Lagarde) und Erziehung (Langbehn). Dazu kam die Verstädterung der deutschen Landschaft.[12] Langbehn und Lagarde haßten die Stadt, besonders Berlin, als Brutstätte des Modernismus, und die Wandervögel taten es ihnen nach. Ihnen war, wie dem jungen Berliner Expressionisten Heym, die Stadt ein menschenfressender, d.h. *menschliches* Leben verheerender Moloch. Daß die Idee der Jugendbewegung in Berlin-Steglitz zündete, hat seine besondere Logik. Das neue Wanderlied zeugt vielfach von dieser Erfahrung:

---

10 Georg Götsch, einer der aktivsten Führer der bündischen Zeit, spricht einmal von der Faszination des Theaters, die nicht in die deutsche Gegenwart, sondern in «sehnsüchtige, zielstellende, prophetische Zeiten» gehöre: «die Zeiten der Verwirklichung haben Genüge am hellen täglichen Leben.» Die Kultur der Kunst wie der historischen Wissenschaften ist vorbei, «ich suche den bewegteren, heißen Urgrund der Dinge», so Götsch als Sprecher dieses neuen Sturm und Drang, «ihre erkaltete, tote Oberfläche, nach der ich gar nicht gefragt habe, wird mir täglich ... als Wissenschaft und Kultur gepriesen und durch Zerlegen deutlich gemacht. Zerlegen und besprechen aber kann man nur Leichen. Ich will mit dem leben, was mit mir geboren ist, worüber man noch nicht sprechen kann, was noch nicht erlaubt oder verboten ist ...» Und Götsch beschwört diese neue Erlebnisrealität folgendermaßen: wer will Kunstbegeisterung von dieser Jugend verlangen, «wenn sie alles wirklich aus sich herausleben darf? Beim nächtlichen Schwimmen im schilfduftenden See; bei stürmischer Ostseefahrt auf dem sturzseeüberschütteten kleinen Kohlendampfer; auf erklettertem Alpengipfel über durchwanderten Gewittern ...; in Zeltnächten, wenn draußen im zugigen Ruinenturm das Lagerfeuer flackert; ... im duftenden Heuboden der Wassermühle, wo das brausende Wasser einen in den Schlaf singt; im Flammenstoß, wo ein Lied zu rechter Stunde hundert Herzen und Hände zusammenreißt; auf sonnenfleckigen Waldwegen im Gespräch mit dem Freunde, tiefer packend als der gewaltigste Dialog der griechischen Tragödie ...» (*Dokumente* III, 1692/1694).
11 *Rembrandt als Erzieher* (Leipzig: Hirschfeld, 1890).
12 Die städtebildende Industrialisierung hatte in Deutschland spät eingesetzt, hatte dann aber die übrigen Länder mit einer Maßlosigkeit überholt, die das gebildete Bürgertum abgeschlagen hinter sich ließ.

> Aus grauer Städte Mauern
> Ziehn wir durch Wald und Feld . . .
> (*Die Mundorgel*, Nr. 170)
>
> Einer Woche Hammerschlag,
> Einer Woche Häuserquadern
> Zittern noch in unsern Adern,
> Herrlich lockt der Sonnentag.
> (*Bruder Singer*, S. 203)
>
> Wir kommen aus verfallenen Bereichen,
> Die Spuren schwemmte Dunkles zu.
> Geaichte wir, mit der Verdammnis Zeichen,
> Geschieden wir von Schlaf und fauler Ruh.
> (*Der Turm*, Nr. 319)

Oder auch das stammelnde Tagebuch eines jungen Ergriffenen:

> Werden wie der Baum, wie die Himmelsbläue – wer's könnte! Aber dahinten . . . Menschen, Menschen laut, arm, gierig, zerrissen – Städte, Straßen – stampfende Hämmer – Millionen unsichtbare Hände – die sich ausstrecken nach einem Unbekannten, nach einer Erlösung, nach einer Erfüllung – und du selbst . . . (W. Jantzen, *Die lyrische Dichtung*, S.108).

Kein Wunder, daß der Fahrende Schüler des unverändert idealromantischen Mittelalters Leitfigur wurde. Karl Fischer führte eine Hierarchie von «Pachanten» (verderbt aus «vagans») ein; er selbst, als Bundesführer, war «Oberpachant,» die Mitglieder «Scholaren» oder «die Horde.» Ein Gemisch aus altem Vaganten- oder Kundenjargon, häufig auch stilistischen und grammatisch-historischen Imitaten der kernig naiven Volkssprache Jörg Wickrams *(Rollwagenbüchlein)* und Hans Sachsens,[13] und Gymnasiastenslang begründete die bundeigene, dem Außenstehenden oft unverständliche Sprache.

Der Vagant also, der heimatlose Abenteurer zu Lande und zu Wasser, spielt die Hauptrolle in den selbstgemachten, doch immer den Liedgenres des 16. und 17. Jahrhunderts nachempfundenen Fahrtensongs. Er ist die Symbolfigur eines unbändig freien, allen Stürmen des Daseins bis zum Untergang ausgesetzten Menschseins. Die Abtrennung von der Welt der Arbeit und des Kapitals ist radikal. Das ist entscheidend, denn es ist der entschiedene Schritt hinaus über den alt-romantischen Wanderlied-Typus des Müllerburschen.[14] Wandervogel heißt Armutsgelübde und Freiheit von Bedürfnis. Der Kunde/Vagant kehrt niemals zurück ins gemachte Bett, und er steht außerhalb der bürgerlichen Moral. Er ist immer unterwegs mit und in der Natur, zu immer neuen (Selbst-)Offenbarungen. Er ist rauh, wild, verwittert bis zur Unkenntlichkeit,

---

13 Beide wurden Lieblingsautoren. Der «Fahrend Schuler im Paradeis,» unzählige Male vorgeführt, begründete geradezu eine neue Theatertradition: das Laienspiel.
14 Selbst Eichendorffs echter Landstreicher, der «Taugenichts,» ist bekanntlich eine Figur der Versöhnung, die «alles, alles gut» macht. Zum Thema Wandervogel und Landstreicher vgl. die guten Bemerkungen von Hans Blüher, *Wandervogel*, I, lllff.

– das genaue Gegenbild bürgerlicher Verweichlichung und affluenter Degeneration. Hier einige Proben:

> Was gehn euch meine Lumpen an?
> Da hängen Freud und Tränen dran.
> Was kümmert euch denn mein Gesicht?
> Ich brauche euer Mitleid nicht.
> Hoppla o he, weit in die See...
> (*Der Turm,* Nr. 128)
>
> Wilde Gesellen, vom Sturmwind durchweht,
> Fürsten in Lumpen und Loden,
> Ziehn wir dahin, bis das Herze uns steht,
> Ehrlos bis unter den Boden.
> Fiedel, Gewand in farbigen Pracht,
> Trefft keinen Zeisig ihr bunter!
> Ob uns auch Speier und Spötter verlacht,
> Uns geht die Sonne nicht unter.
> (*Die Mundorgel,* Nr. 177)
>
> Was sollen wir aber trinken? Wir haben keinen Wein.
> Der Beutel hängt uns leere, es muß geschieden sein...
> Wir wolln zu Land ausfahren, wohl über das weite Meer.
> Nach Fahrten, kühnen Fahrten, gelüstet uns gar sehr.
> (*Der Turm,* Nr. 310)

Der Widerspruch in dieser Projektion darf freilich nicht übersehen werden: Zur Vagabunden-Romantik gehören die Trink- und Liebesfreuden.[15] Die aber werden nur vereinzelt und topologisch geduldet. Diese seltsamen Vaganten sind nämlich in Wirklichkeit lebensreformerische Abstinenzler. Die antibürgerliche Provokation wird überhöht von einer den Gattungsrahmen sprengenden Pflichtstrenge, einem Idealismus der Charakterbildung und leibseelischen «Reinheit». Der preußische sozialpädagogische Idealismus Kants und vor allem Fichtes, jener Auftrag der Erneuerung des «Volksgeistes» durch die Jugend in den *Reden an die deutsche Nation* steht hier Pate – was das Meißner-Fest deutlich erweist. Wandervogel sein hieß alles andere als Lebensgenuß oder Sichtragenlassen vom Daseinsstrom. Es hieß Engagement in der und für die Gemeinschaft, die elitistisch jedes moralisch fragwürdige Element oder Mitläufertum ausschied. Im Eros der *Gefolgschaft,* die sich zum Gau, zum Bund, zum Volk steigern sollte, lag das Heil, – nicht in der individuellen Liebeserfahrung. Die hätte die Gemeinschaft gesprengt.[16] Die blaue Blume des

---

15 Die letzteren vor allem spielen, wie Jost Hermand gezeigt hat, im literarischen Umkreis der Neuromantik die hervorragende Rolle: «Der neuromantische Seelenvagabund,» a.a.O., S. 105-10.

16 Natürlich wurde auch das Mädchenwandern eine Realität; die weibliche Jugend bedurfte der Emanzipation ja noch dringender als die männliche. Es geschah aber sehr zögernd, meist durch die Schaffung abgeschlossener Mädchenbünde, und nach endlosen Diskussionen der «Mädchenfrage.» Und das gemeinsame Wandern wurde «entschärft» durch eine konstitutio-

Novalis, das vom Wandervogel adoptierte Sehnsuchtssymbol, hat mit der Liebeserfüllung nichts mehr zu tun. Die *unio mystica* des Individualismus ist gänzlich verdrängt und ersetzt durch die der Volksgemeinschaft. Die Vagabundenrolle, wildromantischer als in der alten Romantik, blieb Dichtung.

Dazu kommt ein zweites: die Fiktion der Bindungs- und Heimatlosigkeit. Sie ist Teil des Als-ob der «Fahrt.» Dem Ausflug des Wandervogels folgt aber in Wirklichkeit immer der Heimflug ins bürgerlich-elterliche Nest. Die Beziehungen zur Elterngeneration sind zwar ideologisch schlecht, praktisch aber recht gut und einträglich. Schon Karl Fischer schuf den Dach- und Schutzverband der Eltern, die zeichneten, finanzierten und staatliche Deckung ermöglichten. Nur so war ja die Idee der Selbsterziehung im geltenden Rechtssystem zu realisieren. Diese Fürsorge verschaffte aber der autonomen Jugendkultur nicht nur die Lebensbasis, sondern auch eine Belastung. Es stellte sich nämlich heraus, daß die geistige Abhängigkeit der Elterngeneration von dieser Jugend noch größer war als die materielle der Jugend von den Eltern, und daß der Kulturpessimismus der deutschen Intelligenz nur auf eine derartige Botschaft gewartet hatte. So drängten sich die zumeist ungebetenen geistigen Fürsprecher und Ideologen von allen Seiten heran, die Feste und Tagungen der Bewegung (auf denen die Jugendlichen dann zu entscheiden hatten, ob sie sich zum *Eros* des Ludwig Klages oder des Hans Blüher bekennen sollten) wurden zu nationalen, in allen Zeitungen vieldiskutierten Ereignissen. Die «konservative Revolution» hatte ihr Zentrum und Lieblingskind. So wurde von außen – trotz oft heftiger, ja explosiver Abwehrversuche – der Mythos der Bewegung gewoben, oder mindestens mitgewoben, und es ist oft schwer zu entscheiden, wo ein Gedanke eines prominenten Sprechers dieser Bewegung «aus dem Herzen sprach» und wo nicht.

Andererseits ist die Gunst dieser Umstände nicht gering zu veranschlagen. In den zwanziger Jahren reichten die Gönner und Geldgeber bis in die einflußreichsten Regierungsspitzen: der preußische Kulturminister Dr. Becker beispielsweise wurde ein enger Freund der Jugendführer Georg Götsch und Rolf Gardiner, fühlte sich in bündischen Kreisen zu Hause und ermöglichte der Sozialarbeit der Bewegung die Realisation weitreichender Volksbildungspläne. Die Bünde bzw. ihre Ortsgruppen besaßen bald eigene Stadtheime (gern in Wehrtürmen u.ä.), wo sie ihre «Nestabende» hatten, und malerische Landheime (alte Wassermühlen, Bauernkaten) oder, besonders gern, mittelalterliche Burgen. Die Mehrzahl der deutschen Burgen wurden von der deutschen Jugendbewegung, vor allem vom Jugendherbergswerk, erworben und ausge-

---

nelle Kameraderie (und Unisex-Kluft), die das Mädchen als Geschlechtswesen entmachtete. Hans Blüher in seinem Buch über *Die deutsche Wandervogelbewegung als erotisches Phänomen* (Berlin: Ruhland, 1912) hat den homoerotischen Sinn der Bewegung zweifellos überinterpretiert. Ein idealer und verhalten physischer Gruppen- und Gefolgschaftseros ist aber überall unverkennbar.

baut. Die staatlich-politische Etablierung der ersten Romantik im preußischen Staats- und Kulturbereich wiederholt sich in der letzten.

Die bürgerlich-idealistische Jugend war, wie kaum verwunderlich, gänzlich und programmatisch unpolitisch. Der Krieg riß sie unvorbereitet und unaufgeklärt aus ihrem «Jugendreich.» Was sie ihm zu geben hatte, war die reine Begeisterung einer mystisch hingebenden Vereinigung ihres Daseins mit dem bedrängten Volks-Ganzen. Von den Wandervogelsoldaten fielen (prozentual) doppelt so viele wie vom übrigen Heer. Für den völkischen Idealismus bedeutete das Fronterlebnis einen schlimmen Schock: war dies ihr «Volk,» diese fremden, vulgären Menschen, die ihnen ihre Zoten und Prostituierten aufdrängten? Immer wieder sprechen die Feldbriefe von der Tiefe dieser Enttäuschung,[17] die zur erneuten Isolation, d.h. zur Bildung und Organisation des «Feldwandervogel» führte. Man ist wieder zusammen und lebt in den alten Zeiten. Im übrigen bedeutet ihnen der Krieg eine sittliche und physische Bewährung. Der Feldwandervogel nimmt unendliche Mühen auf sich, für andere, weniger Gehärtete, er wacht am längsten, entbehrt am meisten und fällt zuerst – immer gleichen heiteren Mutes bis zum letzten Ende. Ich beschreibe hier Charakter und Schicksal des Leutnants Ernst Wurche, des Helden und Freundes in Walter Flex' *Der Wanderer zwischen beiden Welten: Ein Kriegserlebnis*. Flex schrieb den kleinen von der bündischen Nachkriegsjugend vielgelesenen Roman, das Idealporträt des Feldwandervogel, zum Andenken an den toten Freund im Felde, unmittelbar bevor er selbst fiel.

Der Krieg brachte der Jugendbewegung *nicht* den Zusammenbruch ihres völkischen Idealismus, nur seine Revision. Die neue, bündische Phase bedeutet den überfälligen Schritt in die politische Realität, und zur Kultur- und Sozialarbeit. Der Geist des Meißner-Festes behält dabei seine Gültigkeit. Auf dieses Ereignis müssen wir darum zunächst zurückblicken.

Die Vereinigung von vierzehn akademischen und Schüler-Bünden, die im Sommer 1913 zu einem «Fest der Jugend» auf dem Hohen Meißner (nicht weit von Kassel) aufrief, nannte sich die *Freideutsche Jugend*. Eine Öffnung nach oben hatte sich vollzogen. Die studentischen Verbände, sowie die Zwanzig- und Dreißigjährigen, die nun Einlaß fanden, sorgten für die Vergeistigung der Bewegung und für die Aufnahme romantischer Literatur und Philosophie. Das «Prinzip Jugend» hatte sich durchgesetzt, es war zur Parole und zum Fanal geworden. Niemand findet mehr etwas dabei, wenn sich Eugen Diederichs als fünfundvierzigjähriger «Vagantenvater» mit Kunststudenten durchs Saaletal bettelt[18] und dabei Pläne schmiedet für die Organisation des Festes.

---

17 Vgl. die Hinweise und Briefauszüge bei Walter Laqueur, *Young Germany,* S. 88ff.; bei Jakob Müller, *Die Jugendbewegung,* S. 200ff.; H. Buddensieg, *Dokumente* I, 213f.
18 E. Diederichs, «Aus meinem Leben,» *Namen und Werke,* a.a.O., S. 84.

Dieses freideutsche Fest macht in den Reden und Diskussionen zum ersten Mal das erwachte historische Selbstbewußtsein der Jugendbewegten als Vollender der «deutschen Bewegung» (Hermann Nohl) allgemein sichtbar. Überall will man anknüpfen, den im Dunkeln verlaufenen Weg des romantischen Idealismus und seiner Nationalpädagogik wieder aufnehmen und zu Ende gehen. Programmatisch feiert man den hundertsten Jahrestag des Sieges über Napoleon, der «Befreiung des Vaterlandes vom fremden Joch» (*Dokum.*, I, 91). «Wir fühlen,» heißt es in den Aufrufen, «daß vieles von dem, was die Dichter der Freiheitskriege besungen, was Fichte und Stein gesonnen und gewollt haben, heute noch der Erfüllung harrt.» Und die jugendlichen Kräfte sind nun da, die «zu innerlicher nationaler Erneuerung drängen» (ebd., S. 92). Einen «Frühlingssturm des Geistes» erwartet Diederichs, «der schon seit einem Menschenalter in Deutschland aus der Dumpfheit zum Lichte drängt.» Gottfried Traub ruft auf, das Fest im Sinne von Fichte zu feiern. Fichte, so erinnert er, ging mit den Jenaer Burschen zum Wartburgfest;[19] er war der geistige Vater jener Urburschenschaft, die eine reaktionäre Geschichtsschreibung so sehr in Mißkredit brachte, und die keinen Teil hatte am kruden Burschenschafts- und Verbindungswesen späterer Generationen. «Frei-deutsch,» erklärt Paul Natorp in seinem Festbeitrag, meine nichts anderes «als was Fichte unter den Worten frei und deutsch versteht, indem er in der Ursprünglichkeit selbsteigener Seins- und Lebensgestaltung den Sinn echter Freiheit und in dem Geiste solcher Freiheit das auszeichnende Merkmal des Deutschen sah.»[20] Fichte eignete sich in der Tat wie kein anderer, das «völkische» Selbstvertrauen der jungen Generation zu heben, und sie zu begeistern mit dem Bewußtsein ihrer Ur-Volkheit und Auserwähltheit. Die Versicherung, daß diesem deutschen Vaterland ein Göttliches einwohne, das geboren werden wolle, und daß aus solcher Begnadung die heilige Verpflichtung erwachse, diesen eigenen Geist erstarken zu lassen und durch die Welt zu verbreiten, – sie ging dieser Jugend zu Herzen.[21] Auch der unfehlbare Weg der Verwirklichung dieses Zieles war durch Fichte (und den kritischen Idealismus überhaupt) den jungen Menschen vorgezeichnet: sie sollten sich nur «selbst bestimmen und nie durch etwas Fremdes sich bestimmen lassen.»[22] Daraus erwuchs die berühmte Meißner-Formel, die Autonomieformel der Freideutschen Jugend:

---

19 *Dokum.* I, 111. Gründungsjahr und Wartburgfest: 1815.
20 Natorp bezieht sich hier auf die siebte der *Reden an die deutsche Nation,* in der Fichte den Unterschied zwischen deutsch und nichtdeutsch darin sieht, «ob man an ein absolut Erstes und Ursprüngliches im Menschen selber, an Freiheit, an unendliche Verbesserlichkeit, an ewiges Fortschreiten unseres Geschlechts glaube, oder ob man alles dieses nicht glaube, ja wohl deutlich einzusehen und zu begreifen vermeine, daß das Gegenteil von diesem allen stattfinde» (*Sämmtliche Werke* [Berlin: Veit, 1846], III, 2, S. 374). Den Pessimismus, Agnostizismus, Determinismus, Materialismus etc. in der deutschen Gesellschaftskultur versteht Fichte als heterogene «Ausländerei» (ebd., 359–77).
21 Achte Rede. Ebd., S. 383.
22 *Bestimmung des Gelehrten,* ebd., VI, 297.

> Die Freideutsche Jugend will nach eigener Bestimmung vor eigener Verantwortung mit innerer Wahrhaftigkeit ihr Leben gestalten. Für diese innere Freiheit tritt sie unter allen Umständen geschlossen ein. (*Dokum.*, I, 109)

Für Gustav Wyneken, den wohl bedeutendsten Sprecher der Bewegung, bedeutet das die «Erlösung von der Passivität» (*Dokum.*, I, 122), diesem Keim der Vernichtung im gesellschaftlichen und kulturellen Gesamtleben. Der Durchdringung aller realen Sphären des Jugendlebens, also vor allem der schulischen Einrichtungen, mit aktiver «Jugendkultur» war seine Freie Schulgemeinde verpflichtet. Auch hier steht Fichtes (und hinter ihm Pestalozzis) Gedanke der Nationalerziehung aus *einem* eigenen Sinn und Ursprung Pate.[23]

Die radikalste Position in diesem Kampffeld gegen Fremdbestimmung, Objektivismus, Intellektualismus, Historismus bezog aber wohl, unter den Beiträgern zum Meißner-Fest, Ludwig Klages. Für seinen Kultus schöpferischer Lebenskraft ist der Geist-Begriff nicht mehr tragfähig. In der allverbindenden Liebeskraft der Seele allein liegt das Heil. Die deutschen Romantiker aber waren ihre Botschafter und Zeugen: «Kaum hundert Jahre sind es her, daß sie wie aus heimlichen Brunnen der Tiefe in vielen Herzen wirklich aufs neue hervorquoll und die unvergeßlichen Träume jener jünglingshaften Weisen und Dichter trug, die man mißverstehend Romantiker nennt. Ihre Hoffnungen trogen, der Sturm ist verrauscht, ihr Wissen verschüttet, die Flut verebbt und „die Wüste wächst"» (*Dokum.*, I, 103). Der Geist des frühen Nietzsche (der *Unzeitgemäßen Betrachtungen*) spricht hier, wenn auch gefährlich irrationalistisch vereinseitigt. Und kein Vermittler des idealistischen Geistes hat so stark auf die Jugendbewegung gewirkt wie Nietzsche, der den «Bildungsphilister» demaskierende Nietzsche genauso wie der künderische, der Zarathustra-Nietzsche.[24]

*

Wenn Ludwig Klages recht hat mit seinem Diktum, die vernichtende Tendenz der Weltgeschichte liege in der Erhebung der «begreifenden Wachheit» über den Traum (*Dokum.*, I, 102), dann war die begreifende Wachheit, das sozialproduktive Engagement der *bündischen Jugend* (1918–1933) nach der Kriegserfahrung der Niedergang der Bewegung. Das Gegenteil war offenbar der Fall.

Der Ausgang des Krieges bedeutete für die Nachkriegsjugend die endgültige geistige und politische Bankrotterklärung der «Alten». Sie fühlte sich auf die eigene geistige Durchdringung der deutschen Situation, auf ihre politische

---

23 Fichtes Forderungen nach einer unabhängigen, selbstversorgenden Landerziehung wurden erst von der Jugendbewegung erfüllt, besonders durch das Landsiedlungswesen, das Landschulheim, die Freie Schulgemeinde (*Reden*, S. 422ff.). Die Nationalerziehung der «deutschen Bewegung» von Fichte bis Wyneken meint nicht mehr Aufklärung und Empirie, sondern Etablierung eines «festen und gewissen Geistes» (S. 400).
24 Auch Nietzsche wendet sich in seiner Kulturkritik immer wieder, wie Fichte, an die deutsche Jugend, die allein den Kulturzerfall aufhalten könnte. Vgl. die Basler Vorträge von 1872 «Über die Zukunft unserer Bildungsanstalten» (*Krit. Gesamtausg.*, [Berlin: de Gruyter, 1973], III, 2).

Verantwortung, auf die Notwendigkeit strafferer Organisation und praktischer Aufbauarbeit verwiesen. Die Freideutsche Autonomieformel hatte sich der progressiven «Bündigung» zu unterwerfen, das autonome Subjekt verschob sich von der Person zur Gruppe. Die verpflichtende Bindung an Gruppe und Führer, dem von «Trabanten» umschrittenen Träger der «Flamme» (Stefan George), wurde zum Grundgesetz eines erneuerten, strengeren Ethos. Georges Elitismus, sein Bund-Konzept, Führerprinzip, die geistige und organisatorische Strenge, die Idee des Neuen Reiches haben zweifellos eine bedeutende (und noch unerforschte) Wirkung auf das neue Selbstverständnis der Bewegung gehabt. Nichts hätte ihr freilich ferner stehen können als Georges Esoterik, sein Ästhetentum, sein Wort-Kultus. Der Jugendbund wollte Mitte von Kraft und Wirkung in der sozialen Gegenwart sein. Auch war das Führerprinzip keineswegs absolut. George war da so wenig Vorbild wie Hitler der Vollender. Die Bünde waren durchaus spezifische, organische Gesinnungs- und Funktionsgemeinschaften. Das wird im letzten Teil dieser Studie deutlicher werden.

In der Weimarer Zeit kam die Jugendbewegung auch erst zu ihrer ganzen erstaunlichen Breitenwirkung. Wenn man die vielfachen Zahlenberechnungen der Literatur vergleicht, kommt man etwa zu folgendem Bild: ca. 100 000 Jugendliche gehörten um 1925 zur Kernzone der «freien» (d.h. konfessionell, politisch etc. unabhängigen) Bünde. Etwa das Vierfache dieser Zahl machte die organisierte katholische, protestantische und Arbeiter-Jugend aus, die nun – verwandelt von jener Kernzone – in die Jugendbewegung einging. Dazu kommt eine halbe Million aktiver Nichtmitglieder, sowie etwa vier Millionen Mitläufer (bzw. -wanderer). So gelangt man zu dem Wirkungsfaktor fünfzig. Konfessionelle Bünde wie der «Quickborn» unter Romano Guardini wurden bald vorbildlich für ihre Haltung und Kulturarbeit, und die bisher auf «Klassenkampf» beschränkten proletarischen Organisationen hatten auf einmal ein erfülltes Jugendleben mit Volkstanz und Nestabend, Wandern und Singen, Sonnenwendfeiern und Lagerfeuern. Hermann Claudius konnte für die Arbeiterjugend das Lied schreiben, das dann von der ganzen Bewegung als *ihr* wesenseigenes Lied zurückgenommen wurde:

> Wann wir schreiten Seit an Seit
> und die alten Lieder singen
> und die Wälder widerklingen,
> fühlen wir, es muß gelingen:
> mit uns zieht die neue Zeit!
> ...
> Wort und Lied und Blick und Schritt,
> wie in uraltewgen Tagen
> wollen sie zusammenschlagen.
> Ihre starken Arme tragen
> unsre Seelen fröhlich mit.
> (*Bruder Singer,* S. 203)

Das Lied wurde und wird, wie bekannt, vom kommunistischen Nachkriegsdeutschland requiriert. Es ließ sich aber ebensogut «völkisch» verstehen und singen. Daß die Jugendbewegung hier latent ambivalent war, wurde offenbar, als sich die Freideutsche «Einheitsfront» auf ihrer Hofgeismarer Tagung von 1920 im Zuge der revolutionären Ereignisse der politischen Forderung des Tages stellte. Sofort bildeten sich die Fronten, die sich im stürmischen Verlauf der Tagung[25] von keinen freideutschen Beschwörungen und Manövern mehr überbrücken ließen. Die Freideutsche Jugend mit ihrer idealen Einheitsvision zerbrach im Grunde an diesem Ereignis: der tragischen Ankunft der Idee auf dem Boden der politischen Wirklichkeit.

Die politisch-kulturelle Verzweiflung gepaart mit idealistischem Erweckungspathos wurde zur Hauptkategorie der Rezeption – und Produktion – romantischer Geistesgeschichte. So las man Fichte, machte man Nietzsche zum geistigen Vorbild, und entdeckte zuerst den bis dahin unbekannten Hölderlin.[26] Es gab vielleicht keine mehrgelesene und -zitierte Textstelle aus der romantischen Literatur als Hyperions, des tragisch scheiternden Volkserziehers, Einkehr bei den Deutschen. Sicher erklärt es den ungeheuren Erfolg des Machwerks *Wiltfeber, der ewige Deutsche: die Geschichte eines Heimatsuchers* in der Jugendbewegung, daß der Autor Hermann Burte es verstanden hatte, diese Nietzsche- und Hölderlin-Effekte zu kombinieren und ins Maßlose zu steigern. Wiltfeber ist ein Zarathustra, der aus der Fremde heimwehgeplagt zurückkehrt und «unter die Deutschen» tritt. Und nun wird Hölderlins Katastrophe der «Heimkehr des Genius in sein Volk» kitschig-christlich zum Weg auf den «Marterberg,» dessen Gipfel erreicht ist, als die Preisrichter eines deutschen Turnfestes die siegfriedartigen Bestleistungen des Heimkehrers mit dem 23. Platz quittieren.

Die jugendbewegten Leser sahen in diesem Opus zweifellos das eigene frustrierte Sendungsbewußtsein gespiegelt, und ein echoloses Liebesverlangen nach einer nichtexistenten Volks-Gemeinschaft. Auch der zweite große Erfolgsschlager der bündischen Jugend, Hermann Poperts *Helmut Harringa*, enthüllt manches über die Psychologie der Bewegung. Poperts Abstinenzlerbund *Vortrupp* war unter den vierzehn Gastgebern des Meißnerfestes gewesen. Wieder haben wir die pathetische Antithese: Harringa, der herrliche, nordische Held einerseits, und andererseits die Scheußlichkeiten des (alkoholisch, sexuell und rassisch) vergifteten und sich zersetzenden Volkskörpers. In der oft zitierten Lebensmaxime des Walter-Flex-Helden Ernst Wurche, «Rein bleiben und reif werden,» müssen wir beides sehen: die angstbesetzte, romantisch-idealistische Fallhöhe, und einen lebensreformerischen Ansatz, der historisch produktiv wurde.

---

25 Der Vorgang wurde ausführlich beschrieben von dem Teilnehmer Wilhelm Ehmer: «Die Hofgeismarer Tagung,» *Dokum.*, I, 230–43.
26 Die Freunde Norbert von Hellingrath und Ludwig Pigenot schufen ihre bahnbrechende Hölderlin-Ausgabe bekanntlich im Geist und Umkreis der Jugendbewegung.

Die Wirkung dieser künstlerisch fragwürdigen Produkte beweist, daß das literarische Bewußtsein der Bewegung ein ethisches und religiöses, niemals ein ästhetisches war. In diesem Sinne auch befriedigten die Bauerndichter Johannes Schlaf, Friedrich Lienhart und Gustav Schröers einen «völkischen» Bildungsbedarf. Genauso, nämlich als Energiespender, alle Form überspringend, las man Stefan George, Rudolf Alexander Schröder, Rudolf Borchardt und die Brüder Jünger (die selbst Wandervögel waren). Der Expressionismus war diesen Lesern zu zersetzend, und nur die Beschwörungen eines Heym, Trakls Hölderlin-Nähe und Barlach hatten einen gewissen Erfolg. Zur Literatur der alten Romantik hatte man da ein viel unmittelbareres Verhältnis. Man denke nur an die Zahl der Vertonungen und Nachahmungen von liedhaften Eichendorff-Texten.

Von den «Neuromantikern» kam außer Stefan George nur Hermann Hesse zu einem bedeutenden Einfluß, was bei seinem besonderen pädagogischen, der Jugendbewegung in Schriften, Briefen, Rezensionen, Aufrufen zugewandten Elan nicht verwunderlich ist. Dazu kommt die zentrale Bedeutung des (romantisch inspirierten) Jugend-Themas im Frühwerk: das entfaltete innere Universum der eigenen Jugend in einer fremden und starren Welt, die Zentralidee der Selbstwerdung, und die erlösende Kraft der Natur. Hesse wurde auch zum entscheidenden Vermittler Nietzsches.[27]

Hesse und die Brüder Jünger in ihren Frühphasen, Manfred Hausmann und Paul Alverdes gehörten zum unmittelbaren Einzugsbereich, zur «latenten Jugendbewegung» (Müller, S. 161). Genauso wesentlich aber blieb die trennende Kluft: der Eigen-Sinn der Neuromantiker, denen es um Innerlichkeit, Imagination und Individuation ging, und nicht um «Bündigung» als Mittel und Ziel der Welterlösung. So erklärt es sich, daß die neuromantischen Autoren, die sich der Bewegung genähert oder angeschlossen hatten, sich sämtlich wieder von ihr lösten und ihre eigenen Wege gingen. Der wandernden Jugend andererseits hatte ausgerechnet Hesse den Weg mit einem Gedicht gewiesen, das zu ihrem Motto wurde:

> Seltsam, im Nebel zu wandern!
> Einsam ist jeder Busch und Stein,
> Kein Baum sieht den andern,
> Jeder ist allein.
> (*Gesammelte Werke* [Frankfurt: Suhrkamp, 1970], I, 27)

---

27 Vgl. die explizit pädagogische Rezension des Nietzsche-Buches von Ernst Bertram, und den Aufruf «Zarathustras Wiederkehr,» der den Überwinder Zarathustra in die deutsche Nachkriegszeit versetzt. S. auch Ch. Völpel, *Hermann Hesse und die deutsche Jugendbewegung*, S. 74–82, 161ff., 175–181.

Man las hieraus die moderne Katastrophe menschlicher Isolation und Richtungslosigkeit, und die Aufforderung, sich auf der Nebelwanderung zu suchen, zu ertasten, zu verbinden, um des Wandersinnes gewiß zu werden.²⁸

*

Wir kommen zur Kultur- und Sozialarbeit der Bewegung, die allein ihrem romantisch «völkischen» Idealismus die Überzeugungskraft verleiht. Ihre außerordentliche Vielfalt kann hier nur exemplarisch dargestellt werden.

An erster Stelle ist die *Jugendmusikbewegung* zu nennen. An ihrem Anfang stand das Volkslied und der vorzügliche, die *Wunderhorn*-Sammlung an Breitenwirkung weit übertreffende *Zupfgeigenhansl* von Hans Breuer. Die Auswahl beschränkte sich auf die beste deutsche Liedtradition vom 15. bis zum 18. (Schwergewicht auf dem 16. und 17.) Jahrhundert. Sie brachte eine allgemeine Kultivierung und Geschmacksreinigung des Volksgesangs, die historisch ohne Beispiel ist. Die Sammlung *und* ihre Wirkung wurden ermöglicht durch einen begeisterten romantischen Konservativismus, wie er etwa aus Hans Breuers Vorwort zur 10. Auflage spricht: «Was ist das alte, klassische Volkslied? Es ist das Lied des ganzen, in sich noch geschlossenen Menschen, der alle Entwicklungsformen und -möglichkeiten – in nuce wohl – noch in sich trug, der nur recht von Herzen zu singen brauchte, um dem ganzen Volke Herzenskünder zu werden» (*Dokum.*, I, 66). Dazu kam, daß diese neue Liedpflege zum ersten Mal dem *musikalischen* Phänomen Volkslied gerecht wurde – für Herder wie für Brentano und Arnim hatte es nur ein literarisches Interesse. Eine noch heute mustergültige Satzkunst entfaltete sich, und Fritz Jöde, Walther Hensel, Cesar Bresgen, Armin Knab, Walter Götz, Karl Marx u.a. entwickelten aus dem alten Liedgut einen großen Reichtum neuer Volkslieder. Wandergemeinschaft und Volkslied wurden eins und trugen und stärkten sich gegenseitig.

Die Jugendbewegung breitet das Singen völkisch-konsequent durch ganz Deutschland aus. 1925 gibt es 600 jugendbewegte Singgemeinden. Das Schulliederbuch *Der Musikant* bringt den Durchbruch an den Schulen. Eine musikalische Fortbildungsbewegung für Volksschullehrer setzt ein, 1930 sind praktisch alle Musiklehrstühle der neuen pädagogischen Hochschulen mit Dozenten aus der Jugendmusikbewegung besetzt. Zahlreiche Jugend- und Volksmusikschulen entstehen. Die Landerziehungsheime werden aktiver Teil der Bewegung; ihr Ziel: «Durchdringung des gesamten Schullebens mit Musik und musikalischem Geist» (*Dokum.*, III, 1675).

Das musikalische Gemeinschaftserlebnis der Jugendbewegung war ein fundamental religiöses. Die Wendung zur alten Musik, «die als Sinnbild der besten Kräfte unseres Volkes von jeher untrennbar war von deutscher Frömmigkeit» (G. Götsch, ebd., 1668), war eine entschiedene Abkehr von moderner

---

28 Als Dokument dieser bezeichnenden Fehldeutung vgl. R. Mirbt, «Blätter der Erinnerung» (*Dokum.*, III, 1701).

Konsum-Musik. Eine Kirchenmusikbewegung – Choralmusik und Bach-Pflege vor allem[29] – entwickelte sich. Die Zuwendung zur Renaissance- und Barockmusik wirkte geradezu umwälzend auf das gesamte deutsche Musikleben; eine barock orientierte Hausmusikbewegung entfaltete sich bis in unsere Gegenwart, genauso wie die Pflege alter Musik auf alten Instrumenten. So wurde die Jugendbewegung auch führend im Instrumentenbau; die Laute/Guitarre und die Blockflöte wurden zu Volksinstrumenten.[30]

Neue Maßstäbe in ganz Europa setzte auch das Musikheim Frankfurt/Oder. Musik wurde hier in eine «musische Bildung» integriert, die in fachfreien Kursen Bewegung, Musik und Sprache als Einheit verstand und vermittelte, «gegen die Unfruchtbarkeit einer aus den Fugen geratenen, rhythmusfremden Welt.» «Die Mehrzahl der Lehrgangsteilnehmer,» so wird berichtet, erfuhr eine so nachhaltige «Auflösung aller versteinerten Vorstellungen, daß sie geradezu in einen Krisenzustand verfielen» (*Dokum.*, I, 253).

Das Beispiel der Musikbewegung offenbart den sozialtherapeutischen Sinn eines kulturellen *Dilettantismus,* dessen Konzept nach seiner vernichtenden Entwertung durch die klassische Ästhetik von der Basis her rehabilitiert wird. Dieser naturhafte Dilettantismus setzt nicht imitierend Kunst voraus: er ist im Gegenteil ein ursprungshaft expressives Tun und Mittun, das sich dann vielfach bis auf ein Kunst-Niveau steigert. Er erlöst das isoliert verhärtete Gemüt, das jugend-bewegt seine kollektiven Energiequellen wiederfindet. Das ist die romantische Idee, die nun in Deutschland mit einem ganzen Netz von freien Gemeinschaftsschulen und -einrichtungen in die Praxis umgesetzt wurde.

Auch die von Martin Luserke und Rudolf Mirbt begründete *Laienspielbewegung* verstand sich aus dieser Idee heraus. Bezeichnend auch hier der formale und stoffliche Rückgriff auf die Frühzeit der «Volkskultur»: Totentanzspiele, Hans Sachs. Wieder steht die Gemeinschaftsidee im Zentrum: «Laienspiel ist nichts anderes als Gemeinschaftsspiel: Spiel aus der Gemeinschaft, in der Gemeinschaft, für die Gemeinschaft» (Mirbt, *Dokum.*, III, 1674). Und auch hier herrscht der Totalitätsgedanke: die untrennbare Einheit von Sprache, Bewegung, Musik.[31] Waren schon das Wandern und die Naturerfahrung

---

29 Der Fall Bachs ist besonders interessant. Die deutsche Romantik (Mendelssohn) hatte seine religiöse Geistigkeit wiederentdeckt; die romantische Jugendmusikbewegung befestigte seine wirkliche allgemeine Pflege, aus der ein populärer Bach-Kultus entstand.

30 Zur Blockflöte: der Steglitzer Wandervogel Peter Harlan baute sie 1921 einem alten Museumsstück von Denner nach; vgl. *Namen und Werke*, IV, 83. Bekannt wurde Harlan als «Wandervogelklampfenbauer,» Meister historischer Zupfinstrumente, und Herr auf Burg Sternberg, wo er noch nach dem letzten Weltkrieg ein «Asyl» mittelalterlich musischen Lebens unterhielt. Ich habe die Burg zu sonntäglichen Matineen mehrmals besucht und kann bezeugen, daß man sich dem Reiz dieser romantischen Rekonstruktion – bei allen Vorbehalten – kaum entziehen konnte.

31 Martin Luserke machte auch theatergeschichtlich Schule mit seinen gruppenbewegungsrhythmisch expressiven Shakespeareinterpretationen. Und Ernst Ginsberg berichtet, daß damals fast alle später berühmten Schauspieler im Laienspiel bühnenreif wurden. (In der Holtorf-Gruppe spielten z.B. außer Ginsberg noch Matthias Wiemann, Werner Finck, Ruth Hellberg,

Selbstbegegnung in der Gemeinschaft, so ist das jetzt im Laienspiel in einem noch kulturintensiveren Maße der Fall. Wie Brecht, aber aus diametral entgegengesetzten Gründen, räumt die Theorie und Praxis des Laienspiels alles illusionistisch Theatralische hinweg: Vorhang und (symbolische) Rampe, historisierendes Kostüm, Make-up, Bühnenbild. Ein paar Kerzen (im Freien die Fackel) genügen. «Wir können das neue Reich nicht bauen, wenn wir ein überlebtes zum Maßstab nehmen» (ebd., S. 1679). So ähnlich (wenn auch nicht vom «Reich») sprach Brecht ein paar Jahre später, als er *seinen* Neuanfang mit dem Lehrstück machte. Dieser aber bestand in der analytischen Verweisung auf die kollektive Außenwelt, das Laienspiel hingegen in der synthetischen Dar-stellung einer kollektiven Innenwelt. Diese Darstellung geschieht also nicht aus dem Prinzip Aufklärung und Veränderung, sondern aus «leidenschaftlicher Ergriffenheit,» «Treue,» «Hingabe» (ebd., S. 1678) an den gemeinsamen inneren Gott. Die Laienspielidee romantischer Provenienz kommt der Kulturpsychologie C.G. Jungs nahe. Immer aber steht im Hintergrund die volks-heilsgeschichtliche Schau: die Erschließung und Bildung von Kraft-Zellen «für den großen Körper, der einmal die Gesamtheit in ihrer Mannigfaltigkeit lebendig vereinigt» (ebd., S. 1690).

Die Botschaft des «Jugendreichs» wird offenbar, in den zwanziger Jahren, zur Botschaft der «Volksbildung» überhaupt. Es geht um den neuen Menschen, der nicht mehr geleitet werden will «von Thron, Rednerpult, Lehrerkatheder, Bühne oder Konzertpodium aus.» Denn «keine Macht von außen kann Inneres wirklich bewegen» – so lautet die für die ganze Bewegung charakteristische, antimaterialistische und antirationalistische Formel. Masse muß Volk werden, «das *sich selbst* vertraut und sein Leben aus eigener Kraft schöpfend gestaltet wie einst das stolze Bürgertum der Stadtzeit, das sein inwendiges Himmelreich wieder aus sich herauszubauen verstand» (*Dokum.*, III, 1694). Das ländliche Siedlungswesen, das in zahlreichen Mini-Staatsgründungen Ackerbau und Viehzucht mit geistigen Projekten verbindet,[32] ist bezeichnend für diese restaurative Revolution.

Nur stichworthaft seien hier noch die weiteren Hauptrichtungen der bündischen Kultur- und Sozialarbeit erwähnt. Die Rede vom «Volkskörper» meinte konkret ein neues Körperbewußtsein: Volks- und Bewegungstanz, ja eine Art «Tanzwut» (*Dokum.*, III, 1712) breitete sich aus. Das Werkschulheim, das Werkstudententum wurde begründet. Der volkssoziale Idealismus richtete im ostdeutschen Grenzland Arbeitslager von Bauern, Arbeitern und Studenten ein, die (wie das *Boberhaus* unter der Leitung von Adolf Reichwein) auch eine

---

Veit Harlan u.a.). Was kaum erstaunt: Ginsberg rühmt den produktiven *Ensemble-Geist* des Laienspiels, der sein ganzes Leben geprägt habe (vgl. Ginsberg, «Erinnerungen,» *Dokum.*, III, 1706f.).

32 Die Siedlung Schwarzerden z.B. war eine Gymnastikschule mit musischen und sozialpflegerischen Lehrfächern. Sie besteht noch heute. Den ersten Anstoß zu solchen sozialproduktiven Keimzellen hatte Fichte gegeben; vgl. Anm. 23.

Überfremdung durch «Gastarbeiter» verhindern halfen. Volksbildungsheime wurden zu Volkshochschulen, – eine der zukunftsreichen Leistungen der Bewegung. Aus ihrem Geist, aus der Finanzkraft des Ministeriums Becker und unter Führung der jugendbewegten «Beckerjungen» (parlamentarisches Witzwort) entstanden die pädagogischen Akademien. Wenn man die jugendeigenen Errungenschaften hinzusetzt: die Schüler- und Studentenselbstverwaltung (AStA), die Jugendschriftenbewegung (Versorgung mit guter Lektüre, Bearbeitung alter Volksbücher und -sagen u.a.) und das Jugendherbergswerk (Begegnung auf Massenbasis), – dann beginnt sich das Bild der realisierenden Spätphase der deutschromantischen Bewegung zu füllen.

Das Ende ist bekannt, wenn auch immer noch nicht sicher gedeutet. Die Krisenjahre 1930–1933 brachten eine Spaltung der Jugendbewegung. Zahlreiche radikalvölkische, nationalistisch indoktrinierte oder opportunistische Jugendgruppen strömten der Hitler-Jugend zu. Der im bündischen Geist gefestigte Kern, d.h. die überwältigende Majorität der bündisch Aktiven, war sich der unüberbrückbaren Rivalität bewußt und widerstand den immer drohenderen Aufforderungen der HJ, «endlich ihre Abkapselung aufzugeben und sich der großen nationalen Freiheitsbewegung anzuschließen» (*Dokum.*, I, 518), – zumindest, nach erzwungenem Anschluß, passiv. Die alte Bewegung widersprach der neuen Organisation in jedem Punkt: mit ihrer Autonomieforderung, ihrer Überparteilichkeit, ihrem Aristokratismus. Anderseits übte die Hitler-Propaganda – das Pathos der Tat, die Rhetorik der nationalen Erlösung und Erfüllung – eine bedeutende Anziehung aus, und viele sahen im idealen Lichte dieses Versprechens die HJ als vorläufiges, krisenbedingt notwendiges Übel.

Das Jahr 1933 brachte die Befreiung von all diesen Ungewißheiten. Die bündische Jugend wurde zum Staatsfeind erklärt. Die Radikalität der Äußerungen und Maßnahmen des an sich weichlichen Baldur von Schirach setzt den Befehl eines «Führers» voraus, für den «Wandervogel» zum Kennwort des immer gefährlichen (weil nie zu kontrollierenden) romantischen Phantasten werden sollte. «Wir kündigen unseren unerbittlichen Kampf der bündischen Jugend an,» so lautete von Schirachs Osterbotschaft 1933, «die nichts als ichbezogen ist und vom ersten bis zum letzten Mann einer reaktionären Weltanschauung lebt» (*Dokum.*, III, 1260). Das Dekret traf die Bündischen wie ein Schlag aus dem Hinterhalt. Sie sahen nun klar: dieses «Dritte Reich» segelte mit dem Verdienst *ihrer* Arbeit, mit *ihren* Organisationsstrukturen, Begriffen und Symbolen davon in die Geschichte und ließ sie ohne Sinn und Zweck zurück. Viele, sehr viele sprangen unter der Schockwirkung noch auf, in der Hoffnung auf irgendeine Aktionsbasis. Zu einem Einfluß kam niemand, verfolgt wurden viele, und manche bis zum bitteren Ende des Widerstands.[33] Die

---

33 Die bekanntesten Widerstandsgruppen, an denen bündisch Aktive sich maßgeblich beteiligt hatten, waren der «Kreisauer Kreis» und die «Weiße Rose.»

physische und ideelle Liquidation der Jugendbewegung war das erklärte Ziel, und der Chefideologe Alfred Bäumler hatte auf seine Weise schon recht mit seiner Feststellung, die Jugendbewegung sei nichts als die letzte Emanzipationsbewegung des sterbenden Individualismus gewesen (zit. Laqueur, S. 210). Der «deutsche» Weg der Kultur des Humanismus war zu Ende. Von der Schuld mangelnder Entschlußkraft, von der Unfähigkeit, der geschichtlichen Fehlentwicklung eine nicht bloß theoretische «Bündische Einheitsfront» entgegenzusetzen und ernstzumachen mit dem politischen Ethos des Idealismus, ist diese seine letzte Phase nicht freizusprechen.

Es bleibt nur noch, in einer Schlußbetrachtung die Hauptmomente und -motive jener Jugendkultur romantischer Provenienz zusammenzustellen. Die Analyse kann dabei das im entwickelnden Teil dieser Studie sachlich Verstreute wieder vereinen.

Das Wandern

Wandern meinte zunächst ein Hinauswandern aus jenem Bereich versteinerten und verfremdeten Lebens, der Stadt, und ein Hineinwandern in den natürlichen Ursprungsbereich der Natur, des Landes und Volkes. Es war also Selbstbefreiung und Selbstbegegnung zugleich: man erwanderte sich selbst. Dieses Selbst verstand sich in immer umfassenderen Ursprungssphären als: Individualität = Gemeinschaft = Volk = Menschheit = Gottheit. Die Richtung dieses Unterwegsseins ließ sich im Gemeinschaftswandern erleben und finden. Die Zweckfreiheit des Wanderns wurde als das beglückende Geschenk des ganzen, unverstellten Daseins empfunden (Gegensatz: die elterliche, schulische, städtische Zweck- und Arbeitswelt). Daß die Jugendlichen so ihre Weltwirklichkeit erfuhren und sich an ihr bewährten, kommt hinzu: Naturkenntnisse, volks- und landeskundliche Erfahrung, ein intimes «Heimat»erlebnis, Anpassungsfähigkeit, Mitverantwortung, Ausdauer, Härte und Widerstandskraft.

Die Antithetik der wandernden Sehnsucht wird erneuert:

> Kameraden, fremde Welten
> wachen nachts bei unsern Zelten,
> wenn die Feuer tiefgebrannt,
> Kameraden, fremde Welten
> singen leis von unserm Land.
> (*Der Turm*, Nr. 294)

Ausfahrt ist Einkehr, Selbst- und Heimaterfahrung vermittelt durch Sehnsucht.[34] In der Einheit von Fernweh und Heimweh entfaltet sich eine eigentüm-

---

34 Bei fast allen Aktiven der Bewegung blieb dieser Trieb lebenslang bestehen (wie das biographische Handbuch ausweist). Bei vielen wurde daraus ein weltumspannendes und oft sozialproduktives Reiseleben (wie etwa im Falle Adolf Reichweins und Klaus Mehnerts). Mehnert ist ein

liche Dynamik, die sich etwa im Wechsel von «Fahrt» und (eigenem, nicht elterlichem!) «Nest» bzw. «Nestabend» ausdrückt. Sie ist die ewige Unruhe, an deren Ende auch hier die «blaue Blume» steht. Deren innere Gewißheit ist das Leben des Lebens:

> Ach, Blümlein blau, verdorre nicht ...
> (*Zupfgeigenhansl,* S. 67)
>
> ... die Blume zu gewinnen
> ziehn wir ins Land hinein.
> Es rauschen die Bäume, es murmelt der Fluß,
> und wer die blaue Blume finden will, der muß
> ein Wandervogel sein.
> (*Die Mundorgel,* Nr. 168)

Die rhythmische Gelöstheit des Wanderns schafft einen Einklang mit Natur und Welt, der das in ihr «schlafende Lied» weckt. Die rhythmische Bewegtheit und Musik, die «singenden klingenden Wellen / des vollen Lebens» werden real erwandert, die nicht nur bei Eichendorff, sondern auch in den Müller-Liedern und bereits im *Ofterdingen* zuerst thematisch wurden. Ein sinnlich bewegtes und zugleich allverbindendes Körpergefühl entsteht, das sich als

Emanzipation des Leibes (Tanz)

erfährt. Das Hinauswandern aus Stadt und Schule bedeutete nämlich auch die jugend-bewegte Befreiung des Leibes aus der Haft des Geistes, – die letzte Konsequenz des Anti-Intellektualismus. Schon für Fichte entfaltet das Ich in sich den Leib, das eigentliche Tat-Prinzip. Nietzsche aber geht da viel weiter, insbesondere im *Zarathustra,* dem Lesebuch der Jugendbewegung. «Untergehen will euer Selbst,» zürnt Zarathustra, «darum wurdet ihr zu Verächtern des Leibes!»[35] Orientierung im Dasein ist nur möglich am Leitbild des Leibes. Die Fortbildung dieser Umwertung der Werte haben wir schließlich in Stefan Georges Vergottung des Leibes, als der sichtbaren Ankunft des Mythos.

Die Wandervögel bekamen diese Begründungen ihrer Praxis nachgeliefert (Blüher, Wyneken), als schon die am freien leiblichen Selbstgefühl orientierte Schönheits-, Kraft-, Bewegungs- und Bekleidungskultur sich durch ganz Deutschland verbreitete. Aus dem Umkreis der Meißner-Jugend entwickelte sich eine völlig neue Schule der Gymnastik: eine rhythmisch expressive, z.T. improvisatorische Bewegungsgestaltung.[36] Die Lebensreform- und Abstinenz-

---

gutes Beispiel: der bedeutende Politologe wurde nie müde, auf Reisen zwischen den Blöcken zu deren gegenseitigem Verständnis beizutragen; dabei blieb er (bis zu seinem Tod im Jahre 1984) «völkisch» entschiedener Deutscher, tief gebunden an seine Schwarzwaldheimat.

35 *Kritische Gesamtausgabe* (Berlin: de Gruyter, 1968), VI, 1, S. 36f.
36 Die Schulen von Rudolf Bode und Hinrich Medau hatten bald – und haben noch – Weltruf. Beider Auffassung von gymnastischer Körperkultur war eine *musikalische.*

bewegung, ebenfalls in der Meißner-Jugend wurzelnd, hing mit dem neuen Körpergefühl aufs engste zusammen. Die Selbsterfahrung der Jugend war Körpererfahrung, – und das galt immer im Hinblick auf das umfassende Selbst der Gruppe und des Volkes. Man denke an die Bedeutung des Zusammenrückens im Feuerkreis, an das Leben mit der Landbevölkerung, Schlafen im Heu der Bauern und Helfen beim Pflügen des Bodens, Durchmessen der Wälder und Berge etc. Das ganze bündische und völkische Wesen ist begreiflich zu machen als das «Wiederfinden des eigenen Körpers und des ... Bundes mit ihm» (Wyneken, *Der Kampf*..., S. 156). Wandern, singen, werken[37] wollte diese Lebensdynamik zunächst, aber letztlich wollte sie *tanzen*. Zarathustra, der Prophet des Leibes, war der Tänzer des Lebens.

Tanzende Bewegtheit als Urlebendigkeit des Lebens ist eine romantische Vision. In der Frühromantik, aber auch bei Eichendorff (vor allem im *Taugenichts!*) sind es die Künstler, die sie wiedererwecken.[38] Was in der alten Romantik poetische Prophetie blieb, drängt in der neuen in die Realität. Alle Berichterstatter des Meißner-Festes sprechen von dem seltsamen Schauspiel der jugendlichen Abgesandten, die aus allen Winkeln Deutschlands auf dem Berge zusammenwanderten und dort – Tausende miteinander – ins Tanzen kamen, so allgemein und pausenlos, daß manchen Älteren «das ewige Herumgehopse» auf die Nerven ging. Eine «Reigen»-Renaissance, gefördert von geistigen Führern wie Romano Guardini, entwickelte sich, und auf etwas tieferem Niveau zog Friedrich Muck-Lamberti mit den Anhängern seiner «Neuen Schar» von Stadt zu Stadt, um neues Leben, Liebe und Freude zu ersingen und ertanzen. Das Ergebnis: nicht nur die Bevölkerung wurde ergriffen, in Straßen und Gassen, von der tanzenden Liebe und Freude, sondern die Kirchen selbst öffneten sich den Massenspektakeln. Der Freiheitskampf «des Lebens wider den Begriff» (Wyneken) verstand sich als religiöse Erweckung, – das genügte den Pfarrern, die Muck ihre Kirchenschlüssel aushändigten.

Das Fest

Die Wanderschaft wollte zum Tanz werden, und der Tanz zum Fest. Tanz und Fest stellten eine besonders innige Konsequenz jugendbewegter Dynamik des

---

37 Die für Schule und Haus so folgenreiche Neuentdeckung des Hand-Werks (Holz-, Leder-, Metall-, Bodenbearbeitung) hat hier ihren erlebnishaften Ursprung. Das Selbst-Gefühl des Leibes im Werk wurde durchaus erotisch erfahren, – Ferdinand Hodlers bekannter *Holzfäller* (1910) macht diese Dimension gut sichtbar.
38 Vgl. Novalis' Konstruktion jener Urzeit, in denen die Dichter selbst die Steine «in regelmäßig tanzende Bewegungen hingerissen» und «tanzende Scharen von Fischen und Meerungeheuern» hervorgelockt haben (*Werke*, hrsg. H.-J. Mähl und R. Samuel [München: Hanser, 1978], I, 257f.). Weitere Beispiele: die tanzenden Sterne in Arkturs Palast (ebda., S. 341); die vom Dichter zu dem Grad erweckte Natur, daß sie «tanzte und weissagte» (ebda., S. 207). Ähnlich der Tanz als Augenblick höchsten Lebensglücks («Schwanings Fest,» ebda., S. 319). – In W. Müllers «Wanderschaft» (!) tanzen «die Steine selbst, so schwer sie sind.»

Selbst in der Lebens-Gemeinschaft dar. So wie die erste Lebensfahrt des jungen Ofterdingen im Fest gipfelt («Der Lebensgenuß stand wie ein klingender Baum voll goldener Früchte vor ihm»), so gipfelten die Jugendfahrten in Festen, an denen man teilhatte wie an einer Kommunion. So beging man Maifeste, Sonnenwendfeste, Bundesfeste u.a., deren Ekstasis gesteigert wurde durch (Gipfel-, Ruinen-) Einsamkeit, Nacht, Fahnen und Fackeln, Feuer, Feuersprüche und -reden. Der Wanderer trat ein in diesen zeitlosen Raum der Lebensfreude und der begeisterten Gemeinschaft. Auf dem ritualisierten Programm standen außer der Hauptsache, Tanz und Gemeinschaftsgesang, das Laienspiel, Wettspiel und -kampf, Rede und Poesie, deren Ziel eine stärkste Verdichtung des Gemeinschaftserlebnisses war.

Gemeinschaft, Gefolgschaft

war sicher noch vor der «Natur» der erste ideale Ansporn und kategorische Imperativ der Bewegung. Einsamkeit, Isolation, die in der Romantik noch aesthetisch kultiviert werden konnte, ist in der Moderne tödlich geworden; daher die Doppeltendenz zum Konservativismus *und* Sozialismus, und die Kampfansage gegen den Liberalismus. Entscheidend war, daß die ganz im romantisch-organischen Sinn verstandene Gemeinschaft erst aus dem Rahmen der modernen Arbeitswelt herausgelöst und elementaren Lebensbezügen (Wandern, Spiel und Gesang, Landarbeit, Handwerk) zugeführt werden mußte, um wieder «zu sich» zu kommen. Aus dem Momentum und der Multiplikation solcher Keimzellen konnten – das war der feste Glaube – Industriegesellschaft, Stadt und Volk[39] re-organisiert werden. Die Wander-, Kultur- und Arbeitsgemeinschaft auf der Suche nach ihrem Selbst war somit nach außen hermetisch abgeschlossen und nach innen zugleich charakteristische Einheit und Totalität. Die Ausrichtung der Gruppen-Sphäre auf ihre symbolische und energische Mitte, die der «Führer» besetzte, weist in vielem auf die Sympathie- und Liebeslehren der jungen Gefühlskultur im 18. Jahrhundert (etwa bei Schiller) zurück: der Gruppeneros war die Macht, die die Versprengten der Zivilisation aneinanderband im Hinblick auf ihr in dem magnetischen Zentrum verborgenes Selbst. Dieses Zentrum hatte sich verleiblicht: im Führer (der nur ca. fünf Jahre älter als der Durchschnitt sein durfte). In der bündischen Zeit entwickelte sich um den Führer ein mythischer Kultus, der von Hans Blühers

---

39 Vgl. die letzte Strophe eines anonymen Gedichts in der Zeitschrift der *Deutschen Freischar,* Bd. 5, H. 2, Weihnachten 1932(!): «Und nun, gestärkt von Mühen, harter Wache, / Vertrauenswürdig durch den Glanz der Feuer, / Durch Sorge um die andern gut und tüchtig, / Durch Horchen und Gehorchen eingeweiht, / Wagt Schar um Schar sich rückwärts in die Städte» (zitiert nach Pross, *Jugend* ..., S. 405). Die historische Konstellation ist nicht ohne tragische Ironie.

gefährlicher Applikation deutscher Genielehre vorbereitet war.[40] Praktisch beruhte die Führer-Wahl jedoch auf Gegenseitigkeit. Außer seinem Charisma hatte der Führer seine Fähigkeit unter Beweis zu stellen, den Spielraum der Möglichkeiten in der Gruppenzusammensetzung zu erkennen, zu ergänzen, und zu aktivieren.[41] Immer wiederkehrende Desiderata eines Führers waren: tatkräftige Begeisterung, Verständnis und Mitgefühl, Charisma, totales Engagement, Organisationstalent. Der Führer, der dies nicht zu leisten vermochte, konnte abgewählt werden, wie das schon dem ersten Gründer Karl Fischer geschah. Für die «Führer, befiehl, wir folgen»-Ideologie war die Jugendbewegung ein dürftiger Boden. Dem widerstand auch das regulative Phänomen einer zweiten, geistigen Führungsschicht (Natorp, Avenarius, Wyneken, Hesse, George, Förster, Spitteler, Niemöller, Scheler u.a.).

Wie wenig konformistisch das Gemeinschaftsideal war, läßt sich gut an einer spezifischen Leistung ablesen: seinem formenden Einfluß auf das Lied. Hier führte es nämlich zu einer Überwindung des herrschenden homophonen Chorgesangs, und zwar nicht nur durch die Wiederentdeckung des quasi-polyphonen *Kanon*,[42] sondern auch durch die Erneuerung der Madrigal- und A-capella-Kunst des 16. Jahrhunderts. Der chorische Harmonie-Begriff, der einer Führungsstimme alle übrigen sklavisch unterordnet, war unerträglich geworden; der neue Gemeinschaftsstil verlangte: Harmonie durch Polyphonie.[43] Zu einer hochentwickelten Kunst gelangte auf diese Weise der Volkslied-Satz (für Gesang und Instrumente), der von Jöde, Hensel, Götsch, Knab, Gneist, von Knorr, Marx, Distler und vielen anderen vom Zwang vertikaler Funktionsharmonik befreit wurde. Auch waren nach außen, vorm «Publikum,» keine Fassaden mehr zu errichten: man sang nur miteinander und füreinander. Der Zweck der soziologisch so beziehungsvollen Satzreform war die *Befreiung der Einzelstimmen,* die sich nun mit der Führungsstimme melodisch und rhythmisch auseinandersetzen (wechselnd duettieren, Liedmelodiephasen kanonisch aufgreifen oder komplementärmelodisch bzw. -rhythmisch interpretieren usw.), so daß eine viel reichere, spannungsvollere Einheit entsteht. Hier ein einfaches Beispiel von Walther Hensel:

---

40 Blüher verkündet in seinem Buch *Führer und Volk in der Jugendbewegung* (Jena: Diederichs, 1918) das Schöpfer-Vorrecht eines ursprünglichen Führertums aus Gottes Gnaden. Ein solcher Führer wählt sich sein Volk (und nicht umgekehrt) – problematische Wirkungen der idealistischen Geschichtsphilosophie.

41 Rudolf Kneips Handbuch *Jugend der Weimarer Zeit* (1974) verzeichnet fast 1200 eingetragene Bünde, – was allein schon ein Maß Demokratie gewährleistete, das jeden Vergleich mit der späteren Hitlerjugend ausschließen sollte.

42 Ursprünglich aus dem Vulgärlied des Mittelalters entstanden. Zur Liebligsgattung aller gemeinsam Singenden wurde der Kanon erst durch die Jugendmusikbewegung (1926 erschien die erste große Sammlung, *Der Kanon*, von F. Jöde).

43 Jöde sprach vom «reinen Beieinander mehrerer ihrem Wesen nach gleichwertiger Stimmen» in den Madrigalen, – «im Gegensatz zu jener harmonischen Bedientenstruktur, wie sie ... bis zum Überdruß die liedertafelnde Männerchorliteratur aufwies» (*Dokum.*, III, 1645).

Das Aufrecht Fähnlein. Kassel, 1933

Volk

Die Volksidee war der Jugendbewegung Fanal, Leib und Seele, Ursprung und Ziel der Kulturgemeinschaft.

«Volk» war zunächst ein kultur- und sozialkritischer Terminus, Protest-Wort der Verselbstung und Verinnerlichung gegnüber dem anonymen Materialismus und «Amerikanismus» der Zeit. Die ideale Einheit Persönlichkeit-Gruppengemeinschaft-Volk hatte nichts gemein mit dem faschistischen «Du bist nichts, dein Volk ist alles.» Dennoch gehört das «ideologiekritische» Zerrbild von der völkischen Jugend-Stimmung, die «trotz ihrer romantischen Verbrämung» auf einen Präfaschismus hinauslaufe,[44] zur immer noch gängigen kritischen Ausrüstung. Das Umgekehrte käme der Sache näher: auf romantischen Idealismus läuft sie hinaus, und Hitlers Faschismus war ihr «raffiniert organisierter Mißbrauch» (wie ein Jugendbewegter 1931 schreibt[45]). «Volk» war diesen seelischen Heimatsuchern das feste Haus der geschichtlichen Menschheit, in dem allein sie ganz *bei sich* sein und schaffen konnten. Die universale «Menschheit,» bei Schiller noch primäre Denkmöglichkeit, wurde der Heidelberger Romantik schon zur Abstraktion, und der hundert Jahre jüngeren Jugend vollends zum nichtidentifizierbaren Idol. Greifbar, und erwander-

---

44 Hermands bekanntes polemisches Verfahren verbaut ihm vollends den Zugang zu einem pathetisch idealistischen Phänomen wie der Jugendbewegung (vgl. dagegen: Hans Raupach in seinem Nachwort zur Dokumentensammlung, III, 1744). Wenn man nicht mehr daran interessiert ist, Erfahrung von Wahrheit in der Geschichte aufzusuchen, an die es sich lohnt zu erinnern: wozu dann historische Kritik?
45 «... so mißbraucht er das Verständnis für das Volkstum im Dienste seines Rassenevangeliums, er mißbraucht die Jugendbewegung und ihre Sehnsucht nach Führung und Ganzheit ...» (Pross, *Jugend* ..., S. 404).

bar mit Leib und Seele, waren ihr aber das Land, die Wälder und Felder der Menschen, die ihre eigene Sprache sprachen. Wenn Hermand also im Begriff dieser Landschaft nur das faschistische Potential, das «germanisch Volkhafte» sieht (ebd.), dann ist das so unrecht wie irreführend. Gewiß stellte sich diese mit der ganzen Skala seelischer Passion (Innigkeit–Sehnsucht–Stolz–Triumph–Ekstase) besetzte Heimat-Liebe ihr expressives Vokabular zusammen, und «germanisch» gehörte dazu. Ihre Sprecher nahmen dergleichen Vokabeln naiv aus ihrer politischen Umgebung wie aus dem Vorbild der Romantik, um sie mit ihrer hoch bewegten Innerlichkeit zu erfüllen. Sie verblieben, politisch gesehen, in ihrem «Jugendreich,» und dessen oft phantastische Dekoration mit Ritter-, Reichs- und Gralssymbolen rechne man ihnen nicht mit grimmigem ideologiekritischem Sarkasmus vor. Mit der Geschichte des innerlich-antirationalen Enthusiasmus, deren letzten großen Wellenzug wir hier vor uns haben, tut man sich heute schwer; man ist nicht bereit, dieser Bewegung die gleiche poetische Gerechtigkeit widerfahren zu lassen, die man etwa den Hainbündlern in ihrer sicheren historischen Distanz zugesteht, obwohl diese an sich weit bedrohlicher bramarbasierten. Zum Mißtrauen berechtigt allein die historische Einsicht Thomas Manns *(Doktor Faustus, Deutschland und die Deutschen),* daß auf dem Boden des Irrationalismus auch unschuldige Triebe der Kultur und Sprache die Neigung haben, dämonische Früchte hervorzutreiben. «Volk» ist der bezeichnendste Fall. Die Problematik der Jugendbewegung lag nicht darin, daß man ihnen die Sprache stahl, sondern daß diese Sprache sich so leicht stehlen ließ.

Grundsätzlich ist festzuhalten, daß sogar die rassistisch-chauvinistische Rhetorik sowohl des völkischen Nationalismus der Zeit als auch der geistigen Väter, der romantischen Früh- und Vorzeit, die der Jugendbewegung weit übertraf. Fichtes Gleichsetzung von «Volk,» «Charakter» und «deutsch» (von Görres, Adam Müller, Arndt u.a. zu schweigen) fand wenig Anklang; selbst das vaterländische Erweckungslied «Flamme empor!» der frühen Burschenschaften wurde fürs Liederbuch bündisch entschärft. Auch das sogenannte Rassenproblem, eminentes Politikum der Zeit, wurde wenig diskutiert. Dem Judentum brachte man das konventionelle Mißtrauen entgegen, während man mit Juden befreundet war. Jüdische Jugendliche spielten in der Bewegung immerhin eine größere Rolle als weibliche. Die politische Bremswirkung religiös fundierter Begriffe wie «Geist» und «Gewissen» war eine bedeutende, die Furcht vor dem Verlust der Wahrheit und Reinheit ihrer Volkwerdung herrschte sogar im aktivistischen Kern der Bewegung. Die Tragödie ihres Geistes lag nicht in seiner faschistischen, sondern im Gegenteil: in seiner machtverweigernden Tendenz. Die Künder der sozialen Urheimat hatten nur ein ideelles «Volk,» – keine Partei, keinen Staat, keine Nation.

Autonomie

Das Autonomiebegehren schon des Wandervogels hatte eine doppelte Wurzel: das Verlangen nach Freiheit von ideologiekritischer Herrschaft und die «romantische» Erfahrung der Visions- und Produktivkräfte des Selbst. Beides konvergierte in der Idee der Selbsterziehung. Um sie zu realisieren, schirmte man sich durch ein eigenes Heim- und Wander-, Kultur- und Arbeitsleben nicht nur gegen den schulischen und elterlichen Herrschaftsbereich ab, sondern auch, mit immerbereitem Argwohn, gegen ideologische Überfremdung durch die «Älteren,» die für den Überbau sorgten. Das konnte zum Ausschluß einer so bedeutenden Persönlichkeit wie Gustav Wyneken führen. Man sang, musizierte und laienspielte für sich selbst, man diskutierte, publizierte, feierte sich selbst. Der romantische Idealismus des «in uns ist alles!» spann und entfaltete sich noch einmal spontan aus dem Herzen, nur sehr wenige waren sich der Tatsache bewußt, daß man den deutschen Weg der autonomen Humanität zur Lösung der politisch-sozialen Probleme (erst Mensch, dann Staat) zum bitteren Ende ging. Andererseits: woran hätte eine gefühlsstarke Jugend in einer zerrissenen und verflachten Zeit glauben sollen, wenn nicht an sich selbst und seine Möglichkeitswelt? Die Einsicht freilich, daß der Menschliche, der sich der unser Zusammenleben bestimmenden Politik enthält, eben damit Politik macht, nämlich die der Unmenschlichen, – diese Einsicht war auch der letzten Phase des Idealismus nicht zugänglich.

Romantik

Wir schließen mit unserem Leitbegriff. Noch einmal wird durch die deutsche Jugendbewegung ein universal- und heilsgeschichtliches Bewußtsein produktiv, und zwar in der traditionellen Verbindung mit dem sentimentalen Regreß, dem Mediävismus und Germanismus, mitsamt seiner Burgen-, Ritter-, Reichs-, Zünfte- und Vagantenszene. Diese Burgen waren nicht bloß ideologisches Dekor: sie wurden tatsächlich restauriert, bezogen und erneut zu Bollwerken – gegen eine denaturierte und vampyrisch andrängende Gesellschaft. Die Sehnsucht nach dem verlorenen Lebensganzen beherrschte diese Jugend, nach *Totalität* in der Gemeinschaft, Wiedervereinigung des rational und zivilisatorisch Getrennten, und Re-generation des sich versteinernden Daseins aus seinem lebendigen Ursprung. Dieser Ursprung war letztlich, wie ein Jahrhundert zuvor, eine mystische Erfahrung, gleichviel ob er in der Natur, im Selbst der Volksgemeinschaft oder in der Musik gesucht und gefunden wird. Das musikalische Erlebnis kam ihm sicher am nächsten, und die Regeneration einer musikalischen Volkskultur wurde zur größten Leistung der Bewegung. Die romantische Uridee der Wiedergeburt des gesamten Daseins aus dem Geiste der großen Lebenseinheit (für die literarische Romantik: aus der Poesie) führte zunächst zu der Schaffung eines insularen «Jugendreichs» als der «unerschöpflichen Quelle der Kraft, der Heiterkeit, des Glücks, des stets neuen Schönen. Das Jugendreich ist die Rettung vor dem Verfall» (*Dokum.*, III, 409). Dieses Jugendreich war ein utopischer Ort, von der Zeitwirklichkeit so rein geschieden wie die Dichtung der alten Romantik. Dahinter aber stand schon zu Beginn die Idee des «Volkes» als der realisierten, organisierten Totalität. So wird verständlich, daß die neuen, zuerst jugendeigenen, ganzheitlichen Lebens- und Kulturformen («musische Kultur» als Einheit von Sprach-, Musik- und Bewegungskultur, das Fest als Lebens-Fest, usw.) in der bündischen Zeit zu umfassenden, die gesamte «Volksgemeinschaft» einschließenden Organisationen und Institutionen drängten. Volkskultur, (Volks-)Pädagogik und Sozialarbeit waren die drei Hauptrichtungen dieser öffentlichen Wirksamkeit.

Es geht nicht an, diese große Kultur- und Sozialleistung zu trennen von der «romantischen» Imagination, ihrer produktiven Voraussetzung. Das aber tut die (monopolartig herrschende) politisch-historische Kritik nahezu geschlossen. Das Beiwort «romantisch» wird hier meist abwertend gebraucht (im Sinne von «phantastisch» oder «romantisierend»), bestenfalls freundlich ironisch. Die Einheit dieser vielgestaltigen Bewegung deutlich zu machen, und zwar als die letzte Welle deutsch-romantischer Humanität, die sich moderner Verfremdung und Vermassung entgegenwarf, war der Zweck der vorliegenden Studie.

* * *

Bibliographie

Es werden nur diejenigen Titel aufgeführt, die (1) bei der Entstehung dieser Arbeit anregend wurden, und (2) sich grundsätzlich zur Einführung in das Gesamtphänomen Jugendbewegung eignen. Alle übrige Literatur (einschließlich Romantiker, Nietzsche, Hesse usw.) siehe Anmerkungen. Dem Zweck der Einführung dienen auch die Kurzkommentare.

Becker, Howard Paul. *German Youth: Bond or Free*. New York: Oxford University Press / London: Paul, Trench, Trübner, 1946.
 Erste umfassende nichtdeutsche Stellungnahme zum Problem «Jugendbewegung und Nationalsozialismus» nach dem Krieg; einseitig, von bedenklich großem, prägendem Einfluß. Schwungvoll witzige und für einen kritischen Leser nützliche Darstellung.

Blüher, A. *Wandervogel: Geschichte einer Jugendbewegung*. Berlin: Weise, 1912. Ders., *Die deutsche Wandervogelbewegung als erotisches Phänomen*. Berlin: Ruhland, 1914. Ders., *Führer und Volk in der Jugendbewegung*. Jena: Diederichs, 1917.
 Blühers literarisch nicht unbedeutende Darstellungen sind zu den Quellentexten der Bewegung zu rechnen; sie trugen zu ihrem «Mythos» und Selbstverständnis bei. Besonders die letzten zwei Bände sind oft tendenziös und mit Vorsicht zu genießen.

Borinski, Friedrich und Werner Milch. *Jugendbewegung: Die Geschichte der deutschen Jugend 1896-1933.* Frankfurt: Dipa, 1967
Die noch im Kriege geschriebene Studie ist eine der besten und prägnantesten der ganzen Literatur. Die natürliche Wahl für jemanden, der sich einen raschen Überblick verschaffen und ein Urteil bilden will.

Helwig, Werner. *Die blaue Blume des Wandervogels: Vom Aufstieg, Glanz und Sinn einer Jugendbewegung.* Gütersloh: Mohn, 1960.
Helwig war Insider: das romanartig geschriebene Buch vermittelt viel von der inneren Gestimmtheit und Motivation der Bewegung.

Jantzen, H., Hrsg. *Namen und Werke.* Frankfurt: Dipa, 1972ff.
Die bisher fünf Bände bieten Kurzbiographien, Selbstdeutungen, Veröffentlichungen und mehrfache Porträts der prominentesten Jugendbewegten.

Kindt, Werner, Hrsg. *Dokumentation der Jugendbewegung* (Abk. *Dokum.*). Düsseldorf: Diederichs, 1963ff. I: *Grundschriften* (1963); II: *Die Wandervogelzeit* (1968); III: *Die bündische Zeit* (1975).
Die ausgezeichnet redigierte, sehr umfangreiche Dokumentensammlung ist die Grundlage jeder künftigen Beschäftigung mit der Jugendbewegung. Weitere Bände sind in Vorbereitung.

Kistner, Albert. *Die deutsche Jugendbewegung.* Katalog Nr. 68, Buchh. Edelmann. Nürnberg 1960.
Einzige die Gesamtbewegung umfassende Bibliographie. Der gedruckte Katalog, in seiner Vollständigkeit nicht leicht zu überbieten, führt 3583 Titel auf.

Kneip, R. *Jugend der Weimarer Zeit: Handbuch der Jugendverbände 1919-1938.* Frankfurt: Dipa, 1974.
Ca. 1100 Bünde und Verbände werden präzis nach ihrer Geschichte, Zielsetzung und Leistung beschrieben.

Laqueur, Walter Ze'ev. *Young Germany: A History of the German Youth Movement.* London: Routledge & Paul, 1962.
Zweifellos die bisher beste und ausgewogenste historische Gesamtdarstellung, und die erste durchgreifende Korrektur der Auffassung Howard Beckers. Das kulturelle Engagement, besonders die Jugendmusikbewegung, kommt freilich zu kurz.

Mohler, Armin. *Die Konservative Revolution in Deutschland 1918-1932: Ein Handbuch.* Darmstadt: Wissenschaftliche Buchgesellschaft, 1972.
Mohler gliedert die bündische Bewegung in aufschlußreicher Weise in das Gesamtphänomen des politischen Konservatismus der zwanziger Jahre ein. Die zweite Hälfte des Buches ist eine vorzüglich lesbare Auswahlbibliographie mit vielfach kommentierenden Hinweisen.

Müller, Jakob. *Die Jugendbewegung als deutsche Hauptrichtung neokonservativer Reform.* Zürich: Europa, 1971.
Das kaum beachtete, etwas schwerfällig geschriebene Buch ist eine Fundgrube aufschlußreicher Daten, Fakten, Gesichtspunkte. Als kritische Leistung unoriginell.

Pross, Harry. *Jugend-Eros-Politik: Geschichte der deutschen Jugend-Verbände.* Bern: Scherz, 1964.
Die einseitig politische Perspektive führt zu vielfach ungerechten Urteilen. Trotzdem: eine der kenntnis- und materialreichsten, bestgeschriebenen Darstellungen. Besonders fruchtbar: die reiche Auswertung der Verbandszeitschriften. Nützliche Anhang-Tabellen.

Rosenbusch, Heinz Stephan. *Die deutsche Jugendbewegung in ihren pädagogischen Formen und Wirkungen.* Frankfurt: Dipa, 1973.
Logischer, klar organisierter Zugang zum Gesamtphänomen vom entscheidenden pädagogischen Gesichtspunkt aus.

Stern, Fritz Richard. *The Politics of Cultural Despair.* Berkeley: University of California Press, 1961. – Deutsche Übersetzung Bern: Scherz, 1963.
Das scharf kritische, aber höchst anregende Buch gibt den Hintergrund der Jugendbewegung: «the rise of the Germanic Ideology.» Stern erreicht mit seinen drei Porträts (de Lagardes, Lang-

behns und van den Brucks) eine Beziehungsdichte, die auf eine Pathographie der kulturkritischen Reaktion in der deutschen Moderne vor 1933 ausläuft.

Wyneken, G. *Der Kampf für die Jugend.* Jena: Diederichs, 1920. Sammlung der Reden dieses bedeutendsten pädagogischen Theoretikers der Jugendbewegung.

Zitierte Liederbücher (in der Reihenfolge ihres Erscheinens):

Breuer, Hans, Hrsg. *Der Zupfgeigenhansl.* Leipzig: Hofmeister, 1908.

Hensel, Walther, Hrsg. *Das Aufrecht Fähnlein.* Kassel: Bärenreiter, 1923, ²1933.

Jöde, Fritz, Hrsg. *Der Kanon, ein Singbuch für alle.* Wolfenbüttel: [1925] Kallmeyer, ²1959.

Schilling, Konrad, Hrsg. *Der Turm.* Bad Godesberg: Voggenreiter, neubearb. Aufl. 1956.

Moser, Hugo, u.a., Hrsg. *Bruder Singer.* Kassel: Bärenreiter, neubearb. Aufl. 1959.

Corbach, Dieter, u.a., Hrsg. *Die Mundorgel.* Köln: Mundorgel Verlag, [1953] Neuausg. 1982.

(Die letzten drei Sammlungen, die zuerst kurz nach dem Krieg erschienen, wurden wegen ihrer Reichhaltigkeit und Zugänglichkeit gewählt.)

Kunststadt München
Von der Entstehung und der Dauerhaftigkeit
eines romantisch-literarischen Mythos*

WOLFGANG FRÜHWALD, *Universität München*

«Aber München. Das gar nicht mehr so sehr leuchtet, eher etwas bösartig unter seinen Kuppeln sitzt. Bei Regen im Englischen Garten, wenn das bayerische Wasser von den grünen Bäumen tropft, oder bei Sonnenschein in dieser ungeheuerlich klaren Föhnluft mit den geradezu beängstigenden Fernblicken auf hundert Kilometer entfernt liegende blaue Bergspitzen.» So beginnt das fünfte Kapitel von Ernst Augustins Roman *Raumlicht: Der Fall Evelyne B.,*[1] der nicht nur ein Schlüsselroman der Münchener Psychiatrie, nicht nur ein autobiographischer Lebensbericht des Psychiaters Ernst Augustin ist, sondern auch eine Parabel von der Begegnung des modernen Autors mit der Poesie. Ein solcher Beginn bedeutet doch wohl, daß der berühmte Anfang von Thomas Manns Erzählung *Gladius Dei* (aus dem Jahre 1902) zu einem geflügelten Wort geworden ist, durch dessen kenntliche Entstellung man in Deutschland noch knapp 80 Jahre nach seiner Entstehung die Aufmerksamkeit eines lesenden Publikums erregen kann.

---

* Dieser Geburtstagsgruß aus München versucht, die Stadt München mit den zentralen Forschungsgebieten Hans Eichners zu vereinen und untersucht deshalb den aus romantisierendem Geiste geborenen, von Thomas Mann literarisch fixierten und von der Tourismus-Industrie noch immer werbewirksam propagierten Stadt-Mythos Münchens. Gelegentlich ergeben sich dabei Überschneidungen mit meinen folgenden Arbeiten:
«Ästhetische Erziehung. Idee und Realisation der Kunstpolitik König Ludwigs I. von Bayern am Beispiel der «Walhalla,» *Hölderlin-Jahrbuch* (1980/81), 295–310; «„Der christliche Jüngling im Kunstladen". Milieu- und Stilparodie in Thomas Manns Erzählung *Gladius Dei,*» *Bild und Gedanke. Festschrift für Gerhart Baumann zum 60. Geburtstag*, hrsg. Günter Schnitzler in Verbindung mit Gerhard Neumann und Jürgen Schröder (München: Fink, 1980), S. 324–42. Zu diesem Aufsatz ist die von Hans Rudolf Vaget in seinem informationsreichen und klugen Kommentar zu Thomas Manns Erzählungen (München: Winkler, 1984) gefundene Quelle von *Gladius Dei* nachzutragen: «Madonna. Novelle» von Max Grad, *NDR* 7 (1896), 988–99; zu den Quellen von *Gladius Dei* vgl. auch Walter Schmitz, «„Der Tod in Venedig". Eine Erzählung aus Thomas Manns Münchner Jahren,» *Blätter für den Deutschlehrer,* 1 (1985), 12 und 18. Hinweise auf den Stadtmythos Münchens finden sich auch in meinem Katalogbeitrag über «Märzenbier und Seidenhimmel. Zur Darstellung der Stadt-Persönlichkeit Münchens in der deutschen Nachkriegsliteratur,» *Trümmerzeit in München. Kultur und Gesellschaft einer deutschen Großstadt im Aufbruch 1945–1949*, hrsg. Friedrich Prinz (München: Beck, 1984), S. 228–34.
1 Ernst Augustin, *Raumlicht: Der Fall Evelyne B. Roman* (Frankfurt: Suhrkamp, 1976), S. 187.

«München leuchtete,» beginnt die von der wissenschaftlichen Kritik recht stiefmütterlich behandelte Erzählung: «Über den festlichen Plätzen und weissen Säulentempeln, den antikisierenden Monumenten und Barockkirchen, den springenden Brunnen, Palästen und Gartenanlagen der Residenz spannte sich strahlend ein Himmel von blauer Seide, und ihre breiten und lichten, umgrünten und wohlberechneten Perspektiven lagen in dem Sonnendunst eines ersten, schönen Junitages.»[2] Das geflügelte Wort, dem wir hier das Attest seines Ursprungs hinzugefügt haben, wie es sich für die Formeln des Bildungsdialektes nun einmal seit Büchmanns Kodifizierung dieses Dialektes gehört,[3] erweckt bei Thomas Mann und seinem modernen Parodisten nicht allein die Assoziation des seidenen Föhnhimmels, sondern auch die einer Spiegelung der Natur in Münchens Kultur. Der letzte Absatz nämlich von Thomas Manns erstem Kapitel der Erzählung *Gladius Dei* – die einer ganzen Reihe literarischer Texte, der «München-leuchtete-Literatur,» den Namen gegeben hat[4] – lautet:

> Die Kunst blüht, die Kunst ist an der Herrschaft, die Kunst streckt ihr rosenumwundenes Zepter über die Stadt hin und lächelt. Eine allseitige respektvolle Anteilnahme an ihrem Gedeihen, eine allseitige, fleißige und hingebungsvolle Übung und Propaganda in ihrem Dienste, ein treuherziger Kultus der Linie, des Schmuckes, der Form, der Sinne, der Schönheit obwaltet... München leuchtete.[5]

Der Glanz also, in welchem München nach dem Willen dieses Erzählers erstrahlt, ist der Glanz einer «Kunststadt,» und Thomas Mann hat die Elemente dieses häufig gebrauchten Terminus, der in den Jahren zwischen 1905 und 1914 und wieder seit 1975/76 einer Inflation ausgesetzt ist, recht genau analysiert.

Wer um 1900 von der «Kunststadt München» sprach – das waren etwa die Brüder Heinrich und Thomas Mann, Paul Heyse, Ludwig Thoma, Josef Ruederer, Max Halbe und viele andere – meinte

– zunächst die künstlerisch-architektonische Gestalt Münchens, die Stadt als ein Kunstwerk, das einem großen kulturpolitisch-erzieherischen Gedanken gehorcht und in dieser romantisierend-antikisierenden Form wohl einmalig ist in der Welt;

– er meinte aber auch München als eine Stadt der Künstler, eine Stadt insbesondere der bildenden Kunst, das heißt eine als Kunstwerk erbaute und bewußt geplante, von Künstlern mit Leben erfüllte Stadt. Die bayerischen Regen-

---

2 Thomas Mann: «Gladius Dei,» *Die Erzählungen,* Bd. 1, Moderne Klassiker (Frankfurt: Fischer, 1967), S. 149.
3 Für Georg Büchmann, dessen *Zitatenschatz des deutschen Volkes* erstmals 1864 erschienen ist, gehörten diese Atteste des Ursprungs zur Definition des geflügelten Wortes.
4 Terminus nach Dieter Albrecht, in Max Spindler, Hrsg. *Bayerische Geschichte im 19. und 20. Jahrhundert 1800 bis 1970,* Erster Teilband, *Staat- und Politik* (München: Beck, 1974), S. 349, Anm. 3. Diese «München-leuchtete-Literatur» ist bisher noch nicht im Zusammenhang dargestellt.
5 «Gladius Dei,» S. 151.

ten und die Erbauer der Stadt gehörten dabei nicht nur zu den Mäzenen der nobilitierten und mit offiziellen Ehren überhäuften Künstler, sondern waren, seit König Ludwig I., auch selbst ausübende, meist dilettierende Künstler.

– Er meinte schließlich München als eine Stadt des Kunsthandwerkes und des Kunstbetriebes, als Kunstmarkt, auf dem die Künstler gefragt waren, auf dem sie durch jährliche Ausstellungen bekannt gemacht wurden, auf dem sie durch Reproduktionen ihrer Werke verbreitet, durch Ankäufe ihrer Werke aus der Hof- und Staatskasse sozial abgesichert, durch Einladungen zur Hoftafel sozial aufgewertet und durch die Nobilitierung der Angesehensten dem Verdienstadel zugezählt wurden;

Diese Art von Kunststadt war so recht eine Stadt nach dem Herzen Thomas Manns, der – darin ganz Neuromantiker – durch Kunst zu Ruhm und Ansehen gelangen wollte und auch gelangte. Er hat Repräsentation zu den Aufgaben des Künstlertums gezählt und jenen messerscharfen Grat zwischen Amusement und Skandal beschritten, auf dem nur große Künstler sicheren Schrittes gehen können, die meisten in Lächerlichkeit oder Bedeutungslosigkeit abstürzen. Die Madonna, welche in *Gladius Dei* im Schaufenster «des weitläufigen Schönheitsgeschäftes von M. Blüthenzweig» steht – «Die große, rötlichbraune Photographie stand, mit äußerstem Geschmack in Altgold gerahmt, auf einer Staffelei inmitten des Fensterraumes. . . . eine durchaus modern empfundene, von jeder Konvention freie Arbeit. Die Gestalt der heiligen Gebärerin war von berückender Weiblichkeit, entblößt und schön»[6] – ist nicht nur Inbegriff der renaissancistischen Madonnen- und Porträtmalerei an der Wende vom 19. zum 20. Jahrhundert; in der bekannten, auf Tiecks und Eichendorffs Venusbilder ebenso wie auf Heinrich Heines Formel «Unsere liebe Frau von Milo»[7] zurückzuführenden Mischung von Venus und Madonna, von femme fatale und Patrona Bavariae, ist sie das berückend zweideutige Symbol der verführerischen Kunststadt München, und sogar kenntlich-unkenntliches Bild jedes der berühmten weiblichen Malermodelle, jeder Angehörigen der «Lebenden Schönheitsgalerie» von Lady Blennerhasset über die Gattin von Fritz August von Kaulbach und Lolo von Lenbach, bis zu Frau von Poschinger, zur Gattin von Franz Stuck und der Baronin von Wimpffen.[8] In Bayern, so meinte um

---

6 «Gladius Dei,» S. 153. Thomas Mann hat die Darstellung der Madonna gegenüber seinem Quellentext erheblich gemildert und sich offenkundig bei der Beschreibung des Bildes selbst an Theodor Mundts Beschreibung einer «Madonna de Sevilla» orientiert (vgl. Frühwald, «Der christliche Jüngling,» S. 340, Anm. 21). Dies nimmt Vagets Entdeckung der Quelle für die ganze Erzählung nichts von ihrer Überzeugungskraft, doch hat die vor Wonne bebende, «sich wie in verzücktem Krampfe in den Gras- und Haidekrautbüscheln» festhaltende Maria aus der «Novelle» Max Grads in Thomas Manns geschmackvoller Darstellung keine Parallele.

7 Zu Joseph von Eichendorffs Venusbildern vgl. die anregende und schlüssige Darstellung Hans Eichners, «Joseph von Eichendorff,» *Handbuch der deutschen Erzählung,* hrsg. Karl Konrad Polheim (Düsseldorf: Bagel, 1981), S. 172–77; Heines Formel aus dem Nachwort zum *Romanzero.*

8 Zur «Lebenden Schönheitsgalerie» vgl. *München und die Münchener. Leute. Dinge. Sitten. Winke.* (Karlsruhe: F. Bielefeld, 1905), S. 72f.

diese Zeit der Münchener Student Jean Giraudoux, gebe es kaum Bilder büßender Magdalenen, dagegen Bilder der Jungfrau Maria mit dem Kinde Jesus in Fülle.[9] Der notorische Epiker Thomas Mann hat nur ein Drama publiziert: *Fiorenza* (1905), für das er seit Herbst 1899 historische Studien betrieb; dieses Drama aus dem mediceischen Florenz aber, das auch als Parodie der renaissancistischen Kunststadt-Atmosphäre in München gelesen werden kann, befestigte Thomas Manns Stellung im Salon Pringsheim in der Arcisstraße 12, wo sich – den Kulturführern der Zeit nach zu schließen – die «Haute finance» und die «Bühne» trafen. In diesem Salon hat Thomas Mann am 6. November 1904 aus seinem Drama vorgelesen, am 3. Oktober dieses Jahres schon hatte er sich mit Katja Pringsheim, der Tochter eines der reichsten Männer Münchens, verlobt.[10]

So ist auch der erste Satz der bis heute berühmtesten München-Novelle Thomas Manns *Der Tod in Venedig* (1912) – «Gustav Aschenbach oder von Aschenbach, wie seit seinem fünfzigsten Geburtstag amtlich sein Name lautete ...»[11] – unter anderem als ein Wink an den an der Schwelle des Thrones stehenden Prinzen Ludwig von Bayern zu lesen, er möge mit dem Autor dieser Erzählung so verfahren, wie der in der Erzählung apostrophierte deutsche Fürst mit Gustav Aschenbach verfahren war. Diesem war es «innerlich gemäß, und er lehnte nicht ab, als ein deutscher Fürst, soeben zum Throne gelangt, dem Dichter des „Friedrich" zu seinem fünfzigsten Geburtstag den persönlichen Adel verlieh.» Der Zusammenhang von Ruhm und Kunst, der, in der deutschen Romantik erstmals forciert, im Bayern Ludwigs I. zur Grundlage des neuen Staates gemacht wurde, spielt – als ein romantisches Erbe – eine nicht zu unterschätzende Rolle im Werke Thomas Manns. Tony Buddenbrooks' Apologie des Adels gegenüber ihrem Bruder Tom ist nicht nur ironisch zu interpretieren: «Ja, Tom, wir fühlen uns als Adel und fühlen einen Abstand und wir sollten nirgend zu leben versuchen, wo man nichts von uns weiß und uns nicht einzuschätzen versteht, denn wir werden nichts als Demütigungen davon haben, und man wird uns lächerlich hochmütig finden.»[12]

Thomas Mann, der in München, der «unliterarischen Stadt par excellence,»[13] energisch den Anspruch der Wortkünstler auf die Gleichstellung mit den Malern, den Architekten und Bildhauern, der «Aschenbach» mit den Kaulbach und Lenbach forderte, der sich darüber ärgerte, selten eine Buch-

---

9 Vgl. Roger Bauer, «Das wiedergefundene München. Jean Giraudoux und die „bayrische Ewigkeit",» *Neue Zürcher Zeitung*, 27. April 1984, S. 37.
10 Zu den Daten vgl. Hans Bürgin und Hans-Otto Mayer, *Thomas Mann. Eine Chronik seines Lebens*. (Frankfurt: Fischer Taschenbuch, 1974), bes. S. 29.
11 Thomas Mann «Der Tod in Venedig,» *Erzählungen* I, S. 338. Das folgende Zitat ebd. S. 347.
12 Vgl. dazu Thomas Mann, *Buddenbrooks. Verfall einer Familie*, 5. Teil, 10. Kapitel.
13 Vgl. Peter de Mendelssohn, «Ein Schriftsteller in München,» *Thomas Mann 1875-1975. Vorträge in München – Zürich – Lübeck*, hrsg. Beatrix Bludau, Eckhard Heftrich und Helmut Koopmann (Frankfurt: Fischer, 1977), S. 19. Brief Thomas Manns an Otto Grautoff von März 1896.

handlung betreten zu können, ohne begrüßt zu werden: «Guten Tag, Herr Kunstmaler, was darf es sein?», hätte die Nobilitierung durchaus verdient; denn ihm ist gelungen, was nur wenigen Dichtern der Moderne seit dem 18. Jahrhundert gelungen ist: einem Mythos literarisch Ausdruck zu geben und ihn dadurch im Bewußtsein der Menschen erst zu verankern, dem Mythos des in der Blüte seiner Kunst leuchtenden München. Im Grunde haben erst die Künstler der Jahrhundertwende, und unter ihnen vor allem Thomas Mann, jene stärker im Unbewußten als im Bewußten wirksame Vorstellung verbreitet, in welcher ein literarisch stilisiertes München, ein München, welches mit der historischen Realität nur wenig gemeinsam hat, in Literatur und durch Literatur lebt. Diese Auffassung Münchens als Manifestation kollektiver und immanenter Paradiesesvorstellungen hat den historisch lokalisierbaren Niedergang der Kunststadt, seit etwa 1914, die brutale Besitznahme der Stadt durch die Nationalsozialisten als Stadt ihrer «Bewegung,» die der inneren Zerstörung folgende äußere Zerstörung durch die Bomben des Zweiten Weltkrieges und – jedenfalls bisher – sogar die Kommerzionalisierung überstanden.

*

Der amerikanische Erzähler Thomas Wolfe, der seit 1924 seine Europa-Liebe entdeckt, dem «neuen» Deutschland Adolf Hitlers aber nach der Berliner Olympiade mit Abscheu den Rücken gewandt hat, fragt in seinem der Entdeckung des Lebens und der Welt gewidmeten Roman *The Web and the Rock*: «How can one speak of Munich but to say it is a kind of German heaven? Some people sleep and dream they are in Paradise, but all over Germany people sometimes dream that they have gone to Munich in Bavaria. And really, in an astonishing way, the city is a great Germanic dream translated into life.»[14] Dies ist der genaue, freilich leicht satirisch getönte Ausdruck eines fast antiken Vorgangs in der Stadt München, die durch Ludwig I. antikisierend umgebaut und erneuert wurde. Durch Dichterwort entsteht aus einem in romantisierenddidaktischer Absicht erbauten Stadtensemble eine kollektive Identifikationsfigur, ein Stadtmythos, der die Menschen so zu verzaubern vermag, daß sie sich – fast gegen ihren Willen – gebannt fühlen und ihr Leben diesem Zauber anheimgeben. Daß dies ein von den Fremden geschaffener Mythos ist, von Dichtern geschaffen und von Dichtern verbreitet, daß es ein den LabyrinthMythen der Antike und der Sage vom Tannhäuser im Venusberg gleichsam nachgebildeter Mythos ist, den die Einheimischen mit Befremden, oft genug auch mit Haß und Erbitterung bekämpften, ist sozialpsychologisch leicht zu erklären. So ist Richard Wagner, der problematische Erneuerer und Vollender romantischen Mythendenkens, nach dem Abschluß seiner Oper *Tannhäuser* und während der Arbeit an *Tristan und Isolde* – dem Beginn der musikalischen

---

14 Thomas Wolfe, *The Web and the Rock* (New York and London: Harper, 1939), S. 650 (Beginn des Kapitels «The Pension in Munich»).

Moderne aus dem Versuch zur Aktualisierung und zur Radikalisierung romantischer Liebes- und Todesmythen –, fast notwendig nach München gekommen und von «den Münchenern» aus der Stadt wieder vertrieben worden. Thomas Mann konnte darin 1933, nach dem *Protest der Richard-Wagner-Stadt München,* die Antizipation des eigenen Schicksals sehen.[15] Wagner soll es ja am 25. März 1864 in München ähnlich ergangen sein, wie den entzückten Betrachtern der aphrodisischen Madonna im Schaufenster der Kunsthandlung am Münchener Odeonsplatz, wie Gustav von Aschenbach beim Anblick Tadzios; auf der Flucht vor seinen Wiener Gläubigern soll er auf der Durchreise in München vor einem Schaufenster mit dem Bild des jungen Königs stehen geblieben sein, «in „ungemein schwieriger Lebenslage" von Schönheit gerührt.»[16]

In neueren sozialgeschichtlichen Untersuchungen wurde nachgewiesen, daß die erste Hälfte des 19. Jahrhunderts eine Zeit war, in welcher verstärkt historische Phänomene mythisiert wurden. «Die Angst, die durch unerwartete „Bewegung" im 19. Jahrhundert hervorgerufen wird, muß offensichtlich gebannt werden. Mythisierungen sollen dabei helfen.»[17] So entstanden zugleich mit der «ästhetischen Transformation historischen „Wissens"» jene Stadtmythen, unter denen der jungdeutsche Mythos des arkadisch-elysischen Paris und der romantische Gegenmythos von Paris, dem «Labyrinth, / Das schrecklicher als jenes alte ist, / In dessen ausweglosem Pfadgewind', / Ein scheußlich Ungeheur den Wandrer frißt,»[18] nur ein besonders auffallendes Beispiel ist; er wurde um die Jahrhundertwende in München aus neuromantischem Geist erneuert und werbewirksam parodiert.

Die Charakterisierung Münchens als irdisches Paradies, durch den erst in den dreißiger Jahren, nach der Machtergreifung durch die Nationalsozialisten, desillusionierten Deutschland-Enthusiasten Thomas Wolfe, wäre kaum auffällig, hätte nicht Jean Giraudoux 1922 in dem Roman *Siegfried et le Limousin* von «l'éternité bavaroise» gesprochen und damit das Stichwort vom bayerischen Himmelreich gegeben. Roger Bauer hat mit liebevoller Feder die Münchener Zeit von Giraudoux in der Amalienstraße 14, über dem Café Ste-

---

15 Vgl. zur Dokumentation der Vorgänge Hartmut Zelinsky, *Richard Wagner – ein deutsches Thema. Eine Dokumentation zur Wirkungsgeschichte Richard Wagners 1876–1976* (Frankfurt: Zweitausendundeins, 1976), S. 192ff.
16 Martin Gregor-Dellin, *Wagner-Chronik. Daten zu Leben und Werk* (München: Hanser, 1972), S. 107.
17 Jürgen Link und Wulf Wülfing, Hrsg., *Bewegung und Stillstand in Metaphern und Mythen. Fallstudien zum Verhältnis von elementarem Wissen und Literatur im 19. Jahrhundert* (Stuttgart: Klett, 1984), S. 13 (Einleitung). Das folgende Zitat ebda.
18 Der Mythos des arkadischen Paris findet sich z.B. in Börnes *Briefen aus Paris,* der Gegenmythos in Clemens Brentanos Gedicht «Nimm hin den Faden durch das Labyrinth» (aus diesem 1826 geschriebenen, 1838 erstmals gedruckten Gedicht stammen die zitierten Verse). Vgl. auch Luigi Forte, «Schriftsteller und Stadt im 19. Jahrhundert,» *Propyläen Geschichte der Literatur,* Bd. 5 (Berlin: Propyläen, 1984), 512–34.

phanie, nachgezeichnet.[19] «L'éternité bavaroise» ist auch bei Jean Giraudoux jener Mythos vom irdischen Glück, der den Zeitgenossen der zwanziger Jahre, nach Krieg, Revolution und inmitten eines wirtschaftlichen Niederganges ohnegleichen, in den goldenen Jahren der Sicherheit, im München der «späten Regentschaft»[20] beheimatet schien. Vom Abglanz dieser Jahre lebt der Mythos des leuchtenden München bis in unsere Tage.

Thomas Mann ist es in diesen Jahren gelungen, an einer Nahtstelle der Geschichte, an der Grenze zwischen Aufstieg und Niedergang der Kunststadt, dort also, wo realiter München seinen Rang als Kunstwerk, Künstlerstadt und Kunstmarkt an Berlin abzugeben begann, den Mythos des leuchtenden München zu etablieren, so daß selbst jene Berliner, Dresdener und anderen nord- und ostdeutschen Flüchtlinge, die 1945 in die zerstörte Stadt strömten, diesen Zauber noch zu spüren, ja von ihm gezogen zu sein glaubten. In Erich Kästners Glossen und Aufsätzen aus dem Jahre 1945 zum Beispiel ist das zerstörte München eine ungemein lebenskräftige Stadt, eine Stadt der Hoffnung und der Zukunft, in der sich 1945 rund 2500 Schauspieler drängten, um die Wiedereröffnung der Theater zu erwarten:

> Noch denken viele an die Glanzepoche Schwabings, Wedekinds und der ruhmreichen Skandinavier zurück. Und der Ausblick in einen neuen gelobten Kulturabschnitt wärmt schon heute ihr zärtlich für die Kunst schlagendes Münchener Herz. – Und so mag es also nicht vergeblich sein, daß in manchem kalten, zugigen Zimmer ihrer alten, zerborstenen Stadt die Köpfe rauchen![21]

Wolfgang Koeppen, der (heute, 1986) als ein Achtzigjähriger in der Widenmayerstraße wohnt, ist vor 40 Jahren (1946) in München – nach eigener Auskunft – einfach hängengeblieben:

> Vielleicht war es der Föhn, der mich antrieb, der vielbesungene bayerische Himmel, in dessen Licht ich durch das Siegestor ging, vielleicht der Schnee, durch den ich Albertus Magnus barfuß wandern sah, der selbst als Bischof von Regensburg mehr den Vaganten, den Chaoten von einst, zugeneigt war als der satten Selbstzufriedenheit in den Mauern.[22]

Er blieb in München, weil er *sein* Paradies hier gefunden hatte, «die in München immer mögliche Berührung des Irdischen mit dem Überirdischen im Sinne des Novalis, diese kühne und gefährliche Vermählung von Materie und Geist, Unruhe und auch die Künste schaffend, die von der Unruhe leben.» Auch Wolf Wondratschek, 1943 in Rudolstadt geboren, mit weit über 100000 verkauften Gedichtbänden ein ungewöhnlich erfolgreicher Lyriker, der sich in

---

19 Jean Giraudoux, *Siegfried et le Limousin,* Les cahiers verts 14 (Paris, 1922), S. 88.
20 Thomas Mann, *Doktor Faustus. Das Leben des deutschen Tonsetzers Adrian Leverkühn erzählt von einem Freunde,* Kapitel 23.
21 Erich Kästner, *Gesammelte Schriften,* Bd. 5 (Köln: Kiepenheuer & Witsch, 1959), S. 312. (Der *Münchener Theaterbrief,* aus dem das Zitat stammt, wurde im Oktober 1945 geschrieben.)
22 Wolfgang Koeppen, «Die Vollendung eines Schicksals. Dankrede für die Verleihung des Kulturellen Ehrenpreises 1982 der Stadt München,» *Süddeutsche Zeitung,* 17./18. Juli 1982, S. 102.

Lebensstil und künstlerischem Ausdruck zu Wolfgang Koeppen hingezogen fühlt, lebt seit über 10 Jahren in Schwabing – und meint noch immer, er sei nur auf der Durchreise. Dieser nicht nur ungewöhnlich erfolgreiche, sondern auch ungewöhnlich begabte Gegenwartslyriker, der zusammen mit anderen Münchener Autoren die Tradition der Schwabinger Bohème wieder aufgegriffen hat, der sich nicht seßhaft macht und immer wieder – aufbruchsbereit – in Kleidern und mit den Schuhen schläft, rühmt an München, daß «nirgendwo sonst in Deutschland» das, «was man Zeit-Verschwendung nennt, so ernst genommen [wird] wie hier. Ein wenig anders scheint hier die Sonne. Mehr als sonstwo scheint sie den Menschen bewußt zu machen, daß sie ihr Leben genießen sollen. In Schwabing hat man, gewissermaßen, die Pflicht dazu, es zu tun.»[23] Aus Trotz blieb er in München, «der Schriftsteller, ... der Aufgegebene», aus Trotz gegen die Überheblichkeit all jener, welche München «die unnötigste Stadt Deutschlands» nennen:

> Ihre Überheblichkeit, mir und meinem Wohnort gegenüber, beantwortete ich in den darauffolgenden Jahren mit Gedichten. Ihr Schauplatz war Schwabing. Ihre Helden waren die Menschen, die ich hier traf. Sie waren nicht besser, nicht wichtiger als die Menschen anderswo, aber es waren die, die ich kannte. Gut genug, um dieses Jahrzehnt portraitieren zu können. Zudem war es meine eigene Generation, gerade nah genug, um sie aus der Distanz heraus scharf sehen zu können.

*

Erich Kästner, Wolfgang Koeppen, Wolf Wondratschek, Paul Wühr, Bernhard Setzwein und manchen anderen Schriftsteller in München könnte man noch jener Kategorie zuordnen, unter der Schwabing seit den neunziger Jahren des 19. Jahrhunderts gesehen wurde, als es eine «Massensiedlung von Sonderlingen» genannt wurde; wenn aber selbst ein so wenig zu Rausch und Überschwang neigender Geist, wie Wilhelm Hausenstein, von der «Stadtpersonalität» Münchens spricht, deren Wesen als «Zusammenkunft» benannt werden könne, so bedeutet dies die Lebendigkeit eines modernen Mythos, der liebenswürdig und gefährlich zugleich ist und nur von den dagegen offenkundig immunisierten einheimischen Bewohnern der Stadt auch heute noch nicht nachvollzogen werden kann. Für Hausenstein war München «sozusagen ein prästabilierter Ort der Begegnungen, der Harmonisation,» die Geschichte Münchens «eine Geschichte der Konzentration künstlerischer und wissenschaftlicher Geister»; Glanz und Bewußtsein von Kunst lagen für ihn auf dem Antlitz dieser Stadt, die ausgezeichnet sei durch eine grundlegend christliche Natur, durch Liberalität und durch eine übernationale Universalität. Auch Hausenstein also ist dem Zauber einer Denkfigur der Dekadenz erlegen: dem Mythos, daß aus allen Untergängen Schönheit zu gewinnen sei.

---

23 Wolf Wondratschek, «Servus, Schwabing,» *GEO Special*, Nr. 6 (5.XII.1984), 130–32. – Zu den nachfolgenden Zitaten Hausensteins vgl. Frühwald, «Märzenbier ...,» (Anm. *), S. 230f.

Es ist von jeher das Bestreben romantisch-idealistischen Dichtens gewesen, mythenschaffend [...] rend in die Realität einzugreifen, um dann selbst [...] ückzutreten, welches gleichsam sein eigenes Leben [...] zu leben beginnt. Einen solchen literarisch fun[...] Clemens Brentano am Rhein begründet, als er – [...]igen Sagengut – den Mythos von der zauberischen [...] aus dem Echo des Rheinfelsens und dem Namen des [...] entwickelte. Bis heute lebt der Rheintourismus vom [...] Sirene, die an der tiefsten und der gefährlichsten [...]vo noch die Salmfischer des 19. Jahrhunderts den Ni[...], mit ihrer Schönheit die Schiffer in den Tod lockt. [...] Mythos, antiken Orakelwundern vergleichbar, hat Brentano noch im Alter geschaffen, als er – durch den Mund der stigmatisierten Nonne Anna Katharina Emmerick – das Sterbehaus Mariens in Ephesus lokalisierte.[24] Einen solchen Mythos hat dann der Neuromantiker Thomas Mann verkündet, als er, fünfzig Jahre eigenständiger Kulturentwicklung in Süddeutschland in die glückliche Formel des leuchtenden München bannend, den Mythos der Friedensstadt, der Stadt des irdischen Glücks und der Lebensfreude, kurz: einen profanen Paradiesesmythos prägte, den er noch im *Doktor Faustus* zitieren konnte:

> Wovon ich spreche, ist das München der späten Regentschaft, nur vier Jahre noch vom Kriege entfernt, dessen Folgen seine Gemütlichkeit in Gemütskrankheit verwandeln und eine trübe Groteske nach der anderen darin zeitigen sollten, – diese perspektivenschöne Hauptstadt, deren politische Problematik sich auf den launigen Gegensatz zwischen einem halb separatistischen Volkskatholizismus und einem lebfrischen Liberalismus reichsfrommer Observanz beschränkte...[25]

In *Doktor Faustus* hat Thomas Mann jene Entwicklung mit einbezogen, die er in *Gladius Dei* schon geahnt hatte, ohne daß ihm die Propagandisten geflügelter Worte darin gefolgt sind. Als nämlich wenige Jahre nach dem Abklingen der «München-leuchtete-Literatur» die «Revolution der Dichter» in München den Mythos in reale Politik umzusetzen versuchte, als gleichsam die romantisierende Schwabinger Vorstellung des irdischen Glücks das Modell eines anarchisch-individualistisch-poetischen Staates werden sollte, wurden die problematischen Elemente des Mythos offenkundig. Die versuchte Etablierung eines Schiller und der deutschen Romantik nachempfundenen, neuen goldenen Zeitalters im Deutschland des 20. Jahrhunderts führte im April 1919 in München zu einer kurzlebigen kommunistischen Diktatur und schließlich zu jener Rache der Freikorps-Truppen an den Begründern der Münchener Räterepublik, in der nationalsozialistischer Terror präfiguriert war und die nackte Mordlust triumphierte.

24 Vgl. dazu Werner Vordtriede, «Clemens Brentanos Anteil an der Kultstätte in Ephesus,» *DVjs*, 34 (1960), 384–401.
25 Thomas Mann, *Doktor Faustus*, Kapitel 23.

Am 4. Juni 1919 wurde einer der noch lebenden Führer der anarchistischen Phase dieser Räterepublik Bayern, der Dramatiker und Lyriker Ernst Toller, hinter einer Tapetentüre in der Wohnung seines Freundes, des Kunstmalers Reichel (in der Schwabinger Werneckstraße), verhaftet. Toller, der später den blutigen Irrtum des Räteexperimentes erkannt und bedauert hat, beschreibt in seiner (schon) im Exil, 1933, erschienenen Autobiographie *Eine Jugend in Deutschland* die Szene dieses Ereignisses:

> Bilder werden abgenommen, durch die Türritzen dringt Licht. Ich stoße die Tür auf, ich sehe Kriminalkommissare und Soldaten.
> – Sie suchen Toller, ich bin's.
> – Hände hoch! schreit ein Soldat.
> ... Ein Soldat fällt auf die Knie, richtet mit quellenden Augäpfeln das Gewehr auf mich, entsichert und hält die zitternden Finger am Abzug.
> – Sie sind ...?
> – Ja, ich bin Toller. Ich werde nicht fliehen. Wenn ich jetzt erschossen werde, wurde ich nicht auf der Flucht erschossen. ...
> Wie ich an meinen Gastfreunden vorbeigeführt werde, sage ich, um sie vor Verhaftung zu schützen:
> – Diese Menschen wußten nicht, wer ich bin.[26]

In dieser Beschreibung ist alles enthalten, was die johanneische Szene der Verhaftung Jesu im Garten jenseits des Baches Kidron kennzeichnet: die Erkennungsfrage; das Bekenntnis; das Erschrecken der Rotte, die mit Stricken und Banden ausgezogen ist, Jesus zu fangen; die Fesselung; die Bitte des Gefangenen für seine Freunde; und – im weiteren Fortgang des Textes – auch das «Crucifige» des verführten Volkes.

Der Dichter, der als Erlöser des Volkes dessen Befreiung aus Banden und Knechtschaft verkündet hat, wurde von eben diesem Volk gefangen, mißhandelt, dem Tode überliefert. Dies ist – auf biblischer Folie – der Antimythos des leuchtenden München. Jene, die ausgezogen sind, einem Mythos politische Konkretion zu verleihen, werden von einem Volk ans Kreuz geschlagen, welches den Mythos Münchens hinnimmt als ein Element zur Hebung des Fremdenverkehrs, welches die politische Realisierung dieses Mythos aber verweigert. Der Paradiesmythos des irdischen Glücks hat irdische Erlösermythen gezeugt, die in ihrer Realitätsferne Angst und Aggression hervorriefen, und endeten wie alle Mythen und selbst die Geschichte der Erlösung. Toller hat im Exil die wirklichkeitsfremde Literarisierung der politischen Revolution als einen der Gründe für deren Scheitern erkannt, er hat sich vom Räteexperiment Landauer'scher Prägung abgewandt und in der Stilisierung der Verhaftungsszene nach johanneischem Muster doch wohl jenen expressionistisch-

---

26 Vgl. das Kapitel «Flucht und Verhaftung» in Ernst Tollers Autobiographie *Eine Jugend in Deutschland* (Amsterdam: Querido, 1933), und dazu Wolfgang Frühwald, «Exil als Ausbruchsversuch. Ernst Tollers Autobiographie,» Manfred Durzak (Hrsg.), *Die deutsche Exilliteratur 1933–1945* (Stuttgart: Reclam, 1973), S. 492f.

aktivistischen Messianismus kritisiert, an dem er zwar selbst einmal teilgehabt hatte, dessen Gefahren er aber im nationalsozialistischen Todeskult nun deutlich vor Augen sah. Als Tollers Autobiographie im Querido-Verlag in Amsterdam erschien, war München längst zur «Kunststadt des deutschen Reiches» proklamiert worden.

In München traf man die Vorbereitungen dafür, daß die Matthäus-Kirche, die erste Kirche der evangelischen Gemeinde, der nationalsozialistischen Großmannssucht zum Opfer fiel, daß auch in der Ludwigstraße brutale Lücken in das kunstvolle Bau-Ensemble Klenzes gerissen wurden, daß der Königsplatz durch jene «Ehrentempel» verunstaltet wurde, in denen der blutige Mythos des 9. November 1923 den Mythos eines leuchtenden München ganz in sich aufnahm, der Todesmythos den ihm verwandten Lebensmythos völlig überformte. Es ist, als sei das Ende der Erzählung *Gladius Dei* historische Realität geworden, wo der strahlende Himmel von blauer Seide von der schwefelgelben Gewitterwand überdeckt wird, «die von der Theatinerstraße heraufgezogen war und in der es leise donnerte.» Ein «breites Feuerschwert» stand in dieser Wolkenwand, «das sich im Schwefellicht über die frohe Stadt hinreckte ...»[27]

*

Dabei hatte alles mit einem großen, romantisierenden Kunstgedanken begonnen. König Ludwig I. von Bayern, der ein Fürst europäischen Ranges werden wollte, hatte erkannt, daß nach Napoleon mit Waffentaten kein Ruhm mehr zu gewinnen war. Ihm blieb daher nichts anderes, als der Mäzen Europas zu werden. So baute er das trotz Säkularisation und bayerischem Königtum im Schlaf der Vormoderne schlummernde München zu einer Stadt aus, die Deutschland so zur Ehre gereichen sollte, «daß keiner Teutschland kennt, wenn er nicht München gesehen hat.»[28] Die im Norden von Friedrich Gärtner – nach römischem Vorbild –, im Süden von Leo von Klenze – nach florentinischem Vorbild – in fünfunddreißigjähriger Bauzeit ausgebaute Ludwigstraße bildet das Modell dessen, was künftig unter Kunststadt verstanden werden sollte. Wilhelm Pinder meinte: «Die Ludwigstraße in München ist eine der schönsten Straßen Deutschlands, obwohl sie kaum ein ganz schönes Haus besitzt. Aber das Ganzheitsgefühl, das die Geschoßhöhen nur leise variiert, dies eben entscheidet. Proportionen, Rhythmus, Farbe, Werkstoff, Umrißverwandtschaft, sind Elemente dieser ganzeinheitlichen Einheit.»[29] In der Münchener Ludwigstraße verkörpert sich die groß gedachte und großzügig ins

---

27 Thomas Mann, «Gladius Dei,» S. 162.
28 Heinz Jürgen Sauermost, *Bilder zur Kunst Ludwigs I. Sonderbeilage der Münchner Ärztlichen Anzeigen für das Rahmenprogramm zum 30. Bayerischen Ärztetag vom 7. bis 9. Oktober 1977.*
29 Vgl. Oswald Hederer, *Die Ludwigstraße in München* (München: Eher, 1942), S. 92.

Werk gesetzte Idee eines Künstlerstaates mit dem Ziel ästhetischer und religiöser Erziehung des Menschen, der so in Kunst und mit Kunst leben sollte, daß Moral und Staatsgesinnung veredelt würden. Daß die Religion in dieser architektonischen Didaxe eine herausgehobene Rolle zugewiesen bekam, ist bei aller klassizistischen Grundhaltung das romantisierende Element in diesem Ideengebäude. Wer die Ludwigstraße, empfangen von der Bavaria auf dem Löwengespann, durch das Siegestor kommend, durchschreitet, sollte den Weg der abendländischen und der deutschen Geschichte gehen, den Weg von Rom (von der Kopie des Konstantinbogens und den römischen Brunnen vor der Universität) nach Florenz (zur Kopie der Loggia dei Lanzi in der bayerischen Feldherrnhalle am Odeonsplatz), vom Süden in den Norden, von der Antike in die Renaissance. Er sollte – und dieser künstlerische Gedanke stellte sich im Laufe der langen Baugeschichte her, in die der König selbst immer wieder gestaltend und anregend eingegriffen hat – auf deutschem Boden den Wurzeln der Kultur in der Antike begegnen und sollte auf dem Weg der Geschichte (in der Ludwigskirche) das Christentum als die alles überragende, Anfang und Ende signierende Kraft erkennen. Nicht Aneignung von Tradition also ist der allmählich sich entfaltende Baugedanke dieses Königs, sondern – ganz in romantischem Geiste gedacht – Aktualisierung und Verlebendigung des Vergangenen, damit die Kontinuität der abendländischen Geschichte von der griechisch-römischen Antike bis in die unmittelbare Gegenwart herein zu erkennen ist, und der Mensch in der Erkenntnis dieser Kontinuität auch seine Identität als Individuum und als Mitglied einer historisch gewachsenen Gemeinschaft erfährt. Erst dem Kunstschönen gegenüber wird das Individuum sich als Mensch und als Glied einer Gemeinschaft erfahren, die an der Kette der abendländischen Tradition hängt. Von der «Walhalla» (bei Donaustauf) über Kelheim und München bis in die Rheinpfalz hinein zeugen die Bauten Ludwigs I. noch heute von dem kunstdidaktischen Gehalt einer durch die politischen Ereignisse des Vormärz und der Märzrevolution dann zerstörten Idee.[30]

Die Liebhaber des alten München, wie etwa der Maler und Zeichner Ludwig Emil Grimm, haben die neue Ludwigstraße «etwas langweilig»[31] gefunden, sie verstanden, weshalb die Münchener die auf den Wiesen vor der Stadt errichtete Alte Pinakothek, ihrer etwas abgelegenen Lage wegen, spöttisch die «Dachauer Bildergalerie» nannten; die Jüngeren aber, Heinrich Heine oder gar Gottfried Keller, haben sogleich angefangen, an jenem Mythos zu «stricken,» der dann eben Thomas Mann in *Gladius Dei* bewogen hat, die Geschichte des me-

---

30 Oswald Hederers (von Ideologie freies) Buch von 1942 ist noch immer die umfassendste Darstellung der Baugeschichte der Münchener Ludwigstraße. Vgl. jetzt auch Frank Büttner, «Die Planungsgeschichte der Ludwigskirche in München,» *Münchner Jahrbuch der bildenden Kunst,* 3. Folge, Bd. 35 (1984), 189–218.

diceischen Bußpredigers Girolamo Savonarola ironisch in der antikisierenden und renaissancistischen Kulisse des «nördlichen Südens» zu wiederholen. Heinrich Heine hat – im Gegensatz zu Ludwig Emil Grimm, welcher sich nur im Schatten der Frauentürme wohlgefühlt hat – den Anblick des Domes «barbarisch» genannt, da er sich «in stiefelknechtlicher Gestalt» über die Stadt erhebe und «die Schatten und Gespenster des Mittelalters in seinem Schoße» verberge. Beim Anblick der Ludwigstraße jedoch war es ihm, als würde ihm «eine schwere Perücke vom Haupte genommen und das Herz befreit von stählerner Fessel. Ich spreche hier von den heiteren Kunsttempeln und edlen Palästen, die in kühner Fülle hervorblühen aus dem Geiste Klenzes, des großen Meisters.»[32] Gottfried Keller hat dann (bei des grünen Heinrichs Einzug in München) endgültig jenen Ton getroffen, der seither die «München-leuchteteLiteratur» beherrscht.[33]

Von Heines und Kellers Lobpreis der «im letzten Abendscheine» glühenden großen Hauptstadt, aus deren «Kirchen und mächtigen Schenkhäusern ... Musik, Geläute, Orgel- und Harfenspiel» erschallt, führt zur MünchenLiteratur der Jahrhundertwende eine gerade Linie, nachdem Theodor Fontane das Stichwort von den geistig toten und «verbierten» Einheimischen und den Künstlern als einer Nebenbevölkerung gegeben hatte.[34] In dieser Literatur der Jahrhundertwende, die gleichwohl den Charakter Münchens als einer Stadt der Maler, Bildhauer, Architekten und Musiker nicht verändern konnte, sind alle Elemente eines leuchtenden München, zwischen den Polen des seidenen Föhnhimmels und der Bierseligkeit, erhalten: die Lebensfreude, das ZeitHaben und das Sich-Zeit-Nehmen, die Fülle der Feiertage, das Leben und Leben-Lassen, was sich auch dadurch beweist, daß die «Nebenbevölkerung» von den Einheimischen lange Jahrzehnte hindurch geduldet wurde; ein eher passiver Kunstverstand der Einheimischen, nicht so sehr die aktive Kunstförderung durch die Stadt und den königlichen Hof war Münchener Realität. Josef Ruederer, Zeitgenosse Thomas Manns, im Unterschied zu ihm aber (1861) in München geboren (und gestorben, 1915), hat in einer seiner *Münchener Satiren* von Bierheim, einem «stattlichen Pfahlbauerndorf von fünfhunderttausend Einwohnern im Süden des Reiches,» berichtet:

> Nur dunkle Sagen melden noch aus der Urnacht, daß die Bierheimer Menschen waren, die breitspurig über den Bürgersteig tappten, immer nach links auswichen, den Schutzmann Schandi nannten und deshalb für äußerst gemütlich galten. Auch rühmt man ihre Ehrfurcht vor reichlichem Essen und nicht minder ihre Begeisterung für Bier- und Kaffeehäuser. Ihre Straßen waren, der damaligen Zeit entsprechend, in einem Urzustand von Dreck;

---

31 Adolf Stoll (Hrsg.), *Ludwig Emil Grimm: Erinnerungen aus meinem Leben* (Leipzig: Hesse & Becker, 1911), S. 479.
32 Vgl. Heinrich Heines *Reise von München nach Genua* (= *Reisebilder*, 3. Teil), Kapitel 2, und das Ende des 10. Kapitels im 3. Teil von Gottfried Kellers Roman *Der grüne Heinrich*.
33 Die folgenden Zitate aus Kellers *Der grüne Heinrich*.
34 Vgl. de Mendelssohn (Anm. 13), S. 17.

ihre Frauen waren dagegen um so sauberer. Und was ein richtiger Bierheimer war, hatte stets eine ausgesprochene Vorliebe für große Geweihsammlungen. Daß sie fortwährend Bilder kauften, wird allerdings bestritten; doch scheint sich zu bestätigen, daß sie Maler und Bildhauer wenigstens nicht des Burgfriedens verwiesen. Handel trieben sie so gut wie gar nicht; den Nationalökonomischen Jahrbüchern zufolge muß aber eine ziemlich rege Fremdenindustrie bestanden haben, die in kräftiger Exploitierung des Einzelindividuums wie der Massen bestand. Die zahllosen Feste, die Bierheim veranstaltete, kamen dabei in bester Weise zu Hilfe, denn der Umsatz in Ansichtskarten und Laugenbretzeln stieg um solche Zeit ebenso wie der Absatz an Met und welschen Getränken, die krachten, wenn man die Flaschen aufmachte.[35]

*

Zum Mythos des leuchtenden München also gehört der Gegenmythos, die Darstellung der von den zuströmenden Künstlern in ihrer «Gemütlichkeit» als unheimlich, als «grantig,» als unverständlich, anarchisch und brutal charakterisierten Einheimischen. Ihr Schimpfvokabular ist meist, wie Oskar Panizza 1897 meinte, der Metzgersprache entnommen, was die Rede von «Isar-Athen» als einen blutigen Irrtum erweise.[36]

Auch der Gegenmythos aber ist unverkennbar ein Mythos, der sich zu dem des leuchtenden München verhält wie das Bild zum Gegenbild, wie der Zerrspiegel zum Original; noch deutsche Wahlkämpfe aus jüngster Zeit wurden mit solch mythisierenden Klischees bestritten. Sie reichen von Thomas Manns wortmächtiger Beschreibung des wortkargen, aber gehorsam-tatkräftigen Herrn Krauthuber – «ein Sohn des Volkes von fürchterlicher Rüstigkeit»[37] – über Karl Arnolds böse Karikatur des bayerischen Spießers aus dem *Simplicissimus,* bis zu Herbert Achternbuschs bissiger Behauptung, daß 70% aller Bayern Anarchisten geworden seien und deshalb die CSU wählten. Karl Arnold hat diesen anarchisch-separatistischen Grundzug der Bayern 1923, nach dem gescheiterten Hitlerputsch, in der Figur eines am Wirtshaustisch sitzenden Spießers dargestellt, der ohne Hals, mit Seehundbart und Knollennase, die mit dem Königswappen versehene Pfeife in der Hand, hinter einem halb geleerten Bierglas sitzt und – statt durch zwei Augen den Betrachter durch zwei Hakenkreuze ansieht. Darunter aber stehen die für das Jahr 1923 fast prophetischen Verse:

> Mei' Ruah möcht' i hamm und a Revalution,
> A Ordnung muaß sei' und a Judenpogrom,
> A Diktator g'hört hera und glei' davo'g'haut:
> Mir zoagen's Enk scho', wia ma Deutschland aufbaut'.[38]

---

35 Josef Ruederer, «Der Hohe Schein. Ein prähistorischer Epilog aus alten Urkunden gesammelt,» in Josef Ruederer, *Münchner Satiren* (München und Leipzig: Müller, ²1907), S. 41f.
36 *Abschied von München. Ein Handschlag von Oskar Panizza.* (Zürich: Schabelitz, 1897), S. 4f.
37 Thomas Mann, «Gladius Dei,» S. 161.
38 Titelblatt der Zeitschrift *Simplicissimus,* München, 3. Dezember 1923.

Mythos und Antimythos haben ihre prägende Kraft bis heute nicht verloren. Ernst Augustins Roman *Raumlicht* (1976) zeugt davon ebenso, wie Paul Wührs Gegenmünchen (1970), wie die Münchenbücher, die noch immer auf dem Humus dieser Mythen entstehen. Noch immer sind die Pole Seidenhimmel und «Verbierung» zu erkennen, doch sieht die Gegenwartsliteratur nicht mehr davon ab, daß es den «Sündenfall» dieses Mythos gegeben hat, daß das Stereotyp des «leuchtenden München» nicht wiederholt werden kann, ohne an Kurt Huber und die «Weiße Rose,» an ihre Denunzianten und ihr grausames Ende zu denken. Allein den Geschwistern Scholl und ihren Freunden hat Hannah Arendt zugestanden, «in einer einzigen verzweifelten Geste» das, was man in Deutschland einst Gewissen genannt hatte, «in der Öffentlichkeit kundgetan» zu haben.[39]

So hat Ernst Augustin, mit den von Thomas Mann übernommenen Stereotypen, das leuchtende München in ein kochendes München verwandelt. Er sieht die dunkelgelben Gebäude der Ludwigstraße von den dunkelgelb gekachelten Untergrundbahn-Schächten unterfangen und die Kulisse der Kunststadt nur noch als nostalgisches Gegenbild zur Realität des Stadtplanes: «Eine auf der Karte senkrecht verlaufende achtspurige Hauptachse, die zwei Autobahnringe durchschneidet, den mittleren und den äußeren Ring, wobei der mittlere sechzehnspurige der mörderischste ist.»[40] Doch in der so charakterisierten Stadt gelingt, wenn nicht die Heilung, so doch die Stillung einer schwer psychotischen Patientin, begegnet der Dichter der Poesie, wie der Arzt der Kranken; denn in dieser Stadt gibt es noch immer ein «Trotzdem»:

> Trotzdem. Wenn an warmen Sommerabenden die zweihundert Türme schwarz vor den apfelsinenfarbenen Alpen stehen. Und sich durch eine Luftspiegelung auch noch das abendliche Verona über die Alpen hereinspiegelt – an vier Tagen im Jahr sind sogar die Glocken zu hören –, wenn an den vier Tagen München an allen vier Ecken durch eine überirdische Beleuchtung brennt, dann gibt es sogar Straßen, die wie früher aussehen.

In der Gegenwartsliteratur also erscheint nochmals der Mythos vom leuchtenden, vom in überirdischer Beleuchtung brennenden München, in welchem der Glanz der Kunst und das Feuer des Infernos nie mehr voneinander zu trennen sein werden. Ob symbolistisch verschlüsselt, ob satirisch gebrochen, ob experimentell zur Wörterstadt gefügt, immer ist diesen Mythen eines die Zeit überdauernden Stadtcharakters von München jener Grundzug des (bedrohten) irdischen Paradieses eigen, in dem Leben erlebt und erfüllt werden kann; die Freude am bloßen Dasein, an der menschenwürdigen Existenz scheint in dieser Stadt «trotzdem» zu Hause. Nichts anderes meint Wolf Wondratscheks Gedicht *Kleinhesseloher See (im Englischen Garten),*[41] das an alle Phasen der

---

39 Hannah Arendt, *Eichmann in Jerusalem. Ein Bericht von der Banalität des Bösen* (München: Piper, 1965), S. 138.
40 Ernst Augustin, *Raumlicht,* S. 188f. Das folgende Zitat ebd.
41 Das Gedicht in dem Anm. 23. zitierten Aufsatz von Wolf Wondratschek, S. 132.

Geschichte des Münchener Stadtmythos erinnert: an Ludwig I., jenen romantisierenden Künstlerkönig, der den Garten gegründet und die Stadt zu einem Kunstwerk ausgebaut hat; an die großen Dirigenten, die aus der Stadt hinausgeekelt wurden; an Rilke, der 1919 München fast fluchtartig verlassen mußte, weil ihm Sympathien für die Räteregierung nachgesagt wurden; an Thomas Mann, der 1933 durch den heuchlerischen Protest scheinbarer ehemaliger Freunde gegen seine Rede auf Richard Wagner aus München ins Exil getrieben wurde; an Bertolt Brecht, der als Schüler von Karl Valentin und Freund Lion Feuchtwangers in München bescheidene Erfolge hatte, aber Ruhm und Einfluß in Berlin gesucht hat; und an Hitler, der die Kunststadt sich und seiner «Bewegung» einverleibte und dies alles – außer der Erinnerung – zerstörte. Durch die Parodie von Lyrik- und Prosatönen der Münchener Literatur zu Beginn unseres Jahrhunderts stellt sich Wondratschek in die Tradition der «München-leuchtete-Literatur,» deren beste Werke durch die parodistische Aneignung mythischer Denkfiguren gelungen sind. So endet das Gedicht notwendig mit der Beschwörung einer «trotzdem» immer wieder und immer noch möglichen, vom Dichter besungenen «Freude am Leben»:

«Da liegt der See,
die Zeiten ziehn darüberhin
wie tiefe Wolken.

Im Hintergrund,
im Eid der Ewigkeit,
die Alpen.

Hier gingen große Dirigenten
und hatten endlich die Hände
in den Hosentaschen.

Hier ging Rilke
und wollte sich wie Gott verschwenden
und litt, daß er dem Schwan
nicht ebenbürtig war,
der wie im Wahn an ihm vorüberglitt.

Und dann und wann kam Thomas Mann
und fütterte die Enten.

Bertolt Brecht hatte ganz andere Pläne,
ohne Wahn und ohne Schwäne.
Er studierte beim Starkbier
die einfachen Leute.

Das gleiche tat Adolf Hitler;
er hatte bis heute beim deutschen Volk
den größten Erfolg.

Da liegt der See –
die Menschen drehen ihre Runden
vorbei an Schwänen, Enten, Hunden
und murmeln Nichtssagendes
über die Freude zu leben.»

Hans Eichner – A Bibliography

Hans Eichner was born in Vienna on 30 October 1921; after the *Anschluß* he succeeded in escaping from Austria to Belgium and finally reached England in 1939. After a period of internment in Australia he was able to return to England and study at London University, taking his B.A. and Ph.D. at University College. He taught at Bedford College for two years before emigrating in 1950 to Canada to take up an appointment as Assistant Professor of German Language and Literature at Queen's University at Kingston. He rose to be Head of Department at Queen's but left there in 1967 in order to assume the Chairmanship of the Graduate Division and subsequently the Chairmanship (1975–85) of the Department of Germanic Languages and Literatures at the University of Toronto.

During his long and extraordinarily distinguished career in Canada Hans Eichner has received many honours, of which the following are the more notable:
Fellow of the Royal Society of Canada, 1967
Gold Medal of the Goethe Institute, 1972
Hon. LL.D., Queen's University, 1974
Honorary Professor of Humanities, Calgary University, 1978–
William Riley Parker Prize, Modern Language Association of America, 1983

Publications

1. Books, chapters in books, articles, and published papers.

«The Place of *Doctor Faustus* in the Works of Thomas Mann,» *GLL,* NS, 1 (1948), 289–302.
«Bemerkungen zur Form von Goethe's 'König in Thule',» *Monatshefte,* 47 (1951), 405-408.
«Aspects of Parody in the Works of Thomas Mann,» *MLR,* 47 (1952), 30–48.
«A Note on the Cloud Girl in *Finnegans Wake,*» *ES,* 35 (1954), 1–3.
«The Poetry of Franz B. Steiner,» *GLL,* NS, 7 (1954), 180–84.
«The Supposed Influence of Schiller's „Über naive und sentimentalische Dichtung" on Fr. Schlegel's „Über das Studium der Griechischen Poesie",» *GR,* 30 (1955), 260–64.

«Friedrich Schlegel's „Alarcos" in the Light of his Unpublished Notebooks,» *MLN,* 71 (1956), 119-22.
«Friedrich Schlegel's Theory of Romantic Poetry,» *PMLA,* 71 (1956), 1018-41.
«Thomas Mann and Goethe. A Protest,» *PEGS,* 26 (1957), 81-92.
Friedrich Schlegel, Literary Notebooks 1797-1801. Edited with introduction and commentary. London: Athlone Press and Toronto: University of Toronto Press, 1957. Pp. 342.
«Friedrich Schlegel und wir,» *DR,* 44 (1958), 646-56.
«Neues aus Friedrich Schlegels Nachlaß,» *Jahrbuch der Deutschen Schillergesellschaft,* 3 (1959), 218-43.
Reading German for Scientists. London: Chapman & Hall; New York: Wiley, 1959. Pp. XII + 207. (Co-author with Hans Hein.)
Kritische Friedrich-Schlegel-Ausgabe, vol. IV: *Ansichten und Ideen von der christlichen Kunst.* München-Paderborn-Wien: Schöningh, 1959. Pp. LVI + 273.
«Friedrich Ast und die Wiener Allgemeine Literatur-Zeitung», *Jahrbuch der Deutschen Schillergesellschaft,* 4 (1960), 343-57.
Thomas Mann. Eine Einführung in sein Werk. Bern: Francke, 1953. Pp. 124. Second, revised edition, Bern: Francke, 1961.
Kritische Friedrich-Schlegel-Ausgabe, vol. VI: *Geschichte der alten und neuen Literatur.* München-Paderborn-Wien: Schöningh, 1961, Pp. L + 434.
Kritische Friedrich-Schlegel-Ausgabe, vol. V: *Dichtungen.* München-Paderborn-Wien: Schöningh, 1962, Pp. CXVI + 544.
«The Meaning of „Good" in Aesthetic Judgments,» *British Journal of Aesthetics,* 3 (1963), 301-316.
Four Modern Authors: Mann – Rilke – Kafka – Brecht. Toronto: Canadian Broadcasting Corporation, 1964. Pp. 91.
«The Genesis of German Romanticism,» *QQ,* 72:2 (1965), 213-31.
«Internierungslager und Lageruniversität,» in: *Verbannung. Aufzeichnungen deutscher Schriftsteller im Exil.* Hrsg. v. E. Schwarz und M. Wegner (Hamburg: Christian Wegner, 1964), p. 115-21.
«„Camilla:" Eine unbekannte Fortsetzung von Dorothea Schlegels Florentin,» *Jahrbuch des Freien Deutschen Hochstifts,* 1965, S. 314-68.
«A National University,» *Saturday Night,* 81:6 (June 1966), 46-48.
«Unbekannte Briefe von und an Friedrich Schlegel,» *Journal of English and Germanic Philology,* 65 (1966), 511-15.
«Zur Deutung von *Wilhelm Meisters Lehrjahre,*» *Jahrbuch des Freien Deutschen Hochstifts,* 1966, pp. 165-96.
Kritische Friedrich-Schlegel-Ausgabe, vol. II: *Charakteristiken und Kritiken I.* München–Paderborn–Wien: Schöningh, 1966, Pp. CXX + 460.
Friedrich Schlegel, *Gespräch über die Poesie* (ed.) Mit einem Nachwort von Hans Eichner. Stuttgart: J.B. Metzler, 1968 (Nachwort: 1*-25*).
«Thomas Mann und die deutsche Romantik,» in: *Das Nachleben der Romantik in der modernen deutschen Literatur,* ed. Wolfgang Paulsen. Amherster Kolloquium zur modernen deutschen Literatur, 1968 (Heidelberg: Lothar Stiehm, 1969), 152-73.
«Friedrich Schlegels Theorie der Literaturkritik,» *ZfdPh,* 88 (Sonderheft, Jan. 1970), 2-19.
(With Richard Samuel) «Unpublished Letters by Friedrich Schlegel and Karl von Hardenberg to Georg Andreas Reimer,» *Seminar,* 6 (1970), 128-17.
Friedrich Schlegel. New York: Twayne, 1970. Pp. 176.
«The Novel,» in: *The Romantic Period in Germany.* Essays by Members of the London University Institute of Germanic Studies. Ed. S. Prawer. London: Weidenfeld and Nicolson, 1970.
«Dichterische Absicht und literarische Deutung,» in: *Psychologie und Literaturwissenschaft,* ed. Wolfgang Paulsen. Viertes Amherster Kolloquium zur modernen deutschen Literatur, 1970 (Heidelberg: Lothar Stiehm, 1971), pp. 56-78.
«Zwei unbekannte Briefe Thomas Manns,» in: *Studies in German – in Memory of Robert L. Kahn,* ed. Hans Eichner and Lisa Kahn, Rice University Studies, 57:4, (Fall, 1971), p. 39-46.
Studies in German in Memory of Robert L. Kahn. Ed. Hans Eichner and Lisa Kahn, Rice University Studies, vol. 57, no. 4, Fall 1971. Pp. 134.

«The Eternal Feminine: An Aspect of Goethe's Ethics,» in: *Transactions of the Royal Society of Canada,* Series IV, vol. IX: 1971 (Toronto, 1972), 235–44.
„Romantic" and its Cognates. The European History of a Word (ed.). Toronto: University of Toronto Press, 1972. Pp. 536.
«Introduction,» «Germany: Romantisch – Romantik – Romantiker,» and «Chronology,» pp. 3–16, 98–156 and 501–513 in *„Romantic" and its Cognates...*
«Friedrich Schlegel's Theorie der Literaturkritik,» in: *Romantik heute* (Bonn-Bad Godesberg: Inter Nationes, 1972), p. 18–30.
«Friedrich Schlegel's Theory of Literary Criticism,» in: *Romanticism Today* (Bonn-Bad Godesberg: Inter Nationes, 1973), p. 17–26. (Translation of «Friedrich Schlegels Theorie der Literaturkritik».)
Kritische Friedrich-Schlegel-Ausgabe, vol. III: *Charakteristiken und Kritiken II.* München-Paderborn-Wien: Schöningh, 1974. Pp. XCVI + 380.
«The Eternal Feminine: An Aspect of Goethe's Ethics,» in J.W. v. Goethe, *Faust,* tr. Walter Arndt, ed. by Cyrus Hamlin. New York: W.W. Norton, 1976. (Reprint of «The Eternal Feminine...»)
«Thomas Mann and Politics,» in: *Thomas Mann. Ein Kolloquium.* Ed. H.H. Schulte and G. Chapple. (Bonn: Bouvier, 1978), p. 5–19.
Analecta Helvetica et Germanica. Eine Festschrift zu Ehren von Hermann Boeschenstein. Ed. A. Arnold, H. Eichner, E. Heier and S. Hoefert. Bonn: Bouvier, 1979. Pp. 392.
«Zur Deutung von *Wilhelm Meisters Lehrjahren,*» in: *Goethes Wilhelm Meister. Zur Rezeptionsgeschichte der Lehr- und Wanderjahre,* ed. Klaus F. Gille (Königstein: Athenäum, 1979), p. 277–91. (Abridged reprint)
«In Defence of Literature,» in: *Humanities in the Present Day,* ed. J. Wood and H.G. Coward (Waterloo: Wilfried Laurier Press, 1979), p. 75–89.
Friedrich Schlegel, *Literarische Notizen 1797–1801.* Hrsg., eingel. und kommentiert von Hans Eichner. Frankfurt: Ullstein: [1980]. (Reprint of *Friedrich Schlegel, Literary Notebooks...* with the Introduction and commentary translated into German.)
[Editorial contributions, with George Whalley:] «Thomas Abbt,» «Athenaeum», in: S.T. Colleridge, *Collected Works,* vol. 12, pt. I: *Marginalia* I (Princeton, 1980), p. 3–6, 131–153.
«Zur Integration der Gedichte in Eichendorffs erzählender Prosa,» *Aurora,* 41 (1981), 7–21.
«Joseph von Eichendorff,» in: *Handbuch der deutschen Erzählung,* ed. K.K. Polheim (Düsseldorf: Bagel, 1981), p. 172–91 and 578–81.
Kritische Friedrich-Schlegel-Ausgabe, vol. XVI: *Fragmente zur Poesie und Literatur I.* München-Paderborn-Wien: Schöningh, 1981. Pp. XXIX + 689.
«The Rise of Modern Science and the Genesis of Romanticism,» *PMLA,* 97 (1982), 8–30.
«Greatness, Saintliness, Usefulness. Character Configuration in Goethe's Oeuvre», in: *Goethe's Narrative Fiction.* The Irvine Goethe Symposium (Berlin & New York, 1983), p. 38–54.
Friedrich Schlegel, *Gemälde alter Meister.* Mit Kommentar und Nachwort von Hans Eichner und Norma Lelless. Darmstadt: Wissenschaftliche Buchgesellschaft, 1984. Pp. 224.

2. *Reviews*

Barker Fairley: Goethe's Faust, in: *QQ,* 60 (1953), 581–83.
Barker Fairley: *Heinrich Heine* and *Goethe. Selected Poems,* in: *QQ,* 62 (1955), 309–12.
Friedrich Schlegel: *Schriften und Fragmente,* ed. Ernst Behler, in: *QQ,* 64 (1957), 452–53
Roy Pascal: *The German Novel* and Ronald Gray: *Kafka's „Castle,"* in: *QQ,* 65 (1958), 149–51.
Fr. Schlegel: *Wissenschaft der europäischen Literatur,* ed. Ernst Behler (= Kritische Friedrich-Schlegel-Ausgabe, vol. XI), in: *GR,* 34 (1959), 308–11.
Krisenjahre der Frühromantik, ed. Josef Körner, vol. III, *JEGP,* 60 (1961), 148–50.
Hölderlin: *Selected Verse,* with ... Prose Translations by Michael Hamburger and Barker Fairley: *Wilhelm Raabe,* in: *QQ,* 68 (1962), 697–98.
Ludwig Wittgenstein: *Tractatus Logico-Philosophicus* ... with a new translation by D.F. Pears and B.F. McGuinness, in: *Dialogue,* 1 (1962), 212–16.
Heinrich Nüsse: *Die Sprachtheorie Fr. Schlegels,* in: *JEGP,* 62 (1963), 870–72.
Ronald Gray (ed.): *Kafka. A Collection of Critical Essays* (1962), in: QQ, 70 (1963), 291–92.

Klaus Briegleb: *Ästhetische Sittlichkeit. Versuch über Friedrich Schlegels Systementwurf zur Begründung der Dichtungskritik,* in: *JEGP,* 62 (1964), 308.

H.W. Bruford: *Culture and Society in Classical Weimar. 1775–1805,* in: *QQ,* 71 (1964), 131–32.

Friedrich Schlegel: *Lucinde. Ein Roman.* Hrsg. und mit einem Nachwort versehen von K.K. Polheim, in: *JEGP,* 63 (1964), 573–74.

«A New View of Heine,» in: *UTQ,* 34 (1965), 197–200.

H.W. Seiffert: *Untersuchungen zur Methode der Herausgabe deutscher Texte,* in: *JEGP,* 64 (1965), 359–63.

François Hemsterhuis: *Lettre sur l'homme et ses rapports avec le commentaire inédit de Diderot.* Texte établi, présenté et annoté par Georges May, in: *Dialogue,* 4 (1965), 254–356.

Henry Hatfield: *Aesthetic Paganism in German Literature,* in: *QQ,* 72 (1965), 576.

Walter H. Sokel: *Franz Kafka – Tragik und Ironie,* in: *JEGP,* 64 (1965), 783–85.

Michel Dentan: *Humeur et création littéraire dans l'oeuvre de Kafka,* in: *JEGP,* 65 (1965), 135–36.

F.M. Barnard: *Herder's Social and Political Thought,* in: *Dialogue,* 4 (1966), 550–51.

K.K. Polheim, *Die Arabeske. Ansichten und Ideen aus Friedrich Schlegels Poetik,* in: *Euphorion,* 60 (1966), 415–17.

Thomas Mann: *Sieben Manifeste zur jüdischen Frage,* in: *Germanistik* 8 (1967), 438–39.

H. Bürgin und H.O. Mayer: *Thomas Mann, Eine Chronik seines Lebens,* in: *Seminar,* 3 (1967), 161–62.

Friedrich Schiller: *On the Aesthetic Education of Man . . .* Ed. and tr. E.M. Wilkinson and L.A. Willoughby, in: *UTQ,* 38:1 (1968), 103–04.

Wittgenstein und der Wiener Kreis: [Conversations recorded] by F. Waismann. Ed. B.F. McGuiness, in: *Dialogue,* 7 (1968), 480–81.

Werner Weiland: *Der junge Friedrich Schlegel oder Die Revolution in der Frühromantik,* in: *Germanistik,* 10 (1969), 842.

Joh. Chr. Gottsched: *Ausgewählte Werke,* hrsg. Joachim Birke, vols. I and IV, in *JEGP,* 54 (1970), 138–40.

Deutsche Romantheorien, ed. Reinhold Grimm, in: *GRM,* NF, 20 (1970), 232–33.

Andreas Huyssen: *Die frühromantische Konzeption von Übersetzung und Aneignung,* in: *Germanistik,* 11 (1970), 749–50.

Joh. Chr. Gottsched: *Ausgewählte Werke,* hrsg. v. Joachim Birke, vols. II and III, in: *JEGP* 70 (1971), 360–61.

A.W. Schlegel, *Vorlesungen über das akademische Studium. Bonner Vorlesungen,* ed. Frank Jolles, vol. I, in: *Seminar,* 8 (1972), 141–42.

Eckhardt Heftrich, *Novalis: Vom Logos der Poesie,* in: *GQ,* 45 (1972), 762–63.

Friedrich Schlegel, *Lucinde and the Fragments,* tr. Peter Firchow, in: *GQ,* 46 (1973), 478–81.

Bernhard Leitner, *The Architecture of Ludwig Wittgenstein,* in: *Dialogue,* 13 (1974), 388–89.

Thomas Mann, *Notizen zur Felix Krull . . . und anderen Werken,* ed. H. Wysling, in: *Germanistik,* 15 (1974), 718.

D.J. Farelly, *Goethe and Inner Harmony,* in: *Germanistik,* 15 (1974), 647.

Erich Kahler, *The Germans,* in: *QQ,* 81 (1974), 624–26.

Martin Brunkhorst, *Shakespeares „Coriolanus" in deutscher Bearbeitung,* in: *CLS,* 12 (1975), 421–23.

Hermann Meyer, *Natürlicher Enthusiasmus. Das Morgenländische in Goethes Novelle,* in: *Seminar,* 11 (1975), 123–24.

Mythology and Humanism: The Correspondence of Thomas Mann and Karl Kerényi, tr. A. Gelley, and *An Exceptional Friendship. The Correspondence of Thomas Mann and Erich Kahler,* tr. R. and C. Winston, in: *QQ,* 82 (1975), 633–35.

Horn of Oberon. Jean Paul Richter's School for Aesthetics, introd. and tr. by Margaret R. Hale, in: *Dialogue,* 14 (1975), 727–29.

Werner Kohlschmidt, *Geschichte der dt. Literatur von der Romantik bis zum späten Goethe,* in: *Monatshefte,* 68 (1976), 72–73.

Goethe, *The Autobiography,* introd. by K.J. Weintraub, and E.M. Oppenheimer, *Goethe's Poetry for Occasions,* in: *HAR,* 27 (1976), 212–14.

Marianne Schuller, *Romanschlüsse in der Romantik,* in: *Germanistik,* 17 (1976), 226.

Jane K. Brown, *Goethe's Cyclical Narratives. Die Unterhaltungen deutscher Ausgewanderten and Wilhelm Meisters Wanderjahre,* in: *Germanistik,* 18 (1977), 160.

T.J. Reed, *Thomas Mann: The Uses of Tradition* in: *Journal of Modern History,* 49:2 (1977), 335-37.
Albert Fuchs, *Le «Faust» de Goethe,* in: *Modern Philology,* 75 (1977), 95-96.
J.C. Gottsched, *Ausgewählte Werke,* ed. P.M. Mitchell, vol. 7, pt. 1-2, in: *JEGP,* 76 (1977), 78-79.
Martin Swales, *The German Novelle,* in: *UTQ,* 47:1 (1977), 89-90.
S.S. Prawer, *Karl Marx and World Literature,* in: *QQ,* 84:4 (1977), 677-78.
Margaret Scholl, *The Bildungsdrama of the Age of Goethe,* in: *Monatshefte,* 70 (1978), 187-88.
Thomas Mann, *Tagebücher. 1933-34,* in: *Germanistik,* 19 (1978), 533.
J.C. Gottsched, *Ausgewählte Werke,* ed. P.M. Mitchell, vol. 6, pt. 1-4, in *JEGP,* 78 (1979), 596-99.
Marshall Brown, *The Shape of German Romanticism,* in: *Seminar,* 16 (1980), 261-62.
Glyn Tegai Hughes, *Romantic German Literature,* in: *Germanistik,* 21 (1980), 136.
Klaus W. Jonas, *Die Thomas-Mann Literatur. Bd. II. Bibliographie der Kritik 1956-1975,* in: *JEGP,* 79 (1980), 422-23.
David B. Richards, *Goethe's Search for the Muse,* in: *Germanistik,* 21 (1980), 343.
Theodore Ziolkowski, *The Classical German Elegy 1795-1950,* in: *Seminar,* 17 (1981), 320-21.
Richard Brinckmann, ed., *Romantik in Deutschland. Ein internationales Symposion,* in: *CRCL,* 8 (1981), 543-44.
Thomas Mann, *Tagebücher,* 3 vols.: 1918-21, 1935-36, 1937-39, in: *Germanistik,* 22 (1981), 875-76.
W.V. Ruttkowski, *Nomenclator litterarius,* in: *Seminar,* 18 (1982), 143-44.
«Neue Bücher über Goethe» (Review Article), in: *Monatshefte* 74 (1982), 327-34.
Thomas Mann, *Tagebücher, 1940-43,* in: *Germanistik,* 23 (1982), 515.
Benno von Wiese, *Ich erzähle mein Leben. Erinnerungen* and Hans Mayer, *Ein Deutscher auf Widerruf. Erinnerungen,* in: *Arbitrium,* 1 (1983), 121-26.
Ivar Sagmo, *Bildungsroman und Geschichtsphilosophie. Eine Studie zu Goethes Roman „Wilhelm Meister",* in: *Germanistik,* 24 (1983), 110.
J.C. Gottsched, *Ausgewählte Werke,* vol. 7, pt. 4 *(Ausführliche Redekunst: Kommentar),* in: *JEGP* 82 (1983), 417.
Sulpiz Boisserée, *Tagebücher,* hrsg. v. H.-J. Weitz, Bd. I & II, in: *JEGP,* 83 (1984), 284-85.
Eric A. Blackall, *The Novels of the German Romantics,* in: *JEGP,* 83 (1984), 602-04.
Ricardo Blanco Unzué, *Die Aufnahme der spanischen Literatur bei Friedrich Schlegel,* in: *Arbitrium,* 2 (1984), 184-86.
J.C. Gottsched, *Ausgewählte Werke,* vol. V, pt. 1-2 *(Erste Gründe der gesamten Weltweisheit),* in: *JEGP,* 84 (1985), 82-84.

3. *Broadcasts*

«Thomas Mann and Music.» BBC Third Programme, March, 1949.
«James Joyce: Ulysses.» Nordwestdeutscher Rundfunk, Nachtprogramm, September 1949.
«Die Literaturkritik. Ein Vortrag über das Moderne an Friedrich Schlegel,» Westdeutscher Rundfunk, 29 October, 1963.
«Four Modern German Authors: Thomas Mann, Kafka, Rilke, Brecht.» Seven lectures, Canadian Broadcasting Corporation, December, 1963/January, 1964.
«German Romanticism.» Seven lectures, Canadian Broadcasting Corporation, 3 February - 17 March, 1967.

The rich legacy of German Romanticism is the focus of the sixteen essays by North American and European scholars written expressly for this volume. Although most of the essays are concerned with the echoes of Romanticism in literature and especially in the works of individual writers (e. g. Büchner, Mörike, Nietzsche, Thomas Mann, Hesse, Musil, and Christa Wolf), the political and philosophical implications of Romantic thought and ideas as well as their influence on the fine arts are examined. The book is a tribute to Hans Eichner, one of the most outstanding scholars in the field of Romanticism.

The editors all teach German Language and Literature at Canadian universities: the University of British Columbia (M.S. Batts), Queen's University at Kingston (A.W. Riley), and the University of Toronto (H. Wetzel).